American Literary Realism
and the Failed Promise of Contract

American Literary Realism
and the Failed Promise
of Contract

Brook Thomas

UNIVERSITY OF CALIFORNIA PRESS

Berkeley / Los Angeles / London

University of California Press
Berkeley and Los Angeles, California

University of California Press, Ltd.
London, England

© 1997 by the Regents of the University of California

Parts of some chapters of this book draw on previously published material.
    Chapter 3: "The Construction of Privacy in and around *The Bostonians*," *American Literature* 64 (1992): 719–47.
    Chapter 5: "The Risky Business of Accessing the Economy of Howells's Realism in *The Rise of Silas Lapham*," *REAL* 11 (1995): 227–53.
    Chapter 7: "Tragedies of Race, Training, Birth, and Communities of Competent Pudd'nheads," *American Literary History* 1 (1989): 754–85.

Library of Congress Cataloging-in-Publication Data

Thomas, Brook.
    American literary realism and the failed promise of contract /
Brook Thomas.
        p.   cm.
    Includes bibliographical references and index.
    ISBN 0-520-20647-9 (alk. paper)
    1. American fiction—19th century—History and criticism.
2. Realism in literature.   3. Literature and society—United States—
History—19th century.   4. Promise (Law) in literature.   5. Social
ethics in literature.   6. Contracts in literature.   7. Law in literature.
8. Social status in literature.   I. Title.
PS374.R37T48   1997
810.9′12—dc20   96-3719
                                                              CIP

Manufactured in the United States of America
9 8 7 6 5 4 3 2 1

The paper used in this publication meets the minimum requirements of American National Standard for Information Sciences—Permanence of Paper for Printed Library Materials, ANSI Z39.48-1984.

To Jayne

Contents

Preface

This book continues my work interrelating legal and literary history in the United States. A previous book, *Cross-examinations of Law and Literature,* focused on the years prior to the Civil War. This one looks at the end of the nineteenth century and the first few years of the twentieth. My general method remains the same. By "cross-examining" legal and literary history, I hope to present a perspective on both that is absent when they are studied separately, as they usually are. As a result, I tell a story about the culture and society, of which both legal and literary history are a part, that would not be told otherwise. That story is by no means the only story to be told. Nonetheless, it is, I believe, one that is worth telling.

If there is continuity between my earlier book and this one, there are also differences. The relation between law and literature did not remain static. Changes in it necessitate a different organizational principle. The first book juxtaposed important legal figures and their cases with important literary figures and their stories. Close family and class connections between the two professions enabled this structure. If by the 1850s the intricate alliance between lawyers and men of letters in the early years of the republic had broken down, close biographical connections remained. Those connections did not disappear, but increased professionalization did contribute to a growing split. In this book, rather than pair figures, I have structured material by bringing into relation contract, which took priority in the law, and realism, which was the major innovation in literature. Thus, if my first book claimed generally to bring together law and literature of a particular period, this one is concerned with specific aspects of both.

That concern is not, however, perfectly balanced. I rarely examine in depth specific cases involving contract law. I am instead interested in the importance that legal thinkers gave to contract as a way of understanding social relations. In contrast, I do closely examine selected literary texts. This imbalance betrays my training as a literary critic. I hope that this disciplinary bias does not discourage members of the legal profession curious enough to start reading the book. The first two chapters are designed in part to keep those readers interested. If they have not read all the literary works that I treat, they should not despair; many literary critics have not either. I hope that my readings of literary works will enrich—and perhaps alter—legal scholars' understanding of the period's legal history. For those interested specifically in contract, the subtle sense of human agency suggested by realistic works should be especially challenging.

My identification of myself as a literary critic points to another difference between this work and my earlier one. When I began that book, I, along with many others, was still struggling to figure out how to take literary studies beyond formalism. An influx of continental theory had successfully complicated New Critical readings, but that theory often seemed to breed a formalism of its own while retreating from pressing social and political concerns into a realm of textuality inaccessible to those without initiation into its special language. My work on law and literature was my effort to move beyond formalism by connecting the study of literature with important legal issues of antebellum America.

Today it is hard to characterize literary studies as a retreat from the political and social. This book is as much concerned with both subjects as my previous one was. Nonetheless, it much more directly addresses what some consider a formalist's question: why do some literary works retain their power of engagement more than others?

A work's power of engagement, I will argue, is not solely dependent on a willing listener; it also comes from the structural relation by which a work binds readers to the issues it treats. One answer to my question, then, is that for a work to retain its power of engagement, it has to entangle readers in a world as complicated as the world of history, rather than deliver them to an untangled and secure position from which to judge events both within and outside the text. If I am correct, such power, while dependent on the particular issues treated, cannot be measured solely by the political positions that a work takes on them.

To argue that a work's power of engagement cannot be judged solely by its political positions needs explanation, and not simply because we can rarely determine with certainty a work's politics. My point is not that there is an ahistorical category of the literary. On the contrary, what today we call the literary has a specific history. But, as the literary has been historically constituted, it has become a form of discourse that is not identical with political positions. Some argue that such discourse is impossible. But surely there are socially and historically defined differences between a political stump speech and a Henry James novel. We can, of course, take a political position on whether we should continue to value an institution like the literary. For some, a discourse that does not have as its primary goal the taking of explicit stands on particular issues, is not worth maintaining. On the contrary, I argue that, because we already have so many institutions that allow us to declare our politics, literary discourse can serve an important political function in our society, not because it serves as a guide to political action, but because it creates a space in which our political beliefs can be tested and challenged by the dramatization of hypothetical events.

To be sure, this is not the only function of texts generated and read within the realm known as the literary. Furthermore, there are many other ways in which political beliefs can be tested and challenged: for instance, by directly confronting and debating opposing positions or by experiencing, observing, and reading about historical events. Nonetheless, my own experience as a reader and teacher convinces me that the way provided by literature is valuable. The works treated in this book, both realistic and nonrealistic ones, are important to me because reading them in conjunction with legal history contributed to my rethinking of the role of contract. That rethinking marks another difference between this book and the one on the antebellum period.

When I finished that book I was convinced that contract in the law was simply a tool to legitimate an unfair regime of market-based economics. As the "failure" in the title of this book indicates, I have not completely abandoned that view. Yet, as the "promise" in the title indicates, I have modified it. An important way in which I came to appreciate the "promise of contract" was by experiencing the "contract" that realistic texts offer their readers. The techniques that realists developed to engage their audiences are among their most important contributions to the construction of the literary as presently defined. Through a series of comparisons, I will argue that the implied contract between a work of realism and its reader differs from that offered by other works written at the time. One result is that, whereas nonrealistic works are also "literary," they do not tap the same literary potential tapped by selected works of realism. Those who want to hear my explanation of how the realists tap that potential and how in doing so they pose challenges to both defenders and critics of contract are invited to read on. *Caveat lector.*

Acknowledgments

Grants from the American Council of Learned Societies and the Woodrow Wilson Center gave me a year to finish writing a book that had been in the works for a number of years. *American Literary History*, *American Literature*, and *REAL* gave permission to reprint parts published before. Audiences at the John F. Kennedy Institute of the Free University in Berlin, Pennsylvania State University, Johns Hopkins University, the Law and Literature Group at Harvard University, and the Center for the Study of Cultures at Rice University provided helpful feedback. Lawrence Douglas, Morton Horwitz, Gary Jacobsohn, Robert Post, and David Rabban lent their attention to some legal points. I also thank the historians Casey Blake, Thomas Haskell, Sarah Maza, and especially Amy Stanley, who provided a careful reading of the entire book and also team-taught with me a course at an early stage. The following literary critics commented on parts of early drafts: Jonathan Arac, Jonathan Auerbach, Sacvan Bercovitch, Marshall Brown, Stuart Culver, Wai-Chee Dimock, Geoffrey Hartman, Ross Posnock, Gary Scharnhorst, and Eric Sundquist. I am especially grateful to Martha Banta and Robert Levine for their shrewd suggestions for improvement of the entire manuscript. Steven Mailloux gave excellent publishing advice at a crucial moment. I owe William Murphy of the University of California Press a special debt of gratitude for going far beyond any contractually prescribed obligations in order to make the book available to the public in a timely fashion.

CHAPTER I

Introduction

I

Legal historians often refer to the late nineteenth century in the United States as the Age of Contract; ~~literary historians as the Age of Realism~~. Period labels can deceive. Contract was not all that was at stake in the law; not all works written were realistic. Nonetheless, these labels have proved useful because they signal trends. Even revisionists in law and literature relate alternative explanations of the period to contract or realism. In this book I bring contract and realism themselves in relation to one another in the hope of learning something about both, as well as about late nineteenth-century culture and society in the United States.

I use the term *contract* in the general sense of a mutually agreed upon exchange of obligations that, as the word's roots imply, draws people together. In Anglo-Saxon law a contract is enforceable only when some formal sign of the agreed upon exchange, known as consideration, is available. What fascinated ordinary people of the late nineteenth century, however, was not the legal doctrine of consideration but the idea of contract as a mode of social organization in which people freely bound themselves to others by binding themselves to the fulfillment of obligations.

At this point symmetry demands that I define my use of the term *realism* as well. But because my contribution to an understanding of American literary realism depends on my definition of contract's promise, I ask the reader's indulgence as I defer my discussion of this vexed

1

term for the moment. Suffice it to say that recently neither contract nor realism has fared well in some scholarly circles. The predominance of contract in law continues to be condemned for legitimating the inequities of laissez-faire, or, as others will have it, proprietary, capitalism. Literary realism, once seen as posing challenges to those inequities, is now seen in complicity with them because it aided and abetted in the production of disciplined, middle-class subjects. My study supports the contention that the law of contract legitimated social and economic inequities. It also establishes a connection between works of realism and such legitimation, not because they faithfully represented the intricacies of contract law, but because they were produced within the framework of contractarian thought that Owen Fiss has shown dominated law at the time.[1] But even though realism and contract are related, their connection complicates recent assessments of both. It does so, I argue, because selected works of realism both evoke what my title calls the promise of contract and dramatize its failure to be sustained.

What I mean by the promise of contract can be clarified by Sir Henry Maine's famous 1861 proclamation that "the movement of the progressive societies has hitherto been a movement *from Status to Contract.*"[2] For Maine, traditional societies determined people's duties and obligations according to status. For instance, in medieval society both peasant and lord were assigned clear-cut, if different, duties and obligations according to the hierarchical social class into which each was born. In contrast, contractual societies undermine those hierarchies by determining duties and obligations through negotiations among contracting parties.

Maine's statement had special meaning for the United States in the late nineteenth century. Convinced that the United States was the most progressive of progressive societies, William Graham Sumner in 1883 boasted, "In our modern state, and in the United States more than anywhere else, the social structure is based on contract, and status is of the least importance."[3]

Contract's promise is twofold. First, a society ruled by contract promises to be dynamic rather than static. Not bound by inherited status, individuals are free, on their own initiative, to negotiate the terms of their relations with others. Contract does not promise equality of conditions, but it does promise equality of opportunity. As Sumner puts it, "A society based on contract is a society of free and independent men, who form ties without favor or obligation, and co-operate without cringing or intrigue. A society based on contract, therefore, gives the utmost room and chance for individual development, and for all the self-reliance and dignity of a free man. That a society of free men, co-operating under contract, is by far the strongest society which has ever yet developed the full measure of strength of which it is capable; and that the only social improvements which are now conceivable lie in the direction of more complete realization of a society of free men united by contract, are points which cannot be controverted."[4] By promising individuals equal chance to develop, contract claims to produce an equitable social harmony that has been achieved through a network of immanent and self-regulating exchanges rather than a social order imposed artificially from above. The smooth functioning of such a network depends on the second sort of promise alluded to by my title.

The second meaning of the promise of contract involves the sanctity of promising itself. To put one's signature on a contract seems to entail the making of a promise, with all of the connotations of trust involved. The association between promising and contract gives a contractual society a moral foundation that results not from preconceived notions of status but from the duties and obligations that individuals impose on themselves in their dealings with other members of society. Radically conceived, therefore, contract promises an immanent, rather than a transcendental, ordering of society.

Sumner and other conservative defenders of contract did not, I hasten to add, adhere to this promise. Instead, they invoke a transcendental, natural standard to limit the contractual liability of the primary beneficiaries of a changing economy. That standard also legitimated the persistence of status in a world claiming to be ruled by contract. Maine might have stressed the transformation from status to contract, but in fact the transformation was never complete. Sumner himself implicitly admitted status's persistence when he noted that "in a state based on contract sentiment is out of place in any public or common affairs. It is relegated to the sphere of private and personal relations, where it depends not at all on class types but on personal acquaintance and personal estimates."[5] Writing on *What Social Classes Owe to Each Other,* Sumner was at pains to argue that any residue of inherited status had nothing to do with class. But in relegating sentiment to the private sphere he implied that status persisted in gender relations. It also persisted in another area that remains of great concern to us in late twentieth-century America: race. Furthermore, despite Sumner's objections, status also affected class relations, although here the question of inherited status is indeed complicated.

Sumner did not deny the existence of classes. For him the competition fostered by contract led to a division between people. But because all were given equal opportunity, that division was natural, not based on caste. In a contractual society, Sumner might argue, economic success dictated a man's social status rather than social status dictating his economic position. But as Karl Polanyi points out, it is a mistake to think of class only in terms of economic interest. "Purely economic matters such as affect want-satisfaction are incomparably less relevant to class behavior than questions of social recognition. . . . The interests of a class most directly refer to standing and rank, to status and security; that is, they are primarily not economic but social."[6]

As *The Rise of Silas Lapham* indicates, wealth alone is not the final measure of social status. Even so, the genteel elite, represented by the Coreys in this novel by William Dean Howells, still felt threatened by the revaluation of status brought about by the period's realignment of economic power. The elite's anxiety was shared by workers who, even when granted more earning power, faced the threat of becoming dependent wage earners rather than relatively independent craftsmen. William Forbath has shown that the period's labor movement was not simply about wages and hours of work. It was also animated by principles of classical republican virtue associated with an artisanal economy where workers owned their means of production.[7] As late as 1883 the majority of workers in industry were skilled craftsmen employed in shops of twenty to thirty workers. For instance, the workers that Henry James highlights in *The Princess Casamassima* are a bookbinder and a pharmacist.[8] The realists themselves shared workers' worries. Along with other professional writers, they were bound to publishing firms by contractual agreements.[9] Furthermore, the "status rebellion" described by Richard Hofstadter was felt most markedly when the rise of corporations threatened to make members of the middle class salaried workers.[10] Indeed, what Alan Trachtenberg calls the "incorporation of America" is another reason why contract failed to live up to its promise.[11] Corporate forms of organization, in which individual members submit their legal identities to the corporate whole, are quite different from contractual ones, in which people form associations while retaining their legal identities. Contract might have reigned in the law during this period, but it reigned over an economy that was turning into a corporate rather than contractual one, or, to be more accurate, one of "corporate liberalism" that worked out a complicated alliance between corporate and contractual capitalism.[12] That alliance did not eliminate the status of class, but it did transform it. For instance, since a corporation is a legal person, a labor contract between Standard Oil and a worker trying to avoid unemployment would be dealt with as one negotiated between equal bargaining partners.

If contract promises free and equal exchange among all individuals and thus equality of opportunity, the increase in corporate influence and the persistence of status in race, class, and gender—even if manifested in different ways—made delivery on that promise impossible. Instead, contract's promise could be evoked ideologically to create the illusion of equitable social relations when in fact they retained a residue of inherited and realigned hierarchy.[13] In latter chapters I elaborate on reasons for contract's failure. For now, however, I need to indicate how works of literary realism can evoke contract's promise.

Two poignant examples occur in works that establish both Mark Twain and James as realists. Both works derive much of their force from scenes that hold out the promise of replacing relationships of status with more equitable, "contractual" ones. One such scene occurs in *Adventures of Huckleberry Finn* after Huck tricks Jim into believing that the difficulties they experienced on the raft while traveling through a dense fog resulted from a dream. Realizing that his trick has betrayed Jim's trust, Huck apologizes, even though doing so means humbling himself to "a nigger." Until this scene Huck and Jim's relationship was governed by their socially assigned status: Jim's as a slave; Huck's as a free white. With Huck's apology, their relationship promises to be one of free and equal individuals bound together by mutual benefit and trust, so long as they remain on the raft, uncontaminated by the hierarchical order of the shore world.

A similar moment of promise occurs in James's *The American*. James's hero, Christopher Newman, the self-made man who has conquered the world of American business, seeks the hand of the beautiful daughter of an aristocratic French family, the Bellegardes. Looked down on by his lover's mother and elder brother, Newman elicits from them a promise that they will not interfere with his courtship. Told nonetheless that the mother will not enjoy having her daughter marry him, Newman is unconcerned. " 'If you stick to your own side of the contract we shall not quarrel; that is all I ask of you,' said Newman. 'Keep your hands off, and give me an open field. I am very much in earnest, and there is not the slightest danger of my getting discouraged or backing out. You will have me constantly before your eyes; if you don't like it, I am sorry for you. I will do for your daughter, if she will accept me, everything that a man can do for a woman. I am happy to tell you that, as a promise—a pledge. I consider that on your side you make me an equal pledge. You will not back out, eh?'"[14]

There is no better symptom of Newman's innocence than his belief in "the contract" that he has entered into with the Bellegarde family, which does nothing more than remove status as a consideration in determining whether he is worthy of marrying the woman he loves and who loves him. Part of that innocence grows out of Newman's past success in an economic sphere in which the social status of contracting parties was supposedly irrelevant. Though in *The American* James demonstrates that in Europe, at least, that ideal does not extend to the business of marriage, in subsequent works he suggests that status affects even business affairs.

If these two scenes evoke contract's promise, the works in which they occur fail to sustain it. That failure has important implications for our contemporary situation. Contract may be in disrepute in some academic circles, but not all, as evidenced by its sophisticated defense by Charles Fried, Ronald Reagan's former solicitor general, in *Contract as Promise*, as well as by the influence of the law-and-economics movement with its model of rational (that is, market-based) decision making.[15] Furthermore, as the 1994 electoral success of the "Contract with America" demonstrated, the idea of contract remains popular with many voters. The Republicans' "Contract" appealed to both aspects of the promise of contract. First, the metaphor of a contract capitalized on voters' discontent with broken promises in past campaigns. The symbolic act of signing something called a contract signaled its supporters' intention to keep their word. Second, a contractual relation between politicians and voters implied that they were on equal footing, that there was no hierarchical relation between the governed and those governing. Indeed, the popularity of the "Contract" with white males indicated the extent to which its provisions appealed to those worried that, by determining one's worth on the basis of status, not merit, programs such as affirmative action undermine the promise of equal opportunity for all citizens. Although they may not welcome the lesson, supporters of the "Contract" certainly have much to learn from the realists' dramatization of why contract failed to live up to its promise.[16]

But they are not the only ones with something to learn. As works of realism explore the possibility of presenting a world in which people are bound together contractually, they bring us to its limits. Those opposed to contract might want to call these presentations immanent critiques that expose the contradictions of contractual thought by working within its premises. But whereas works of realism enable such criticism, they do more than pose a challenge to contract's defenders. They also challenge those who dismiss contract as discredited and inherently corrupt. Evoking the promise of contract, the works of realism that I examine are not written in opposition to contract. Indeed, insofar as they link contract's failed promise to the persistence of status, they leave open the possibility that status is more of a problem than is contract. To be sure, strong historical evidence suggests that to initiate a reign of contract in a world in which status persists is to perpetuate social and economic hierarchies. Nonetheless, contract's promise persists as something to be reckoned with.

One of my goals in writing this book is, therefore, to invite contract's advocates and detractors to experience how works of realism, in presenting both the promise and failure of contract, suggest ways in which it can be reimagined. In the end such readers might reconfirm their beliefs that contractual thought is inherently superior or inherently flawed. But if so, I hope that reading this book will help contract's advocates avoid the causes of its past failures, and help contract's detractors better address the aspirations of the many in our culture who still sense its promise.

II

That lofty goal expressed, I am brought back to reality by the need to define how I designate a work in this period realistic. In 1889 Albion W. Tourgée, the lawyer/novelist who would represent Homer Plessy before the Supreme Court, argued, "On every novelist rests alike the same obligation of truth-telling. 'Realist,' 'Naturalist,' 'idealist,' 'romanticist,' only that and nothing more, can be demanded of them—that they paint life as they see it, feel it, believe it to be." His quarrel with the realists, he declared, focuses on their claim to possess the only view of truth.[17] Tourgée's point is well taken. Many artists try to present realistic visions of the world. Any judgment of whether or not a work is realistic depends on the sense of reality in which one operates. Since a sense of reality can change from author to author and critic to critic, why give some works the privileged label of realism?

One way of responding to the insight that realism is a convention as much as any other presentation of reality is to describe the particular sense of reality that self-proclaimed realists perceive.[18] In the nineteenth century it was frequently defined in terms of empirical facts. For instance, writing on the visual arts, Linda Nochlin claims that prior to the nineteenth century, artists concerned with verisimilitude "were looking through eyes, feeling and thinking with hearts and brains, and painting with brushes, steeped in a context of belief in the reality of something other and beyond that of the mere external, tangible facts they held before them." In the nineteenth century, however, artists lived in a world that came "to equate belief in the facts with the total content of belief itself."[19]

David Shi has drawn on this belief to provide an inclusive definition that allows him to make an interdisciplinary case for the coherence of an Age of Realism.[20] Concerned with differences as much as with coherence, my approach is quite different from Shi's. If Shi brings diverse figures and movements under the label of realism on the basis of commonalities, I emphasize distinctions between works that share common themes and even close attention to social detail. Those distinctions result in an exclusive definition that tries to account for what we experience in reading some works that we do not experience while reading others written at the same time. That difference, I argue—and in doing so make my contribution to discussions of American literary realism—is linked to how works of literary realism evoke the promise of contract.

Contract's promise to generate an immanent, rather than transcendental, ordering of society suggests that how "facts" are ordered is more important than simple attention to them. What distinguishes works of realism in the period is their horizontal rather than vertical ordering of the facts of social life. Not positing a governing moral order to the world, they evoke the promise of achieving a just social balance by experimenting with exchanges and negotiations among contracting parties. My claim is not that the realists self-consciously set out to embody that promise in their work. It is simply that, working within the framework of contractarian thought, they evoke it in their attempts to write the truest stories possible. In turn, an understanding of that promise enhances our appreciation of the contribution made by realists working in the American context.

One of the most important effects of ordering a work horizontally rather than vertically is that it alters the relation between reader and text, what some critics call the readerly contract.[21] The terms of the realists' implied contract are noteworthy. Winfried Fluck has argued that realists abandon the use of paternal guidelines for their readers. For them, the ideal role for the literary work is no longer that of a "guardian figure" but a "conversational partner."[22] Rather than prescribe a code of behavior, such a work includes readers in a dialogue in which judgments of actions are constructed through a process of negotiation and exchange. As Edith Wharton puts it, the "literary artist," unlike the "professed moralist," allows the reader to "draw his own conclusions from the facts presented."[23]

The issue is not just about didacticism or readerly participation, since many works are not didactic and readers participate in all works of literature. It is about how the reader is positioned within the world of the text. As Erich Auerbach has shown while writing about nineteenth-century realism in general, a horizontal ordering principle levels the hierarchy of styles present in other works, thus making available "the unprejudiced, precise, interior and exterior representations of the random lives of different people."[24] Readers who enter such a world participate in a moral economy in which people potentially stand on an equal footing with one another.

That world is generated by certain literary techniques developed by the realists. An obvious one is James's emphasis on showing rather than telling. James's abandonment of an omniscient perspective for a limited point of view can be—and has been—seen as a challenge to the transcendental view of the world.[25] Drawing on Ross Posnock's important distinction between a technique of central consciousness and belief in a centered consciousness, we can see why James's innovation is not, as Fredric Jameson charges, a bourgeois "strategy of containment."[26] James develops this technique to explore what Tony Tanner identifies as a typical situation in his works: "a person confronting new facts with an old vision, or set of values or system of belief, and experiencing a convulsion of values because the old 'vision' will not adequately account for the newly perceived facts."[27] Making readers undergo a similar experience, the Jamesian point of view forces them to negotiate their way through a world without clear-cut moral signposts.

As different as Twain is from James, he too presents us with worlds in which the moral guideposts of an outdated paternalism are challenged. For an example, we can compare Twain's *Huckleberry Finn* with Thomas Bailey Aldrich's *The Story of a Bad Boy*. Howells praised Aldrich's book for showing "what a boy's life is . . . with so little purpose of teaching what it should be."[28] Nonetheless, unlike Twain, Aldrich does not tell his story from the boy's perspective. The narrator is an adult looking back on his youth. We know from the start that the boy has become the respectable adult whose measured voice mediates an earlier experience. Our travels with Huck take place without that paternal guidance.

To be sure, the leveling process dramatized in their works worried the realists, who feared that it was producing a society lacking discrimination. Nonetheless, in their best works they refused to react to it by falling back on a preexisting moral order, which is not to say that they were equally successful in all areas of experience. For instance, works by James are generally more effective than works by Twain in challenging a natural moral order in terms of gender. In contrast, Twain's works, more than James's, challenge received notions about the status of race. But these differences do not undercut my approach; they instead highlight the need to differentiate, even among the realists themselves. They had different visions, and whereas Howells tends to unite the three, James and Twain often seem at odds. To respect their differences is to enable critical comparisons.

In making possible these critical comparisons, my definition of realism trusts the tale, not the teller. That trust leads to a number of paradoxes. For instance, although most of the works in the period that formally embody contract's promise and failure are written by acknowledged realists, not all works written by them do so with equal force. Some of their lesser works do not do so at all. Thus, according to my definition, not all works written by "the realists" embody the full potential of realism. At the same time, Kate Chopin's *The Awakening,* often called naturalistic, to a greater extent does embody it.

Since these paradoxes are bound to cause confusion, it might seem wise to find a label other than realism. I do not for two reasons. First, a new term is likely to create confusion of its own. Second, the realists deserve credit for developing the technical innovations that allow us to evoke what I am calling the promise of contract. Acknowledging those innovations, my definition has the payoff of enabling needed discrimination.[29]

For instance, it allows us to distinguish works of realism from those of sentimental fiction. Recently some critics have argued that the sentimentalists' detailed portrayal of everyday, domestic life qualifies them as realists. Rich in verisimilitude, their descriptions, nonetheless, continue to be ordered by their authors' faith in a transcendental, usually religious, moral order. The realists' technical innovations helped to free their presentations from subordination to such an order.[30] My point is not that we should stop reading works of sentiment. As should become clear, I have read my share. But, as we read them, we should acknowledge the ordering principle of the world that we are invited to enter.

Attention to how details are ordered also leads us to recognize a weakness in Richard Chase's argument that American naturalism is simply realism with a "necessitarian ideology" and George J. Becker's definition of naturalism as "no more than an emphatic and explicit philosophical position taken by some realists."[31] As realistic as the details of naturalism may be, those details are subordinated to a governing ordering principle. For instance, in an excellent reading of Dreiser's styles, Sandy Petrey argues that *Sister Carrie* has two linguistic registers. On the one hand, there is the "dominant style" identified by "what Auerbach calls a paratactic structure" and "the prevalence of lexical choices from the vocabulary of everyday life." On the other, Dreiser provides "hypotactic passages of moral speculation which periodically interrupt [the language of realism]."[32] Dismissing the hypotactic passages as the language of false consciousness, Petrey attempts to salvage Dreiser's novel by claiming that it points out the irreconcilability between the styles. But even though the two may be irreconcilable for Petrey, they were not for Dreiser, who continued to structure the real according to a moral order.

Defining realism in terms of the promise of contract also points to its difference from what we can call the fiction of republican virtue. Such fiction extends an eighteenth-century tradition that used literature ethically, politically, and aesthetically to fashion citizens for a virtuous republic.[33] *The Bread-Winners* by John Hay, *Democracy* by Henry Adams, and novels of the "plantation school" by Thomas Nelson Page are examples. To be sure, Hay and Adams shared ethical and political beliefs with writers who produced works of realism. Nonetheless, their aesthetic presentation of fictional worlds continues to imply the existence of a moral order that *should* govern the republic, even if, as in the case of *Democracy,* it is embodied in a woman and a gentleman lawyer from Virginia excluded by their moral principles from political power in Washington. Works of realism challenge the tradition of republican virtue, not by abandoning the quest for a just social order, but by trying to imagine it horizontally rather than vertically. In works of realism there is no "right reason" governing the world.

The distinction between horizontal and vertical balancing helps to differentiate realistic works in this period from works of romance. An example is Melville's *Billy Budd*. Composed during the period of realism, Melville's novella has the trappings of romance. As Michael Rogin puts it, "As is true for romance, the mundane world left to itself cannot provide meaning."[34] In a romance, as in *Billy Budd*, meaning of the everyday, no matter how realistically rendered, must be sought in a transcendent world. Granted, the narrator warns us that *Billy Budd* is no romance, and Melville's plot suggests that the higher world to which it appeals has itself been emptied of meaning. Thus, *Billy Budd* anticipates those works of modernism, which Georg Lukàcs, drawing on Walter Benjamin's notion of allegory, describes as presenting a concrete sense of everyday life devoid of significance.[35] To be sure, Twain and James each in his own way served as a model for various modernist writers, Twain through his use of the vernacular, James through his mastery of psychological realism. Nonetheless, my point is that a vertical appeal to meaning is, for the most part, underplayed in the works of realism that I examine.

Of course, it is not totally absent, and critics lodged within Chase's romance thesis have been intent on arguing that in fact the repressed soul of American realism remains the romance.[36] Works of realism, so the argument runs, demystify imaginative visions of romance by positing a more realistic world. Nonetheless, because the realistic world that they posit is itself an imaginative construct, realists are ultimately forced to acknowledge the reality of romance as the foundation of their works. The project of realism, it seems, is condemned to fail.

Like so many others, works of realism do participate in a process of demystification. For instance, *Huckleberry Finn* challenges Tom Sawyer's bookish interpretation of the world.[37] Likewise, *Silas Lapham* mocks sentimental fiction, while in James's works characters undergo an education in illusion. But to define realistic works in terms of demystification is ultimately to leave us with no way to distinguish them from others. Once we start to demystify, most works of literature can be shown to repeat the same process of seeking to represent reality only to acknowledge consciously or unconsciously their failure to do so.

Critics lock themselves into an undifferentiated reading of realism by focusing on a vertical axis of analysis. Continuing to seek a work's supposed foundational first principle only to undermine it, they confirm over and over again what they claim to know from the start: foundations are constructed.[38]

The fixation on exposing the constructed nature of foundations may lead to an undifferentiated view of realism, but it forces me to clarify my claims about the readerly contract. After all, if no work can successfully re-present reality, even the vertical ordering principles of nonrealist works can be exposed as constructs, leaving all readers in the position of fashioning a world without solid foundations. If so, there seems to be nothing unique about the readerly contract with works of realism.

But there is. Works like *Moby-Dick* and *The Scarlet Letter* question transcendental guarantees, but the space that they create for readerly participation is a space of indeterminacy generated by metaphysical or epistemological uncertainty. It results, in other words, from a hermeneutics of suspicion that questions the vertical order that the works seem to posit. In contrast, in works of realism as I have defined them participation results from readers binding themselves to a work's horizontal axis, one that tries to imagine the creation of an equitable social order through interpersonal exchanges. It results, in other words, not from having a work's fictional foundations exposed, but from readers exposing themselves to a world of social relations without foundational principles of order.

To argue that works of realism lack foundational principles of order flies in the face of the commonplace assumption that realists found their works on the claim that they represent reality itself. But it is a mistake to assume that all share the "fantasy," in Jean-François Lyotard's words, "to seize reality."[39] In philosophy Hilary Putnam takes pride in calling himself a realist, even though he does not subscribe to a correspondence theory of truth.[40] But in literary criticism too many critics continue to assume that realists try to find language that corresponds to a preexisting reality.[41] Far from assuming the existence of a self-contained reality that can be seized, the realists that I treat present reality as a process-in-the-making. They share what Laurence B. Holland calls James's "determination to forge or shape a changing world, to create a society, to take his place in a community-in-the-making by joining in the process of making it."[42] A theory of representation adequate to these writers can draw on the German *Darstellung,* which means representation, a presentation, and a theatrical performance. Not trying to *seize* reality, they *present* or *perform* it.[43]

By focusing on the realists' efforts to forge a social and aesthetic balance horizontally, I move away from readings that demonstrate why works of realism inevitably fail to re-present reality. Instead, I emphasize the sense of reality that realists do present.[44] To be sure, their works continue to demystify assumptions about fixed foundations. They also present a sense of failure. But the failure that I focus on is not the failure to present a Cartesian foundation of certainty. It is instead the failure to sustain the promise that an equitable social order can be constructed on the basis of interpersonal exchanges lacking the regulation of transcendental principles.

The realists' reticence to adopt a transcendental position of judgment has opened them to charges of complicity with the status quo. A common early complaint was that they did not offer model characters.[45] A generation later Van Wyck Brooks argued that Twain was simply a humorist, not a full-fledged satirist, because he lacked a clear-cut alternative to the world that he mocked.[46]

If earlier critics faulted realists for failing to resist the breakdown of a moral social order, recent critics complain that they participate in subtle forms of ideological control that enforce the status quo. This view has been influenced, on the one hand, by Roland Barthes's claim that realism castrates desire by privileging a bourgeois sense of what is possible and, on the other, by Michel Foucault's fascination with discourse as a modern technology of control.[47] For instance, Nancy Armstrong and Leonard Tennenhouse argue that "the violence of an earlier political order maintained by overt social control gives way to a more subtle kind of power that . . . works through the printed word upon mind and emotions rather than body and soul."[48] Secret agents of the police, realists turn out to enact fantasies of surveillance enforcing normative behavior. Intent on measuring the "cultural work" done by literature, Philip Fisher concludes that "in its rituals every state is a police state."[49] Even when a writer self-consciously demystifies the "realist policing of the real," as James does in *The Princess Casamassima,* he doesn't get off the hook. "This police work," according to Mark Seltzer, "is finally remystified, recuperated as the 'innocent' work of the imagination."[50]

The problem with this police academy approach to realism is highlighted in Seltzer's characterization of James's work. When someone claims that James sees his works as "innocent," I have to wonder who is involved in mystification. The answer to such charges is not to claim that the realists were innocents either at home or abroad. In any work implying a vision of the polis, some form of policing goes on. What the critics of counterespionage fail to acknowledge, however, is that their criticism of novelistic surveillance has no power unless it assumes the ideal of a utopian world of free and equal exchange unconstrained by regulatory forces—a vision, in other words, that comes very close to what I have called the promise of contract. Indeed, these critics' distrust of regulation is even stronger than that of most laissez-faire thinkers who fully acknowledged the need for some—if limited—police powers for the state. Given the utopian vision enabling their demystifications, such critics might learn from the way works of realism relate to contract's promise.

My point is not that works of realism are somehow outside of ideology. On the contrary, by engaging readers in a world of conflicting views, none of which is adequate, they can be said to generate citizens for life in a liberal democracy. Nonetheless, even if readers are subjected to the structure of these works, that subjection is different in kind from the experience of works that try to teach readers a moral lesson or, through more subtle forms of policing, make them conform to a unitary "logic" of an age.

To be sure, to expose unacknowledged forms of policing and literature's complicity with them is to do valuable work. But its limits are indicated by the types of questions that such work leaves unasked. Unless we are prepared to advocate a return to an "earlier political order" that maintained control through overt violence because it was somehow more "honest" in its display of power, our present situation forces us to ask: of the various social visions presented, which are the most equitable and on what basis do we judge their equity? By interrelating a discussion of works of American literary realism with the promise of contract, this book raises such necessary, if ultimately unanswerable, questions. A summary of my argument follows.

III

The next chapter introduces the paradox that contract, radically conceived, promises a more equitable society by abandoning transcendental guarantees for equity. In order to explain this paradox I discuss contract's link with promising, which is thought of as a dynamic, interpersonal creation of duties and obligations rather than as an activity receiving its sanctity from God's witness. Evoked by the horizontal ordering principle of works of literary realism, this radical promise is betrayed by legal thought of the period. One reason for that betrayal is the transcendental moral sanction granted to contract as a result of the battle over slavery in the Civil War. That moral sanctity is linked to the period's notorious legal formalism. Using three 14th Amendment cases,

I show how the formalists claimed to use science to discover foundational principles rooted in the nature of things. An important component of such formalism was the establishment of distinct boundaries among different spheres of social activity, with contract having "natural" reign in only the economic and political spheres, not, for instance, in the domestic sphere where status still ruled. Such boundaries established clearly delineated limits to human responsibility for social and economic inequalities, limits that the realists' evocation of contract's intersubjective promise call into question.

Chapters 3 through 8 present close readings of various literary texts. A separate chapter is devoted to each of the three most prominent realists: James, Howells, and Twain. The other three examine and compare novels concerned with contractual relations written by nonrealists. These three chapters are important to my argument, since they highlight the distinctive nature of realist texts, which is not simply thematic treatment of contract, but formal embodiment of its promise and failure.

The chapter on James juxtaposes *The Bostonians* and *The Aspern Papers* as a way of exploring complications posed to contractual thought by the marriage contract, a special sort of contract that at the time constructed a relation of status between husband and wife. This chapter takes as its point of departure reflections on the relationship between the domestic sphere created by the marriage contract and the right to privacy that was first articulated in American law shortly after the publication of James's two works. It concludes by distinguishing what is mistakenly called James's belief in a work of art's autonomy from his defense of a work's privacy. Chapter 4 compares two works that offer very different portrayals of both labor unrest and marriage: John Hay's *The Bread-Winners* and Elizabeth Stuart Phelps's *The Silent Partner*. As different as the two are, both present worlds governed by a transcendental principle of moral order: in *The Bread-Winners*, a classical republican sense of right reason, in *The Silent Partner*, an evangelical sense of God's higher justice.

These two works differ, not only from James's novels, but from Howells's *The Rise of Silas Lapham*, which is the topic of the fifth chapter. As it interrelates plots concerning the worlds of business and romance, Howells's novel challenges a formalism that tries to establish clear-cut boundaries between the two. It also defies critics who try to account for its action by positing a unified, governing logic. Instead, by adopting a form that tries to remain true to a world of temporality that renders all formal solutions subject to revision, this novel explores the difficulty and necessity of assessing individual responsibility in an economy of the unaccountable.

The first three chapters of literary analysis examine the role of contract in the domestic and economic spheres. The next two introduce the complications of race. The first of these two contrasts Howells's presentation of an interracial marriage in *An Imperative Duty* with two novels by Charles Chesnutt, one about an interracial love affair—*The House Behind the Cedars*—and one about the effect of race on the economy of the New South—*The Colonel's Dream*. Chesnutt shrewdly analyzes how racial status undermines contract's promise of equal economic opportunity, and a number of his literary techniques match the realists at their best. But ultimately his works are governed by a transcendental sense of right reason that provides him and his implied readers with a position from which to judge questions of racial justice. It is precisely such a position that the dramatic action of Twain's *Pudd'nhead Wilson,* discussed in chapter 7, denies us. This chapter compares the dramatic action of Twain's novel with the logic of *Plessy v. Ferguson* (1896), the case declaring "separate but equal laws" constitutional. It also contrasts Twain's work with *Pactolus Prime,* a novel written by Tourgée, Plessy's attorney and a critic of realism. More progressive on racial politics than any of the realists, Tourgée offers us an ideal opportunity to explore the question of whether or not our judgment of realistic texts should rest solely on the political point of view that they present.

Chapter 8 turns to a topic that did not captivate the primary interest of the realists: the threat posed to contract-based relations by the rise of corporations. Concerned with the perceived loss of individual independence, the chapter looks at two neglected novels: David Graham Phillips's *The Cost* and Francis Lynde's *The Grafters*. Both evoke traditional values of autonomy while actually constructing a new version of the autonomous self that contributes to a "politics of character."

This chapter helps to clarify the realists' relation to "progressive" political thought. In an excellent book Amy Kaplan argues that realism was a way of "imagining and managing the threat of social change."[51] As fitting as this description is, there is a tendency to read it as evidence of the realists' conservatism and their fear of progressive reform. But unless we assume a teleological view of history, not all social change is positive, not all progressivism that liberating. Insofar as one of the most important changes occurring during the end of the nineteenth century was the ascendancy of corporate capitalism, for the realists to imagine a sense of individual agency and responsibility that resists incorporation might not be so reactionary. To be sure, it has become increasingly popular to accuse the realists of clinging to a nostalgic belief in the autonomous subject. In contrast, literary naturalists are said to respond to the new consumer-oriented economy. Although a detailed analysis of the complexity of literary naturalism is beyond the scope of this study, I argue—in opposition to critics such as Walter Benn Michaels and James Livingston—that the realists, unlike the naturalists and writers such as Phillips and Lynde, present works that allow us to imagine a sense of individual agency without assuming the existence of an autonomous self.[52]

In my final chapter I lend support to the argument that social and economic changes in the late nineteenth century helped to generate new forms of subjectivity. But I challenge accounts based on simple oppositions between two types of subjectivity, whether they oppose the subjectivities of producer and consumer economies; a cult of sincerity and one of performance, character and personality; modern and postmodern selves; or individual autonomy and corporate interdependence. The point is not that such distinctions lack importance but that turning them into binary oppositions generates narratives of transformation that are far too simple. History is much messier. Comparing a sense of agency implied by works of realism with many others available at the time, I link it, with the aid of Hannah Arendt, to the interpersonal activity of promising that is so important to the utopian possibilities of contract. The primary literary text for the final chapter is Kate Chopin's *The Awakening*. But *The Awakening* also poses a challenge to even a reimagined sense of contract: can it deal with the labor involved in the delivery of children into the world? Or, to rephrase the question, how can what seems to be an essentially synchronic mode of contract deal with the problematics of inheritance and the responsibility of providing future generations with the promise of a better life?

IV

This summary indicates that, although I am clearly interested in the relation between literature and history, my argument does not conform to a traditional sense of what constitutes historical criticism. To begin with, rather than attempt to use realism as the writers of the time used the term, I develop my own definition in an effort to explain how the works that I treat maintain their power to engage readers today. Interested in the persistence of that power, I do not trace the rise and fall of realism as a movement. Furthermore, my focus is not on the trajectory of individual authors' careers. While recognizing the importance of an author's development, I look primarily for textual moments in which the failed promise of contract is most poignantly dramatized. It is these moments that allow me to make connections between works of literature and the Age of Contract in the law. But even they are organized only loosely chronologically.

These aspects do not mean that my study lacks an implied diachronic narrative. Like many cultural critics writing today, I link important shifts in subjectivity to a transformation from proprietary capitalism and its focus on production to corporate capitalism and its focus on consumption. I do, however, challenge the clear-cut breaks that too many of those writing about that transformation imply. The shift from production to consumption is no more absolute than was the shift from status to contract. Furthermore, I challenge many interpretations of the transformation's significance, just as in the next chapter I challenge progressivism's interpretation of the significance of important 14th Amendment cases. My challenge is based in part on a strategy of concentrating most of my analysis on three historical moments.

The first is the mid-1880s. Indeed, the 1885 *Century Magazine* contains a number of the works that I look at: it serialized *The Rise of Silas Lapham* and *The Bostonians* and published George Washington Cable's "The Freedman's Case in Equity," Henry Grady's response, and an excerpt from *Adventures of Huckleberry Finn*. This moment also saw much of the Civil Rights Act of 1875 struck down by the Supreme Court in 1883; the election in 1884 of the first Democratic president after the Civil War; a heated debate over divorce; the Haymarket affair; the formation of the American Federation of Labor in 1886; Sumner's articulation of his laissez-faire doctrine in 1883, which I have been citing; and the publication of Christopher Tiedeman's *A Treatise on the Limitations of Police Powers in the United States* in 1886. And it saw the Supreme Court guarantee corporations 14th Amendment protections and thus, in the name of contract, help to undermine contract's domination just as it reached the height of its power. I cluster another group of texts around *Plessy v. Ferguson* (1896). Finally, my corporate chapter examines two texts written in 1904, while my study is framed by *Lochner v. New York* (1905).

If my concentration on these three moments illustrates various trans-formations, it also enables a synchronic analysis whose details do not always fit into forward-moving diachronic narratives. Although I se-lected the works that I did because they help to advance my narrative, their complexity poses a challenge to diachronic narratives, including my own. Indeed, the failure of stories about historical transformations to account for all details of history and literature is part of the story I want to tell, since it reminds us of aspects of the past that, in resisting translation into the present, persist as a challenge to our present con-structions of reality.

To be sure, some readers will object that my selection of works leaves too many out. If, for instance, I had chosen *Iola Leroy* rather than *A House Behind the Cedars,* or Edith Wharton rather than Henry James, I would have been forced to tell a somewhat different story. My re-sponse is twofold. First, the story that I tell is not the only story to be told. Unlike others, I do not claim to discover a logic that accounts for every text produced in the age. At the same time, I think that my story is an important one, one that would remain untold if contract in the law and realism in literature were not put in relation to one another. Readers will have to decide if they agree that it is a story worth telling.

Second, selecting other works would not have substantially altered my claims about either the failed promise of contract or a potential within realistic texts that distinguishes them from other texts written at the time. As I have already explained, I chose the realistic works that I did, not because they are representative of a career, but because they dramatize that potential, a potential not found in even all works written by the realists. I chose the nonrealist works in part because of the pressure they put on my thesis. For instance, it was not at all clear to me when I began whether Chesnutt's texts relied on a transcendental or-dering principle or not. On that issue *Iola Leroy* does not present the same problem of judgment.

The pressure that works of realism continue to place on our assump-tions brings me to the possible objection that my emphasis on these works' readerly contract is ahistorical. At stake is the role literary texts play within historical criticism. For many, the historical criticism of literature means bringing historical evidence to bear on the reading of texts and the use of literary texts as historical evidence. Historical evi-dence gives readings a context lacking in pure formalism, which in turn allows works of literature to illustrate historical transformations or the felt life of a period.

Such criticism is important and is crucial to my project. Nonetheless, it raises the nagging question of why works of fiction are given the status of historical evidence. It would seem that those intent on an accurate understanding of the past would be better advised to rely on the evidence of nonfictional texts. To be sure, an important part of understanding the past is to understand the stories that people tell one another about the world they inhabit. For this task works of fiction do provide important evidence. But they also have the capacity to contribute to a redefinition of what we mean by historical criticism.

The sense of historicity that we get from studying literature can be more than an understanding of the past or of how the past led to the present. It can also generate a sense of the present itself as a moment of history, one that future generations will judge on the basis of the possibilities it created. To think of a sense of historicity as an attitude toward the present as much as toward the past suggests that literary texts can do more than provide historical evidence. By involving readers in the construction of their worlds, they allow them to experience how judgments and actions of the past, conducted without certain knowledge of their consequences, help to determine the shape of the future.

If literary texts have the capacity to invite readers to participate in the responsibilities of historical judgment, we still need to ask why some texts written in the past raise questions that continue to engage us, while others remain of interest mostly as period pieces. One answer lies in their way of confronting crucial anthropological questions. For instance, as much as the meaning of death might change from culture to culture and historical period to historical period, death remains a fact of life that everyone must face. Other questions, however, are more specifically historical, since they involve issues that a particular culture has not yet resolved.

The works of realism that I examine retain the power to engage us today in part, I argue, because for our culture the promise of contract that they evoke is still open. To be sure, it is not the only issue treated by texts in the past that is still open. But it is one worth careful attention. One result is that the contract that a work of realism creates with its readers is similar to what in law is called an aleatory contract, one open to chance. As historical contingencies lead us to renegotiate our relation to the work, we are confronted with the historicity of the present and the responsibilities entailed in imagining a more equitable social order in a world presented to us without fixed moral guidelines.

It should go without saying that our contract with the work is never completely successful, that we will never produce perfectly balanced readings. Nonetheless, our failure to sustain contract's promise in our readings of realistic works opens us to the insight that they do not simply present us with a self-contained logic that we can then judge. Instead, in reading them we are transported to a much more uncertain mental territory, one with the capacity to force reconsideration of our presuppositions about how social relations are constructed.

Linking works of literary realism to contractual thought does more than expose contradictions in the period's boundary ideology. It also indicates what is lost in the failure to realize contract's promise. Much would be gained if contemporary critics would acknowledge that loss. Not to do so is to abandon a way of measuring social justice that relies on standards created by interpersonal agreement, not transcendental principles. For instance, the book most responsible in the period for calling attention to the injustices perpetuated against Native Americans, Helen Hunt Jackson's *A Century of Dishonor,* draws its moral force from broken promises made in treaties. Similarly, a recent work of history condemns American slavery with its title: *Without Consent or Contract.*[53] When Martin Luther King Jr. proclaimed that the architects of the Declaration of Independence and the Constitution signed a "promissory note" that has not yet been paid to all Americans, he also evoked contract's promise.[54]

To be sure, earlier in the century Roscoe Pound correctly noted that "wealth in a commercial age is made up largely of promises. An important part of everyone's substance consists of advantages which others have promised to provide for or to render to him; of demands to have the advantages promised which he may assert not against the world at large but against particular individuals."[55] But the pervasiveness of contract in the economic realm should not lead to the error that plagues even the best recent criticism. That error surfaces in Hugh Collins's claim that contract law assumed the "justice of an order of wealth and power established through exchange relations. This faith stems from the belief that the market order establishes equality in the place of social hierarchy and reciprocity instead of exploitation."[56] Almost imperceptibly, Collins identifies all human exchanges with market exchanges. Critics linking literature to the market make the same mistake. To be sure, the rise of the market influenced all areas of human life. But it did not completely determine them. We should remember, as

Hannah Arendt reminds us, that not all exchanges are strictly market exchanges.[57]

In the late nineteenth century contract failed to deliver on its promise, in part because legal theorists did not consider the effect of exchanges *between* the market and other spheres of action that continued to be governed by status. The resulting exploitation should not, however, cause us to subsume all exchanges under market exchanges. Nor should it lead us too hastily to abandon the sense of responsible individual agency linked to the exchange of promises. The realists' retention of this "promise" of contract has particular poignancy today because it points to one of the most important failures in contemporary criticisms of contract. Conflating contractual human agency with the human agency assumed by a laissez-faire system of governance, critics influenced by poststructuralism too often allow cultural conservatives to monopolize discussions of an individual's duties and obligations, of individual responsibility and blame. Indeed, despite important differences, there are affinities between various poststructuralist accounts of the cultural-constructedness of the self and the notion of selfhood that serves the corporate liberalism that helped to displace the ascendancy of contractual liberalism in American social thought. Literary realists offer a much more complicated notion of selfhood and human agency than they are often given credit for.

One of the ironies of an almost exclusive concern with the cultural constructedness of the self is that it risks returning us to a situation in which a person's worth is determined by social status. Unless we want to abandon ourselves to a world in which identity is inevitably determined by one's race, class, or gender, we need some alternative vision of measuring a person's worth. Recognizing the role that status plays in political and economic as well as social exchanges, the realists, nonetheless, continue to present in their works the promise of what Howells calls "that republic of letters where all men are free and equal."[58]

My point is not that the realists are radical social egalitarians. They are not. Their sense of free and equal is closer to Justice Sandra Day O'Connor's when she argues that the constitutional guarantee of freedom of religion means that people's religious beliefs should not affect their political standing.[59] Rarely explicitly political in their works, the realists are most interested in the possibilities of freedom within civil society, which Michael Walzer defines as the "space of uncoerced human association and also the set of relational networks—formed for the sake of

family, faith, interest, and ideology—that fill this space."[60] Presenting
the relations in that space, the realists remain intrigued by the promise
of contract. To be sure, their works dramatize the failure of that promise; nonetheless, it has not been completely laid to rest. It persists as a
force to be reckoned with in contemporary negotiations about how our
society should be more equitably ordered. Its persistence helps account
for challenges that works of realism continue to pose to us. The next
chapter begins by exploring one of the most important challenges, how
to determine an equitable order when deprived of equity's traditional
appeal to higher law.

CHAPTER 2

Contract and the Road from Equity

I

A Modern Instance, Howells's first important work of realism, begins in a rural New England town called Equity. Complete with an Academy that simulates a "classic facade,"[1] Equity evokes a nostalgic image of the early years of a republic striving to establish a reign of classical virtue in the pastoral setting of the new world. A necessary component of this republican ideal is a country lawyer who serves as a patriarchal protector of justice, figured by Howells as Squire Gaylord. Gaylord's daughter Marcia mixes new world and classical virtue through a "demure innocence" that qualifies "the Roman pride of her profile" (MI 6).

That mixture is, however, not ready for modern complexity. Equity, we are told, is "a good deal behind the age in everything" (MI 9). Out of fashion even for a country lawyer, Squire Gaylord dons "the cassimere pantaloons, the saturn vest, and the dress coat, which old fashioned lawyers still wore, ten years ago" (MI 14). More important, the patriarchal protection that he offers his daughter is no match for the exciting figure of modernity, Bartley Hubbard. Bartley captures Marcia's heart and steals her away against the Squire's will. Bartley and Marcia marry and move to Boston where he begins a career as a journalist. In Equity Bartley had planned to read law with the Squire. The ancient profession of the law with its emphasis on precedent starkly contrasts journalism with its focus on fleeting moments in the present.

Nonetheless, by the book's end the Squire seems to have his revenge when he travels to Indiana to defend Marcia against Bartley, who, having abandoned his wife, unscrupulously files for divorce in his new home. During the trial the Squire unleashes powerful oratory of the sort that is in a state of decline in the East but "is still a passion in the West" (MI 443). Moving his audience, he demands justice as both an attorney and a father. His address to the court is, however, his final act of inspiration. Finishing, he collapses, permanently paralyzed. Shortly thereafter he dies under the care of his daughter in retreat in Equity.

It is no accident that Howells names his rural New England town Equity. Equity, as defined by Aristotle, is the "sort of justice which goes beyond the written law."[2] To recognize the need for equity is to acknowledge the failure of any society fully to embody justice in its laws. That failure points to a conflict between the good and the just. Laws are enacted to bring about what is good for society, but what is good for all of society is not necessarily just in every case. Since strict application of the law can actually lead to cases of injustice, some institutional structure seems necessary for people to turn to when the narrowness of the law provides no relief. As Joseph Story puts it, Aristotle's definition of equity "must have a place in every rational system of jurisprudence, if not in name, at least in substance."[3] The institutionalization of equity is, however, complicated.

Appeals to equity acknowledge the failure of humanmade laws fully to embody justice. Nonetheless, any institutional structure devised to correct the fallibility of the law is itself a human product and thus fallible. Indeed, equity grows out of the recognition of human fallibility. "Equity," according to Aristotle, "bids us be merciful to the weakness of human nature."[4] Founded in natural justice, equity cannot simply be translated into human terms. Thus, there is no guarantee that institutions constructed to provide equitable relief will be any more equitable than the legal system. A discrepancy remains between the general notion of equity described by Aristotle, Grotius, and Pufendorf, and the institutional forms of equity "recognized by the mere municipal code of a particular nation."[5]

That discrepancy causes special problems in democracies. Although there is no guarantee that a democracy's laws fully embody justice, they have legitimacy because they supposedly express the voice of the people. Any institution given the authority to make exceptions to democratically enacted laws risks deriving its legitimacy from a source other than that of the people. For instance, in Anglo-American countries matters of equity were supposedly decided in courts of chancery that originally derived their authority from the lord chancellor of the king of England. Such courts, Renaissance apologists claimed, served as the conscience of the king, who was God's minister of justice on earth.[6] But if courts of chancery were supposed to guarantee equitable relief, their association with the crown opened them to charges of elitism. A system of equity that was supposed to provide justice not accounted for by the narrowness of the written law developed its own set of written procedures. It became in effect a parallel system of law. As Blackstone put it, "The systems of jurisprudence, in our courts of law and equity, are now equally artificial systems, founded on the same principles of justice and positive law, but varied by different usages in the forms and mode of their proceedings."[7] Associated with the Crown, courts of equity were viewed with distrust by many Americans. In addition to having a history that marked them as aristocratic, these courts threatened to perpetuate outdated governmental paternalism.[8]

Equity's potential paternalism is suggested by Howells's Squire Gaylord, whose very name evokes the landed aristocracy of England. If, on the one hand, the town of Equity evokes the image of an agrarian republic intent on establishing a reign of classical virtue, on the other, it evokes the image of a static, hierarchical society in which the "right reason" of a governing elite gives it access to higher laws of justice unavailable to the people at large. The breakdown of Equity's order dramatized in *A Modern Instance* is thus double edged. Promising freedom from an aristocratic paternalism that blocks democratic development, equity's breakdown also threatens the moral foundation on which the United States promised to construct a more equitable and virtuous society.

This conflict is registered in the Squire's effort to defend his daughter from Bartley's suit for divorce. Once the country's most liberal, Indiana's divorce laws had been accused by conservatives of threatening the social fabric and the sanctity of marriage. But in 1873 they were rewritten, forcing Bartley to lie in order to get a divorce legitimating his irresponsible actions as a husband.[9] Thus there is a certain nobility about the Squire's defense of Marcia. Nonetheless, in typical Howellsian irony the Squire is motivated more by an Old Testament sense of revenge than a consideration of mercy. Furthermore, when we return to Equity at the end of the book, it is to bury the Squire. Howells may wonder where in the modern world we are to turn when the narrowness of the law provides no relief, but he also satirizes the paternalistic and static world view on which equitable appeals had traditionally been based. Condemning Bartley Hubbard's actions, Howells, nonetheless, shares his "discontent with the narrow world of Equity" (MI 9).

Like Aristotle, Howells recognizes the potential injustice of human-made laws. They seemed especially fallible given the political corruption of the 1870s. The question he faces in *A Modern Instance* is how to correct that fallibility. One approach, represented by the Squire, is to evoke a higher moral code to guarantee equitable results. Another is to trust the democratic process to correct itself. As a theater manager tells Bartley, "I believe in what Grant said: 'The quickest way to get rid of a bad law is to enforce it'" (MI 268). For Howells, journalism dramatizes this conflict. One man for whom Bartley works believes that "the press is a great moral engine, and that it ought to be run in the interest of the engineer" (MI 262). In contrast, Bartley feels that a newspaper is not obliged "to be superior in tone to the community" (MI 264).

Where Howells stands is not completely clear. Not fooled by populist rhetoric appealing to the public, he recognizes that it is frequently self-serving. For instance, when Bartley asks someone else whether he believes that a paper "ought to be run in the interest of the public," he responds, "Exactly—after the public has paid" (MI 262). Pleasing the public does not necessarily serve the good or the just, but it can reap profits. In Howells's America, "democratic" appeals to trust the public were more often than not invitations to follow the dictates of a marketplace ruled by contract. Nonetheless, if Howells worries about the direction such a world is taking, it is clearly triumphing over the static code of morality associated with Equity.

Contract's double-edged role in modernity's dilemma is illustrated by the effect that it had in determining people's responsibility for their actions. In a status-based society, people assumed unspoken duties and obligations determined by rank and standing. In contrast, contract implies a universal standard in which everyone has the same duties to everyone else—even strangers. But the democratic ideal of universal duties that all owe to all was severely limited by the workings of contract law that held people responsible only for actions considered legally binding. As a result, people could violate unspoken codes of behavior without legal reprisal.

For instance, when Bartley and a fellow journalist express an interest to write the life story of a rural philosopher named Kinney who has befriended Bartley, Kinney trusts them not to, noting simply, "I'm amongst gentlemen" (MI 312). Not contractually constrained, Bartley ignores this gentlemen's agreement and writes the article anyway. Furthermore, he sells it to a rival paper. When the owner of his paper confronts him, Bartley makes clear that he has no duties other than those spelled out in his contract. "I wrote [the article]," he responds, "out of time, and on Sunday night. You pay me by the week, and all that I do throughout the week belongs to you. The next day after that Sunday I did a full day's work on the Events. I don't see what you have to complain of. You told me when I began that you would not expect more than a certain amount of work from me. Have I ever done less?" (MI 323). Bartley's actions might seem unjust and unfair—a violation of unspoken agreements and loyalties—but they are legal.

A *Modern Instance* registers the divided reactions to the movement from status to contract. Whereas that movement evoked the promise of contract by challenging undemocratic hierarchies, it also seemed to undercut the foundation for traditional appeals to equity, leaving the workings of the market to arbitrate justice. That divided reaction is reinforced by Ferdinand Tönnies, whose distinction between *Gemeinschaft* and *Gesellschaft* was influenced by Maine, whom he praised as one of the first sociologically minded legal historians.[10] Tönnies, however, regretted the loss of face-to-face personal relations associated with *Gemeinschaft*. Émile Durkheim also argued that the contractual relations of the modern *Gesellschaft* generated anomie as well as solidarity. Contract promises a dynamic society allowing for individual advancement, but it also generates insecurities. Etymologically status is related to standing. Preassigned status in traditional societies gave people a secure knowledge of where they stood. A contract-based society undercuts the security of a grounded sense of identity. For instance, when the Squire visits Boston, "he suffered from the loss of identity which is a common affliction with country people coming to town" (MI 241).

If traditional societies were held together largely by unspoken agreements sanctified by tradition, the dynamism of contractual societies undercut many of those bonds. One result was the increased importance of promises, which is illustrated early in A *Modern Instance* when Marcia and Bartley imagine exchanging letters to agree on a rendezvous to go sleigh-riding. To Bartley's suggestion that he sign his "affectionately," Marcia responds, "And *I* think it had better be Truly." "Truly, it shall be, then," Bartley agrees. "Your word is law—statute in such case made and provided" (MI 12). Bartley's major fault is his inability to stay true to his word in interpersonal relations, a fault that undercuts the considerable promise that Howells finds in him.[11]

Bartley's fault points to how much contractual society depends on people fulfilling their obligation to deliver on the contracts that they promise. If people entering into contracts lack the constancy of character necessary to fulfill their promises, a society bound together by contracts threatens to fall apart. That threat compels us to examine in more detail how the promise of contract is linked to the act of promising.

Promises are traditionally said to alter our moral situation by placing obligations on us. For instance, unlike a gift, a promise implies a future obligation. Stanley Cavell has, however, challenged this view. For Cavell, promises do, indeed, spell out commitments, but what binds, he argues, are commitments, not promises.[12] If Cavell is correct, it would be wrong to see a society held together by promises. Instead, society is bound together by commitments, some of which promises simply name.

David Hume, however, offers a different view.[13] Hume, like Cavell, does not think that all obligations derive from promises. He is not, therefore, a contractarian. Nonetheless, for Hume promises do *add* to the already existing, everyday commitments by ritually enacting a commitment and by representing the conditions under which the commitment will be performed. As such, promises are especially important in establishing commitments to those beyond our immediate circle of friends and family. Indeed, distance seems to be a vital part of the dynamic of promising, since a promise is almost always evoked when delivery on an obligation involves a delay. Promises, therefore, are ideally suited for the transfer of goods that are absent in either time or space. Someone may promise to deliver part of a crop not yet harvested or a cow three miles away.

Deferred obligations raise the question of why we should trust promises. For Hume, the answer lies in the ritual of a handshake often used to seal promises. That ritual enacts an exchange in which the promisor hands over to the promisee his reputation as a responsible person. Because the promisee holds the promisor's reputation in his hands, the promisor subjects himself to the penalty of "never being trusted again in case of failure."[14]

Hume helps to clarify the promise of contract in two ways. First, he makes clear that it does not depend on belief in an original social contract posited by thinkers such as Hobbes, Locke, and Rousseau. A contractual promise for Hume is not the only form of human commitment. In his historical narrative, promising is not the original social artifice, but the third. Indeed, Maine can speak about a progressive movement from status to contract because human society did not originate with contractual obligations.[15]

Second, Hume helps to separate the radical promise of contract from dependence on transcendental sanctions. The obligation to honor a promise is often considered a duty to God. For Hume, however, promissory obligations result from negotiations among individuals, not from an external authority. As much as people continue to evoke a transcendental appeal when talking about the sanctity of promising, the promise of contract, as I describe it, tries to do without it. The social implications of that promise have been forcefully argued by Thomas Haskell.

Haskell stresses how important promising is to humanity's moral sense of itself by quoting Nietzsche in *The Genealogy of Morals*. "To breed an animal *with the right to make promises*—is this not the paradoxical task that nature has set itself in the case of man? Is it not the real problem regarding man?" Agreeing with Nietzsche that "*conscience*" is the name of the "privilege of *responsibility*" that gives a man sovereignty over himself so that he can keep his promises,[16] Haskell goes on to argue that, "not until the eighteenth century, in Western Europe, England, and North America" did societies appear "whose economic systems depended on the expectation that most people, most of the time, were sufficiently conscience-ridden (and certain of retribution) that they could be trusted to keep their promises. In other words, only then did promise keeping become so widespread that it could be elevated into a general social norm. Only to the extent that such a norm prevails can economic affairs be based on nothing more authoritative than the obligations arising out of promises. And a growing reliance on mutual promises, or contractual relations not based on status, custom, or traditional authority comes very close to the heart of what we mean by 'the rise of capitalism.'"[17]

Haskell's historical narrative tends to confirm Maine's argument about the movement from status to contract. Haskell, however, makes a further claim. He associates the private responsibilities created by a contractual society with the rise of humanitarianism at the end of the eighteenth century. "At the most obvious level, the new stress on promise keeping contributed to the emergence of the humanitarian sensibility by encouraging new levels of scrupulosity in the fulfillment of ethical maxims." In addition, as suggested by Hume, a society held together by the dynamics of promising taught people "to attend to the remote consequences of [their] acts both spatially and temporally."[18]

Ideally, each person was responsible for maintaining social well-being, since broken promises could disrupt society's moral fabric and thus jeopardize the lives even of strangers.

Haskell's link between the rise of humanitarianism and the rise of a market economy under capitalism has, to be sure, provoked controversy, since it seems to contradict so much empirical evidence that capitalism perpetuates inhumane practices. But Haskell is not arguing that the emergence of the humanitarian sensibility that accompanied the rise of capitalism meant that exploitative practices were abolished. He is instead trying to account for the conditions in which what Hume called the sentiment for humanity could take on the status of a universal norm. We should not forget that in the late nineteenth century Adam Smith's *Theory of Moral Sentiments* was at least as popular as *Wealth of Nations*. The sentiment for humanity is linked to an aspect of capitalism and market society that has increasingly become the target of moralistic attacks: its stress on the individual.

The adjective "individual" to designate the existence of a separate entity was rarely used before the seventeenth century; that is, before the rise of modern capitalism. If critics have stressed individualism's self-interestedness, Durkheim noted another effect. Individualism, he writes, "is the glorification not of the self but of the individual in general. It springs not from egoism but from the sympathy for all that is human, a broader pity for all sufferings, for all human miseries, a more ardent need to combat them and mitigate them, a greater thirst for justice. Is there not herein what is needed to place all men of good will in communion?"[19] Durkheim does not unequivocally endorse individualism. He is especially harsh on atomistic and egotistical individualism. But he does recognize how individualism can create bonds among people. For him the concept of the individual in general allows us to recognize the commonality of individuals in particular. As such, it works against the differentiations perpetuated by the preassigned roles and statuses of traditional societies.[20]

To Durkheim's observations we can add that a social ritual binding together "the cult of individualism" is the promise. Indeed, although Durkheim is critical of defenders of "freedom of contract" such as Herbert Spencer, the contractual thought that he attacks lacks an emphasis on bonding.[21] The ritual of promising grants to contract the sort of bonding that Durkheim seeks. When two people, of whatever social class, shake hands to seal an agreement, they symbolically enact an equal standing, at least in terms of this particular transaction. Indeed, by handing over their reputations as trustworthy people to one another, they submit themselves to be measured by the same standard of accountability. This ritual act dramatizes a crucial aspect of contract's promise.

The link between contracts and promising is a fairly recent development. Before the twelfth century, promises between individual parties were rarely considered by the king's courts. Even as a few contractual relations gained legal sanction, they were often circumvented by what today we would consider torts, or consideration of wrongs enacted by a private party. Into the eighteenth century, the law of contract remained a minor part of the legal system, appearing in Blackstone's *Commentaries* (1765) as little more than an appendage to the law of property. During the late eighteenth and nineteenth centuries, however, with the rise of a market economy, contract law rapidly expanded. It also underwent a subtle shift that reinforced the importance of promising.

"Traditionally," Haskell summarizes, "liability had rested on a combination of promise and consideration. Promise alone, the mere fact of a voluntary and deliberate declaration of intent to do something, was not enough. What made a promise binding was consideration, proof that there had been 'adequate motivating circumstances'—such as a fee or other concrete benefit—to induce the promisor to give his promise." Consideration never dropped out of contract law. But during the reign of Lord Mansfield over British courts in the second half of the eighteenth century, promises made seriously were enough to count as consideration in commercial contracts. To allow the voluntary will of individuals legally to bind commercial agreements was to contribute to a change in the nature of contract law. As Haskell puts it, "Originating as a kind of tort, contract now took on its modern status as the antithesis of tort: obligations created not by law but by private agreement."[22]

It is, I would argue, no accident that the Scottish philosopher Hume lived about the same time as the great Scottish jurist Lord Mansfield.[23] The promise of contract develops out of a concrete historical situation in which the notion of contracts and promises merged. Contract might, as *A Modern Instance* dramatizes, undermine appeals to a higher standard of equity, but radically conceived it promises to generate equitable relations through a system of immanent exchanges. Nonetheless, without a merger with promising, contract's promise disappears. Indeed, without it contract theory might justify the sovereign state of Hobbes. Historically, however, a third option was taken. Unable to do without transcendental guarantees, classical liberalism legitimated contract as part of a social order based on the laws of nature. Before turning to how doing so altered notions of equity, we need to explore from a slightly different perspective why sustaining the radical promise of contract causes such anxiety.

II

If status-based societies are held together mostly by commitments that precede promises, promising has the potential to open these relatively closed communities to transactions with strangers by providing a mechanism for the ritual creation of new commitments. At the same time, because the value of one's reputation as a reliable person is so crucial to promising, the expanded community that promising helps to generate retains the ideal of trust so important to status-based societies.

Promising adds to existing commitments, but it also tends to transform the nature of communities bound by unspoken commitments. It does so by destabilizing the foundation on which those commitments are based. In status-based societies commitments are sanctified because the human order, through an elaborate, organic network of spiritual and symbolic relations, is implicated in a cosmic moral order. Insofar as, with Hume, we see promising as a human artifice, not a sacred obligation, it severs the link made between the human and the cosmic order. Arising from exchanges among individuals, promising contributes to a human rather than divine explanation of commitments. In so doing it invites a reexamination of the commitments that it supplements. On the one hand, that reexamination has the progressive force of undermining the existence of hierarchical, status-based relations. On the other, it tends to make even those living in close proximity relate to one another as if they were strangers. As a result, previously unspoken commitments get turned into contractual ones. Paradoxically, therefore, promising both extends the trust that helps to bind closed communities and contributes to conditions in which the unspoken foundation for that trust is threatened.

In market societies, which depend so much on contracts, a great deal of anxiety is generated over whether people will keep their promises. That anxiety helps to account for the frequency with which characters who stick to their word at any cost are associated with more traditional societies. There is, for instance, the Southerner Colonel Woodburn in Howells's *A Hazard of New Fortunes,* Twain's First Families of Virginia in *Pudd'nhead Wilson,* and James's Valentine de Bellegarde in *The American*. On the one hand, such characters suggest that a stable social world cultivates people whose word does not fluctuate. On the other, they point to the narrow and arbitrary foundations of such stability. Serving as a progressive force that exposes such narrowness, the rise of the market also threatens to undermine the stability seemingly necessary to bind a society held together by promises.

Defenders of contract did not gaily construct a social vision on a foundation of instability. Confronted with and contributing to the destruction of traditional social foundations, those living in a market economy felt the need for alternative foundations for both personal conduct and the world at large. Thus, as P. S. Atiyah has observed, it is no accident that the Age of Contract was also an Age of Principles.[24] Supposedly based on natural laws, these principles governed the physical universe, ethics, jurisprudence, the political economy, and the domestic economy. Because they could "refer to rules of moral conduct as well as to law-like uniformities of nature," these principles, in Haskell's words, "bridged the widening chasm between nature and morality."[25]

This appeal to natural foundations has consequences for the relation between status and contract in the new market economies as well as the relation of those economies to questions of equity. One reason that courts of equity came under fire in the United States was that, traditionally, they reserved the authority to interfere with business contracts that seemed unfair. Nonetheless, in the nineteenth century equitable interference occurred less and less. For instance, Story quotes from Blackstone to underscore a point about the limits of equitable appeals: "'If a person of ordinary understanding, on whom no fraud has been practiced, makes an imprudent bargain,' writes Lord Wynford, 'no Court of justice can release him from it.'"[26]

Statements like this have been interpreted as proof that questions of morality and justice were sacrificed to market expediency, especially with the rise of formalism in the second half of the nineteenth century. Indeed, Atiyah has a section entitled "The Rise of Formalism and the Decline of Equity."[27] Howells helps to dramatize the effects of such a decline in *A Modern Instance*. Nonetheless, as Howells's novel indicates, the situation is complicated. In a society held together by promises, there is a strong moral imperative to make people honor their word, especially if it was felt that a market economy was the best way to provide social justice. Sophisticated defenders of commercial societies did not ignore questions of equity, they provided new answers to them. For an example we can turn to perhaps the most influential political economist, Adam Smith.

Smith was trained in the natural law tradition of Grotius and Pufendorf that helped to define equity jurisprudence. His concern for justice compelled him to confront two paradoxes. In an early "draft" of *Wealth of Nations,* he wondered how, "in the midst of so much oppressive inequality," was it possible to "account for the superior affluence and abundance commonly possessed even by [the] lowest and most despised member of civilized society, compared with what the most respected and active savage can attain to?"[28] Similarly, he noted that the ideal of civic virtue was almost always maintained by slave labor. In Plato's ideal republic, the productivity of labor would have been so low, he speculated, that it would have required a "territory of boundless extent and fertility" to maintain its guardian class.[29] These two paradoxes led Smith to conclude that, whereas individuals could be virtuous, the ideal of a virtuous society cost too much. Admitting that commercial societies could not provide distributive justice, he nonetheless claimed that their ability to satisfy basic needs fulfilled the requirements of "strict justice." As two recent commentators summarize, "Modern commercial society was unequal and unvirtuous but it was not unjust. It did not purchase civic virtue at the price of misery for its poorest members. However unequal men might be, in property and citizenship, they could be equal in access to the means to satisfy basic needs."[30]

If Smith's defense of commercial societies did not abandon considerations of justice, his conclusion that it was achieved through economic means did alter the status of equity. Societies that can provide only "strict justice" would seem to cry out for equitable remedies for specific situations. But to allow courts to interfere in business contracts would be to undermine the regularity and predictability needed by a market economy. One result was the decrease in equitable interference that we have examined. But there was also the extraordinary suggestion by Lord Kames in Scotland to use equity's relative freedom from precedent to overturn common law practices that blocked the needs of the market economy.[31] Using equity to support the market would of course undermine its potential to correct injustices perpetuated by the market. Nonetheless, Kames's proposal makes clear that many advocates of commercial society sincerely believed that it was the best guarantee for overall justice. What gets lost, however, is the distinction between affairs of the market and a higher form of justice that was the basis of Aristotle's sense of equity. Indeed, it is now the market that is justified by higher law.

My point is not to endorse such a theory of the market, which fails to sustain the radical promise of contract. But we do need to understand why its proponents felt that it was fair. One reason has to do with its relation to status. Traditionally equity takes into consideration the specifics of individual cases, including details of person. We should not forget that, in a world in which someone's identity was largely determined by one's social standing, details of person included considerations of status. In contrast, Smith's sense of economic fairness virtually ignores status. When he wonders why the "industrious and frugal peasant" in a commercial society could live better than an "African king, the absolute master of the lives and liberties of 10,000 naked savages,"[32] he might well ask if his fictional African king would, even so, have changed places with an English peasant. But he does not, because, for him, in the economic realm what matters is economic well being. The democratic potential in discounting status gives an added dimension to Lawrence Friedman's excellent summary of how the law of contract served the interests of classical liberal thought.

According to Friedman, the "pure" law of contract is "blind to details of subject matter and person. It does not ask who buys and who sells, and what is bought and sold." This "abstraction of classical contract law," he argues, "is a deliberate renunciation of the particular, a deliberate relinquishment of the temptation to restrict untrammeled individual autonomy or the completely free market in the name of social policy. The law of contract is, therefore, roughly coextensive with the free market. Liberal nineteenth-century economics fits in neatly with the law of contracts so viewed. It, too, had the abstracting habit. In both theoretical models—that of the law of contracts and that of liberal economics—parties could be treated as individual economic units which, in theory, enjoyed complete mobility and freedom of decision."[33]

Status theoretically had no role in the marketplace, but it was not completely abolished from consideration. As recent legal historians have argued, classical liberalism was not simply a theory of market relations. It replaced status by contract only in the economic sphere. In other realms, status continued to receive natural legitimation. Indeed, in the late nineteenth century legal thinkers developed a sophisticated system that claimed to determine scientifically the natural boundaries between various spheres of social activity. The aim of this "boundary" thought was to minimize governmental interference by allowing individuals to act freely in accordance with laws of natural necessity *appropriate to each sphere*. With natural boundaries reinforced by law, laissez-faire legal science hoped to create conditions in which the social system would, more or less, run by itself.[34] Furthermore, because the boundaries drawn between spheres were based in nature, someone's status in one realm was said to play no role in the economic sphere—which is why, as Friedman points out, the "pure" law of contract is "blind to details of subject matter and person."[35]

The natural foundation of boundary thought did not restore the organic network of spiritual and symbolic relations of precontractual societies. Instead, it legitimated the social order that had arisen as a result of an expanding market economy. Summarizing Durkheim, Dominick LaCapra writes that modern societies "dissociated institutional spheres from one another (family, job, politics, religion, and so on), defined often depersonalized roles in functionally specific ways, and furthered technological mastery and the accumulation of economic goods. . . . In modern society differentiations tended to be detached from one another in relatively clear and distinct, Cartesian compartments of activities and boxes of experience."[36] The principles of boundary thought grounded those differentiations in natural law. As a result, legal thought failed to live up to the promise of contract that is evoked by works of literary realism in the period. To see results of that failure we can turn to three 14th Amendment cases.

III

After the 13th Amendment abolished slavery and involuntary servitude, the 14th Amendment in effect granted citizenship to former slaves, provided federal protection for citizens, and forbade states from depriving people of life, liberty, or property without due process of law or from denying them equal protection of the laws. Its protection of property most directly links the amendment to the triumph of contract. If a major conflict in antebellum years had been between the North's system of contractual labor and the South's system of slave labor, the first right listed in the 1866 Civil Rights Act was the right to make and enforce contracts, thus guaranteeing freedmen's ability to contract their labor to gain property. The 14th Amendment was designed in part to leave no doubt that the 1866 Act was constitutional. The identification of freedom with a system of contractual labor confirms Eric Foner's argument that the period's definition of freedom must be seen in relation to slavery.[37] Indeed, the postbellum period saw the sanctification of "freedom of contract."

An example of how far that concept would be extended in the economic sphere is found in *Lochner v. New York* (1905). *Lochner* involved a New York law protecting workers in bakeries by limiting hours of employment to ten hours a day or sixty hours a week. The Supreme Court declared the law unconstitutional for interfering with their freedom of contract. In depriving workers of the right to earn wages by contracting their labor, such laws violated the 14th Amendment and were "mere meddlesome interferences with the rights of individuals."[38] But the Court did not worry about a state law meddling with the rights of individuals in *Plessy v. Ferguson* (1896), when it upheld Louisiana's law mandating "equal, but separate" cars for whites and "coloreds" on intrastate railroads.

From our present perspective the Court's appeal to the 14th Amendment to deny a state the power to limit work hours after it refused to evoke it to deny a state the power to mandate racial segregation, seems the height of hypocrisy. Indeed, *Lochner* and *Plessy* are often used to tell the story of how the Court abandoned the original intention of the 14th Amendment, which ostensibly was the socially responsible one of guaranteeing equality for newly freed African-Americans, in order to institute a class-based regime of laissez-faire economics. As a result, dissenters in both cases, Justice Oliver Wendell Holmes Jr., in *Lochner,* and Justice John Marshall Harlan, in *Plessy* and *Lochner,* have been lionized by many critics of laissez-faire constitutionalism. But this story is generated by an anachronistic opposition between an amoral market run by a logic of cost-accounting and a moral realm of social relations. Within the Anglo-American tradition, the person most responsible for perpetuating this opposition is C. B. Macpherson.

In his highly influential account of the "possessive individualism" of classical liberalism, Macpherson dismisses any appeal that liberals make to human values as a leftover residue of "traditional" thought inconsistent with the "logic" of the market. But what Macpherson sees as mere residue was in fact a vital part of much liberal thought. As a result, those following Macpherson often neglect connections that laissez-faire thinkers saw between morality and economics. Indeed, if laissez-faire thought had not integrated elements of what J. G. A. Pocock has called the tradition of republican virtue, it may not have triumphed. To be sure, in England the tradition of republican virtue was for the most part anticommercial. But, as we shall see in chapter 4, virtue in the United States was frequently linked to liberal economics.[39]

For late nineteenth-century laissez-faire theorists, freedom of contract was an ethical concept, making possible the moral development of human beings. A perfect confirmation of the moral superiority of a contractual conception of human affairs was the issue of slavery. If there was ever any doubt about the virtues of contractual labor, the Civil War dispelled them for most Northerners. Embodying the principles of Northern economic federalism, the 14th Amendment signaled the victory of virtue over the evils of slavery.

Not an example of amoral positivism, late nineteenth-century legal formalism was deeply rooted in a moral view of the universe. The Court did not move away from the morally responsible social intent of the 14th Amendment toward an immoral, or at best amoral, economic interpretation for the simple reason that the amendment was economic and moral from the start.

Morality, however, was not confined to economics, and Herbert Hovenkamp is somewhat misleading when he argues that civil rights after the Civil War were limited to "(1) the right to equality of treatment in court trials and of access to the agencies of the state; and (2) a set of distinctly *economic* civil rights, namely, the right to make contracts and the right to own property."[40] Civil rights were more narrowly defined then than now, but if their possibilities were as narrow as Hovenkamp claims, there would have been no 1875 Civil Rights Act that forbade various discriminatory acts based on race. To be sure, in 1883 the Supreme Court did declare most of the 1875 Act unconstitutional. But it based its decision on limits to federal guarantees, not on the impossibility of having a wider definition of civil rights. The 1875 Act forbade acts by private parties against one another, but the 14th Amendment forbade actions by individual *states* against persons or citizens. The intent of the amendment, the Court ruled, was not to sanction interference by the federal government in exchanges among private parties. It was to make sure that individual states—that is, governmental entities—did not deny individuals certain rights.

This interpretation, which closely follows the precise language of the amendment, reveals how much the 14th Amendment was guided by the goal of limiting governmental interference into the private lives of individuals.[41] Granted, it does give the federal government increased control over the actions of *state* governments. But granting centralized control to the federal government over the states was perfectly consistent with the desire to have the country conform to a uniform set of economic conditions so as to enhance "natural" conditions of trade and exchange. After all, if one crucial dispute between North and South had been over the right of all individuals—white and black—to make contracts and own property, another was over the issue of states' rights. Self-consciously, Congress passed the Civil Rights Act in 1866 modeled on the Fugitive Slave Act of 1850, which provided a precedent for legislation in which the federal government enforced rights previously protected by the states. As Senator Lyman Trumbull of Illinois put it, "Surely we have the authority to enact a law as efficient in the interests of freedom, now that freedom prevails throughout the country, as we had in the interest of slavery when it prevailed in a portion of the country."[42] The 14th Amendment helped to declare the North victorious on both the issue of contractual labor and of federal control of the states.

Rather than illustrate how the morally noble cause of African-Americans was abandoned to advance the discredited cause of laissez-faire economics, the Court's 14th Amendment decisions reveal how intricately the North's defense of African-American rights was linked to a belief in the moral superiority of a system based on the right of men to contract their labor. To insist on that linkage is not to deny that United States society, the Court, and the Republican Party abandoned the cause of freedmen, but it is to suggest a different explanation for that abandonment. That explanation is more complex than Albion W. Tourgée's claim that his party simply abandoned human rights for dimes and dollars.

For many, the problem was that in the years following the Civil War most freedmen seemed incapable of taking advantage of the moral improvement afforded by newly won economic and political rights. For instance, Charles Sumner, confining himself to the right to vote, proclaimed that the 15th Amendment had "chained [the freedman] to the chariot-wheel of American progress."[43] In terms of *Plessy*, the Court—and many other people at the time—felt that, having granted newly freed slaves political and economic rights allowing them to develop the full moral capacity of human beings, the nation had fulfilled its obligation. If blacks failed to capitalize on their opportunities, they were in large measure responsible. In the meantime, the Court saw in the 14th Amendment a chance to make the law of the land conform to a theory of political economy proven morally superior by the Civil War. It did so by interpreting the due process clause as guaranteeing not only procedural but substantive economic rights.

Discussing the clause in *Commentaries on Law* (1884), Francis Wharton writes, "The provisions contained in these amendments, bearing distinctively on the negro race, are comparatively ephemeral in character, while the clause before us is likely to be permanent, and to permeate the whole business systems of the Union."[44] The amendment's real importance for Wharton was its guarantee that state legislatures could not interfere with private business. Rather than view the Court's economic interpretation of the 14th Amendment as a move away from morality, we need to see it as implementing the moral victory of Northern principles. It is perhaps no accident that a prominent dissenter in a number of 14th Amendment cases, Justice Harlan, came from the South. Likewise, an overlooked significance of Holmes's *Lochner* dissent is that, forty years after the Civil War, it questions the moral sanctity of economic principles associated with the victorious North. It is possible that the progressive challenge to laissez-faire economics could not have taken place until the victory of Northern principles was severed from its moral foundation.

Before turning to Holmes's complicated relation to that challenge, we need to examine another 14th Amendment case to see how the political economy was bolstered by a vision of social relations determined by status. *Bradwell v. State* (1873) involved a challenge to an Illinois law forbidding women to practice law. Myra Bradwell sued, arguing that the law violated her 14th Amendment rights, including her right freely to contract her labor as she wished. By an eight to one majority the Supreme Court decided that the Illinois law was constitutional. Justice Bradley's concurring opinion in *Bradwell* is especially revealing. Bradley agrees that the 14th Amendment protected "the right to engage in any lawful employment for a livelihood." But, he counters, any state has the right to exercise its police powers, if it does so for the public good and treats all similar people equally. The humanmade (or civil) law passed by the Illinois legislature was a reasonable use of police powers because it corresponded to the laws of nature concerning the different capabilities of men and women. Bradley's reasoning deserves extended quotation.

The civil law, as well as nature herself, has always recognized a wide difference in the respective spheres and destinies of man and woman. Man is, or should be, woman's protector and defender. The natural and proper timidity and delicacy which belongs to the female sex evidently unfits it for many of the occupations of civil life. The constitution of the family organization, which is founded in the divine ordinance, as well as in the nature of things, indicates the domestic sphere as that which properly belongs to the domain and functions of womanhood. The harmony, not to say identity, of interests and views which belong, or should belong, to the family institution is repugnant to the idea of a woman adopting a distinct and independent career from that of her husband. . . . The paramount destiny and mission of woman are to fulfill the noble and benign offices of wife and mother. This is the law of the Creator. And the rules of civil society must be adapted to the general condition of things, and cannot be based upon exceptional cases. . . . In the nature of things it is not every citizen of every age, sex, and condition that is qualified for every calling and position. It is the prerogative of the legislator to prescribe regulations founded on nature, reason, and experience for the due admission of qualified persons to professions and callings demanding special skill and confidence. This fairly belongs to the police power of the state; and, in my opinion, in view of the peculiar characteristics, destiny, and mission of woman, it is within the province of the legislature to ordain what offices, positions, and callings shall be filled and discharged by men, and shall receive the benefit of those energies and responsibilities, and that decision and firmness which are presumed to predominate in the sterner sex.[45]

For thinkers like Bradley it was folly and bad policy to legislate against the natural laws governing the market, but it *was* reasonable for a state to use its police powers when its laws corresponded to the laws of nature governing the domestic economy.[46] According to the majority in *Plessy*, similar laws governed the social order regarding race.

The Court, Justice Brown writes, disagrees with Plessy's belief "that social prejudices may be overcome by legislation, and that equal rights cannot be secured to the negro except by an enforced commingling of the two races." The Court believes instead that "if the two races are to meet upon terms of social equality, it must be the result of natural affinities, a mutual appreciation of each other's merits and a voluntary consent of individuals."[47] The majority's distrust of attempts to find legislative solutions to social problems is not surprising. What is curious is its need to state this distrust in a case in which it defends the right of a state legislature to do so. After all, at issue is a state law *requiring* the separation of the races on railroad cars. Like Bradwell, Plessy merely asks that a state not be allowed to make discriminations based on a category of status such as race or sex. But in *Plessy*, as in *Bradwell*, the Court reveals that, insofar as a form of status is part of the natural, moral order, legislation reinforcing it is a reasonable use of police powers.

The 14th Amendment, Brown declares, was "undoubtedly" intended "to enforce the absolute equality of the two races before the law." Nonetheless, "in the nature of things it could not have been intended to abolish distinctions based upon color, or to enforce social as distinguished from political equality, or a commingling of the two races upon terms unsatisfactory to either."[48] Louisiana's Jim Crow law simply reinforced natural social distinctions between whites and "coloreds."

Far from showing that the Supreme Court sacrificed a moral interpretation of the 14th Amendment to an amoral one dictated by a cost-accounting logic of the market, *Plessy, Bradwell,* and *Lochner* are governed by the Court's enforcement of a moral order that continues to posit the existence of status in the social and domestic realms, status that supposedly does not affect the guarantees of "freedom of contract" in the economic realm and equality in the political realm because these are governed by different natural laws. *Plessy* even suggests that when demands of the market came into conflict with a state's assumed "moral" order of the races, economic efficiency was sacrificed. Some railroads, for instance, opposed the Louisiana law because it forced them to have extra cars. As we will see, segregation's economic inefficiency was a major theme in a post-*Plessy* novel by Charles W. Chesnutt. Nonetheless, rooted in the natural order, the Louisiana law was allowed to stand. Indeed, contrary to common assumptions, it is not laissez-faire constitutionalists who separate law and economics from morality, but the famous *Lochner* dissenter Holmes.

IV

More than any other figure, Holmes illustrates the complicated relationship between contract and orthodox laissez-faire thought. If laissez-faire thinkers relied on principles to bridge the widening gap between nature and morality, Holmes challenged the Cartesian effort to found the study of law on first principles. In perhaps his most-quoted passage, Holmes declared, "The life of the law has not been logic: it has been experience." Elsewhere he vigorously denied that laws have their origin in some "brooding omnipresence in the sky."[49] Holmes's effort to free law from a reliance on first principles was part of a larger campaign to separate law from morality. Holmes did not urge people to act immorally. He was instead intent on freeing the study of law from its subordination to moral philosophy so as to make it more responsive to actual social needs. As a result, Holmes is an important figure in what Morton White called the "revolt against formalism."[50]

Generated by what today is called antifoundational thought, this revolt would come to include pragmatists, new historians, and literary and legal realists.[51] It is no accident that the legal realist Roscoe Pound begins an essay distinguishing law in books from law in experience by citing a scene from *Huckleberry Finn*.[52] But similarities should not cause us to neglect important differences between the literary realists and Holmes. One difference is indicated by Holmes's relation to boundary thought. On the one hand, he admits that a legal boundary line "looked at by itself . . . seems arbitrary." On the other, he argues that "the great body of the law consists in drawing such lines." Since for him "there is no mathematical or logical way of fixing [those lines] precisely, the decision of the Legislature must be accepted unless we can say that it is very wide of any reasonable mark."[53] More important, his theory of contract differs crucially from the evocation of contract's promise in works of literary realism.

Works of realism, I argue, challenge the formalism of contract law by presenting promising as an interpersonal act that is grounded in neither a scientific appeal to the laws of nature nor a moral appeal to God's witness. But whereas the utopian promise of contract cannot do without a link between contract and promising, Holmes could not think of promising without transcendental sanctions. As a result, he felt that if law was to free itself from moral philosophy, it was necessary to sever contract's association with the moral connotations of promising. Pointing out that a contract was originally treated more like a tort than a voluntary promise, he argued that "the duty to keep a contract at common law means a prediction that you must pay damages if you do not keep it—and nothing else. If you commit a tort, you are liable to pay a compensatory sum. If you commit a contract, you are liable to pay a compensatory sum unless the promised event comes to pass, and that is all the difference."[54] The significance of Holmes's comparison is made clear by the title of an 1880 work by Thomas M. Cooley: *A Treatise on the Law of Torts, or the Wrongs which Arise Independently of Contract*.[55] By severing contract from promising, Holmes restored its relation to torts. To understand contract, indeed all law, Holmes looked pragmatically at effects, not intentions, which he felt was the province of morality.

But, if Holmes challenged formalist efforts to found human action on principles of moral philosophy, through his definition of consideration he formalized contract in another way. According to prevailing doctrine, consideration was established whenever a promisor received a benefit from a transaction or a promisee suffered a detriment. As we have seen, under Lord Mansfield promises between private individuals had been ruled to be enough to make contracts legally binding. Taking great historical liberties, Holmes reinterpreted the leading British case of *Raffles v. Wichelhaus* (1864) so that he could argue that a meeting of the minds was not enough to establish consideration, since the "law has nothing to do with the actual state of the parties' minds."[56] Instead, consideration was established only if certain external criteria were met. In his own words, "The whole doctrine of contract is formal and external."[57]

Holmes's formalization has consequences for contractual liability. For Holmes liability was absolute. "The only universal consequence of a legally binding promise is, that the law makes the promisor pay damages if the promised event does not come to pass." Liability was absolute, but Holmes severely limited it by making a promise legally binding only when it conformed to designated formalities. Furthermore, because the law dealt only with formal consideration, subjective motivation became legally irrelevant. A well-intentioned contract breaker was as legally bound to pay the same damages as a greedy one. Indeed, everyone had the right "to break his contract if he [chose]," so long as he paid damages.[58]

According to Grant Gilmore, Holmes's theory of contract became orthodox doctrine. For instance, its denial of subjective intentions made possible the abstractions described by Friedman. But if Holmes challenged the laissez-faire connection between moral philosophy and the law, how could he be responsible for most powerfully formulating its theory of contract? He could, because boundary thought gave his theory of contract a moral foundation that his own antifoundationalism denied.

Holmes's dissent in *Lochner* was not an attack on the formalization of contract that he helped to bring about. It was instead directed against the moral foundation that the Court insisted on granting it. Holmes did not claim that his description of contract law implied a particular theory of economics or morality. According to him, the only incentive that people had to fulfill their contractual obligations was that they would be punished if they did not. A positivist in important respects, Holmes often seems to offer no reason to obey the law other than the fact that it expresses the sovereign power of the people. As a result, Holmes usually felt that economic disputes should be decided in the political realm of majority rule, not by reference to a theory of natural rights. In *Lochner,* for instance, Holmes countered the Court's defense of a person's right to the "freedom of contract" by defending the "right of the majority to embody their opinions in law." "This case," he asserted, "is decided upon an economic theory which a large part of the country does not entertain." In fact, Holmes does leave open the possibility of overruling the majority in a democracy, but only when "a rational and fair man would admit that the statute proposed would infringe fundamental principles as they have been understood by the traditions of our people and our law."[59]

Even with this important exception, Holmes's dissent reveals that judges who claimed to distrust paternalism in fact paternally protected an economic—and moral—order from popular threats to it.[60] Holmes's challenge to such paternalism did not, however, evoke the radical promise of contract. It did not, because Holmes's formalization of contract freed it from more than the yoke of a transcendental moral philosophy. It also severed it from the intersubjective construction of morality implied by Hume's account of promising. If for Hume promising adds to, and thus transforms, the commitments holding social relations together, for Holmes there is nothing special about contractual promises. For Holmes, the only authority binding contractual obligations is the sovereign power of the state, a view that has caused some to link him with Hobbes.[61] Unlike Hobbes, however, Holmes accepts a democratic sense of sovereignty, not because it is morally superior, but because it is the system in which he operates. Holmes's defense of sovereignty raises the possibility that the almost religious reverence for the United States Constitution results because for some it has reoccupied the position formerly held by equity as a guarantor of justice. But even if it has, it has not solved the dilemmas presented by appeals to equity.[62]

Comparing law and equity Ralph A. Newman argues that "equity corrects the law by applying, in circumstances where the ordinary rules would lead to unwarranted hardship, considerations of what is fair and just." Nonetheless, he goes on, "when all law emanates from popular sovereignty, it is nonsense to think of law as having to correct itself."[63] As Holmes's *Lochner* dissent makes clear, popular sovereignty in the American tradition need not be defined simply as majority rule. It can also be located in "fundamental principles as they have been understood by the traditions of our people and our laws." In the United States today, more people appeal to the constitutional embodiment of those principles than to equity. For Morton J. Horwitz, "the idea of a Constitution as fundamental law is one of America's important contributions to civilization. The written constitutions, promulgated in the states after 1776, seem to have embodied a new understanding of a constitution, not simply as an arrangement or frame of government, but as fundamental law more basic than ordinary legislation."[64]

Those linking the Constitution with the Declaration of Independence tend to base the country's fundamental law, like equity, in natural law. But others adopt a view much closer to the promise of contract by arguing that these principles were generated by mutual agreement of the people. It is these agreements that bind citizens together as a distinct entity. But a self-consciously modern age questions whether new generations are bound by past agreements. Are they free to interpret constitutional principles to make them agree with new social realities, or must they adhere to the intent of the framers? Thus for Horwitz, "the contemporary crisis in constitutional law" has one basic question: "how can the idea of fundamentality be rescued from its historic association with fundamentalism? How, in other words, is it possible legitimately to incorporate changing ideals or values, or dynamic meanings or understandings of the world, into constitutional doctrine that aspires to fundamentality?"[65]

That question causes Horwitz to compare *Lochner* and *Plessy* and the Court's later rationale for not honoring them. Indeed, he suggests an answer in Holmes's *Lochner* dissent. "Justice Holmes," he writes, "did not betray his belief in immutable constitutional principles to the whims of the majority. Such an exchange would have been inconsistent with what became his First Amendment jurisprudence. Justice Holmes and Brandeis were steadfast in their demand for fundamentality in the First Amendment at a time when not only the Supreme Court, but also dominant legal opinion, were willing to justify virtually all legislative restrictions on unpopular speech."[66] But Horwitz's effort to find a solution to our constitutional legitimation crisis in Holmes's *Lochner* dissent ignores the similarity between his rationale for overruling a state law and that used by the *Plessy* majority to justify Louisiana's Jim Crow law. If Holmes appeals to the standard of "the traditions of our people and our laws" as understood by a "rational and fair man," *Plessy* appeals to the standard of "reasonableness" as defined by the "established usages, customs and traditions of the people."[67] Furthermore, the Court was about to adopt the "rule of reason" to determine the limits of monopolistic corporate control. Horwitz's effort to transfer appeals for a more just social order from principles of equity to those of constitutionalism does not solve the problem of determining that order in a modern world deprived of transcendental appeals.[68]

Holmes, like the literary realists, challenges appeals to transcendental principles of equity. Ultimately, however, he needs to posit his own vertical ordering principle, which he finds in a theory of popular sovereignty that makes him sound sometimes like a defender of constitutional principles and sometimes like a legal positivist. His theory of contract illustrates his need for such a principle. Unable to imagine promising without transcendental supports, he abandons the link between promising and contract and relies on the sovereign power of the state to enforce contractual obligations. In contrast, the literary realists dramatize how the rituals of promising have the power to construct the sort of intersubjective commitments described by Hume. As a result, in late nineteenth-century America it is in their works, not concrete laws, that contract's promise is most powerfully evoked. It fails in them, not because it falls short of a transcendental standard, but because it cannot be sustained by a network of immanent exchanges among social, economic, and political realms. That failure suggests the continued need of the law, even a constitutionalism sanctioned by the authority of popular sovereignty, to correct itself.

V

I call this chapter "Contract and the Road from Equity" because, as Howells's *A Modern Instance* dramatizes, existing institutional structures for equity were based on a static, status-based view of the world. Participating in the challenge to that view, Howells's first realistic work wrestles with the difficulty of fulfilling contract's promise in a world in which a modern, contract-based economy undermines traditional institutional structures and communal relations used to guarantee equity. The rest of my book tries to face the challenge posed by *A Modern Instance* through close readings of various literary works of the period.

These works are not a guide to the details of contract law in the period. Nonetheless, they can help us to understand the cultural context in which contract reigned. One reason is that their "thick descriptions" give us a better insight into the complicated effects of status than the relatively "thin descriptions" of the law.[69] For instance, Holmes asserts: "The reason why a lawyer does not mention that his client wore a white hat when he made a contract, while Mrs. Quickly would be sure to dwell upon it along with the parcel gilt goblet and sea-coal fire, is that he foresees that the public force [backing the law] will act in the same way whatever his client had on his head."[70] If a writer like James might mock some of "Mrs. Quickly's" conventional descriptions of "reality" as much as Holmes does, James's novelistic thick descriptions draw attention to the ways in which seemingly irrelevant details of social life can have unacknowledged influence on how the law enforces contractual obligations. And not only contractual obligation. In 1888 Lelia Robinson worried: "Shall the woman attorney wear her hat when arguing a case or making a motion in court or shall she remove it?"[71]

Works of literature are helpful in another important way. The law of business contracts in late nineteenth-century America did not develop in a vacuum. For instance, as *Bradwell* makes clear, laissez-faire thinkers based civilized society on a particular form of domestic life, in which status rather than contract held sway. A close reading of the period's fiction can deepen our understanding of the implied relation between images of the market and the domestic economy. It is easy to dismiss the love plots of much of the period's explicitly political or economic fiction as simple appeals to the sentimental tastes of readers. But these plots do much more. They help dramatize the larger cultural narrative in which a theory of market relations arose. As we have seen, one of the problems facing a market system based on contract is that in undermining the traditional foundations of a status-based society, that system threatens the constancy needed to bind together one based on contract. For many that constancy was found in the stable moral foundation of the domestic realm. When a work of fiction ends with the sentimental marriage of its political or economic figure, it shows how important the maintenance of a "proper" domestic order was for economic and political order.

Many works of literature are capable of illustrating links between the logic of the market and that of the domestic sphere, but realistic works further our understanding in two specific ways. One involves their relation to boundary thought. If, as in boundary thought, many works of the period posit a higher force that guarantees a balance among various spheres of human activity, works of realism, in seeking an immanent balance, force a consideration of exchanges among the different spheres that boundary thought keeps apart. For instance, James recognizes the impossibility of separating the political from the social when, in a review of E. L. Godkin's *Unforeseen Tendencies of Democracy,* he notes the need to interweave "reference to the social conditions" since "at so many points are they—whether for contradiction, confirmation, attenuation, or aggravation—but another aspect of the political."[72] Similarly, a recent attempt to explain how the theory of contract that reigned in this period was transformed to include consideration of "good faith" draws on and concludes with a work of realism that I do not treat: Sarah Orne Jewett's *The Country of the Pointed Firs.*[73]

A second contribution of works of realism is most prominent in James. In a controversial review in the November 1882 *Century Magazine,* Howells notes of James, "No other novelist, except George Eliot, has dealt so largely in analysis of motive, has so fully explained and commented upon the springs of action in the persons of the drama, both before and after the facts."[74] A year earlier in *The Common Law* Holmes had argued that the law should ignore intention and confine itself to the quantifiable, economic effects of contractual exchanges. In exploring motive, James not only draws attention to an aspect of exchanges that Holmes would discount, he constructs evidence newly considered in the law. Holmes would have contract treated more as a tort. It was, however, not till about this time that courts began to consider psychological damage as a form of tort. James's novels open up a space for the analysis of such damage.[75]

But if works of realism raise questions about the moral consequences of psychological motive and exchanges among different spheres of social action, they do not moralize on them. Their failure to do so can be extremely frustrating, especially when they dramatize the failure of contract to realize the promise that it awakens. Confronted with that failure, it is tempting to seek a transcendental position that would guarantee the equitable relations not provided by the workings of contract at the end of the nineteenth century. For instance, I share the frustration over unfair racial practices detailed in George Washington Cable's "The Freedman's Case in Equity." I also understand the aspirations of women law students and lawyers who in 1886 formed the Equity Club in order to demand equal status in the profession.[76] But I am wary when Cable links a desire to plant "society firmly upon universal justice and equity" with "eternal principles of justice."[77] After all, the Ku Klux Klan also legitimated its actions by an appeal to higher standards of justice.

Eschewing both that higher ground of judgment and the sometimes morally self-satisfied ones generated by contemporary politics, I hope to show how, in dramatizing contract's failure to embody its vision of an equitable social balance, works of literary realism, each in its own way, challenge us to confront the problem of achieving equitable social relations without transcendental appeals. The next chapter explores James's vision of privacy. If a contract was considered an agreement between private individuals, it is important to understand what we mean by privacy.

CHAPTER 3

Henry James and the Construction of Privacy

I

This chapter begins with two scenes from James's fiction that suggest a link between privacy and contractual relations. The first is from *The Aspern Papers,* whose narrator covets the letters that his beloved, dead poet, Jeffrey Aspern, wrote to Aspern's presumed lover, Miss Bordereau, an aged lady who lives with her niece in a large, decaying Venice palace. Before the book begins, the narrator's fellow man of letters had written to the aunt, inquiring about the existence of Mr. Aspern's "literary remains."[1] She had responded first with silence and then by having the niece send a short note asserting that, even if they possessed things of Aspern—which they didn't—they wouldn't dream of "showing them to any one on any account whatsoever." The note ends begging him to "let her alone" (AP 122). Ignoring her request that she be let alone, but lacking the "resource of simply offering them a sum of money down" (AP 11), the narrator travels to Venice and uses his mocked fascination with an attached garden as a "pretext" (AP 11) to rent rooms in the palace. His only chance to procure his "spoils" (AP 11), he believes, is to adopt an assumed name and to rely on "hypocrisy and duplicity" (AP 12).

The scene that interests me involves the deal for the rooms. Pained that "these women so associated with Aspern should so constantly bring the pecuniary question back" (AP 34), the narrator, nonetheless, agrees to pay an outrageous sum and arranges when he should return with the money. Told that Miss Bordereau is always there, but has "her hours" (AP 30), he inquires,

> "You mean the times when you receive?"
> "I never receive. But I'll see you at noon, when you come with the money."
> "Very good. I shall be punctual." To which I added: "May I shake hands with you on our contract?" I thought there ought to be some little form; it would make me really feel easier, for I was sure there would be no other. Besides, though Miss Bordereau couldn't today be called personally attractive and there was something even in her wasted antiquity that bade one stand at one's distance, I felt an irresistible desire to hold in my own for a moment the hand Jeffrey Aspern had pressed.
> For a minute she made no answer, and I saw that my proposal failed to meet with her approbation. She indulged in no movement of withdrawal, which I half-expected; she only said coldly: "I belong to a time when that was not the custom."
> I felt rather snubbed but I exclaimed good-humoredly to Miss Tina, "Oh you'll do as well!" I shook hands with her while she assented with a small flutter. "Yes, yes, to show it's all arranged!"
> "Shall you bring the money in gold?" Miss Bordereau demanded as I was turning to the door (AP 30–31).

The second scene takes place in *The Bostonians,* when the transplanted Southerner Basil Ransom returns to Boston from New York on a business trip and decides to look up Verena Tarrant, whom he had met the year before while visiting his cousin Olive Chancellor, an advocate of women's rights. Basil knows that Olive despises him for his conservative views, but risks a visit hoping to locate Verena. Seeing instead the old abolitionist Miss Birdseye leaving Olive's house, Basil elicits from her Verena's Cambridge address and a promise not to tell Olive that she had seen him. Believing in the "victory of truth" and that Verena will convert Basil "privately," Miss Birdseye assents, saying, "She *will* affect you! If that's to be your secret, I will keep it" (B 221).

Proceeding to Cambridge, Basil finds Verena and goes with her for a long walk through the Harvard campus. At a crucial moment the question arises as to whether Verena will tell Olive of the visit. "How will she know," Basil asks, "unless you tell her?" (B 243). "I tell her everything," responds Verena (B 243), all the while suggesting that she might after all keep the visit secret.

> "Well, if I don't tell Olive, then you must leave me here," said Verena, stopping in the path and putting out a hand of farewell.

"I don't understand. What has that to do with it? Besides I thought you said you *must* tell," Ransom added. In playing with the subject this way, in enjoying her visible hesitation, he was slightly conscious of man's brutality—of being pushed by an impulse to test her good nature, which seemed to have no limit. It showed no sign of perturbation as she answered:

"Well, I want to be free—to do as I think best. And, if there is a chance of my keeping it back, there mustn't be anything more—there must not, Mr. Ransom, really."

"Anything more? Why, what are you afraid there will be—if I should simply walk home with you?"

"I must go alone, I must hurry back to mother," she said, for all reply. And she again put out her hand, which he had not taken before.

Of course he took it now, and even held it a moment; he didn't like being dismissed, and was thinking of pretexts to linger. "Miss Birdseye said you would convert me, but you haven't yet," it came into his head to say (B 244–45).

Later we learn that Ransom's visit, "buried in unspoken, in unspeakable, considerations," becomes "the only secret [Verena] had in the world—the only thing that was all her own" (B 288). Staged around a handshake—the most common gesture standing for the enactment of a contractual agreement—these two scenes would seem to contradict one another in terms of the construction of privacy. In the first, Miss Bordereau guards privacy by refusing to take the narrator's hand. In the second, Basil's taking of Verena's hand creates a private space between them, giving to Verena a secret that is her only possession in the world.

This apparent contradiction seems to invite vigilant critics to unmask James's ideological presuppositions about privacy. But, even though I like to think of myself as vigilant, I will argue that at least part of his seeming confusion is the product of our own confused thinking about privacy. As the author of a legal text on the right of privacy notes, "The word 'privacy' has taken on so many different meanings and connotations in so many different legal and social contexts that it has largely ceased to convey any single coherent concept."[2] Or, as a book coauthored by the lawyer who defended *Ulysses* against charges of obscenity puts it, "The word 'privacy' has different meanings for all of us."[3] The notion of privacy seems to evoke its own private meanings. Given this confused sense of privacy, there still might be some lessons to be learned about the possibilities of contractual relations from James's fictional construction of the private, even if we no longer accept them as lessons from the Master.

II

One reason for the legal confusion over privacy is that law in the United States distinguishes between two kinds of privacy. On the one hand, there is the constitutional right of privacy that protects against governmental actions. On the other, there is the common law or tort right to privacy that protects against actions by other private parties. Constitutional privacy is in large measure a creation of the Warren Court, especially Justice Douglas, who argued that various amendments of the Bill of Rights contain "penumbras," which, when taken together, create "zones of privacy" into which the government should not intrude.[4] For instance, a constitutional right of privacy is the basis of *Roe v. Wade* (1973), the Supreme Court case that limits the government's power to interfere with a woman's choice to have an abortion or not. In contrast, the common law right to privacy grows out of a *Harvard Law Review* essay published in 1890. Its authors, Samuel Warren and Louis Brandeis, like James, attended Harvard. Constructed out of his milieu and at almost the same time that he was writing, this right to privacy would seem to be the one most pertinent to his works.

Brandeis and Warren graduated first and second in their law school class. Warren came from a wealthy Boston family. Brandeis would become the first Jewish member of the Supreme Court. Roscoe Pound is quoted as saying that their article did "nothing less than add a chapter to our law."[5] Its intent was to protect human dignity from the prying of others. They were most concerned about the press' violation of "obvious bounds of propriety and of decency." Condemning the commercialization of gossip that leads to intrusions "upon the domestic circle," the two argue that the "intensity and complexity" of life accompanying "advancing civilization" necessitate "some retreat from the world." If, on the one hand, "man, under the refining influence of culture, has become more sensitive to publicity, so that solitude and privacy have become more essential to the individual"; on the other, "modern enterprise and invention have, through invasions upon his privacy, subjected him to mental pain and distress, far greater than could be inflicted by mere bodily injury."[6]

This hostility to the press has sparked imaginative accounts of the article's origin. According to legend, Warren sought Brandeis's help in response to press coverage of his family's social life. In 1883 Warren married Miss Mabel Bayard, daughter of Thomas Francis Bayard Sr., a senator from Delaware who was nearly nominated for president by the Democrats, although his Southern connections raised suspicion about him with some Northerners. As Secretary of State, Bayard forged a cooperative alliance with Great Britain known as "hands across the Atlantic."[7] It is only appropriate, then, that the famous writer of transatlantic novels, Henry James, knew Bayard's daughter, having met her on a visit to Washington, D.C., in 1882. Impressed by her charm, he wrote to his mother that she and her friends were "such as one ought to marry, if one were marrying."[8] James, of course, did not marry, but the next year Warren did. According to one of Brandeis's biographers, when the Warrens "set up housekeeping in Boston's exclusive Back Bay section and began to entertain elaborately, *The Saturday Evening Gazette,* which specialized in 'blue blood items,' naturally reported their activities in lurid detail."[9] Reporters, we are told, snuck into social affairs as waiters, carrying hidden cameras. For six years, according to the authors of a book on privacy, Warren and Brandeis considered legal means to halt such intrusions, using that time meticulously to arrange "the words that convey the ideas that constitute [their] argument."[10]

This account of the article's origins has since been disputed. Unearthing very few reports of the Warrens' social life, less sympathetic scholars speculate that the actual cause of Warren's outrage was the press's handling of Senator Bayard in 1889.[11] But whether the image of Samuel Warren knocking a camera out of a disguised reporter's hands is a fabrication or not, it is clear that many of the so-called "best men" of the time were concerned about the intrusiveness of the press. For instance, Warren and Brandeis cite a *Scribner's Magazine* article written the same year by E. L. Godkin, the editor of *The Nation.* Godkin argues that the threat to privacy grows out of the development of new technologies of publicity. Admitting that there is "some substance" to the claim that "the love of gossip is after all human," he warns that gossip is no longer confined to the "immediate circle" of someone's acquaintances. Instead, it can "make his name, or his walk, or his conversation familiar to strangers." If oral transmission spared someone the "pain or mortification of knowing that he was gossiped about" because he seldom heard that which "simply made him ridiculous, or trespassed on his lawful privacy, but made no positive attack on his reputation," the wide circulation of papers reveals his imperfections to people hundreds or thousands of miles away, and, worst of all, "brings to his knowledge exactly what is said about him, with all of its details." Thus he must suffer "the great pain of feeling that everybody he meets in the street is perfectly familiar with some folly, or misfortune, or indiscretion, or weakness, which he had previously supposed had never got beyond his domestic circle."[12]

The press's power to affront personal dignity intrigued James. In *The Reverberator* (1888), for example, a vulgar American reporter almost halts the wedding of a sophisticated French-American man to an innocent American woman when he publishes information that she confidentially tells him about the private life of her family-to-be, which, in turn, considers anyone who would give such information to a reporter unworthy of membership in its exclusive circle. Whether or not we can trust a biographer's summary of journalistic accounts of the private life of the Warren family, James's plot indicates that Warren and Brandeis had available vivid, if fictional, accounts of the press's lack of scruples. Their concern was not with libel, which was already covered by the law. Instead, they wanted legal protection against the sort of intrusions that James imagines, *whether the information was true or not*.[13] They sought this protection by claiming that, although it had never been articulated, the common law guaranteed a right to privacy, or, as they put it, "the right 'to be left alone.'"[14]

The political consequences of such a right to privacy in our own day are not clear. Some liberals point to its mugwump origins as proof that it is a relic of an elitist, bourgeois ideology. For evidence they could cite an 1890 editorial in *The Nation* commenting on the Warren and Brandeis article. While deploring violations of privacy, the author is pessimistic about providing for its protection because "in all democratic societies today the public is disposed either to resent attempts at privacy, either of mind or body, or turn them into ridicule."[15] Defense of privacy, in other words, is perceived as undemocratic. But an editorial in *Scribner's Magazine* takes issue with this account. "It is important to note," it insists, "that privacy is not by any means an attribute of aristocracy as opposed to democracy." Nonetheless, the *Scribner's* article confirms those who find the defense of privacy conservative. It begins: "In the great future battle of the world between the two systems of Socialism and Individualism, one of the vital points of difference is to be *privacy*."[16]

But lest we succumb to the identification of privacy with individualism, we should remember John Dewey's argument in 1927 that "the distinction between private and public is . . . in no sense equivalent to the distinction between individual and social, even if we suppose that the latter distinction has a definite meaning." Drawing on the pragmatic

definition of actions by their consequences, Dewey insists: "When indirect consequences are recognized and there is an effect to regulate
them, something having the traits of a state comes into existence. When
the consequences of an action are confined, or are thought to be confined, mainly to the persons directly engaged in it, the transaction is a
private one."[17]

If Dewey's argument is not enough to make us resist equating the
protection of privacy with conservative individualism, the argument of
radical feminist Andrea Dworkin should. Describing media coverage of
rape victims as "the third rape" (after the act itself and the trial),
Dworkin decries the *New York Times* and *NBC News* policy of reporting
the names of victims. "If a woman's reporting a rape to the police means
she will be exposed by the media to the scrutiny of voyeurs and worse,
a sexual spectacle with her legs splayed open in the public mind, reporting itself will be tantamount to suicide." Like Warren and Brandeis
years earlier, Dworkin considers the truth of the reporting irrelevant.
"The media," she says, "use you until they use you up." What the rape
victim needs, she argues, sounding very much like our mugwumps, is
"privacy, dignity, lack of fear."[18]

Similarly, the mugwumps' fear that the threat to privacy was socialism is challenged by the attack on the tort right to privacy by that
staunch defender of free enterprise, Judge Richard Posner. "Very few
people want to be left alone. They want to manipulate the world around
them by selective disclosure of facts about themselves. . . . Reputation is
what others think of us, and we have no right to control other people's
thoughts. Equally we have no right, by controlling the information that
is known about us, to manipulate the opinions that other people hold
of us. Yet this is the essence of what most students of the subject mean
by privacy."[19]

Posner's stand on privacy is consistent with his defense of market
freedom. Indeed, the purpose of Warren and Brandeis's article was to
provide legal protection for those who wanted to keep information
about themselves, true or not, from circulation in the market. Any
consideration of the political effect of their construction of a right to
privacy should take into account their desire to resist the logic of the
market.

To resist that logic the two lawyers distinguished a right to privacy
from property rights. Their need to do so grew out of the relation
between property and contract at the time. Whereas in the eighteenth
century there was a general tendency to assume the intrinsic value of a

piece of property, in the highly developed market economy of the late nineteenth century value was determined by contractual exchanges. Thus, although the law may have protected vested interests of property, the *value* of property was subordinate to the contract relation. The consequences of the reign of contract for a guaranteed right to privacy are best understood if we remember Locke's crucial distinction between life and labor. For Locke labor is alienable from the person and thus becomes a form of property. Life, however, is not alienable. To subordinate the right to privacy to that of property is to make it alienable. But the entire point of a right to privacy is to protect aspects of the personality from circulation in the marketplace. Privacy, therefore, had to be related to an inalienable part of one's personality.

One way of looking at the history of the tort right to privacy is to note how difficult it has been to disassociate it from property.[20] For an example, we can turn to Godkin's argument that reputation is one of man's most valuable possessions, as important or more important for the comfort and happiness of life as "tangible property." For proof he quotes *Othello:*

> Who steals my purse steals trash; 'tis something, nothing;
> 'Twas mine, 'tis his, and has been slave to thousands;
> But he that felches from me my good name
> Robs me of that which not enriches him,
> And makes me poor indeed.[21]

But even though Godkin insists on reputation as being more valuable than money, the courts protected reputation by linking it to tangible property. Because reputation could increase earning power, it, like labor, was a form of property. For instance, one of Albion W. Tourgée's most ingenious attacks on the "separate but equal" law challenged in *Plessy v. Ferguson* was that, in labeling Homer Plessy, who was seven-eighths white, black, the Jim Crow law deprived him of his reputation as a white man, which affected his earning power and consequently violated the 14th Amendment's protection of life, liberty, and property.

If reputation itself is marketable, how can it be an inalienable part of someone's personality? Indeed, the inability to disassociate the right to privacy from property would seem to undercut Warren and Brandeis's claim that an "inviolate self" is capable of resisting the market. As a generation of literary critics has been trained to believe, the very notion of an inviolate, private self is a construct. Students of late nineteenth-century United States culture have used this insight to suggest that far from resisting the logic of the market, the notion of an inviolate, private self is a product of it. For instance, Philip Fisher problematizes the opposition between public and private by arguing that in *The Bostonians* the private self does not preexist the public but is created by disappearing from it. The "genius" of James's novel he asserts, "is not to ask the question of how, out of normal human materials" a performing public self is constructed. "Instead [James] begins with Verena's instinctively public self and asks how, out of this, an intimate and human-scale personality might be won." Verena's "full possession of an individual self," he argues, comes from her final act of disappearing from the public.[22]

Fisher's reading seems to complicate a genteel, mugwump vision of a private, autonomous self that preexists the realm of publicity. It is worth noting, however, that the mugwumps were not quite the essentialists that contemporary critics make them out to be. For Godkin a private self is not an ahistorical self. "Privacy," he maintains, "is a distinctly modern product, one of the luxuries of civilization, which is not only unsought for but unknown in primitive or barbarous societies."[23] Even if we are put off by Godkin's Eurocentric views of civilization and barbarism, we have to acknowledge that they make clear that, for him, a private self is not some preexisting, natural self, but one that is produced by a particular civilization, a self that he feels is well worth preserving. Likewise, the purpose of Warren and Brandeis's article was to demonstrate that the common law is a historically adaptable institution that contains within it principles that provide legal protection against new threats to a particular version of the self. Present commentators almost always overlook the fact that Warren and Brandeis refer to a right *to* privacy, not a right *of* privacy, which is the common phrase today. They shouldn't. The difference is subtle, but a right to privacy implies that unless people are guaranteed the right to be left alone they will not be able to maintain an inviolate personality, whereas a right of privacy, a bit more strongly, implies something that an inviolate personality has as an inalienable possession. A right to privacy is more a creation of the law, a right of privacy more an appeal to natural rights.

My point is that Warren and Brandeis come closer than some give them credit for to Robert Post's very contemporary argument that the issue at stake concerning privacy "is not whether the law ought to protect personality, but rather how the law ought to conceptualize personality for the purposes of legal protection."[24] The mugwumps conceptualized personality in a very particular way and felt that it should be protected. What is interesting when we look at James in conjunction with their concept of personality is that he, too, asserts a notion of personality, but one that challenges the mugwump version. In challenging it he does not, however, reduce it to a pure product of the public sphere or the market. The private self in James *does* respond to new techniques of publicity and a market dominated by contractual relations. But even though those forces shape the nature of the self, they do not completely determine its shape.

The problem with a reading like Fisher's is that it corrects the notion that a private self preexists a public realm by turning the relationship upside down. James's novel works by a "reversal of terms." He underlines a "strategy of self-creation that *inverts* the strategy of publicity and visibility that are the machinery of the celebrity" (my emphasis).[25] The private is formed by disappearing from what must be a preexisting public realm. The legal distinction between the constitutional and tort rights of privacy points to the flaw in such an inversion.

To recall, constitutional privacy concerns violations by the government; tort privacy violations by other private parties. If privacy can be violated by private parties, we cannot rest content with a simple opposition between public and private. Instead, we need to distinguish among different realms of the private. For instance, whereas it makes sense to contrast the private self with the "public" realm of the market, in the late nineteenth century the market was considered part of the private realm into which the public realm of government should not intrude.[26] But even if we grant that the realm of the market was for the most part considered private rather than public, it still makes sense to consider the market *less* private than the domestic sphere into which Verena disappears at the end of *The Bostonians*. It is the almost sacred realm of the domestic circle that Warren and Brandeis and Godkin seem most concerned to protect. They share that concern with Justice Douglas, who in *Griswold v. Connecticut* (1965) appealed to the sanctity of the domestic circle to uphold the right of a married couple to use contraceptives. Waxing eloquent he asks: "Would we allow the police to search the sacred precincts of marital bedrooms for telltale signs of the use of contraceptives? The very idea is repulsive to the notions of privacy surrounding the marriage relationship. We deal with a right of privacy older than the Bill of Rights—older than our political parties, older than our school system. Marriage is a coming together for better or for worse, hopefully enduring, and intimate to the degree of being sacred."[27]

The domestic circle may be considered the most sacred zone of privacy, but, as Douglas's quotation makes clear, it is not an *asocial* realm. Indeed, it is constituted by a contractual relation between husband and wife. The nature of that contract complicates any exploration into the notion of privacy.

III

The marriage contract, lawyers in the late nineteenth century willingly granted, is a special sort of contract. In an 1867 essay Godkin favorably evoked Sir Henry Maine's argument about the movement from status to contract.[28] But the marriage contract raised problems for claims made after the Civil War that, in honoring contract as no other society had, the United States was the most progressive of progressive societies. Involving two mutually consenting adults, it creates, nonetheless, a relationship of status that the Supreme Court called "the foundation of the family and of society."[29] A society supposedly founded on contractual freedom had, in fact, an equally important foundation in a domestic relation of status.

Because the social order depends on proper order in the domestic realm, the contract creating that space has a quasi-public nature. Thus, in an age in which the courts considered interference with market transactions a violation of the freedom of contract, they asserted their right to regulate the marriage contract. Divorce, for instance, was not simply a matter of two individuals who could freely enter or exit a contractual relation. As Justice Thomas M. Cooley of Michigan wrote, "There are three parties to every divorce proceeding, the husband, the wife, and the state; the first two parties representing their respective interests as individuals; the state concerned to guard the morals of its citizens, by taking care that neither by collusion nor otherwise, shall divorce be allowed under circumstance as to reduce marriage to a mere temporary arrangement of conscience or passion. . . . "[30]

Cooley was one of the most respected legal minds of the period. He edited editions of both Blackstone's and Story's *Commentaries.* He is most famous for his *Treatise on the Constitutional Limitations which Rest Upon the Legislative Power of the States of the American Union* (1868), which was one of the most important statements of laissez-faire legal thought. But although he reluctantly interfered with the terms of business contracts between private citizens, he, like most of his generation, believed in governmental regulation of the marriage contract. Cooley is also the person who provided Warren and Brandeis with their crucial phrase, "the right 'to be left alone.'"[31]

As we have seen, Warren and Brandeis link the right to be left alone with the domestic circle, a sanctified private realm supposedly immune to public and private interference. What needs to be emphasized, however, is that the state relinquishes its regulatory power over the domestic circle only after the marriage contract creates the proper status relations. Once the domestic circle is properly ordered, its regulation can be left to husband and wife, who are expected to perform their proper duties, duties established by a clear-cut legal hierarchy.

As some critics of traditional marriage pointed out, the courts' attitude toward marriage was similar to the attitude Southern courts had adopted toward slavery. In both cases, courts tried to guarantee a proper relation of status but refused to interfere with it once it was established.[32] The end of slavery did not mean the end of the courts' attitude toward marriage. In fact, emancipation fueled fears of miscegenation, which led to powerful reassertions of the government's right to regulate the terms of the marriage contract. For instance, in a decision that declared homes the "nurseries of the States," an Alabama court dissolved an interracial marriage. Who, it wondered, can "estimate the evil of introducing into the most intimate relations, elements so heterogeneous that they must naturally cause discord, shame, disruption of family circles, and estrangements of kindred? While with their interior administration, the State should interfere but little, it is obviously of the highest public concern that it should, by general laws adapted to the state of things around them, guard against disturbances from without."[33]

Because the domestic circle had such an important social role, it was established by a contract more public than the business contract. This public contract created a sacred sphere that should not be violated by public or private parties. Private as that sphere might seem, however, it was not a sphere in which husband and wife could legally assert the right to be left alone against one another. On the contrary, the marriage contract created one legal body out of two. James's works can help us sort out the ways that the marriage contract complicated notions of a private personality. It's time, then, to return to the second of the scenes with which I began.

IV

The relationship established between Verena and Basil in Cambridge is defined in part by the contrast between their encounter and the location in which it begins to take shape. Their intimacy is first established in Memorial Hall at Harvard, a semipublic space commemorating the private deaths of the "sons of the university" who gave their lives in public service during the Civil War. As James puts it, "They were discussing their affairs, which had nothing to do with the heroic symbols that surrounded them; but their affairs had suddenly grown so serious that there was no want of decency in their lingering there for the purpose" (B 247).

Their relation is also defined by a contrast with the one that Verena has with Olive. Because Verena ends up promising to marry Basil, most critics assume that the relationship between the two women stands for an alternative to traditional marriage. To a certain extent it does, but we need to see what alternative it suggests. Although Olive would "hate [marriage] for herself" (B 84) because it would bring her into union with a man, she is not necessarily opposed to the *institution* of marriage. Indeed, Verena's initial radical disapproval of the marriage tie "gave her a vertigo" (B 84). She especially "didn't like the 'atmosphere' of circles in which such institutions were called into question" (B 84). Unlike Verena, she is not an advocate of "free union" (B 84).

Olive's negative response to Verena's radicalism reminds us that only a minority of those supporting women's rights clamored for the abolition of marriage. While decrying existing inequalities, the more conservative reformers continued to consider marriage a special form of contract, sanctified by a higher power. The more radical reformers also believed in marriage, but felt that equality could be ensured only if the marriage contract matched the freedom of business contracts. For instance, free love advocate, spiritualist, and first female Wall Street broker Victoria Woodhull, whom James used as a model in "The Siege of London," proclaimed that in marriage, "there is neither right nor duty beyond the uniting—the contracting—individuals."[34]

When Verena and Olive first meet, Verena's ideas are closer to Woodhull's; Olive's more conservative. A traditionalist, Olive idealizes a relationship that requires renunciation. What distinguishes her from other advocates of marriage is that she asks Verena to renounce heterosexual attraction. Verena's temporary renunciation allows their relationship to develop without what many in their society felt was a natural barrier to an egalitarian relationship in marriage. Indeed, the hierarchical status constructed by the marriage contract was justified by "natural" forces of heterosexuality. Freed from such forces, Verena and Olive strive for an egalitarian union.[35] Appropriately, the language describing their relationship evokes the ideals of marriage.

As Olive acknowledges, the "union of soul" (B 80) that she seeks with Verena would take a "double consent" (B 80). Based on mutual consent, their relationship creates a "partnership of their two minds" (B 156). That partnership is not, however, based on radical notions of "free union" (B 84) in which the partners are free to dissolve it at will. Instead, Olive seeks, as in a marriage contract, a promise that "would bind them together for life" (B 110). That she seeks from Verena a promise not to marry would seem to undercut my claim that James uses their relationship to experiment with the possibility of a truly egalitarian "marriage." But her subsequent refusal to accept Verena's spoken promise when it is offered, preferring to "trust" her "without a pledge" (B 137), emphasizes how Olive hopes for a union more tightly bound than the existing marriage contract. The marriage contract, after all, is enforced by law. Olive's idealized bond demands a perpetual renewal based on mutual trust. Coming together in a partnership that compensated for what each lacked, Verena and Olive form an "organic whole" (B 156).

Verena and Olive's relative success in creating one body out of two contrasts with Basil's lone attempt to form a partnership. Having difficulty making ends meet as a Southern lawyer in New York City, "he had formed a partnership with a person who seemed likely to repair some of his deficiencies—a young man from Rhode Island, acquainted, according to his own expression, with the inside track" (B 187).[36] Rather than compensate for Basil's deficiencies—one of which was capital—his new partner grabbed what little money the partnership had and took off for Europe.

As successful as Verena and Olive's "partnership" (B 172) seems by contrast, its very appearance of success allows James to suggest an indirect criticism of the institution of marriage that Olive herself is not willing to make. If Verena and Olive's union creates an organic body that compensates for their respective deficiencies, what it lacks is a space for Verena to call her own. The problem is not simply that Verena's relationship with Olive grants her a public role, whereas her relationship with Basil confines her to a private one. To be sure, Verena and Olive work together to present a voice to the public, whereas Basil will deny Verena that voice. But if the voice is Verena's, it is controlled by Olive. Olive's control is linked to the nature of their domestic life together. Olive is extremely domestic. On his first visit to her, Basil is struck by the tasteful arrangement of his cousin's home. Like the proper wife, "Olive Chancellor regulated her conduct on lofty principles" (B 23). "Her house," we are told, "had always been thoroughly well regulated" (B 173). Whereas Olive's domestic regulation heightens the cultural refinement of Verena, who comes from a most unregulated family, it still leaves her with no space of her own.

To be sure, Verena will not find that space with Basil. James is highly conscious of how the private sphere of the domestic circle creates a realm in which individual privacy is hard to come by. This, indeed, is part of the message of *The Reverberator*. It is easy to read that work as James's attack on the press' intrusion into the private realm of the domestic circle. But James also directs his satire against the proper French-American family, the "house of Probert," that is held together by a delicate "bond" that makes "each for all and all for each" (R 68–69). Acting as a corporate body, it would forbid son and brother Gaston to marry a lovely but unrefined American, who in her innocence betrays family secrets to the press. Family secrets is the right phrase, for everyone in the family knows about them. As imagined by James, this family is so close that no secrets are allowed, although a lot of hypocrisy is. For instance, the family seems willing to relent in its judgment of Francie, if she would only lie and say that she was forced into confiding to the journalist. But innocent Francie insists on the truth, making Gaston choose between his family and his lover. In a crucial scene, his friend, an American artist, advises him to marry, "to save from destruction the last scrap of your independence" (R 205). Gaston's family, he tells him, is rendering him "incapable of individual life" (R 205). Gaston ends up proving his independence by choosing to marry, but, in a typical Jamesian move, that choice creates the conditions for yet another domestic circle. Similarly, in *The Bostonians,* Verena escapes from one domestic relation into another.

In most respects her relationship with Basil promises to be even more confining than her relationship with Olive. In addition to being predicated on her willingness to hold "her tongue" (B 253) and to no longer speak in public, it introduces the force of sexuality into Verena's life, a force that makes it impossible to maintain the delicate balance of equality for which Olive and Verena strive. Indeed, the holding of Verena's tongue and the force of male sexuality are linked early in the book when Olive warns her, "There are gentlemen in plenty who would be glad to stop your mouth by kissing you" (B 136)!

The image of Verena's mouth being stopped by a kiss invites direct comparison with the scene between Basil and Verena in Cambridge. If that scene culminates in a handshake, the act most symbolic of contractual relations between equal partners, the kiss is the act most symbolic of sealing the contract between husband and wife. The nature of Verena's life in marriage is anticipated by the imagery of the final scene. Wrenching Verena from Olive "by muscular force" (B 448), Ransom thrusts the "hood of Verena's long cloak over her head, to conceal her face and her identity" (B 449).

Verena's marriage with Basil does not signal the end of her performing self in favor of a private self, since Verena will continue to perform. The difference is that she will now perform privately for Basil.[37] She has not disappeared from the public realm to assert the "full possession of an individual self,"[38] because the domestic sphere she is about to enter, while decidedly private, will not allow her the space for a self to exist. Indeed, the marriage contract incorporates her into the body of her husband.

The book's ending does not, however, completely deny a space for a private self to be constructed. One occurs, even if momentarily, during the handshake between Verena and Basil.

V

Like the kiss about which Olive warns Verena, Verena's handshake with Basil leads to a holding of her tongue. But whereas the kiss would put an end to her addresses to the public so as to reserve them for Basil, the handshake implies that she will keep her meeting with Basil secret from Olive, another private party. Furthermore, Verena does not submit to her silence, but offers it on the condition that Basil leave her a space of her own. If offering her hand seals a moment of intimacy between her and Basil, it also establishes boundaries. " 'Well, if I don't tell Olive, then you must leave me here,' said Verena, stopping in the path and putting out a hand of farewell" (B 244). To be sure, at first Basil refuses to accept her offer. He even enjoys playing with her and testing her good nature while being "slightly conscious of a man's brutality" (B 244). But Verena's resistance continues, working to control the "natural" brutality that would force itself on her. "Well, I want to be free—to do as I think best. And, if there is a chance of my keeping it back, there mustn't be anything more—there must not, Mr. Ransom, really" (B 244).

Of course, Verena's desire to be "free" can be read ironically in light of the book's ending. Far from offering her freedom, this moment can be read as leading to her subsequent submission to Basil's masculine will. Nonetheless, at this moment a delicate balance is reached; a balance achieved when Basil, despite irritation at "being dismissed" (B 245), takes the hand she once again offers. In James's world a space in which a private self can take shape is constructed in such a balanced moment.

That moment is different from perhaps the most famous moment in American literature sanctifying a private relationship between a man and a woman: the meeting of Hester and Dimmesdale in *The Scarlet Letter.* Whereas Hawthorne's lovers meet in the forest, James's, as we have seen, meet in a semipublic realm. Part of the sanctity of their moment together results from the sanctity of that semipublic space, rather than a withdrawal into nature. Furthermore, whereas Hester and Dimmesdale share privacy because of their illicit sexual union, Verena and Basil create the possibilities of privacy through the establishment of boundaries. As Olive puts it, trying to wrench Verena's secret from her later in the novel, "Verena Tarrant, what *is* there between you?" (B 370). A private personality for James does not result from protecting a self that preexists social relations. Nor does it result from the union of two selves into one that underlies the so-called sanctity of the domestic sphere. It does not even result from disappearance from the public. Instead, it has to do with the creation of a space *between,* a space that establishes connection while simultaneously helping to define the parties involved as individuals.

What in James's story complicates the establishment of this space *between* is that it depends on an empty space *within* the two parties involved. We can see this most obviously with Verena.

Verena's remarkable capacity to establish relationships with people results not from a fullness, but an emptiness, "the extraordinary generosity with which she could expose herself, give herself away, turn herself inside out, for the satisfaction of a person who made demands of her" (B 380). Her role as medium is her most obvious manifestation of this "generosity."[39] She seems capable of speaking the voice of anyone who controls her. Her generosity suggests that James draws on the traditional definition of a woman as an empty vessel, waiting to be filled and given identity by her union with a man. During his first encounter with her, Basil even comes close to attributing "to Miss Tarrant a singular hollowness of character" (B 61). But the "hollowness" defining Verena's essence inhabits other characters as well. Deficiencies, after all, not a fullness, cause Basil, Verena, and Olive to seek out partnerships. Furthermore, if Verena's voice seems capable of being taken possession of by whomever she is around, that very voice seduces Basil, penetrating the core of his being so that he, in turn, wants to take sole possession of it.

Taking possession of another is as much a sin for James as it is for Hawthorne. Unlike Hawthorne, however, he does not imagine an alternative in a moment of organic unity. In contrast, James's alternative balances the generosity that he associates with Verena against the resistance that she displays in her handshake with Basil. Owing much to the ideal of the period's market exchanges, that balanced vision also points to its limits.

The ideological power of contract as a mode of exchange depends on an image of balance in which two free and equal parties willingly consent to a transaction from which both can benefit. But, whereas the exchange ideally leads to financial profit for both, it rules out truly *interpersonal* exchanges because it involves alienable property, which is not part of the parties' essential identities. For James, however, because no essential self exists outside of exchanges, all exchanges are interpersonal and thus affect the very nature of the self. A self cannot achieve definition without a "space *between*" that only interpersonal relations can provide; at the same time, interpersonal relations are impossible without an emptiness *within* the self, an emptiness making one vulnerable to penetrations— and dominations—by another. This image of exchange leads to a very different account of how business contracts lead to profit.[40]

Rather than present a world in which a balanced agreement between equal partners can lead to mutual profit—as Basil hoped for in forming his law partnership—James presents a world in which profit results from imbalances, dominations, and submissions. For James, even in transactions in which both parties reap a financial gain, a personal loss is involved. Indeed, rather than assume a preexisting balance between bargaining partners whose contractual agreement signals a meeting of the wills, James suggests that a balance can be achieved only, as Verena temporarily does, through the resistance of one party to the will of another.

If James's vision of exchanges differs from that of laissez-faire theorists, it also differs from that of the two versions of feminism that we have examined. Feminists like Woodhull embrace the vision of freedom implied by business exchanges and try to extend its logic to the domestic circle so that husband and wife can also relate as free and equal contracting parties. Like Locke, such reformers feel that someone can enter into exchanges and alienate property (or labor as a form of property) without affecting an essential, inalienable self. James, however, presents a self that is defined by the exchanges into which it enters, just as the marriage contract alters the status of the contracting parties. Rather than use the business contract as a model to reform the marriage contract, he uses the marriage contract to suggest that *all* exchanges involve imbalanced structures of the status of the person that they in part construct.

He differs from a feminist like Olive Chancellor because of her belief that exchanges can be properly regulated. James suggests Olive's desire to regulate exchanges by a higher moral order through her name. A chancellor is a judge who presides over courts of equity. Olive so desires an equitable order that, as her sister tells Basil, she would reform the solar system if she could. Nonetheless, she is convinced that a history of past oppressions and wrongs makes it impossible to achieve an equitable balance between men and women. "She considered men in general as so much in the debt of the opposite sex that any individual woman had an unlimited credit with them; she could not possibly overdraw the general feminine account" (B 138). Since for James it is the very nature of interpersonal relations to create obligations for both parties, Olive's belief that accounts between men and women can never be balanced effectively closes off her relations with men. Indeed, if in her relations with women Olive displays so much "generosity, that she liked obligations of gratitude" (B 138), she scarcely recognized any obligation to men. If that belief would seem to affect her relations only with men, it also affects her relation with Verena, since for it to be regulated by Olive's moral standards Verena too must renounce heterosexual relations.

Verena, of course, ultimately cannot make that renunciation, and she pays the price by ransoming her freedom to Basil's masculine domination. Despite this pessimistic ending, however, a momentary balance is achieved when Basil and Verena, in shaking hands, create a space between themselves, a space that both constructs and—so long as it exists—helps to maintain a private self otherwise denied Verena.

VI

James's association of privacy with the creation of a "space between" helps to explain why the scene in *The Aspern Papers* in which Miss Bordereau protects privacy by refusing the narrator's hand is consistent with the scene in *The Bostonians* in which Verena and Basil construct a private space through the act of shaking hands. Whereas Verena and Basil exchange no money, the transaction between the narrator and Miss Bordereau would seem to be no more than a simple exchange of money for rooms to rent. But much more is at stake. The narrator agrees to pay an outrageous price because renting rooms is part of his strategy for taking possession of Aspern's papers. Further-more, he offers to shake hands, not merely to seal a contract, but in an attempt to bridge the gap between Aspern and himself. "I felt an irresistible desire," he admits, "to hold in my own for a moment the hand Jeffrey Aspern had pressed" (AP 30). In refusing to take his hand, Miss Juliana refuses to serve as a link between him and Aspern. She is not, however, protecting Aspern alone. She is also protecting the pri-vacy of what transpired *between* herself and Aspern.

The narrator wants to possess anything to do with Aspern. But Aspern's letters are special in part because they might establish a con-nection between the poet and Miss Juliana. Ironically, however, they can do so only because they record a gap between the two. Lovers, after all, don't write letters while in the midst of an embrace. Thus, whereas Miss Juliana is perfectly willing to sell Aspern's portrait, even if for an extravagant price, she denies the narrator possession of the space that the letters occupy. Indeed, although the narrator possesses Aspern's portrait at the end of the tale, it serves to remind him of his failure. Thinking of it hanging, appropriately, above his writing table, the nar-rator ends the book by admitting, "When I look at it I can scarcely bear my loss—I mean of the precious papers" (AP 143).

This final sentence does more than remind us that any gain in James's world involves a loss. It also draws attention to the many losses that the narrator risked suffering. When the story first appeared in *The Atlantic Monthly* in 1888, the sentence read, "When I looked at it my chagrin at the loss of the letters becomes almost intolerable."[41] The loss here is clearly the letters. The final phrase of the revised version also makes that loss clear, but by reordering the sentence James alerts us to other losses that the narrator might regret: perhaps the loss of the large sum of money that he sent to Miss Juliana's niece with an explanation that he had sold the portrait, or, more likely, the loss of Miss Tina herself, for, as the narrator recognizes early on, one way to get possession of the letters, which were not for sale, was "to make love to the niece" (AP 14). What he had not bargained for was that his duplicitous lovemaking to Miss Tina would cause her to offer herself to him in exchange for the letters.

Although marital and market relations are governed by different contracts, Miss Tina's offer inextricably links the two. The link is even more complicated because Miss Juliana's negotiations for money, which for the narrator taint the sacred name of Aspern, are intended to make Miss Tina more marriageable by increasing her wealth. The narrator thinks that he can procure the letters by making love to the niece, but the aunt is aware of the strategy and seems to encourage it. Furthermore, James hints that Miss Tina might be the issue of the affair between the poet and his lover. If, more than anything, the narrator wants to establish a relation with Aspern, Miss Tina offers him that possibility in, perhaps, more senses than one.[42]

Of course, we will never know whether Miss Tina is Aspern's daughter, but it is clear that the narrator's desire to make contact with Aspern through his papers is deflected by a series of substitutions, first to Miss Juliana and then to Miss Tina. This series of substituted exchanges is enacted in the scene with which we started. When Miss Juliana refuses the narrator's hand, he turns to grasp Miss Tina's, who "assented with a small flutter" (AP 31). The possibility that their handshake could lead to marriage in exchange for the letters demonstrates how the institution of marriage complicates notions of privacy.

For someone who would exchange the "riddle of the universe" (AP 5) for a "bundle of Jeffrey Aspern's letters" (AP 5), a few secrets between lovers are nothing. Ironically, however, the narrator can most successfully violate the private realm between Miss Juliana and her lover by entering into the private realm of matrimony with Miss Tina. If it was commonplace for defenders of privacy to evoke the sanctity of the domestic circle, in the *Aspern Papers* James dramatizes how the domestic circle can itself lead to violations of privacy. Marriage between the narrator and Miss Tina would not protect the family's privacy. On the contrary, it would make it legal for the narrator to reveal family secrets.

After Miss Juliana dies the letters still exist, but Miss Tina, out of respect for her aunt, refuses to show them to the narrator. Talking to him, however, she imagines that her aunt had tried to tell her something about the papers but couldn't. When asked what it might have been she replies,

> "Well, that if you were a relation it would be different."
> I wondered, "If I were a relation—?"
> "If you weren't a stranger. Then it would be the same for you as for me. Anything that's mine would be yours, and you could do what you like. I shouldn't be able to prevent you—and you'd have no responsibility" (AP 133).

Because as Miss Tina's husband the narrator would own her property, he has the chance to establish the connection that he so desires and publish it to the world without taking on the responsibility of legally betraying a trust. But recognizing that the "only way to become possessed was to unite myself to her for life" (AP 141), he concludes, "there was no doubt whatever that I couldn't pay the price. I couldn't accept the proposal. I couldn't, for a bundle of tattered papers, marry a ridiculous pathetic provincial old woman" (AP 137). Later the narrator reconsiders. "It seemed to me that I *could* pay the price" (AP 142). But by then it is too late. Miss Tina has burned the papers "one by one" (AP 142).[43]

In burning the papers, Miss Tina demonstrates her ability to gain a measure of self-worth out of an obvious loss. She becomes, at least momentarily, more than a pathetic old woman precisely when she destroys what gives her value in the narrator's eyes. Her act of resistance foils the narrator's plan to make contact with Aspern. It also reminds us that while making love to her he unknowingly reoccupies, with a difference, the poet's relation to his lover.

What makes Miss Juliana fascinating for the narrator is not merely her contact with Aspern, but the possibility of intimacy *outside* marriage. Indeed, the narrator hopes that in procuring the letters he will be able to confirm his speculation "that Miss Juliana had not always adhered to the steep footway of renunciation. There hovered about her name a perfume of impenitent passion, an intimation that she had not been exactly as the respectable young person in general" (AP 48). Miss Juliana's seduction suggests that her privacy was betrayed when she lost her capacity to resist a willful male. In trying to procure Aspern's papers, the narrator threatens to repeat his hero's violation of her privacy. But in doing so he places her—despite her age—once again in the situation of being courted. This time Miss Juliana has more power to resist. Nonetheless, when the narrator wonders whether lines in Aspern's poetry were a "sign that her singer had betrayed her, had given her away, as we say nowadays, to posterity" (AP 48), he reminds us that in James's world the question of privacy intersects with that of art. If so far I have used James's works to explore the construction of privacy, I would like now to use that exploration to examine how "artistic privacy" in James is related to contractual exchanges. To do so is to make a crucial distinction between artistic privacy and artistic autonomy.

VII

Alfred Habegger has argued that James's concern with privacy is a conservative response to the growth of a democratic press. From his father's exchange in the press with Stephen Andrews, a free love advocate and ally of Victoria Woodhull, James supposedly draws the lesson that "the radical democratic press sought to invade the private life." This association of "social reform with the violation of family life by the press," we are told, is "something negative and powerful and antidemocratic."[44]

Without a doubt, James did associate, in his own words, "the extinction of all sense between public and private" and "the sinking of *manners*" with "the democratization of the world."[45] But it is one thing to recognize James's class snobbery and another to imply that everything done in the name of the public by the popular press is worth defending. Furthermore, in his fiction James does not simply judge the press, he explores ways in which he himself might be complicit with it in its abuses of privacy. That Habegger misses the complications of these Jamesian explorations becomes clear when he lists *The Aspern Papers* as one of the works illustrating how James's "dislike of newspaper vulgarity hardened into a lasting hatred of investigative candor."[46] In a number of works James does mock journalists, but in *The Aspern Papers* he risks turning that mockery on himself, when he undertakes a Hawthornean investigation into how artists and critics can violate the subjects that interest them.

The distinguishing and enabling aspect of James's art, Ross Posnock has argued, is curiosity.[47] And yet it is curiosity that E. L. Godkin cites as the "chief enemy of privacy in modern life." Godkin realizes that his charge is complicated, because "curiosity, in all its larger and nobler aspect, lies at the root of Western, as distinguished from Oriental, civilization." Godkin, however, is speaking of "its smaller, pettier, and more ignoble shape," in which it "became the passion of the Paul Pry and the scandal-monger." The "advent of newspapers, or rather of a particular class of newspapers," he goes on, "has converted curiosity into what economists call an effectual demand, and gossip into a marketable commodity."[48] Sure enough, in *The Reverberator* Mr. Flack is distinguished by his "curiosity" (R 11). Is there a way, we need to ask, to distinguish James's artistic curiosity from that of Flack and the narrator in *The Aspern Papers*?

Before trying to answer that question, we need to see what the two have in common. Gary Scharnhorst has speculated that the ethical questions that James raises about literary biography in *The Aspern Papers* were influenced by the appearance in 1884 of Julian Hawthorne's biography of his parents.[49] Including many family documents, the two-volume work violated his father's wish that no one write his biography. It also sparked controversy for printing a previously omitted excerpt from his father's notebooks on Margaret Fuller's character. The controversy might well have reminded James of Harriet Beecher Stowe's notorious revelation about the secret life of the Byrons.[50] But if Stowe had the excuse that she revealed secrets about a famous author in order to vindicate the character of his wife, Julian seemed to reveal his own family's secrets for personal gain. James's displeasure with Julian for cashing in on his father's fame increased in 1886 when Julian published in the New York *World* allegedly confidential remarks made to him by his father's old friend James Russell Lowell. As a result, Julian became a model for the journalist in *The Reverberator*.[51] In his notebook entries describing his plan for that work, James compares the letter that Mr. Flack, the journalist, will publish to one "as monstrous as Julian H.'s beastly and blackguardly betrayal of J. R. L."[52] Julian also very likely served as a model for the publishing scoundrel in *The Aspern Papers*.

Nonetheless, James's own biography of Hawthorne complicates his relation to the scoundrel. In preparing it, James had arranged a meeting with Julian to see if the son could provide information. James came away disappointed, writing to his brother William that Julian, "gave me very little satisfaction or information about his father."[53] Thus at one stage

Julian frustrated James's attempt to dig up secrets about a famous author's life, just as in James's novella Juliana (the similarity of names is probably not accidental) frustrates the efforts of the narrator.

The influence that Julian might have had on the composition of *The Aspern Papers* suggests that James both identified with the narrator and condemned him. Furthermore, he seems to have had a double relation to the fictional author of his creation, Jeffrey Aspern. In a source for James's story, the prize is papers of Shelley and Byron. But James makes his poet an American, one who "found means to live and write like one of the first" at a time when the "famous 'atmosphere'" that the country "is supposed to lack was not even missed" (AP 50). The latter phrase echoes James's notorious comment in his study of Hawthorne. James does not, however, simply allude to his study. By allowing Aspern to overcome the limitation that he attributes to Hawthorne, he suggests another writer who, like Aspern, abandoned America for Europe: himself. Thus James establishes relationships with both the critic/narrator and Aspern, who, like vulgar journalists, risk violating someone's privacy, one through efforts to possess literary papers and the other through poetry.

But James and his fictional creations are not identical. The link that Warren and Brandeis draw between privacy and art can help us see why. The two lawyers, it turns out, distinguished privacy from property by relying on copyright cases that often involved works of art and letters by artists. To be sure, to claim copyright is to transform a work into a form of property available for circulation through *publication*. Warren and Brandeis were interested, however, in those cases that established the artist's right to withhold publication. That right, they claimed, established the precedent for a right to be left alone. They could rely on these cases because of the special position that artistic creation occupies in our culture. On the one hand, it can be alienated and become a form of property. On the other, prior to its act of alienation, it seems to be coextensive with the life of its creator. To attempt to possess it without his permission, they argued, is not so much the theft of a piece of property—its market value may be worthless—as it is a violation of his personal dignity; that is, his privacy. For them, a work of art was, therefore, simultaneously a potential piece of property and an expression of its creator's innermost self. The importance of distinguishing the right to privacy from property rights is poignantly illustrated when the publishing scoundrel justifies his actions by declaring "Jeffrey Aspern the property of the human race" (AP 63).[54]

James also links art and privacy, but he complicates that linkage by reminding us that an innermost self is itself the product of relationships with others. Warren and Brandeis may evoke an inviolate personality, but in James's world personality is by definition prone to violation. This Jamesian sense of personality implies a different notion of art. Just as an innermost self depends on relationships, so a work of art has no life without them. For James a work is not, as it is for Warren and Brandeis, coextensive with its creator until he alienates it as a piece of property by making it available to the public. It depends instead on what we can call various contractual relations. One is with the author. Recognizing a vital connection between himself and his works, James, nonetheless, grants them a life of their own, rather than maintain paternal control over them. A second contract is between the work and its readers. Indeed, as James knew from revising, an author himself is often a reader. On the one hand, a work's relation to its readers makes it vulnerable to possession. On the other, the work has the capacity to possess its audience.

Furthermore, although the law attempts to maintain a clear-cut distinction between works of fiction and life, allowing authors to guard against libel suits, James also knew that works of art with a mimetic component often involve an urge to appropriate life or some aspect of it. For instance, in *The Reverberator* the artist's portrait of Francie is described as an "act of appropriation" (R 71). Yet it is an appropriation that evokes "no jealousy" in Francie's lover because it made possible "an act of handing over" (R 71). Artistic appropriation for James does not involve taking sovereign possession of the real. It is instead an act that allows for more exchanges. Those exchanges depend on the existence of a space between a work and the very life that it would appropriate, for if a work's act of appropriation were complete it would lose its status as art. In turn, artistic status is not intrinsic, but something defined by a work's relations with author, audience, and world. Its "privacy" depends on establishing a "space between" in at least these three relations.

In his preface to *The Aspern Papers* James worries about such spaces. Indeed, he seems to implicate himself in the betrayal of artistic privacy through his desire, like the narrator, to use art to establish a connection with the past. He takes a "delight," he tells us, in a "palpable imaginable *visitable* past—in the nearer distances and the clearer mysteries, the marks and signs of a world we may reach over to as by a long arm we grasp an object at the other end of our own table" (AP x). The artist's appropriation of a visitable past anticipates the narrator's attempt to establish a connection with Aspern by extending his hand to grasp Miss Juliana's. Her delightfully ironic response in refusing it is: "I belong to a time when that was not the custom" (AP 31). The past lives by its own customs, James implies, which deny our attempts to grasp it.

But if James's story dramatizes that failure, the narrator insists on using art, not only to establish a relation with the past, but to possess it. It is in his acts of possession that the narrator risks violating, not only Miss Juliana's and Aspern's privacy, but the "privacy" of Aspern's poetry as well.

The double nature of art assumed by Warren and Brandeis's understanding of copyright implies that there are two different ways to possess a work of art. On the one hand, someone can hold legal title to it and copyright the earning power brought about by its publication. On the other, someone with no legal claim at all can "possess" a work through an imaginative act of appropriation. The narrator in *The Aspern Papers* tries both. Although he has no chance of copyrighting Aspern's poems, he does hope to possess his letters. That act of possession is in part motivated by his desire to possess the poems imaginatively. Like many critics of the nineteenth century, the narrator reads biographically. He wants to read Aspern's life in his poetry and his poetry as coextensive with the poet's life. The letters, he assumes, will confirm his reading of the poems as revelations about the private life of his beloved poet.

The narrator's view of art is similar to that of *The Bostonians*'s journalist, Matthias Pardon, for whom "all distinction between the person and the artist had ceased to exist; the writer was personal, the person food for newsboys, and everything and every one were every one's business" (B 122).[55] It is also like the highly critical friend created in James's preface, who rebukes James for fabricating the figure of Aspern, who, not only did not exist, but could not have existed. "It was vicious," the critic contended, "to flourish forth on one's pages 'great people,' public persons, who shouldn't more or less square with our quite definite and calculable array of notabilities" (AP xii). To create Aspern and not have him square with a real figure seems to destroy a link with life. Although James responds that given time he could have "perfectly 'worked out' Jeffrey Aspern" (AP xiv), he does not do so. Instead of squaring his fiction with life, he reflects on the different status that public and private figures have in art.

James's imaginary friend and critic condemns his creation of public figures because the public already has expectations about them. In contrast, private figures cause no problem. As James notes, "Mere private figures, under one's hand, might correspond with nobody, it being of their essence to be but narrowly known" (AP xii). Paradoxically, then, a writer of fiction more likely violates the privacy of public rather than private figures. This paradox helps to make possible what is perhaps James's most important contribution to the realist novel: the presentation of psychological realism. Psychological realism with its intrusions into the interior of characters might seem the most extreme invasion of privacy. But exploring the interior of a "private" person who "might correspond with nobody" does not violate anyone. In contrast, to present a figure recognizable to the public risks violating that person's right to be left alone.

Of course, to reveal everything about people would deny them privacy. But, as James demonstrates in his 1892 story, "The Private Life," total revelation proves impossible, not because of an unrepresentable plentitude, but because of a lack at the core of the self.[56] A similar lack within works of art helps to generate their "privacy," which the publishing scoundrel's way of reading fails to respect. As he puts it, "a lodger who had forced an entrance had no *locus standi* as a critic" (AP 34).

A reader who forces entrance into a work of art may sacrifice his standing as a critic; nonetheless, for James there must be a relation between readers and art. Warren and Brandeis link the right to privacy with the existence of a work of art prior to copyright, because they want to separate it from obligations resulting from contract as well as property rights. For them "the doctrines of contract and trust are inadequate to support the required protections" because an "inviolate personality" preexists relations with others.[57] But for James neither a personality nor a work of art has an existence without relationships.

To insist that, for James, artistic privacy depends on spaces between a work and author, reader, and life, might seem to confirm the popular view of James as a proponent of artistic autonomy. But those spaces no more mark a work of art as autonomous as the space constructed between Verena and Basil marks her as autonomous. In James's world, a work of art, like Verena, is defined by the relationships that it enters into. Any private self that Verena has depends on them. At the same time, to efface the space established by those relationships is to violate her privacy. Privacy, in other words, involves that delicately balanced moment in which a self, created through exchanges, is not effaced by them. The same holds for a work of art. Its privacy is not a moment of autonomy in which it can speak for itself. It is preserved instead by maintaining a space that keeps it from being dominated by the very relations that define it. For James, that moment is a moment akin to courtship, as in *The Bostonians* when Verena, so vulnerable to being possessed by others, maintains the power to possess her would-be possessors.

If this notion of artistic privacy helps to answer charges that James is a champion of artistic autonomy, his comparison of Verena to a work of art helps to answer charges that he denies Verena any possible autonomy.[58] Like a work of art, Verena does lack autonomy, but since few would deny that James regards art very highly, that lack does not necessarily mean that James portrays her negatively. To explore the analogy between Verena and a work of art is to understand better James's construction of both.

VIII

Unlike *The Reverberator* and *The Aspern Papers*, in which art is a vital part of James's exploration of the question of privacy, *The Bostonians* doesn't include an actual artist. Nonetheless, James frequently compares Verena to an artist or a work of art. It is Verena, as artist or work of art, who seduces both Olive and Basil. For Olive, "Verena had the disposition of the artist, the spirit to which all charming forms come easily and naturally" (B 115). Verena's charm gives her the appearance of an autonomous work of art whose originality creates its own value. As Mrs. Burrage puts it, "When a girl is as charming, as original, as Miss Tarrant, it doesn't in the least matter who she is; she makes herself the standard by which you measure her; she makes her own position" (B 307). But, as we have seen, Verena's "originality" derives, not from her autonomy, but from a hollowness at her core that makes her dependent on relations. That dependency, in turn, makes her the most fascinating figure in the book. She may not drive the plot, but it is generated by her "generosity." Making her vulnerable to possession by those around her, this generosity also opens her to life. For instance, on the beautiful spring day that Basil visits her in New York, Olive leaves them alone and walks along the streets "barely conscious of the loveliness of the day, the perfect weather, all suffused and tinted with spring" (B 303). In contrast, although Verena is at first nervous about her walk with Basil, once she "was fairly launched the spirit of the day took possession of her" (B 324).

In consciously evoking Verena's role as a medium, her ability to be taken possession of by spirits, this description calls attention to one of the most important strategies in the book. Habegger has noted that the book divides in two.[59] The first half is predominantly a satire of the reformist and spiritualist movements; the second, a psychological exploration of the attractions between Verena and Olive and Verena and Basil. In the first half James satirically discredits the spiritualist vocabulary of magic and the occult associated with Verena. But in the second half he finds himself returning to it as he struggles to describe the seemingly mysterious attractions connecting his major characters. At times his use of it is almost unnoticeable, as when he frequently refers to Verena's "charm." At other times it is quite explicit. Contemplating Basil's success in courting her, Verena "felt it must be a magical touch that could bring about such a cataclysm. Why Basil Ransom had been deputed by fate to exercise this spell was more than she could say—poor Verena, who up to so lately had flattered herself that she had a wizard's wand in her own pocket" (B 385). The vocabulary of magic and spiritualism does more than explain the "spells" cast by characters on one another. It becomes the only vocabulary available to explain the seductive attraction of art. The two, in fact, merge in Verena.

Like a work of art, Verena is always vulnerable to appropriation. But, also like a work of art, her vulnerability generates an openness to life with its own seductive power. Both vulnerability and seduction might seem to derive from Verena's lack of a voice of her own, a lack which makes her a victim of those who would use her to voice their own opinions. But Verena does not lack a voice. Others may speak through her, but the voice that speaks is distinctly hers.

Neither Olive nor Basil is originally attracted to her ideas. Olive, as we have seen, is repulsed by her notions of free union; Basil by almost everything. As he tells Miss Birdseye, "Does a woman consist of nothing but her opinions? I like Miss Tarrant's lovely face better, to begin with" (B 219). Verena's ideas, it seems, are alienable from Verena's body. And more than from her body, from her voice. Under the spell of her voice as she performs in New York, Basil takes for granted that "the matter of her speech was ridiculous. . . . She was none the less charming for that, and the moonshine she had been plied with was none the less moonshine for her being charming" (B 264). Indeed, it is Verena's voice that proves so seductive. For Basil, Verena's voice, not her opinions, represents her "character." As he tells Mrs. Luna, Olive's sister,

"You like me for my opinions, but entertain a different sentiment for my character. I deplore Miss Tarrant's opinions, but her character—well, her character pleases me" (B 421).

But lest we think that only the ideas of a woman seem alienable from the voice that stands for her character, it is important to remember that Verena also separates her attraction to Basil from his opinions. Challenged by Olive about her attraction to a former slave owner, she with "majesty" responds, "I don't loathe him—I only dislike his opinions" (B 371). Just as Basil is seduced by Verena's voice, so she marvels at "how wonderfully he can talk" (B 377). The "spell" that each casts on the other, like the spell that works of art cast on their audience, cannot be explained by mere reference to ideas and argument.

The separability of a work or a character from its ideas seems to return us to a doctrine of individual autonomy by imparting a mysterious essence to both work and character that cannot be reduced to their ideas. Eliot, for instance, praised James for having a mind so fine that no idea could violate it. But this commonplace reading of James's inviolability is more appropriate to Warren and Brandeis's notion of personality and art than James's. Rather than establish autonomy, the failure of a character or work of art to be identical with its ideas forces it into relations of dependency. Autonomy would occur, not when there is a discrepancy between voice and content, but when there is an organic merger of the two. Indeed, the failure to merge the two makes Verena's voice vulnerable to appropriation by others who speak through her as a medium. There is, in fact, no better expression of the emptiness at the core of her being than the discrepancy between her voice and the ideas that it expresses. It is, however, that emptiness that allows her to be both vulnerable and seductive. So too with a novel, especially because its *medium* is language, which by nature cannot be, as perhaps music can be, pure voice.

Constituted by language, a literary work possesses a voice that is not identical to the ideas that it expresses, a discrepancy that renders readers' efforts to reduce it to ideas a violation of its "privacy." At the same time, because language would not be language unless it expressed ideas, any reading that attempts completely to separate a work from its ideas is as flawed as the effort to alienate workers' labor without altering their selves. Just as Verena and a work of art are not identical to the ideas that they express, so workers are not identical to their labor. This lack of identity would seem to indicate that ideas, like labor, are alienable from the essential character of a person or a work of art. Verena should be able, in other words, to enter into exchanges of ideas with Olive or Basil that would leave her essential self untouched. But because she is defined by a lack, not a preexisting autonomy, this is impossible. Part of her self is involved in any exchange that she enters, just as workers' selves are involved in any exchange that they make for their labor. This is most obvious in Verena's prospective marriage with Basil. In marriage Verena's character will be altered because the very structure of the relationship established by the marriage contract is dominated by ideas held by Basil, not negotiated through a free exchange of ideas.

The point, then, is not only that a discrepancy between voice and ideas creates a dependency on relationships, but that people and works are defined by the specific relationships into which they enter. The ways in which Olive and Basil relate to Verena offer two negative models for the contract between reader and text. Possessed by Verena's voice, both Basil and Olive try to possess it. Basil's mode of possession grows out of his recognition of gendered difference, which for him is a hierarchical one of status. Having separated the charm of Verena's voice from what it says, Basil does not care so much to influence its content, which he dismisses as moonshine. For him Verena's voice is a purely formal performance. He merely wants to reserve its performances for himself. In contrast, Olive, in striving for an egalitarian union, demands a perfect merger of form and content. That merger demands a loss of difference. As a result, her way of achieving it becomes in one important respect more proprietary than Basil's. If Basil allows Verena a voice and dismisses its content, Olive appropriates it as a medium to express her own ideas. Thus she is like many readers who use a work of literature as a vehicle to make public their own point of view. Basil reads Verena's voice performatively; Olive constitutively. Basil, as his last name suggests, holds the freedom of Verena's voice in ransom; Olive, as her last name suggests, tries to regulate it according to her sense of an equitable order to the world. For James a contract between reader and text that will preserve a text's privacy depends on resistance to such acts of possession.

Of course, in *The Bostonians* such resistance is not sustained. The balance between a work's power to possess its would-be possessors and their power to possess it seems impossible to maintain. But if "balanced" readings (including my attempt at one in this chapter) are doomed to fail, something is, nonetheless, lost if we abandon the effort to produce them. Trying to define what that "something" is forces me to add some final complications to my argument about the differences between James's and Warren and Brandeis's notions of privacy.

IX

That Warren and Brandeis turn to copyright cases involving works of art to separate privacy from property rights is not surprising. As Renaissance new historicists have argued, the construction of an institutional space known as the aesthetic paralleled the construction of a legal space making way for the institution of modern forms of private property that assume a subjectivity of "possessive individualism."[60] As C. B. Macpherson has shown, this subjectivity is constructed in theories of social contract that implicitly legitimated the rise of a modern market economy. In such a world theorists of the aesthetic claimed that it resisted the market's power to turn everything into a commodity. Warren and Brandeis's use of copyright law to establish an inviolate personality that resists the forces of the market is a specific example of this general argument. Recent critics have challenged the possibility of such resistance. They argue that it is instead produced by the forces it claims to resist. At stake is the very existence of spaces known as the "private" or the "aesthetic."

In part, James confirms the argument against standard notions of both the private and the aesthetic. For him no private personality or aesthetic space exists prior to exchanges. Nonetheless, James continues to hold out for notions of both the private and the aesthetic. James's notions of both may seem as doomed to failure as Warren and Brandeis's effort to separate privacy from property rights. Indeed, just as today the major threat to the two lawyers' concept of a right to privacy is not, as some mugwumps feared, socialism but a market economy that would turn everything, including personality, into a commodity, so the major threat to a Jamesian notion of the aesthetic is the effort by recent critics to subsume it completely under the category of rhetoric and measure its value by the amount of work that it accomplishes in the marketplace of ideas. Unable to resist efforts by readers to possess it, a work of art seems as incapable of maintaining "privacy" as it does of possessing an originating autonomy.

But at this point James poses a challenge to the challengers, for although he adopts the vocabulary of property relations to describe aesthetic relations, he forces us to recognize the difference between possessing a work of art as a piece of property and possessing it through an imaginative act of appropriation. The first is clearly within the realm of legal notions of property. The second, however, is difficult to articulate in legal terms. Indeed, what lawyer would claim that a reader's imaginative possession of a work is a claim to legal ownership over it? This second form of possession does not fit under the law of copyright.

If aesthetic possession cannot be completely separated from legal notions of property, neither can it be simply translated into legal discourse without a loss. It is inseparable because a work cannot be imaginatively possessed without being made available to the public through some form of publication, which brings it into the realm of copyright law. Nonetheless, once we have appropriated James's notion of privacy from his published works, it has no obvious place in the present legal system. The United States's legal system works in part by assigning rights, just as Warren and Brandeis assign a right to privacy to individuals. But to whom would it assign a Jamesian right to privacy, which depends on a space that belongs to no one person although it is a product of human exchanges? Not easily translatable into legal discourse, James's construction of privacy continues to raise questions about how our legal system grants title to a right that it has constructed. Its power to raise questions about aspects of the legal system at the time of its publication forces me to question my appropriation of Verena to construct an allegory of reading.

If there is a difference between legal and metaphoric possessions of works of art, there is also a difference between possessing works of art and possessing people. The law does not totally cover the metaphoric modes of possessing either; it does, however, offer literal ways of possessing both. The former involves the law of copyright, which was being refined as James was writing. The latter involves the law of slavery that had been abolished a generation before the time in which the book is set. Nonetheless, when it has its aging representative of abolitionism grant Ransom access to Verena, this post-Reconstruction book suggests that other forms of legal possession exist. Miss Birdseye hopes that Verena will privately reform this conservative Southerner who grew up in a society that classified master and slave and husband and wife as parallel parts of the law of domestic relations.[61] Instead, Basil persuades Verena to enter into a contract with him that their society feels constructs a private realm. In that realm Verena's artistry, like a work of art in the copyright cases that Warren and Brandeis cite, will be withheld from the public. Verena, however, is not a work of art (although she is constructed by one.) Thus she enters a relationship covered by marriage laws, not copyright. My discussion of the terms of the marriage contract should help to explain why the narrator has good reason to fear that Verena's tears at the book's end "were not the last she was destined to shed" in "the union, so far from brilliant, into which she was about to enter" (B 449).

CHAPTER 4

In the Hands of *The Silent Partner* and Spiritual Regulation in *The Bread-Winners*

I

In *The Bostonians* and *The Aspern Papers* James does not offer a critique of contract. A critique would look more like attacks made a generation earlier against Northern "wage slavery" by defenders of the slave system in the South or Carlyle's anti-modernist attack on the industrial system in England, an attack that caused him to sympathize with the South in the Civil War. To be sure, James does not explicitly endorse contract, but he is intrigued by its "promise" to produce social balance without the regulatory force of some transcendental power. If an important part of James's realism has to do with his refusal to present such a regulatory force in his fiction, that refusal makes it unrealistic for his works to sustain contract's promise to generate egalitarian social relations.

This chapter will place in perspective the connection between James's realism and the promise of contract by looking at two nonrealistic works from the period: John Hay's *The Bread-Winners* (1883) and Elizabeth Stuart Phelps's *The Silent Partner* (1871).[1] Both raise questions about the marriage contract and both address the labor question. Politically, however, they are almost opposed. Vernon Parrington complains that *The Bread-Winners* "is clearly a partisan defense of economic individualism, an attack upon the rising labor movement, a grotesque satire smeared with an unctuous morality—and because of this, a perfect expression of the spirit of upper-class America in those uneasy eighties with their strikes and lockouts and Haymarket riots."[2] Its representation of domestic politics is no more progressive. In contrast, *The Silent Partner* has been praised for its sympathy to labor and its progressive sexual politics. If radical feminists and labor historians don't give it unqualified endorsement—Susan Harris calls it "meliorist" rather than "radical"[3]—no one would claim that it has the same politics as Hay's novel.

Despite their differences, however, the two are more similar to one another than to the realists insofar as both present a world in which social relations are regulated by a transcendental principle. To be sure, they imagine different standards of regulation. Hay orders his moral universe according to principles embodied in law and institutions, whereas Phelps orders hers according to religious principles that divinely sanction questioning of some of the very laws and institutions that Hay supports. Even so, these transcendental perspectives distinguish their presentations of social relations from the realists'. As we saw, James, intrigued by the promise of contract, presents an immanent exploration of social relations that stretches contractual thinking to its limits. Contractual thinking also influences both Hay and Phelps. Hay vigorously defends the freedom of contract in labor relations, and Phelps campaigns for women's contractual equality. In positing a regulatory hand over social relations, however, both violate contract's promise of generating a self-regulating social economy. Their mode of presenting social relations may violate this aspect of the promise of contract, but in both cases it paradoxically serves to legitimate various social divisions generated by the appeal to contractarian ideology of the time. Before analysis, however, we need a brief summary of both books.

II

The protagonists of *The Silent Partner* are Perley Kelso and Sip Garth, young women in their early twenties. Sip is a factory worker; Perley's father owns the factory with Perley's fiancée Maverick Hayle and his father. At the story's beginning both are motherless, and shortly thereafter both lose their fathers. When her father dies, Perley is shocked to learn that she will not automatically inherit his position in the firm. She won't, because the company is "private, not corporate"

(SP 58). In a corporation shareholders give up their individual identity to merge into a corporate body that has a legal identity of its own. But Hayle and Kelso is a partnership, in which various partners maintain their individual identities and relate to one another according to a contractual arrangement that a majority of partners must agree upon. Perley inherits her father's financial interest in the firm, but she does not automatically inherit his role as an active partner in its management since, when he dies, the partnership has to be renegotiated. As the senior partner explains to Perley, "Maverick and I reorganize the firm in our own way: that is our affair. You fall heir to a certain share of interest in the business: that is your affair. It is for you to say what shall be done with your own property. You are even quite at liberty to withdraw it entire from the concern, or you can leave it in our hands. . . . You then receive certain dividends, which will be duly agreed upon, and have thus the advantage of at once investing your property in a safe, profitable, and familiar quarter, and of feeling no possible obligation or responsibility—business obligation and responsibility are always so trying to a lady—about it. You thus become, in fact and in form, if you prefer, a silent partner" (SP 59–60). Perley could try to negotiate a contract making her an active partner, but the other two partners would outvote her. Indeed, it seems to make no sense for her to challenge her role since she is engaged to the junior partner. As soon as she marries, she will relinquish the right to enter into other contracts in her own name. This limit to the contractual rights of married women makes "formal partnerships impossible in the case of husband and wife" (SP 62).

Phelps's plot is generated by Perley's refusal to live the life scripted for her by this father and son. She might be a silent partner legally, but she refuses to leave her affairs in her partners' hands. Her growing friendship with Sip leads her to assume heartfelt, if not legal, obligations and responsibilities for the lives of the mill hands. She breaks her engagement with Maverick and devotes her life to the workers, forming an alliance with the new partner Stephen Garrick, a self-made man who runs the mill efficiently but who still cares for the lives of his hired help. When Garrick in turn offers his hand in marriage, Perley refuses with, "I believe that I have been a silent partner long enough. If I married you, sir, I should invest in life, and you would conduct it. I suspect that I have a preference for a business of my own" (SP 262).

In the meantime, not wanting to bring children into a corrupt world, Sip has refused marriage to a mill worker. Her life is instead devoted to her deaf-mute, younger sister, who is drowned when a flood sweeps through the mill town. With Catty's death, "a singular comfort came to Sip, almost with the striking of her sorrow. She and Catty could not be parted like two speaking people" (SP 279). If Catty was silent in life and yet communicated to her sister, so in death she continues to speak to her. Translating her sister's heavenly message to the world, Sip lives as fulfilled as Perley in her single life and becomes an evangelist, preaching the religion of the poor to the workers.

Hay's anonymously published novel presents a very different world. If *The Silent Partner* focuses on the refusal of an upper-class woman to live the life scripted for her by others, *The Bread-Winners* is driven by a plot that sketches the failure of a working class woman to live a life scripted by herself. The beautiful Maud Matchin does not, like Sip, refuse marriage to preach to the poor, but instead imagines rising in the world by marrying the rich Captain Arthur Farnham. A major obstacle to Maud's dreams is Farnham's refusal to play the role she has imagined for him. Even though Farnham rejects Maud, she still has many admirers, including Sam Sleeny, who lives with her family and works for her father, a modest but skilled carpenter. If Maud finds Sam beneath her, she is intrigued by the deceitful Andrew Jackson Offit, who is a professional reformer and organizer of a labor union called the Bread-Winners. In events that one-sidedly evoke the 1877 railroad strike, Offit encourages striking workers to ransack the rich houses on Algonquin Avenue, where Farnham and his closest neighbors, the widowed Mrs. Belding and her beautiful daughter Alice, live. An ex-army officer, Farnham organizes a private group of Civil War veterans and easily routs the undisciplined strikers.

With the Bread-Winners restored to work, Offit, needing money to win Maud's love, returns to rob Farnham. Knocked unconscious, Farnham is nursed back to life by Alice, who had modestly refused his earlier declaration of love, even though she secretly loves him. In the meantime, Sam, who was framed for the robbery, is arrested, escaping just in time to save Maud from Offit, who tries to force her to run away with him. Sam, a blonde, not quite Billy Buddlike character, strikes out and kills the Claggartlike Offit, and is once again arrested. The jury, however, lets him off on the grounds of "emotional insanity," making sure not to harm his reputation by adding that he was "perfectly sane up to the moment he committed the rash act in question, and perfectly sane the moment after, and that, in our opinion, there is no probability that the malady will ever recur" (BW 307). Freed, Sam plans to marry Maud, who testified vigorously on his behalf. Their proposed marriage is balanced by that of Alice and Arthur, who have finally successfully communicated their mutual love.

III

Hay presents such an unflattering picture of labor unions that it is logical for Parrington to identify him as a partisan defender of "economic individualism." Hay's economic individualism might seem to make him a strict defender of contract. But Hay's satire stems at least as much from certain classical republican values as it does from those of classical liberalism that we usually associate with contractual thought.

The past two decades have witnessed a debate over whether the United States was founded on principles of Lockean liberalism, as argued by Louis Hartz, or those of a transatlantic tradition of humanistic republicanism, as argued by Gordon Wood and J. G. A. Pocock.[4] The liberal interpretation stresses a social contract growing out of a Lockean vision of the state of nature and inalienable individual rights. The republican interpretation stresses a more communitarian ideal, in which individuals achieve fulfillment only through active civic participation that subordinates individual interests to the public good. There is increasing agreement that American political thought consists of a mixture of liberalism and republicanism, although the exact nature of that mixture at various times in the country's history is not always so clear.

For anyone interested in how works of literature in the late nineteenth century relate to a contractual view of society, it is important to be aware of these competing views of the self and social interaction. For instance, friends and correspondents, James and Hay would seem at odds in how they conducted their lives in response to the Age of Contract. Following the republican ideal of virtuous public service, Hay began his career as Lincoln's private secretary and ended it as secretary of state. More in line with liberal celebrations of the "private" citizen, James devoted his career to exploring the private workings of social relations and human interiority. Paradoxically, however, Hay's major work of fiction helps to legitimate what would seem to be liberal notions of contract, whereas James's *The Bostonians* poses a challenge to liberal notions of the self. This paradox cannot be resolved by referring to traditional political beliefs, since more than likely they would have voted along similar lines. Nonetheless, a clue to the different effects of their fiction can be found in statements that both made in 1898.

Supporting an Anglo-Saxon alliance that had "a sanction like that of religion," carrying "always in [its] shadow freedom and civilization," Hay told Theodore Roosevelt that the Spanish-American War "had been a splendid little war; begun with the highest motives, carried on with magnificent intelligence and spirit, favored by that Fortune that loves the brave." James hated the war's violence but reluctantly supported it and an Anglo-Saxon alliance. Rather than see himself as a moral agent forwarding the course of civilization, however, he confessed, "I fear that I am too lost in the spectacle for any decent morality."[5]

If James's fiction results from losing himself within the spectacle in order to explore how it functions, Hay's is guided by his belief in a moral force regulating the course of history and social relations. In conflict with the promise of contract, such a regulatory moral force plays a role similar to liberalism's famous "invisible hand." The link between a guiding "invisible hand" and a governing moral force reminds us that laissez-faire theorists retained a substantial component of classical republican thought. As Herbert Hovenkamp puts it, "Because [Adam] Smith's theory of economic man was thoroughly intertwined with his theory of moral man, liberty of contract was as much an ethical doctrine as an economic one. . . . Smith's moral man worked for his wages, and in Smith's moral universe the wages set by the market were almost always normatively correct."[6] *The Bread-Winners* dramatizes how late nineteenth-century arguments for "economic individualism" borrow from the republican as well as the liberal tradition.

Before turning to a close look at *The Bread-Winners* we need to sketch out the way in which republicanism and liberalism come together in Hay. Their connection is suggested by an aspect of *The Bread-Winners* that would seem to link it with *The Bostonians* and distinguish it from *The Silent Partner*—its satiric undercutting of spiritualism. Spiritualism's rise is an important part of American social history. Though considered heretical by Christian orthodoxy, spiritualists revived a sense of religion in an increasingly secular society. For instance, Hay's Saul Matchin is "an unbeliever in his youth," but turns to "this grotesque superstition" to "fill the vacuum of faith in his mind" (BW 35). In the United States, as opposed to Britain and the Continent, much spiritualism was linked to radical reform through its extreme individualism. According to Ann Braude, spiritualists believed that, "if untrammeled by repressive social or religious strictures, . . . individuals could serve as vehicles of truth because each embodied the laws of nature in his or her being."[7] This individualism led to a distrust of institutions and existing social hierarchies and allowed women to play an important role in the movement.

Both *The Bostonians* and *The Bread-Winners* were written before spiritualism was widely discredited. Margaret Fox delivered its "death blow" in 1888 when she admitted that the mysterious rappings that so many had witnessed as evidence of spirits earlier in the century were produced by her and her sister's cracking toe joints. Nonetheless, by the early 1880s spiritualism was already on the decline. James, Twain, and Howells contributed to its demise by satirizing it in their works. As Howard Kerr notes, "Hay's sceptical account of a séance [in *The Bread-Winners*] was in the realistic vein."[8]

But as much as Hay's satire links him with the realists, it depends on a set of transcendental moral assumptions. We can begin to tease out those assumptions by focusing on the connection Hay establishes between spiritualism and the labor movement. The basis for labor reform, he suggests, is as ill-founded as spiritualism's efforts to emancipate "the world from its old-fashioned decencies" (BW 109). If spiritualists felt that self-fulfillment came through liberation from repressive institutions, Hay feels that such "emancipation" made self-fulfillment impossible. He believes that, rather than allow individuals access to the laws of nature, spiritualism rules out self-sufficiency by encouraging people to be what they are not. Important political consequences follow from Hay's attack on the spiritualist self.

Contemporary critics too often associate notions of self-sufficiency solely with the liberal tradition of possessive individualism outlined by C. B. Macpherson. But classical republicanism also appeals to self-sufficiency. Republican self-sufficiency did not come from protecting individual rights and possessive accumulation. Instead, it came from an individual's ability to subordinate excessive desire and appetites to the control of right reason. Right reason, in turn, was embodied in institutions and cultivated taste. For Hay spiritualism was dangerous because it unleashed the excesses that submission to institutional duty controlled.

Distrust of spiritualism makes sense within the republican context. But the same assumptions that led Hay to distrust spiritualism would seem to cause him to distrust the excesses released by the possessive individualism of liberalism, especially because, as we saw in the last chapter, many spiritualists, like Victoria Woodhull, based their individualist reforms on contractarian beliefs. Hay, however, combines republican and liberal values. How he does so reveals much about the social vision of a dominant wing of the Republican Party.

One way to understand how the merger of republicanism and liberalism was possible is to turn to Macpherson. Intent on stressing the inhumanity of liberal assumptions, Macpherson champions Hobbes over Locke as a philosopher who sees the consequences of liberalism more clearly. Crucial is their different attitudes toward life, labor, and property.

> In emphasizing that a man's labour is his own Locke marked out the extent of his departure from the medieval view and of his acceptance of the bourgeois view expressed so tersely by Hobbes. But Locke fell short of Hobbes in his acceptance of bourgeois values. To Hobbes not only was labour a commodity but life itself was in effect reduced to a commodity; to Locke life was still sacred and inalienable, though labour, and one's 'person' regarded as one's capacity to labour, was a commodity. Locke's distinction between life and labour is a measure of his retention of the traditional values. His confusion about the definition of property, sometimes including life and liberty and sometimes not, may be ascribed to the confusion in his mind between the remnant of traditional values and the new bourgeois values. It is this, no doubt, which makes his theory more agreeable to the modern reader than the uncompromising doctrine of Hobbes. Locke did not care to recognize that the continual alienation of labour for a bare subsistence wage, which he asserts to be the necessary condition of wage-labourers throughout their lives, is in effect an alienation of life and liberty.[9]

Macpherson believes that Locke's "confusion" about the definition of property exposes a contradiction in his thought that results from the presence of a "remnant of traditional values" in a basically "bourgeois" system of thought. But he falls prey to a false sense of periodization when he assumes that it is "traditional" rather than "bourgeois" to place value on life as "sacred and inalienable." "Traditional" values are not simply a residual element of a system that is completely determined by the market. They are a crucial part of bourgeois thought. Thus Macpherson is wrong to conclude that Locke's confusion over the definition of property, "sometimes including life and liberty and sometimes not" is a weakness because it exposes a contradiction between values of an old and new order. On the contrary, Locke's slippery use of "property" has contributed to liberalism's great resiliency, allowing it to use verbal slippage endlessly to defer the resolution of a contradiction that Macpherson feels should be overcome by a new dialectical synthesis.[10]

That slippage has helped to persuade those who have little or no material property that the protection of life and liberty depends on the protection of property. That belief might seem to be the height of ideological distortion, especially in the Gilded Age when social conflict was often seen in terms of an opposition between propertied and laboring classes. But we need to recognize that the appeal to property by people like Hay was, from their point of view, a sincere effort to oppose threats posed by the rapid rise of a market economy. As we saw last chapter, even though the period's legal system seemed to be no more than a self-interested protection of property rights, its appeal to the freedom of contract created problems for those who persisted in eighteenth-century attempts to ground the law on the secure foundation of property. For instance, in the Age of Contract the eighteenth-century belief that intrinsic properties determined the value of an object or a person was increasingly challenged by a system in which value was determined by the market. In such a situation, protection of property can be seen as an effort to preserve "traditional" values in the face of a market economy that threatened to lead to an alienation of life and liberty for all, not just wage laborers.

The success of that appeal depended on liberalism's ability to graft onto the existing rhetoric of republicanism, which was more compatible with eighteenth-century notions of the law. The appeal to republican ideals by defenders of a contractual economy served two purposes. First, it helped regulate the potentially destabilizing forces of a market economy, a stabilization necessary if "traditional" bourgeois values were to be preserved. Second, it helped keep in check the egalitarian promise potentially unleashed by an uncompromising appeal to contract. Crucial in both cases is an appeal to "virtue."[11]

The concept of virtue was an important part of the republican definition of citizenship. A virtuous citizen was one who actively participated in public life by subordinating his special interests to those of the *res publica*. This definition of citizenship presented a powerful challenge to the liberal assumptions of a rising middle class. As Pocock argues, the existence of the republican definition of virtuous citizenship complicates standard accounts of how bourgeois ideology is responsible for "privatizing" the individual. "If indeed capitalist thought ended by privatizing the individual, this may have been because it was unable to find an appropriate way of presenting him as a citizen. 'Bourgeois ideology,' which old fashioned Marxism depicted as appearing with historic inevitability, had, it seems, to wage a struggle for existence and may never have fully won it."[12] Or we might say, in the United States it tried to win it, not by eliminating its enemy from the field, but by merging with it. That merger was possible because Locke too stressed the importance of virtue. For Locke, however, virtue was associated with labor, not disinterested public service. Linking Lockean and republican virtue meant finding a public role for industrious "private" citizens. The Lockean "confusion" over property helped in that task.

Within traditional republican thought the commercial class had a particularly difficult time achieving virtue because it was so dependent on the uncertainties of the market and because it seemed so concerned with self-interested profit. In contrast, the relative independence of a leisurely, landed aristocracy made it a more likely candidate for disinterestedness. The debate between Alexander Hamilton and Thomas Jefferson demonstrates that in agrarian America a republican suspicion of commerce was retained by a large segment of the population. Nonetheless, Jeffersonians especially opposed formation of a leisurely aristocratic class in America. In the United States the landed elite's virtue derived from Locke's explanation of value in terms of labor. Through its industry the country's landed class, so the myth ran, had generated wealth by developing previously unproductive land. Such industry served the interests of the republic, which hoped through development and growth to increase the value of the land it was founded upon. Such development was most likely to occur if all were encouraged to own property that they would in turn make productive through labor of their own. To be sure, such labor could lapse into mere selfish accumulation of personal wealth and luxury, but not if it was checked by the virtues of frugality.

Frugality dictated that surplus wealth accumulated through labor be reinvested to increase the value of one's land. For instance, in *The Chainbearer* James Fenimore Cooper appeals to such virtuous and productive reinvestment to justify the practices of landowners. "Not a dollar of rent," he argues, "ever left the settlement." In addition, "he who got rich was expected to do so by manly exertions openly exercised," not through speculation, which relied on the "dark machinations of a sinister practice of the law."[13] By contrasting the openness of productive labor to the secretiveness of sinister speculation, Cooper indicates how in the United States some, if not all, individuals "privatized" by capitalism were given a "public" role as virtuous, laboring citizens contributing to *common,* as well as individual, wealth.

The Lockean attribution of virtue to labor explains why Hay did not believe that his novel was anti-labor. To be sure, as Hay's son argued, *The Bread-Winners* is a "defense of the right of an individual to hold property, and a plea for the better protection of that property by law and order."[14] Lodged within the progressive attack on laissez-faire thought by critics like Parrington, today's liberals assume that a defense of property was an attack on labor. But Hay and others of his generation would not have condoned such an opposition. In an 1873 dissent that later was more or less adopted as an accepted interpretation, Supreme Court Justice Field quotes Adam Smith: "The property which every man has in his own labor, as it is the original foundation of all other property, so it is the most sacred and inviolable."[15]

Lacking an aristocracy, Americans claimed to be more solidly founded on Smith's principles than countries with a longer history. For instance, *The Bread-Winners*'s most representative member of the propertied class other than Farnham is Mr. Temple, the vice president of a huge mill. Temple's down-to-earth manner and profane language captivated reviewers, who called him an American type that might pass as a laborer in Britain. An 1884 newspaper editorial expresses a commonplace when it argues that the United States has no classes "except good or bad." The only way to destroy the exceptional conditions in which all citizens are "simply and purely workingmen" would be for workingmen to "degrade themselves and pull away the ladder upon which they are to rise by classifying themselves as a sort of inferior part of the whole."[16] In his review of *The Bread-Winners* in the May 1884 *Century Magazine,* Howells, though defending labor unions, confirms this argument. The author, he argues, has no "prejudice against workingmen as workingmen. We are all workingmen in America, or the sons of workingmen, and few of us are willing to hear them traduced."[17]

We should not forget that the founding motto of the Republican Party was "free soil, free labor, and free men." Hay's party existed because it had formed a coalition between the interests of property and labor. The virtuous nature of that coalition was reinforced by its opposition to the national sin of slavery. Property in the North, the Republican Party proclaimed, was founded on the virtues of free, not slave, labor. From this perspective the threat to labor was not necessarily the propertied class but those elements of the working *or* propertied classes that threatened the founding virtue of a reconstructed Republic—the right of men to accumulate property by freely contracting out their labor. As Howells puts it, the real threat is idleness. "It is the idle poor whom our author does not like, whom he finds mischievous, as other writers of romance have long found the idle rich."[18] Writing in 1884 on the legal requirement for employees to "mitigate damages" even when their labor contract had been wrongfully breached, Eugene McQuillan proclaims, "The law . . . will not lend its aid to enable a servant to eat the bread of idleness; it abhors an idle man; idleness is a breach of social duty and moral obligation which the law would rather punish than countenance."[19]

To the obvious objection that there was an important difference between someone who could accumulate property by hiring other people's labor and those whose only property consisted in their labor, Hay could respond with a republicanlike argument about the need to subordinate class interests to the good of the whole. Even if Hay felt that it was wrong to distinguish classes in terms of labor, he did not deny class distinctions. As William Graham Sumner put it in 1883, any attempt to understand the social conditions in the United States must confront the "elementary contradiction, that there are classes and that there are not classes."[20] The interests of class, however, should never outweigh the interests of a nation. What Hay condemns are those who risked undermining the *res publica* by promoting their self-interests. Although he spends most of his energy exposing the partisanship of the working class, he doesn't forget to criticize the rich.

Those who devote their energy purely to private gain also share blame for the sorry state of the country's political health. Hay writes, "In this city of two hundred thousand people, two or three dozen politicians continued as before to govern it, to assess and spend its taxes, to use it as their property and their chattel. The rich and intelligent kept on making money, building fine houses, and bringing up children to hate politics as they did, and in fine to fatten themselves as sheep which should be mutton whenever the butcher was ready. There was hardly a millionaire on Algonquin Avenue who knew where the ward meetings of his party were held. There was not an Irish laborer in the city but knew his way to his ward club as well as to mass" (BW 246–47).

Hay's condemnation of the "rich and intelligent" for not participating in political life helps to protect him from charges that he is anti-labor, but in doing so it reveals a problem in the merger of republican and Lockean notions of virtue. Rather than lead to a more virtuous republic, the merger threatens to privatize virtue. In the meantime, government is left in the hands of unvirtuous people who advance their own interests rather than represent those of the people as a whole. From Hay's perspective republican checks on liberal self-interest no longer seem to work.

In confronting this problem, Hay faces a dilemma that had plagued American political thinkers since what Gordon Wood calls the "end of classical politics" in the early years of the republic. According to Pocock, Wood detects a partial shift

from republicanism to liberalism—from, that is to say, the classical theory of the individual as a civic active being, directly participant in the *res publica* according to measure, toward (if not fully reaching) a theory in which he appears as conscious chiefly of his interest and takes part in government in order to press for its realization, making only an indirect contribution to that mediating activity whereby government achieves a reconciliation of conflicts which is all the common good there is. In this sense, representative democracy involves a recession, on the part of both individual and 'people,' from direct participation in government, of which the 'decline of virtue' is the measure; but it does not involve political quiescence or a lowering of tensions. It also coincides with a vast expansion of party activity and appeal to a highly responsible electorate.[21]

What concerns Hay is that self-interested party activity has increased while the responsibility of the electorate has not. As a result, government no longer fulfills *its* responsibility. When social disorder erupts, the mayor is incapable of containing it because he is controlled by the very forces that cause it. Hay's initial response to this corruption of republican principles was similar to that of his friend Henry Adams who satirizes Gilded Age politics in *Democracy*. In 1877 Hay turned down Garfield's offer to become his private secretary, citing his desire to avoid exposure to "envy, meanness, ignorance, and the swinish selfishness which ignorance breeds."[22] But if Adams's anonymously published novel signals its author's inability to sustain a belief that history is guided by a moral force and anticipates his move toward an ironic, distant perspective on the course of history, Hay's serves as a form of self-criticism and sets the stage for his return to public life. In *The Bread-Winners* a moral force still exists that can restore order to society. Its agents are not, however, elected governmental officials, but Farnham, Temple, and their private army of Civil War veterans. Hay's novel tries to imagine how political power can be restored to the forces of morality.

But *The Bread-Winners* also reveals how the vision underlying Hay's own return to public service assumes a social vision at odds with changed conditions of life in the United States. Hay worries that elected officials do not represent the interests of all of the people, but his essentially republican notion of what constitutes "the people" no longer corresponds with the definition assumed by many of the people he considers self-interested partisans.

IV

Republican rhetoric of civic virtue and active participation in a nonpartisan public life sounds attractive to contemporaries disillusioned with interest-group politics and the demise of the "public sphere." We should not forget, however, that such rhetoric developed in a status-oriented society. Classical republican thought did not claim that all citizens were free and equal bargaining partners with equal social standing. Instead, "the people" were differentiated according to their estates, with each having a distinct quality and function that determined social standing. As the metaphor of "standing" indicates, the status of one's estate was the ground of one's identity. Given this differentiation, the equality of the people was determined by a differentiated people's equal subjection to the *res publica*.

In more democratic America, however, equality was increasingly defined as equality of conditions. As democratic as such a notion seems, it raises crucial questions about "the people" that government is supposed to represent. No longer differentiated according to estates, "the people" becomes a vast, indistinguishable mass. In addition to making it impossible for individuals to display virtue in the classical manner, such a notion of the people raises questions about what constitutes individual identity.

If all people are treated alike, they no longer can be identified by qualities that distinguish them from one another. The danger, as de Tocqueville noted, was for the ego to be defined by public opinion. Self-discovery, he feared, would mean conforming to other people's notions of what someone ought to be and was. Reputation, in other words, began to replace status as the defining characteristic of the individual. What people were reputed to be took on more importance than the standing that they possessed as a birthright. Denied an identity grounded in their estate, individuals found it increasingly difficult to achieve the self-representation so essential for participation in republican government. That participation is even more difficult because the changed notion of "the people" contributed to a realignment of boundaries between the public and the private.

The realm of public opinion that more and more determined people's identities does not correspond with the public sphere of traditional republican thought. Although it is a realm of "publicity," it is still a realm occupied by private citizens, one that includes the marketplace, one in which government, according to laissez-faire thought, should not intrude. The growing importance of this realm helps to explain the paradox that identity in a market economy is simultaneously privatized and made more public. In traditional republican thought, the public sphere is the realm in which citizens give up their private interests in order to participate in government. But the realm of public *opinion* is not the realm of virtuous, disinterested governmental service. Instead, it is one in which private interests are expressed and pursued.

People in Hay's and James's circle responded to publicity's "corruption" of republican ideals by further privatizing identity, just as Warren and Brandeis did by asserting a "right to privacy." But if James constructed a realm of the private that, while dependent on a market definition of the self, cannot be completely determined by it, Hay holds onto a republican belief in a self-sufficient individual who, through the powers of self-representation, can resist corruption by publicity. To understand the importance of self-representation in republican thought we can turn to Rousseau's "Letter to M. D'Alembert on the Theatre."

In that letter Rousseau attacks the actor and praises the orator in terms of their self-representations in public. "What," Rousseau asks, "is the talent of the actor? It is the art of counterfeiting himself, of putting on another character than his own, of appearing different than he is, of becoming passionate in cold blood, of saying what he does not think as naturally as if he really did think it, and finally, of forgetting his own place by dint of taking another's." To the objection that the orator functions in a similar manner, Rousseau responds: "When the orator appears in public, it is to speak and not to show himself off; he represents only himself; he fills only his own role, speaks only in his own name, says, or ought to say, only what he thinks; the man and the role being the same, he is in his place; he is in the situation of any citizen who fulfills the functions of his estate. But an actor on the stage, displaying other sentiments than his own, saying only what he is made to say, often representing a chimerical being, annihilates himself, as it were, and is lost in his hero. And, in this forgetting of the man, if something remains of him, it is used as the plaything of the spectators."[23]

From our postmodern perspective it might seem that Rousseau's celebration of the orator's ability to represent himself is pure illusion. But before we too hastily discount it, we need to recognize that here at least Rousseau is not positing the existence of a pre-social self. Instead, self-representation is possible because the self has a clear-cut social identity. People achieve self-representation when they fulfill the function of their estate. Self-representation is no longer possible when the self ceases to be defined according to one's estate, for then everyone seems to be no more than an actor, playing roles scripted for him or her by others. Frightened by this possibility, Hay links workers' efforts to better their station in life to discredited spiritualism.

Spiritualism encourages people, like actors, to become who they are not. As Hay writes, "The dim light, the unhealthy commerce of fictitious ghosts, the unreality of act and sentiment, the unwanted abandon, from an atmosphere in which these second-hand mystics float away into a sphere where the morals and manners are altogether different from those of their working days" (BW 107–8). This loss of identity becomes a metaphor for what Hay feels is the misguided effort of workers to claim equality of conditions rather than take pride in fulfilling the function of their estate. The result is disruption of the social order. After all, workers cannot virtuously subordinate their interests to the public good when they are busy trying to be someone else. Rather than leading to virtue, their desire to be other than what they are makes them vulnerable to corruption by Satanic figures like Offit, who is a perfect example of the breakdown of the classical republican notion of representation. As a union leader he claims to speak for the interests of the workers. But he himself is not a worker. As he explains to Mr. Matchin, "I don't work at my trade, because I have got a better thing. I am a Reformer" (BW 205).

Through Offit, Hay leaves little doubt as to who is to blame for the corruption of American politics. Offit's real first name is Ananias, but he goes by Andrew Jackson Offit. For Hay and many other Republicans, Andrew Jackson brought about the decline of virtuous, disinterested government. Appealing to nature rather than law, asserting his personal will rather than submitting to his public duty, Jackson was compared to Cromwell and Napoleon, passionate rulers who led well-intentioned revolutions astray. Of course, this is not the only image of Jackson. He is also celebrated as the first truly democratic president.[24] But even the terms by which he is praised help to identify the nature of Hay's social vision. Jackson, we are told, is the founding father of American liberalism. If, on the one hand, that liberalism is celebrated for creating equal conditions for all, on the other, it is blamed for introducing a reign of self-interestedness into American politics. Hay combats that self-interestedness by retaining the hierarchical assumptions of classical republicanism.

If Hay's republicanism is most apparent in his distrust of Jacksonian liberalism and the changed notions of both the self and "the people" that it instituted, a less obvious but equally important assertion of republican assumptions comes in the way that he links domestic politics to the body politic. Once again Rousseau articulates what is at stake.

"Never," Rousseau declares, "has a people perished from an excess of wine; all perish from the disorder of women."[25] Elsewhere he writes, "To be a good husband and citizen a man must have a good, that is to say, obedient, wife, who upholds order in the sphere that is the natural foundation of civil life."[26] In *The Bread-Winners* Maud Matchin's disruption of order in the domestic sphere is intricately linked to that caused by Offit in the economic sphere. Maud's power to cause disruption might seem to result simply from her beauty. But the real cause is that she refuses to live within herself. She is a perfect example of someone who causes corruption by trying to be someone who she is not; that is, to rise above her station in life.

Maud's ambitions are generated by traditional sources. Like many beauties, she is flattered by her own image. When despondent, she needs merely to look in the "glass" to restore "her good humor" (BW 102). Like Madame Bovary, she is also deceived by the romantic expectations expressed in works of fiction. But more than fiction leads her astray. The society and fashion pages of newspapers provide models for her behavior and style of dress. Finally, her high school education, which has prepared her for no useful employment, has fueled her "ignoble ambitions" (BW 307). The presence of such ambition in a beautiful body produces a dangerously exaggerated sense of self-importance. "What *does* a man want," she once asks herself, "when he don't want me" (BW 207)?

Of course, many men do want Maud, and their desire to possess her breeds social chaos. If Maud's ambition to be more than she is unleashes excessive desire in her, her beauty unleashes excessive desires in men no more capable than she is of controlling them. Seeing her, Offit declares, "She beats anything I ever saw. I've *got* to have the money—to suit such a woman" (BW 253). She directly or indirectly causes tension and sometimes violence between Farnham and Sam, Sam and Offit, and Offit and Farnham.

Maud's disruptive power is, however, complicated. Her beauty may give her power over some men, but they in turn have power over her. For instance, if historically many of the most important spiritualists were women, in Hay's novel men control spiritualist activities, and the spiritualist Bott easily deceives naive Maud. Similarly, Offit has power over the woman who has him under her spell.[27] If in the unregulated economy of *The Bostonians* such reciprocity raises the possibility of achieving at least a temporary balance of power, in *The Bread-Winners* it is a sign of desire set loose with no force to control it. Appropriately, both Hay and Howells call Maud "ill-regulated" (BW 307).[28] The disruption caused by ill-regulated desire along with Hay's vision of how it can be contained is illustrated by comparing a scene of a handshake with one of a kiss, scenes with significance unlike that of similar ones in *The Bostonians*.

V

The handshake occurs when Sam is employed to do carpentry work in Farnham's library. Pleased with Sam's work, Farnham praises it, adding, "I know good work when I see it. I worked one winter as a carpenter myself." Feeling that "the voice of a brother was speaking to him," Sam asks where Farnham had worked.

"In the Black Hills. I sawed a million feet of lumber and built houses for two hundred soldiers. I had no carpenters; so I had to make some. I knew more about it when I got through than when I began."
Sleeny laughed—a cordial laugh that wagged his golden beard and made his white teeth glisten.
"I'll bet you did!" he replied.
The two men talked a few minutes like old acquaintances; then Sleeny gathered up his tools and slung them over his shoulder, and as he turned to go both put out their hands at the same instant, with an impulse that surprised each of them, and said "Good-morning" (BW 98).

This handshake is different from the one between Verena and Basil in *The Bostonians,* and not only because it is between two men rather than between a man and a woman. Verena and Basil's handshake creates a moment in which the imbalances between them are momentarily balanced as they enter into an agreement. Farnham and Sam's is not reminiscent of a contract. Instead, it expresses fraternal fellowship, but not between two men of equal standing. To be sure, Farnham's experience as a worker creates a sympathetic understanding between the two. The understanding occurs, however, across clear-cut class boundaries.

For Hay this fraternal handshake between property owner and carpenter contrasts the fraudulent attempt to establish a Brotherhood of Bread-Winners concerned with the interests of only one class. There is, Hay implies, a natural sympathy that grows out of skillful labor. But the almost utopian fellowship symbolized by the men's handshake is upset by Maud. As the narrator makes clear, "A woman had come between them, and there is no such powerful conductor in nature" (BW 91). The scene causing this rift illustrates how Maud's use of her sexuality to rise above her class threatens a harmonious social order.

Uncertain how to pursue her infatuation with Farnham, Maud seeks advice from the spiritualist Bott, who mistakenly thinks that he is the object of her desire. He advises her to reveal her love to her lover. "Down with the shams of a false-hearted society; down with the chains of silence that crush your soul to the dust! If the object of your heart's throb is noble, he will respond. Love claims love. Love has a right to love" (BW 112). Sam warns Maud that "no decent girl" (BW 113) would follow Bott's advice. But she is in love with the idea of "heart meet[ing] heart in mutual knowledge" (BW 112). Alone with Farnham in his rose-house, she reveals her passionate dreams of marriage, only to be greeted by a "frown of amazement and displeasure" (BW 133). About to faint in despair, she is caught by Farnham, who is confronted by the inviting face of a beautiful woman in his arms.

Her head lay on his shoulder in perfect content, and she put up her mouth to him as simply and as sure of a response as a pretty child. He was entirely aware of the ridiculousness of his position, but stopped and kissed her.

Her work seemed all done; but her satisfaction lasted only a second. Her face broke into happy smiles.

"You do love me, do you not?" she asked.

"I certainly do not," he answered; and at that instant the door opened and Mrs. Belding saw this pretty group of apparent lovers on a rich background of Jacqueminot roses (BW 133–34).

Startled, Maud abruptly departs. Passing Sam, who has also witnessed the kiss, she utters, "Hold your tongue, Sam. I hate you and all men" (BW 134).

In *The Bostonians* a male kissing Verena threatens to hold her tongue. In *The Bread-Winners* the opposite happens. Farnham kisses Maud *after* she has asserted her "right to speak her mind as a man" (BW 113). Speaking out in Hay's world does not lead to mutual respect and shared love. Instead, it invites the contempt of her social better, who is not so noble as to resist the temptation to kiss Maud's sensuous lips. None-theless, the scene would be a harmless exposure of Maud's indecent behavior and Farnham's inability to resist sexual temptation except for the reactions of both Sam and Alice Belding.

As we have seen, Sam reacts with a jealousy that makes him vulner-able to Offit's manipulation. Alice has a different response. When Mrs. Belding reports the scene to her daughter, Alice is shocked and feels that Maud "has *spoiled* him" (BW 144). Properly trained in a New York finishing school, Alice would never think of expressing her love to a man until first spoken to. The scene in the rose-house is important to the book as a whole because it serves as a negative model for Alice. Hay leaves no doubt that Alice awakens sexual desire in Farnham, but it is different from that which Maud awakens in men, including Farnham. If Offit's passion for Maud "was entirely free from respect or good will" (BW 248), Farnham's for Alice leads him to a nobler state. And Alice's effect is not confined to Farnham. She embodies the force of order and discipline that controls the disorder and license unleashed by both Maud and the strikers.

When Farnham's private army holds the mob in check, the narrator remarks, "The crowd began to feel the mysterious power which disci-pline backed by law always exerts" (BW 233). Similarly, when Alice rushes to Farnham's aid after he has been struck by Offit, the villain "saw a sight which for an instant froze him with terror. A tall and beautiful form, dressed all in white, was swiftly gliding toward him over the grass. It drew near, and he saw its pale features set in terrible expression of pity and horror. It seemed to him like an avenging spirit" (BW 261).

Hay's social vision is structured by the opposition between Maud and Alice, one unleashing unregulated desire and disorder, the other reg-ulating desire and restoring order. As male-dominated as that social vision is, women play a crucial role in it, for, as we have seen, the natural order of the body politic depends on the natural order of the domestic sphere. Indeed, the wives of the strikers play a vital role in ending the strike. According to Temple, the strikers had been living "in a good deal of style—with sentries and republican government and all that," until their wives arrived. "Every woman went for her husband and told him to pack up and go home. Some of 'em—the artful kind—begged and wheedled and cried; said they were so tired—wanted their sweethearts again. But the bigger part talked hard sense,—told 'em their lazy picnic had lasted long enough, that there was no meat in the house, and that they had got to come home to go to work. The siege didn't last half an hour" (BW 241). Playing at being reformers called the Bread-Winners, the strikers are forced by their wives to go to work and live up to their name.

Wives performing their proper duties are contrasted with Maud's mother, who is largely responsible for her daughter's ill-regulated behavior. "A woman of weak will, more afraid of her children than of her husband" (BW 25), Mrs. Matchin upsets the proper order of the domestic sphere. Social chaos is the result.

Hay is not so naive as to believe that the harm brought about by Maud's improper training can be completely overcome. Even when she is restored to her proper social place at the end of the novel and plans to marry Sam, the narrator is skeptical about the future of her marriage. But if there is doubt about the future of the book's working class marriage, there is little suggested about the future of its upper-class lovers, whose pending marriage signals the restoration of social and domestic order.

VI

The Bostonians also ends with a marriage and the containment of the novel's voice of reform. Like *The Bread-Winners,* it links reform to spiritualism, which is mocked for its fraudulent claims. But the significance of both the final marriages and the satire of spiritualism is quite different in the two works. James's mockery of spiritualist reformers does not rely on Hay's vision of republican self-sufficiency. Instead, as we saw last chapter, one of the most fascinating aspects of *The Bostonians* is James's use of the spiritualist vocabulary that his satire discredits when, in the second half, he struggles to describe the mysterious attractions connecting Verena and Basil. For James the vocabulary of magic and spiritualism seems the only one available to explain the "spells" that characters have over one another.

To be sure, a similar use of a discredited spiritual vocabulary occurs in *The Bread-Winners* to describe the power exerted by Offit over Sam or Maud over men. Offit, for instance, is "under the spell of [Maud's] beauty" (BW 290). More important, however, is the spell that Alice casts on Farnham. As much as Hay insists on the unreality of spiritualism, he concludes his novel by declaring that "love is a dream, and dreams have their own probabilities" (BW 319). Farnham first realizes his love for Alice when he senses "her power over him that filled him with a delicious awe. She represented to him, as he had never felt it before, the embodied mystery and majesty of womanhood" (BW 159). He compares his feeling to "that familiar to the eaters of hashish" (BW 159). Alice's powers, like Verena's, are manifested in her voice. It is her cry that saves Farnham's life by distracting Offit, causing his blow to miss its target. Nursing Farnham, she, like Orpheus—or a spiritualist— uses her voice to restore life to the supposed dead, as she sings a bewitching song. Listening "in transport" to her repeat this song in the final scene, Farnham "was so entranced by the rich volume of her voice, and by the rapt beauty of her face as she sang, that he did not at first think of the words" (BW 311).

This could well be a description of Ransom listening to Verena. That similarity, however, emphasizes the difference between the two works, for Verena does not correspond to Alice but to Maud. Hay mocks spiritualism only to posit the presence of a mysterious power embodied in Alice that regulates the ill-regulated forces that it unleashes. James mocks spiritualism but offers no Alice in return. To be sure, he presents the socially proper Ransom and Olive as forces promising to regulate the ill-regulated life of Verena. Olive, to recall, "regulated her conduct on lofty principles" (B 52); "her house had always been thoroughly well regulated" (B 184). But James mocks such regulated behavior as much, or more, than Verena's lack of regulation. Indeed, Olive's overregulation closes her to life's possibilities, while Verena's openness to life makes her seductive. That openness results from precisely what Hay fears about spiritualism and Maud—an ability to get outside of predetermined social roles.

More than any other character in *The Bread-Winners,* Maud fascinated reviewers. She was compared to Thackeray's Becky Sharp, Howells's Bartley Hubbard, and James's Daisy Miller. James's comments about the book make it clear, however, that he was not very impressed. Verena, I would argue, is his response to Hay's portrait of a beautiful woman raised in an ill-regulated family.[29] In James's version of the story, the Maudlike figure not only succeeds in seducing Farnham, she also exposes his principles of self-sufficiency and discipline as having no more of a natural foundation than the spiritualist-based reform that he despises. Her success does not, however, signal freedom. Verena, like Maud, is eventually controlled. But the containment of James's free spirit in *The Bostonians* carries with it a sense of loss not present in Hay's containment of Maud. However ironically James views Verena, she, nevertheless, evokes a promise that in *The Bread-Winners* is seen as only a threat. If the threat in Hay's work is contained by a mysterious force of good embodied in proper social institutions, the promise in James's is contained by imbalances built into existing gender relations. Those imbalances mean that Verena's openness, her seductive ability to get outside of predetermined social roles, does not free her, but makes her vulnerable to possession by others. Unlike Maud, Verena seduces a proper, well-regulated male, but James's "realistic" work still has the male take "possession" of his charming female in the end.

This restoration of order in both Hay's and James's novels invites comparison with Phelps's challenge to patriarchal order in *The Silent Partner*. Nonetheless, the transcendental sanction that Phelps gives to social relations has more in common with Hay's presentation of a fictional world than with James's. We can see why by turning to scenes in *The Silent Partner* involving handshakes and a kiss; or to be more precise, three handshakes that allow Perley to avoid the dangers of a kiss.

VII

The dangers of a kiss are evident when Perley explains to Maverick why they no longer are, and maybe never were, spiritually united. His kisses, she claims, blinded her to their difference.

"You kissed me, and I did not know it!"
"And if I kiss you again, you will not know it," said Maverick, with an argument of smothered passion in his voice.
"I would rather," said the lady, evenly, "that you do not kiss me again."
Her face in the teapot shone as if a silver veil fell over it. His face in the teapot clouded and dropped (SP 160).

As Olive warns Verena, a kiss from a man can silence a woman who wants to speak. Unlike Verena, however, Perley succeeds, as Susan Harris puts it, in resisting "openly and successfully the sexual magnetism of the male."[30] Rather than give in to Maverick's kiss, Perley tells him that she does not love him. Sensing the awkwardness of his position, Maverick holds out his hand to signal that he remains a friend despite being rejected.

Perley's handshake with Maverick, like Verena's with Basil, is a gesture of farewell. But it has a very different significance. Verena and

Basil's simultaneously sets boundaries and marks the beginning of their intimacy. In contrast, Perley and Maverick's marks the end of their engagement. Perley, in other words, achieves the "renunciation" that Olive asks of Verena, a renunciation, as the image of her face behind a silver veil implies, of sexual desire that both Phelps and Hay find dangerous when not properly regulated. Handshakes that come before and after Perley's farewell scene with Maverick reveal how she finds the strength to resist what Verena seems incapable of resisting.

The first occurs when Perley and Garrick discuss whether it is possible to be identified with management and simultaneously help labor by picking "people out of the mud" (SP 146). When Garrick declares that it is possible, Perley responds:

> "You are not in an easy position, it strikes me, Mr. Garrick."
> "It strikes me—I beg your pardon—that you are not in another, Miss Kelso."
> Stephen Garrick took his leave with this; wisely, perhaps; would have taken his leave with a gravely formal bow, but that Miss Kelso held out to him a sudden, warm, impulsive woman's hand" (SP 146–47).

The next scene occurs after the two have grown closer and Garrick offers his hand in marriage. Perley, however, responds with her refusal to be a silent partner in marriage. Instead, she chooses to be a responding partner to the poor. " 'Shall they call,' she said, 'and I not answer? If they cried, should I not hear?'" (SP 262). With Garrick she seeks fellowship, not marriage.

> "Mr. Garrick!" She faced him suddenly on the dripping lawn. "If a man who loves a woman can take the right hand of fellowship from her, I wish you would take it from me!"
> She held out her full strong hand. The rain dripped on it from an elm-tree overhead. Stephen Garrick gently brushed the few drops, as if they had been tears, away, and, after a moment's hesitation, took it.
> If not in this world in another, perhaps? In any? Somewhere? Somehow?
> "I shall wait for you," said the man. Perhaps he will. A few souls can (SP 262–63).

The transformation of Perley's hand from "a sudden, warm, impulsive woman's hand" to a "full strong hand" signals her developing character. The strength she has gained allows her to reverse typical gender roles. Refusing marriage, she is self-assured, while Garrick must fight away tears. Most important, by extending a hand in fellowship she preserves her independence. Rather than give her hand in marriage, she establishes her right to enter into and out of relations with men. Denied an active partnership in the firm, Perley, nonetheless, insists on contractual equality with men, an equality that she would lose in marriage.

Perley's ability to enter into and out of relations at her own bidding has won the praise of feminist critics. What they have trouble facing, however, is the fact that she finds the strength to refuse to give her hand in marriage because she has already committed her hand to other relations that are decidedly hierarchical, not contractual. The most obvious is her commitment to the "hands" in the mills. Noble, her commitment is not one of equality. Referring to the workers as "my people" (SP 64), she offers her hand to lift them up because they cannot do so on their own. Says one worker, "We're poor folks. We can't help ourselves, ye see. We're jest clutched up into the claws o' capital tight, and capital knows it, just as well as we do" (SP 179).

Perley must also protect the workers from themselves. A dramatic illustration of her doing so comes in a scene that causes the most problem for feminist critics—a scene in which she stops a strike protesting a cut in wages. Perley believes that the workers simply do not understand that lower wages are necessary because of lower profits. To strike is to risk bankrupting the firm and lose all hope of having a job. As the narrator remarks, "There is something noteworthy about this term 'strike.' A head would think and outwit us. A heart shall beat and move us. The 'hands' can only struggle and strike us,—foolishly too, and madly, here and there, and desperately, being ill-trained hands, never at so much as a boxing-school, and gashing each other principally in the contest" (SP 245).

Convinced that the strike would be called off if only the workers understood the situation, Perley persuades Garrick to speak to them. But they want to hear Perley herself, and she obliges. "The people parted for her right and left. She stood in the mud, in the rain, among them. They made room for her, just as the dark day would have made room for a sunbeam. The drunkest fellows, some of them, slunk to the circumference of the circle that had closed about her. Oaths and brickbats seemed to have been sucked out to sea by a sudden tide of respectability. It has been said by those who witnessed it that it was a scene worth seeing" (SP 250–51). Perley speaks; the people trust her; the strike ends.

"Certainly," Harris writes, "the voice that claimed female independence is not the same voice that bids the workers trust their boss." But for Phelps they *are* the same voice. Perley brings social harmony, not because she "starts to sound like a male capitalist,"[31] but because her voice is different from even Garrick's. Phelps's description of the strike scene makes it clear that Perley's ability to communicate trustfully with the workers comes from the same source that gives her strength to declare independence from men. By comparing Perley to a sunbeam among darkness, Phelps reminds us that she speaks as an agent for the most important of all silent partners—God. Communication in *The Silent Partner* is ultimately due to God's grace.[32]

Perley's commitment to God is even more important than her commitment to the poor. When she extends her hand to the poor, Perley is simply following God's bidding. Explaining to Maverick why she feels it necessary to devote her life to the workers, she exclaims, "I have no words to say how these people seem to me to have been thrust upon my hands,—as empty, idle, foolish hands, God knows, as ever he filled with an unsought gift!" (SP 139). Unable to find words to express her feelings to Maverick, Perley, in the strike scene, is given words by God that create harmony and overcome misunderstandings between rich and poor.

Judith Fetterly notes that in Phelps's world, miscommunication results from the mistrust brought about by "power's" dependence on dishonesty. But when the author of *The Resisting Reader* argues that in the strike scene Perley resorts to a traditional, "male" use of power, she seems to offer a willful misreading that refuses to listen to the message that Phelps tries to communicate.[33] In fact, Perley's success in communicating with the workers after Garrick's failure recalls an earlier scene in which Garrick laments, "I suspect there always are and always will be a few rich men, Miss Kelso, who just because they *are* rich men will be forever mistranslated by the suffering poor, and I suspect that I am one of them" (SP 183). Phelps's solution to the mistranslations caused by class difference is suggested a moment later when Perley refuses to accept Garrick's request to talk of something other than "suffering and poverty."

"I do not see—in God's name I do not see—what else there can *be* to talk about in such a world as this! I've stepped into it, as we have stepped out into this storm. It has wrapped me in,—it has wrapped me in!"
The sultry rain wraps them in, as they beat against it, heavily. It is not until a little lurid tongue of light eats its way through and over the hill, and strikes low and sidewise against the wet clovers that brush against their feet, that Perley breaks a silence into which they fall (SP 183–84).

Imagery of dark storms is crucial to the metaphysics of the novel. So too is the "tongue of light" that eats its way through the darkness. Most unusual about this phrase is, of course, the description of light as a tongue. But in Phelps's novel about silences and mistranslations this mixed metaphor gives voice to the image of a ray of light traditionally seen as a sign of God. Untangling those wrapped within the storm of social mistrust, this tongue of light promises to make way for communication, just as Perley, translating God's message of love on the dark day of the strike, creates an atmosphere of social harmony. As Sip reports, "That day there seemed to be a shining to her" (SP 251).

In an 1868 essay entitled "Why Shall They Do It?" Phelps argued that "a woman should be just as much ashamed of having nothing to do as a man." A woman should not, however, act for personal success. We are born, Phelps sermonizes, "mainly to be disciplined and to be of use" in the service of God.[34] Through her "service in a temple" (SP 256), Perley finds fulfillment. Filled as a vessel of God, she has no need for a man in her life. Seeing her "lifted haunting face" on another dark New England day, Garrick admits, "I see no room for me there" (SP 257).

There may be no room for Garrick in Perley's life on earth, but Phelps holds open the promise that the two will be united in another world. Phelps, after all, is the author of *The Gates Ajar,* a spiritualist romance about communication between the living and the dead.[35] Her spiritualism influences her attitude toward marriage, which is not quite as emancipated as it at first seems. Perley may twice refuse marriage, but she is not against the institution of marriage. In fact, like many spiritualists, she idealizes it as a union of two souls fated to come together. Her spiritualist vision does challenge the hierarchical nature of marriage by insisting on the equal status of the contracting parties. Nonetheless, the notion of love that enables such equality is quite conventional.

Explaining to Maverick why he has not "filled" her life as he claims, Perley tells him that she is not really in love with him. " 'If there is any love in the world, Maverick, that ought to be independent of all moods and master of all moods, it is the love that people marry on' " (SP 164). Even so, because Perley considers the vows of marriage sacred, she feels incapable of marrying anyone else. " 'I was fond of you, Maverick. I promised to be your wife. I do not think I could ever say that to another man. The power to say it has gone with the growing away' " (SP 161). The promise that she made to Maverick—a promise that she feels bound to uphold because it is sanctioned by God—plays as important a role in Perley's refusal of Garrick's offer of marriage as her growing independence. That refusal is made easier because the two have the possibility of uniting after death, if their love is strong enough.

Participating in an 1890 debate, Phelps supported the right to divorce "when not to give the right is to commit an undeniable wrong." Nonetheless, the thrust of her argument switches attention from the question of divorce to the question of marriage. Drawing on her belief in homeopathic medicine, she compares divorce to surgery, "necessary at the extremity, never to be tolerated when the milder measure will save the life." The real solution to the divorce question is, she argues, preventive medicine. We need to focus our attention on preventing wrong marriages. If we do, we will "make it all but unnecessary to ask if divorce be right." And what constitutes a good marriage? It is founded on "almighty love"; it grows from a "vision of the purity, of the unselfishness, the patience, the tenderness, the loyalty through sorrow and sickness and ill fortune and fading fairness, and the clash of temperaments, which the marriage-bond requires." Because that bond is sanctified by a "holy power," Phelps denies divorced people the "right of remarriage until death shall give it."[36]

As Phelps's views on marriage make clear, Perley's voice that claims female independence and her voice that asks workers to trust their boss are not different. Both derive from Perley's relation with a heavenly world. Similarly, Sip's refusal of marriage is linked to her ability to find fulfillment by preaching the word of God. In the subplot about Sip the connection between the ability of Phelps's independent women to speak out and their subserviency to the silent partner of God is made explicit.

Believing that her deaf-mute sister has not died but merely passed "out of sight" (SP 291), Sip translates the message of love that Catty sends from heaven. Catty's deaf-muteness reinforces the two most important symbols in the book. An obvious silent partner, Catty depends on her hands to communicate in sign language. If Perley's hand is not available for marriage because it is already committed to God and the poor, Sip's is not available because it is busy caring for and communicating with Catty. The transcendental significance of such communication becomes obvious when Catty dies and Sip's communication with her sister gives Sip access to "the great world of signs" (SP 280) that is heaven.

Through the 1860s in the United States, deafness was considered a tragedy because it cut people off from the Christian community. Sign language was welcomed as a way to give the deaf access to that community.[37] By making silent Catty the agent through whom God speaks, Phelps reverses this view. In her world the nondeaf, not Catty, are cut off from God's word, and it is through understanding Catty's silent message that people will enter the kingdom of God. Phelps's reversal has important social significance because on earth miserable, misunderstood Catty stands for the poor. Excluded and voiceless as they are, the poor should not be rejected, but loved. When Catty dies, Sip's task is to preach her sister's "untranslated message" of love (SP 281).

But if Sip translates her sister's and God's message, her own preaching remains virtually untranslatable into print, for it is expressed in an oral style that "can no more be caught on the point of a pen than the rustle of crisp leaves or the aroma of dropping nuts" (SP 295). Nonetheless, Phelps, herself adopting the role of a silent partner, lends her hand to translating Sip's message to her readership. When she does so, she clearly hopes to elicit sympathy for the laboring poor and to make a case for contractual equality between men and women. Ultimately, however, she sanctions class difference. She does so through her own attempt to communicate to us both the translatability and untranslatability of "the great world of signs."

To translate God's message in Phelps's world is to remind us that all are equal in the eyes of God. As Erich Auerbach has argued, a Christian vision has the potential to undermine the hierarchies of a status-oriented society.[38] This democratic tendency is indicated by Phelps's use of art to unite rich and poor. In *The Bread-Winners* aesthetic taste is clearly a function of class. When Farnham shares some of his imported sherry with the men in his private militia, half refuse because they believe in temperance. The rest call it "d—— poor cider" (BW 236). Furthermore, spiritualism attracts those for whom "the opera, the ballet, and the annual Zola are unknown" (BW 107). When "intellectual ambition" is "not held in check by any educated judgment" (BW 104) and artisans are allowed to indulge in the reading of fiction, social disruption is likely to result, as we see in the case of Maud. In contrast, in *The Silent Partner* workers have an intuitive appreciation of "high" art. When Sip is attracted to an engraving of a Lemude portrait of Beethoven, Perley gives it to her to hang in her room where it serves as a " 'forgetting' in the life of a factory-girl" (SP 195). Later Perley invites workers to her place for evenings of reading Victor Hugo, Burns, and Dickens or listening to Beethoven. Like religion, the spirituality of art levels class difference.

The equality that Christian and artistic leveling makes possible is, nonetheless, similar to the republican notion of equality. As we have seen, equality in the republican tradition means equal submission to the good of the state, not equality of social conditions. Likewise, because

Christian equality cannot be measured in material terms, it involves equal submission to the will of God, no matter what one's social position.

In emphasizing the similarities between republican submission to duty and an evangelical submission to the will of God, I do not want to conflate the two. As Nancy Schnog has astutely pointed out in an analysis of *The Gates Ajar,* Phelps displaces and reimagines the submissive female protagonist as dramatized by Susan Warner's Elizabeth Montgomery in *The Wide Wide World.* Whereas Warner's heroine submits "to the dominant authority of evangelical religion and patriarchal authority," Phelps "uproots and rejects those forms of female de-selfing that operate through internal self-discipline and the sacrifice of personal desire."[39] Indeed, spiritualism becomes for Phelps, as it did for a number of women of the time, a medium of female self-expression not allowed in other realms of society. Spiritualism's potential to challenge the ethic of self-discipline and sacrifice is one reason why Hay saw it as a threat.

Even so, for Phelps the spiritual translation of God's message does not erase class difference. It simply allows communication *across* class lines. In fact, in the strike scene Perley plays a role similar to that of Alice, who in *The Bread-Winners* appears as a figure in white, controlling the disorder caused by Offit. When Perley addresses the workers, her appearance, "so white and still" (SP 251), helps to restore harmony to a world threatened by social disorder. To be sure, Perley, unlike Alice, does not marry. But, like Alice, she considers marriage only with members of her class, while Sip's prospective husband is a fellow laborer. In contrast, Maud is a threat because she wants to marry out of her class. Furthermore, as I have tried to show, both Perley and Sip gain at least part of their strength to refuse marriage from the belief that mutual spirits will be united in heaven.

The relation between heaven and earth imagined by Phelps makes existing class divisions and separations tolerable. Because earth is not heaven, people must be patient and wait for the time when their spirits pass into another, more perfect, world. Thus, although Perley and Sip translate their messages from the same source, they speak different languages on earth. When some of Perley's friends ask about Sip's preaching, she explains, "I undertook to help her at first . . . but I was only *among* [the poor] at best; Sip is *of* them; she understands them and they understand her; so I left her to her work, and I keep to my own" (SP 293). Accepting class difference, Phelps asks for sympathy and love across classes—and a common faith in the power of God to set the world right. Sip preaches this message by relying on a metaphor similar to the one that accompanied Phelps's description of a "tongue of light" shining through the storm that has "wrapped in" Perley and Garrick.

Perley uses the image of being "wrapped in" to explain to Garrick her sense of connection to the poor. All of us, she implies, are wrapped into this stormy world together. In Sip's sermon the metaphor is one of entanglement. Explaining God's power she asks:

"Don't you suppose he *knows* how the world is all a tangle, and how the great and the small, and the wise and the foolish, and the fine and the miserable, and the good and the bad, are all snarled in and out about it? And doesn't he know how long it is unwinding, and how the small and the foolish and the bad and the miserable places stick in his hands? And don't you suppose he *knows* what places they are to be born in and to die in, and to inherit unto the third and fourth generations of us, like the color of our hair, or the look about our mouth?

"I tell you, he knows, he knows! I tell you, he knows where fault is, and where the knot is, and who's to blame, and who's to suffer. And I tell you he knows there'll never be any way but his way to unsnarl us all" (SP 298–99).

Since this tangled world is in God's hands, human fulfillment comes when we put ourselves in his care. Knotted as it is, that order is not translatable into human concepts of equity. Different customs between classes, Sip preaches to the poor, are "none of your business" (SP 299). God knows, she insists, the social position people "are to be born in and to die in" (SP 298).

The seeming contradiction between Phelps's call for contractual equality and her sanction of class difference is resolved by the paradox that God's message is both translatable and untranslatable. The importance of *The Silent Partner* for an understanding of the period's contractual ideology lies in the way in which it uses that paradox to marry classical liberal thought and spiritualist Christianity. If *The Bread-Winners* shows how a late nineteenth-century version of republican thought helped to legitimate the social relations that existed under the reign of laissez-faire liberalism, *The Silent Partner* shows how Christian evangelicalism can do the same, even if it distrusts many of the humanly constructed institutions so important for Hay.

Because human institutions cannot untangle us from the snarls of an entangled world, Sip declares, "Folks may make laws, but laws won't do it. Kings and congresses may put their heads together, but they'll have their trouble for nothing. Governments and churches may finger us over, but we'll only snarl the more" (SP 299). If this distrust of institutions frightened Hay, who retained a republican notion of society governed by human institutions that embodied rational, moral principles, it fed arguments that government should keep *its* hands out of the private affairs ruled by the hand of God.

But Phelps's vision reveals an even more complicated alliance between laissez-faire and evangelical thought than this standard distrust of institutional interference into private lives. It is no accident that just before the strike scene Perley has "been over to put Mill's 'Liberty' [*sic*] into the library" (SP 246). Nor is it an accident that just before Sip refuses marriage Phelps uses a phrase from Mill to describe her potential for human development (SP 290). Although Mill himself eschews a transcendental position from which to regulate his free exchange of ideas in the marketplace, Phelps finds her transcendental vision in harmony with Mill's defense of liberty. Indeed, for her it was the only way to understand Mill's vision of self-development.

Mill assumes that the "cultivation of individuality" produces "well-developed human beings," which is "the best thing they can be." Individual development, he argues, is best cultivated in a society that allows "free and equal discussion." In turn, free and equal discussion will be able to combat the tyranny of majority opinion only if individuals are strong and independent enough to voice their diverse ideas. "In proportion to the development of his individuality, each person becomes more valuable to himself, and is therefore capable of being more valuable to others."[40] Mill, however, never accounts for the origin of the individual who is supposed to develop. In contrast, for Phelps an individual owes his or her origin to God. In fact, for Phelps even this development and independence result from submission to God's will.

Just as Phelps shares Mill's concern about self-fulfillment while differing with him on an account of its source, so she shares Hay's vision of self-fulfillment while differing with his republican account of its source. But despite their differences, Phelps and Hay shared a similar vision of the growing number of alienated workers in postbellum America, whose dependency marked their lack of individual self-sufficiency.

Nostalgic for an artisanal mode of labor, Hay feels that workers need disciplined skills, such as those of a carpenter, to give them clear-cut social roles and identities. For him an undifferentiated workforce that merely hires out unskilled labor is a sign of the country's fall from republican virtue into a state of corruption. Within a Christian tradition,

Phelps also describes the unskilled work force in terms of corruption. Using Catty to represent a "type of the world from which she sprang," the narrator describes it as "the world of exhausted and corrupted body, of exhausted and corrupted brain, of exhausted and corrupted soul, the world of the laboring poor as man has made it, and as Christ has died for it, of a world deaf, dumb, blind, doomed, stepping confidently to its own destruction before our eyes" (SP 277–78).

Granted, Hay does not call for Christian sympathy for workers as Phelps does. That sympathy, however, is elicited by presenting the poor as helpless victims. Hay at least grants them the power to determine their fate within a socially defined role. Indeed, for Hay it is the social responsibility of workers to live up to their name, to fulfill the function of their estate. In contrast, for Phelps there is no possibility of self-representation since, like everything else in her world, workers ultimately have meaning only in relation to "the great world of signs."

A dilemma that the realists faced was how to maintain a notion of responsible human agency without abandoning it to a transcendental God, as Phelps does, or prescribing it according to predetermined social roles, as Hay does. The dilemma is intensified because the period's answer to it—that human responsibility is negotiated among equal bargaining powers—corresponds to the rise of a market economy that threatens traditional notions of both responsibility and human agency.

As Laurence Holland has argued, in James human agency can be preserved, but only at great expense, an expense bordering on the loss of the very self that serves as an agent.[41] In linking the assertion of agency with the risk of self-effacement, James leads us towards modernism. In contrast, his fellow realist William Dean Howells is closer to the progressive vision of the late nineteenth century that links a developmental narrative with the development of morally responsible human agency. But embodying that vision realistically in fiction was easier said than done, because the two most secure escapes from the period's threat to responsible human agency—a transcendental religious vision and a republican moral vision—were for Howells just that—escapes.

This is not to say that Howells didn't respond to both visions. But for him neither was directly applicable to the "modern instance." God's "great world of signs" could not be, and for Howells it never had been, translatable to the world of men. Similarly, a republican vision, as powerful as it once might have been, was not directly translatable to the present situation. For proof we can contrast Hay's and Phelps's solutions to the social disorder of a strike with the failure of both Basil

March's quasi-republican view and the religious beliefs of Conrad Dryfoos and Margaret Vance to resolve the social conflicts dramatized by
the strike in *A Hazard of New Fortunes*.[42] If the lack of direct translatability in Howells's works leaves questions of responsible moral action open to doubt, it also underlines the importance of human agency,
because in Howells's world human agency is located at the moment of
translatability. Precisely because his characters cannot rely on the security of knowing that their actions are grounded in proper Christian or
civic duty, they are responsible for taking the risks of translating their
duties into action. In turn, Howells's responsibility as a realistic novelist
is to translate a vision of such agency into a fictional world.[43]

The stress that I place on human and authorial agency in Howells as
an act of translation is, to be sure, at odds with a commonplace account
of him as a writer who believed that realistic fiction could offer an
unmediated vision of life "as it is." In the next chapter I try to show,
however, that Howells does not passively imitate the contractual world
of late nineteenth-century America. Instead, he participates in what he
hopes will be a responsible aesthetic transaction with it.

CHAPTER 5

The Rise of Silas Lapham and the Hazards of Realistic Development

I

As Tom Corey goes to work for Silas Lapham, his mother worries about his seeming attraction to Silas's daughter, Irene. While not admitting her motive to herself or others, Mrs. Corey decides to pay a second visit to the Laphams, telling her own daughter that "it seemed she ought somehow to recognize the business relation that Tom had formed with the father; they must not think that his family disapproved of what he had done. " 'Yes, business is business,' [says] Nanny, with a laugh. 'Do you wish us to go with you again?' "[1]

The Rise of Silas Lapham is often called the first realistic portrayal of a businessman in American literature, but Nanny Corey's laughing response to her mother calls attention to a problem that occupies the novel's critics: how does its business plot relate to the love plot involving Tom and Silas's two daughters? Nanny's identification of business with business would seem to imply that the business plot could be marked off as a self-contained entity. But her laugh undercuts any such tautological identification by suggesting that business is not quite identical to business. Mrs. Corey may claim that her visit to the Laphams is to recognize her son's business relation, but if business were completely confined to the world of business, she would have no obligation to do so. Instead, her "business" as mother is to give her son's relation her blessing, a reminder that business relations are legitimated by more than purely market relations.

And there is more. Mrs. Corey claims to be visiting the Laphams on business matters, but, as her daughter knows, her visit involves more serious business: the possible romantic relation between Tom and Irene. Woman's business may focus on personal relations whereas man's business focuses on market relations, but Howells's plot makes it impossible to separate the two completely.

Howells dramatizes that impossibility by self-consciously using the word "business" in nonbusiness contexts. For Mrs. Corey the confusion about the object of her son's affections is the Lapham's "terrible business" (SL 265). Silas reminds Penelope that her actions in the matter are "my business and your mother's business, as well as yours" (SL 252). When his wife wants to know about his deteriorating business affairs, Silas rebukes her with, "You mind your own business, Persis" (SL 284). Asked by Jim Millon's wife what she thinks about the possibility of her daughter getting a divorce, Silas responds, "I don't care anything about all that. It's your own business, and I'm not going to meddle with it. But it's my business who lives off me" (SL 296).

And just as "when it really [comes] to business" (SL 317), "business" moves into all realms of action, so romance inhabits the realm of business. Money, Bromfield Corey claims, "is the romance, the poetry of our age" (SL 64). Silas's paint is "more than a business to him; it was a sentiment, almost a passion" (SL 50).

Confronted with this seepage of one plot into another, critics have sought ways to balance the two. For instance, G. Thomas Tanselle refers to "the care Howells has taken to keep the two plots in balance," whereas Wai-chee Dimock wants us to think of "the novel form as a system of symbolic equivalents, in which disparate events tally with each other, compensate for each other, and balance each other out."[2] What these efforts fail to take into account, however, is an imbalance at the heart of Howells's novel, an imbalance that makes itself felt in even the simple effort to make business equivalent to itself. If formalist critics attempted to stabilize that imbalance by offering a reading of the novel as a whole, recent historical critics have tried to stabilize it by expanding the scope of their reading to situate Howells's text within its cultural context. Dimock, for instance, argues that Howells's balancing of "formal arrangements inside [the] novel" has a "direct link" to "social arrangements outside" it and thus reveals the novelist's effort to dispense "poetic justice."[3]

Howells did see a relationship between a work's formal structure and questions of justice, and his sense of justice, like the symbol of Justice holding the scales, involves images of balance.[4] An equitable social order for him would be one of balanced exchanges among individual members. But, as he tries to imagine such a world, he recognizes that in a world of chance, perfect balancing acts are virtually impossible. Critics intent on performing them in their readings of *Silas Lapham,* as ingenious as they may be, neglect this important aspect of Howells's realism. Indeed, they repeat the efforts of Silas, who continually strives to balance his accounts but usually fails. Those failures indicate that the unbalancing accompanying even the simple attempt to make business equivalent to itself cannot be stabilized by expanding the scope of our reading to the entire novel or even to Howells's cultural context. This is not to argue that Howells's text has no cultural and historical implications. But the link between it and its context is not "direct"; their relationship is itself an unstable one. Indeed, the unbalancing in *Silas Lapham* is generated more from Howells's insistence on the contingency of history than, as some might argue, from the rigors of his rhetoric. To be sure, rhetorical slippage can contribute to history's contingency, and when Howells is not rhetorically rigorous his realism rarely works. But his works are most effective when he accepts the responsibility of presenting an economy that is subject to the unaccountable, even though doing so plays havoc with his efforts to construct balanced aesthetic objects.

An economy that is subject to the unaccountable causes special problems for the assessment of morally responsible actions. How, for instance, can people be held accountable for their actions, if they live in an unaccountable world? Indeed, Howells's desire for virtuous action has caused some critics to assume that he advocates a return to an agrarian economy and its secure set of unchanging values. But as his relation to the world of Equity in *A Modern Instance* indicates, Howells knows that such a closed, static world limits human development. If a world subject to chance makes the assessment of responsibility hazardous, it also keeps open chances for development.

Even so, Howells does worry about the selfishness fostered by the desire for economic development. As Thomas Galt Peyser puts it, "Howells was in the difficult position of advocating a strong self that nevertheless complies with the rules of a virtuous society."[5] Rather than take the easy stance of dictating what those rules should be, Howells tries to imagine the possibilities of morally responsible development while conducting what Everett Carter calls his "criticism of unexamined 'fixed principles' and closed systems of morality."[6] That criticism is also directed at preconceptions that readers bring to the text. By keeping open a space for readerly participation, Howells allows them to experience the hazards of his economy of the unaccountable.

To present a self-sufficient, balanced economy is to position readers outside the text, leaving them with few responses other than preconceived judgments about the accuracy of its representation of reality. In contrast, by allowing a space for readers to participate in the text's network of exchanges, Howells discourages fixed judgments about a closed text and invites responses subject to the chance at play within and without it, responses, that is, in which readers become increasingly aware of the importance of responsible judgment for human development and the hazards involved in judgments of responsibility. I hope to provoke such responses in contemporary readers through my analysis of Howells's attempt to provide a realistic account of responsible human *and* economic development in a world of the unaccountable.

II

We can start by looking at why various efforts to balance the book's action fail. Critics as different as Donald Pizer and Dimock do so by appealing to the "economy of pain" that the Reverend Sewell articulates to solve the dilemma in the love plot when Tom declares his love for Penelope, not Irene.[7] Confronted by one heartbroken daughter and one full of guilt, who refuses to see Tom, the Laphams seek Sewell's counsel. Sewell advises Penelope to overcome her false sense of duty that he blames on sentimental novels and accept Tom's offer to marry. For him the solution is pure common sense: "One suffer instead of three, if none is to blame. . . . That's sense, and that's justice. It's the economy of pain which naturally suggests itself, and which would insist upon itself, if we were not all perverted by traditions which are the figment of the shallowest sentimentality" (SL 241).

Sewell's advice does seem to work for this particular situation. It does not, however, apply to all events in the novel. Silas's transactions with his ex-partner, Rogers, for instance, do not adhere to its logic.

In the story's moral climax, Silas refuses to sell potentially worthless stock to Rogers, even though doing so would, without violating the business ethics of his day, save his financial empire and satisfy his wife, who feels that Silas owes his ex-partner a moral debt. Silas has scruples

because he knows that Rogers plans to unload the stock on unsuspecting Englishmen, ill-served by morally questionable agents acting on
their behalf. Pleading that the sale is "my one chance; that if [Lapham
doesn't] meet me on it, my wife and children will be reduced to beg-
gary" (SL 327), Rogers accuses Silas of wanting "to sacrifice [Rogers's
wife] to a mere idea" (SL 328). Of course, according to Sewell this is
precisely the problem with Penelope's refusal to marry Tom. Her "false
ideal of self-sacrifice" (SL 241) causes unnecessary suffering. In both
plots agreements could be reached that would minimize suffering for
everyone except a third party: in one case Irene, in the other rich men
who can well afford the financial losses that they might suffer. But for
some reason the economic logic of the love plot does not work for the
business plot.

If Pizer and Dimock turn to an "economy" to unite the book's
action, Donald Pease turns to the logic of family relations. Noting that
"throughout the novel the different subject positions Silas Lapham
occupied in different social narratives produced mobile social energies
transgressive of any single social logic," Pease finds himself, nonetheless, compelled to offer such a single logic. He finds it in Silas's refusal
to sell to Rogers. According to Pease, by treating English strangers "as
if they were family members rather than business partners," Silas "enacts a scene that refuses the difference between business transactions and
family relations out of which all of these narratives were constructed."[8]
But Pease's reading raises unanswerable questions. Why, for instance,
does Silas protect the interests of his adopted English "family" at the
expense of his real family (or even that of Rogers)? Furthermore, how
does this logic square with Sewell's advice to Penelope to construct a
new family by discounting the suffering of her closest family member—
her sister?

Howells does, as Pease suggests, invite us and Silas to bring the
different social narratives in which Silas is placed "into relationship with
one another."[9] But we need to resist the temptation to erase their
differences so as to fit them under a single logic. A tentative explanation
of their differences is suggested in Howells's *A Hazard of New Fortunes*
when Basil March distinguishes between two worlds of chance. One is
the world of chance in which Conrad Dryfoos is randomly killed as he
tries to halt a violent streetcar strike. "All that was distinctly the chance
of life and death. That belonged to God; and no doubt it was law,
though it seems chance." There is, however, another world of chance
to which March objects, which is "this economic chance world in which

we live and which we men seem to have created" (HNF 436). In *Silas Lapham* Penelope's dilemma results from the chance world of God; Silas's from the economic chance world of men. In the love plot no one, as Sewell insists, is to blame for Tom loving Penelope rather than Irene. The distribution of affections is not something that we can control. In contrast, Silas's actions are not blameless. The distribution of economic opportunity does seem to involve questions of blame and responsibility.

This difference affects the meaning of self-sacrifice in the two situations. Even though she is not to blame, Penelope adheres to a "false ideal of self-sacrifice" (SL 241) in refusing Tom, whereas Silas is incapable of the proper "measure of self-sacrifice" (SL 50) in his dealings with Rogers, even though he is potentially to blame for Rogers's fate. In one case self-sacrifice is folly, in the other it is called for.

The distinction between the two plots does not rule out similarities between Silas's and Penelope's dilemmas. What is common, however, is that a perfect balance cannot be found in either. The love plot suggests why. Balancing the interests of all involved is impossible because it is the nature of a triangular affair to leave the odd person out. The plot of *Silas Lapham* consists of one incident after another in which attempts to balance accounts leave something or someone unaccounted for. We could even say that the plot is driven by Silas's failed desire to make things come out even. Nonetheless, his desire is understandable. Silas does not want to feel in anyone's debt. His image of himself as a self-sufficient, self-made man depends on keeping balanced accounts, especially moral ones.

The image of balance brings us back to the relationship between the formal structure of Howells's novel and the world in which it is produced. If the late nineteenth-century economy disrupted efforts to balance one's accounts, the ideology legitimating that economy, as we have seen, depended on various images of balance. One involved the balancing of different social spheres by what in chapter 2 I called boundary theorists. Another involved contractual relations among supposedly equal economic individuals. To review, we can start with contractual relations.

According to laissez-faire thinking, the economy operated most efficiently and for the benefit of all when it was generated by mutually agreed upon contractual relations among autonomous, self-possessed individuals. Theoretically, such an economy left to regulate itself would generate a natural balance among its individual members and thus correct unnatural hierarchies based on preassigned status. Even so, it was widely recognized that this famous move from status to contract created peculiarly modern anxieties. Traditional societies may have been hierarchical, but the status assigned to various members gave them a secure standing in the world, a world in which everyone was part of an interconnected network linking the social system to a cosmic order. Loosening the traditional communal bonds of *Gemeinschaft,* contract threatened to produce the anomie of an atomized *Gesellschaft.* Crucial to boundary thought, the image of balanced social spheres helped to combat this sense of atomization.

Not confining themselves to market relations, late nineteenth-century laissez-faire theorists assumed that society consisted of more economies than a market economy. For instance, they also recognized the domestic economy, an economy that comes closer to the word's original meaning, which is the control or management of a household. If for them contract governed the market, status continued to rule at home.

Today's cultural critics tend to explain the simultaneous existence of these two spheres as the uneven development of residual, dominant, and emergent forces,[10] but the period's laissez-faire thinkers did not share their temporal metaphor. Instead, they relied on the spatial metaphor of boundaries. What today seems to be uneven development was, for them, the result of different spheres of human activity operating according to naturally different logics. Believing that attempts to guarantee "even" development in different spheres would be unnatural, they tried instead scientifically to determine the boundaries between spheres. A legal system that recognized such boundaries would, they felt, create conditions in which individuals would be free to act in accordance with natural necessity, thus minimizing the need for governmental interference. If contemporary critics assume that "uneven" conditions in different spheres are unjust because out of balance, the period's laissez-faire thinkers relied on boundary thought to balance the various mutually dependent, but different, spheres sanctioned by nature, just as for Sewell the economy of pain "naturally suggests itself" (SL 241). Contract might have broken down the interconnected organism of traditional societies, but the image of balance among spheres of different standing allowed boundary theorists to retain the sense of an organic, if differentiated, society.

Howells's relationship to boundary thought is complicated. On the one hand, he shares its assumption that different situations generate different logics. The logic of the love plot cannot simply be imposed on the logic of the business plot. On the other, the seepage of one plot into the other suggests that the boundaries separating different spheres are fluid, not fixed. If, as Dominick LaCapra argues, "the saying 'Business is business' was a meaningful tautological expression" of the doctrine of separate spheres,[11] the inability to confine business to business in *Silas Lapham* unbalances the balance sought by boundary thinkers. We can see how by looking at Silas's unsatisfactory account of the transaction that ended his partnership with Rogers.

Silas absolves himself of responsibility in forcing Rogers out of partnership by arguing that they agreed to a balanced exchange between free and equal individuals. According to Silas their exchange was a "perfectly square thing" (SL 46). Rogers "got his money out and more too" (SL 46). But even though Silas's action is legal, Mrs. Lapham does not consider their accounts balanced. When she objects that Rogers's lack of money unbalanced their exchange, Silas reverts to the vocabulary of free will. Rogers had a "choice: buy out or go out"(SL 46). When Persis further objects that "it was no choice at all" (SL 46), Silas asserts that Rogers's choice was determined by natural laws of economics. Silas had not taken unfair "advantage" (SL 47), he had simply exploited a "business chance" (SL 47). Mrs. Lapham's rebuke that "it was no chance at all" (SL 47) threatens Silas by implying that the transaction was not square. Her response so throws him off balance that he dogmatically appeals to the separation of domestic and business spheres. "'I'm sick of this,' said Lapham. 'If you'll tend to the house, I'll manage my business without your help'" (SL 47). The book shows the impossibility of keeping those spheres separate even if they should not be collapsed into one another.

Howells's response to boundary thought needs to be distinguished from other possible responses. If Howells had indeed constructed a balanced formal order that submitted both plots to a common logic, he would have remained within the framework of a literary organicism that has complicated relations to various views of the social order. For instance, Marx responded to the alienation of nineteenth-century society by explaining all social formations by relating them to an economic base. Thus what seemed to be a fragmented social order was, in fact, a total one united by the reigning mode of economic production.[12] In contrast, sentimentalists found a unifying force in a metaphysical cosmic order. Influenced by the early Foucault, some new historicists try to explain all social phenomena by a common episteme, which for many is a non-Marxist "logic" of the market.

Howells, however, does not present a social world united by a common logic, but instead one in which the "logics" governing individual spheres are simultaneously different and related. They are, it might seem, in a relation of "relative autonomy." But even this sophisticated formulation fails to do justice to Howells. Although Louis Althusser used it to revise Marx's theory of economic determinism, it lacks an adequate account of temporality.[13] To be sure, notions of spheres and boundaries involve space. But the relations among spheres in Howells's novel are temporal in at least two ways. First, efforts to apply the logic of one sphere to another are acts of translation, acts with a temporal dimension. Second, various spheres are not, as boundary thinkers assumed, fixed over time, but subject to revision.

To insist that temporality is an important part of Howells's aesthetic is, in one sense, not to make a startling claim. The nineteenth century is, after all, a period in which temporal narratives of development predominate. But we can better understand Howells's vision by comparing it to one of the most important accounts of temporal development, the dialectical logic of Hegel as used by Georg Lukàcs to develop a Marxist aesthetic.

Lukàcs champions works of nineteenth-century realism because, for him, they express a Hegelian sense of time, which allows them to distinguish the contingent, fragmented details of social life caused by capitalism from the true, dialectically driven course of history. They do so through a formal structure that organizes significant details into a plot that reveals essential contradictions at work within any historical moment. But for Lukàcs the form of realistic works does more than reveal contradictions. It also gives us a glimpse of a world of balanced social justice achieved through the unfolding of time. Indeed, in Lukàcs's Aristotlean Hegelianism, a balanced symbolic form is the aesthetic counterpart to Hegel's dialectical *Aufhebung*.

In our poststructuralist age it is not surprising to find Lukàcs's Hegelian sense of temporality under attack. If for Lukàcs realism provides a dialectical alternative to existing historical conditions, the "police academy" of critics argues that, by imagining a balanced form in which the contradictions of an age can be *contained,* works of realism legitimate the existing social order. But neither Lukàcs's nor the "police academy" description of realism adequately describes the temporality of Howells's fiction.[14] In *Silas Lapham* there is no ultimate synthesis of contradictions. Rather than an *Überwindung* of contradictions, we have what Martin Heidegger calls a *Verwindung.*[15] The aesthetic counterpart to such a *Verwindung* is not a balanced formal structure that contains all of the individual elements of its plot. It is instead a work in which the plot's temporal movement disrupts efforts, including its author's, to achieve formal balance. This disruption is apparent in the novel's third plot.

III

Akin to the third party that gets left out in a triangular affair, the third plot disrupts efforts to balance the book's main plots. For instance, for Tanselle it is a "serious problem" because it "remains an element not smoothly blended into the larger structure."[16] But Howells's realism forces us to face such problems, even if they are not easy to account for.

The third plot involves Zerrilla Dewey, the daughter of Jim Millon who sacrificed himself in the Civil War so that Silas could live. Feeling infinitely indebted to Jim, Silas supports Jim's wife and Zerrilla by employing the daughter as a secretary. This support becomes increasingly expensive because Zerrilla is married to a sailor who shares her mother's alcoholism.

Bucking the trend of critics who tend to ignore or discount this plot, Dimock argues that its importance *is* its tenuousness. Tenuously connected to the main plots, but revealing a "network of complications and entanglements," it suggests "a world of causal infinitude" in which "human responsibility becomes infinitely problematic." According to Dimock, Silas's decline is precipitated by this dilemma of "unlimited liability," because "the causal universe he inhabits is not only fearfully expansive but also fatally expensive. Moral responsibilities here have a way of becoming financial liabilities." Though this "domino theory of moral responsibility" proves frightening, Dimock argues that Howells suggests a remedy. "If moral responsibilities tend to get out of hand by mutating into financial liabilities, then the solution *must* work in the opposite direction, which is to say, it *must* try to rectify the moral by way of the economic" (my emphasis). She finds this solution in the familiar appeal to the "economy of pain," an economy that not only helps us to "cope with our own suffering," but also "with the suffering of others: cope with it, in the sense of acceding to it, accounting for it, and learning to see it, as Howells says in its 'true proportion.'"[17]

For Dimock, Howells's economy of pain is so embracing that it contains even the tenuous and the contingent, thus helping readers account for suffering. But as powerful as this reading is, it miscalculates the proportion between the third plot and the rest of the story. To be sure, Silas tries to isolate it. He even records his payments to Zerrilla in a separate account book. Nonetheless, Zerrilla's story does not present us with actions almost "completely superfluous" that can eventually be accounted for by an economy of pain. Instead, it presents us with vitally connected actions that, nonetheless, painfully force us to face our inability fully to account for them. For instance, Zerrilla does more than "provoke Mrs. Lapham into a fit of unfounded jealousy"; her story brings aspects of the two main plots into direct conflict with one another.[18] Those conflicts undermine efforts neatly to balance the business and love plots.

A working wife, Zerrilla occupies a space that stretches the period's belief in contract to its conceptual limits by threatening the delicate balance that laissez-faire thinkers maintained between the business and domestic economies. On the one hand, the business realm depended on honoring the right of individuals to contract out their labor for pay. On the other, the domestic realm depended on a contract in which a woman forfeited her right to enter into business contracts because her husband became her legal representative. As more and more women entered the workforce, legal thinkers were forced to face the problem of who owned her earnings. The solution did not lend itself to simple balancing.[19]

Of course, the inequities that the marriage contract posed for women with property were not new. In the antebellum years several states had passed married women's property acts that allowed women to retain property when they married. Such property did not, however, bring the marriage contract into conflict with the business contract. Property earned by working wives did.

To forbid working women from possessing their earnings was to threaten the logic of the business contract. To allow them to do so was to threaten the relationship of status established by the marriage contract.[20] Thus when states began to pass "earnings acts," many defenders of traditional marriage opposed them. At the same time supporters appealed to a situation like that represented in Howells's third plot: a married woman whose earnings are wasted by an alcoholic husband. The fact that Zerrilla's plight seems to leave her with no option but divorce suggests why traditionalists felt threatened by earnings acts. Indeed, the third plot links Howells's novel to a heated debate sparked by a dramatic increase in divorce revealed by the 1880 census. That link in turn forces a reconsideration of our account of the two main plots.

Traditionalists argued that divorce threatened the social fabric by tearing down the family. Those supporting more liberal divorce laws argued that their consideration of the individual was a sign of progress.[21] In *A Modern Instance* Howells had already dramatized the difficulty of balancing competing claims. By returning to the issue of divorce in the subplot of *The Rise of Silas Lapham,* he not only brings the logic of the domestic and business spheres into conflict, he also complicates the situation presented in his love plot.

The love plot is special because it involves no breaking of contractual promises. If Tom and Penelope's pursuit of their love had violated vows Tom had made to Irene in courtship or marriage, Sewell could not so easily have declared that "none is to blame" (SL 241). By placing Zerrilla in a situation in which she can assert herself only by breaking the vows of marriage, Howells points to the limits of Sewell's economy of pain. On the one hand, Zerrilla's husband is to blame for not living up to his marital obligations. On the other, Zerrilla will be blamed if she does not live up to her marriage vows. Reconciling Zerrilla's claim for divorce with Penelope and Tom's claim to pursue their love calls for a revised understanding of marriage and a reconsideration of the distinction between God's and humanity's worlds of chance that allowed us to differentiate between Silas's responsibilities in the business plot and his daughter's in the love plot.

According to the narrator in *Silas Lapham:*

> The silken texture of the marriage tie bears a daily strain of wrong and insult to which no other human relation can be subjected without lesion; and sometimes the strength that knits society together might appear to the eye of faltering faith the curse of those immediately bound by it. Two people by no means reckless of each other's rights and feelings, . . . may tear at each other's heart-strings in this sacred bond with perfect impunity; though if they were any other two they would not speak or look at each other again after the outrages they exchange. It is certainly a curious spectacle, and doubtless it ought to convince an observer of the divinity of the institution (SL 49).

Unsentimentally describing the struggles of marriage, Howells nonetheless lapses into a sentimental view of it as a sacred bond. He is, for instance, much more of a traditionalist than Henry James. But Howells is not a complete traditionalist, as we can see by comparing his attitude toward divorce with that of the spiritualist feminist Victoria Woodhull.[22]

Traditionalists considered marriage a special contract whose vows involved much more than a horizontal exchange between two people. It also involved the promise each party made vertically to God. Thus they resisted arguments that marriage was a civil contract. They particularly opposed laws allowing divorce because these laws undermined a couple's sworn relation to God. In contrast, Woodhull attacked laws that forbade divorce, but not because she denied a divine sanction to marriage. On the contrary, marriage was for her a manifestation of the spiritual force governing the universe. But since that force embodied itself in the bond between husband and wife, not positive law, she felt that once husband and wife no longer sensed the mystical sanction of their relation, their commitment to one another disappeared. Indeed, as far as Woodhull was concerned, laws forbidding divorce constituted an unwarranted governmental interference with the divine spirit.

Howells also opposed absolute prohibitions on divorce, but for different reasons. If for traditionalists the commitment between husband and wife grew out of the sacred nature of the marriage ceremony and for Woodhull it resulted from the sanction of a transcendental spirit, for Howells it was constructed through the couple's horizontal exchange of promises. At the same time, marriage involved more than the couple's immanent relation, because it depended on the mysteries of love. In Howells's next novel, for instance, Sewell, contemplating the requirements of marriage, wonders, "Was love so absolutely necessary?" (MC 334). His wife forcefully responds, "You know that it is *vitally* necessary" (MC 334). Since for Howells the distribution of sexual affection seems beyond human control, marriage for him, as for traditionalists, was an institution in which the chance worlds of God and human beings intersected. But how they intersected was quite different.

In calling marriage a divine institution "that knits society together" (SL 49), Howells grants it a social role that would make him a reactionary if we accept Sir Henry Maine's claim that "the *unit* of an ancient society was the Family, of a modern society the individual."[23] But for Howells, part of the divinity of the institution is that, whereas it might seem to limit the freedom of the parties bound together, it in fact makes possible the mutual growth and development of individuals. Explaining why he plans to marry his intended, a character from Howells's next novel exclaims, "Why am I in love with M. Swan? Because I can't help it for one thing, and because for another thing she can do more to develop the hidden worth and unsuspecting powers of A. W., Jr., than any other woman in the world" (MC 218).

Thus for Howells divorce is not simply a conflict between an individual's need for self-development and society's need to have people honor commitments to divinely sanctioned institutions. Social and individual needs are interrelated as much as opposed. If honoring the commitment to a bad marriage can stunt individual growth, in Howells's world an individual develops as a responsible human agent in part by honoring the commitments he or she has made. In turn, society depends on the sense of duty and obligation most fully developed in individuals tested by institutions like marriage. For Howells, then, unlike Woodhull, a couple should not be released from its vows the moment it senses that its bond is no longer sanctified by a higher spirit. Indeed, for him marriage cannot partake of its divinity without people working to live up to mutually created duties and obligations that have no higher sanction than the promises that they have made to one another. Even so, blind commitment to a marriage in which husband and wife are constitutionally incompatible only serves to undermine the institution's social function by stunting individual growth.

The special status that Howells attributes to marriage not only justifies Zerrilla's difficult decision to seek a divorce, it also helps to explain why Sewell's economy of pain works for Tom and Penelope but not for others. For Tom to marry Irene would be a disaster because it would bind both to a loveless marriage. For Penelope not to assert her "right" to Tom merely because it would hurt Irene also makes no sense. As Silas notes, the original confusion "had already put Irene to the worst suffering" (SL 252). How Irene deals with her imagined loss is a test of *her* character, not Penelope's. Furthermore, if Tom and Penelope do not marry they will give up a rare chance for mutual development and growth that fuses the strengths of the Lapham and Corey families.

By having society held together by an institution partaking of the divine, Howells might seem to impose a moral order on his world, and to an extent he does, certainly more than James. Nonetheless, the way in which Howells conceives of the institution makes the determination of responsibility more complicated rather than less. For traditionalists marriage vows could never be broken, because they were governed by God. For Woodhull they could be broken the moment that the parties sensed the withdrawal of divine sanction. But for Howells neither absolute position will do. Involving commitments created through the exchange of interpersonal vows, marriages never involve a situation in which "no one is to blame." At the same time, no match is so made in heaven that the husband's and wife's interests never conflict. Since the intersection of the chance worlds of God and humanity varies from marriage to marriage, each situation needs to be evaluated on a case-by-case basis. Howells's inability to predict how the worlds of God and humanity intersect in any situation distinguishes him from a boundary thinker like William Graham Sumner.

Sumner makes a distinction very similar to the one made by Howells's March. "Certain ills," he argues, "belong to the hardships of human life. . . . We cannot blame our fellow-men for our share of these" because "God and Nature have ordained the chances and conditions of life on earth once and for all." At the same time, "certain other ills are due to the malice of men, and to the imperfections or errors of civil institutions."[24] These ills do demand a human remedy. Unfortunately, however, from Sumner's point of view, reformers too often confuse the two and hold human beings, especially certain social classes, responsible for eliminating the first class of ills. Avoiding such confusion, Sumner sets clear-cut limits on human responsibility. On the contrary, by suggesting that in marital controversies the chances of life ordained by God and humans intersect in varying proportions, Howells makes determination of responsibility extremely difficult. Furthermore, he does not confine the intersection of the two worlds to marital situations, as evidenced by the original source of Silas's debt to Zerrilla: his relation to her father. The events of the third plot suggest that far from being set by God "once and for all," the limits of human responsibility are always open to question.

Displaying a generosity that he refuses to extend to Rogers, who, his wife claims, also "saved [him]" (SL 47), Silas tries to pay back an infinite debt to the man who saved his life. Infinite as it might be, that debt has little to do with blame. Just as Tom is not responsible for the distribution of his affections, so Silas is not responsible for Jim's fate, which belongs to the chance world of life and death. Silas's debt is linked to that world.

Silas tells Jim's story at a dinner party to illustrate Corey's remark that an individual may go into war "simply and purely for his country's sake, not knowing whether, if he laid down his life, he should ever find it again, or whether, if he took it up hereafter, he should take it up in heaven or hell" (SL 202). Such sacrifice, Sewell admits, helps us "to imagine what God must be" (SL 202). Recalling the ultimate sacrifice, Jim's death calls attention to humanity's infinite debt to Christ, whose story most poignantly dramatizes how the world of God, while different from that of humankind, intersects with it. But if Jim's story dramatizes human beings' infinite responsibility, his daughter's dramatizes the impossibility of paying back an infinite debt such as the one owed to Christ or Jim.

As the alcoholism of Zerrilla's mother and husband becomes a bottomless hole, absorbing all the money that Silas can give, Silas is forced to realize that he can no more successfully translate his moral debts into economic ones than he can successfully buy status in Boston society. Economic factors influence these other realms and vice versa, but they are not equivalent. Furthermore, Silas must learn that as a mere human being he cannot pay back all of his moral debts. To live in a historical world once inhabited by Christ may mean that people live with an infinite debt, but when Silas acts to cut off support to Zerrilla's husband, he dramatizes a paradox: to be a responsible human agent one must draw limits to one's responsibility. Not to do so is to pretend to be a divine rather than a human agent. Such pretense is not, according to Howells, very responsible.[25]

In order to function, every society constructs narratives that establish what it considers responsible limits to responsibility. Some do so by assigning people clearly defined sets of duties and obligations based on status, while others limit obligations to terms negotiated by contracting parties. When Howells suggests that people have an infinite debt that can never be fulfilled, he draws attention to the contingency by which such limits are drawn. By presenting us with situations in which people must act in order to be responsible, he confronts us with the necessity of drawing them. By imagining novel situations that cannot be accounted for by agreed upon limits, he forces us to reconsider and perhaps redefine them, just as the "flawed" third plot of his novel does.

Any consideration of how the formal structure of Howells's fiction relates to questions of justice needs to take into account his concern with such novel situations; that is, situations that cannot be accounted for by existing formal structures or a Hegelian dialectic. Nonetheless, critics, confused by Howells's statements that the function of fiction is to portray men and women as "they really are," ignore the temporal dimension of Howells's sense of reality.[26] The dangers of doing so are illustrated by Walter Benn Michaels's fascinating, but flawed, attempt to draw connections between Howells's aesthetic and the period's economics.

IV

Michaels's reading of Howells is, as he acknowledges, indebted to Leo Bersani. Working within a framework established by Roland Barthes, Bersani challenges arguments like Lukàcs's that champion nineteenth-century realism for opposing the fragmented world created by capitalism. Admitting that the realistic novel offers valuable social criticism by exposing contradictions, Bersani claims that, nonetheless, its final sense of cohesion offers implicit reassurance that contradictions can be contained within a significantly ordered structure inherent in society. Naturalizing the relations historically constructed under capitalism as "the real," realism's balanced formal order serves the status quo by castrating desire for an alternative social order.[27]

Michaels accepts Bersani's account of realism's efforts to achieve a balanced economy within a balanced formal structure, but he offers a different account of capitalism. Capitalism, he argues, does not castrate desire; it generates it. Consumer capitalism, for instance, produces and reproduces subjects with an endless desire to be what they are not. That desire is generated by an economy based on speculation. Building his argument on the precarious foundation of this speculative economy, Michaels performs a dazzling balancing act that links business and love plots through their fear of speculation. The love plot, he argues warns against sentimental fiction whose lack of anchorage in reality arouses dangerous speculative desire, whereas the business plot warns against a capitalist economy that rewards earnings gained through speculation rather than "real" labor. In this reading Howells opposes the dangers of speculation with the agrarian values of self-sufficiency and balance that led to Silas's initial rise and to which he returns at the end of the novel. Aligning Howells's realism with this pre-market notion of character, Michaels claims that Howells thinks of both as sources of inherent values that resist the flux of an inequitable capitalist economy. In contrast, Michaels champions *Sister Carrie,* whose dramatization of the "almost structural impossibility of equilibrium" endorses "the popular economy" of capitalism.[28]

In his response to Bersani, Michaels in effect endorses the formal relations between capitalism, realism, and naturalism established by Lukàcs.[29] According to both, realism tries to resist capitalism, whereas naturalism feeds its logic. But for Lukàcs resistance is possible whereas for Michaels it is not. Realism does not naturalize the status quo.

Instead, it depends on a nostalgic view that a balanced economy based in nature exists as an alternative to the "artificial," speculative economy of capitalism. Although Michaels himself does not engage Lukàcs, we can see this nostalgia in Lukàcs's reliance on an Aristotlean notion of *mimesis*, in which a work of art, through its formal structure, is able to impart a sense of reality more "real" than the contingent world of historical actuality recorded in naturalism's meticulous detail. Linking efforts to oppose the historical reality of capitalism with a belief in such a naturally based, transcendent world of reality, Michaels champions naturalism, implying that in its immersion in the contingent and speculative economy of capitalism it is in effect more realistic than realism.

For Michaels, naturalism's relation to consumer capitalism does not come from an accurate representation of reality. On the contrary, within the "logic" of naturalism there is an inevitable gap between a work of art and what it would represent. It is, however, precisely this imbalance between life and art that serves the interests of capitalism, for it helps to generate mimetic desire, a desire to be what one is not. In naturalism "the relation between art and desire is . . . very different from Howells's in *The Rise of Silas Lapham*, where art, like character, was seen as a kind of still point, a repository of values that resisted the fluctuations and inequalities of industrial capitalism."[30] In contrast, naturalism is not only about consumer capitalism, it also produces ideal subjects for it, subjects constituted by a desire to imitate what they cannot be.

The problem with Michaels's reading is that it allows the Reverend Sewell unequivocally to speak for Howells when, in denouncing sentimental fiction, he proclaims that "the novelists might be the greatest help to us if they painted life as it is, and human feelings in their true proportion and relation" (SL 197). Such an aesthetic, Michaels argues, is essentially a painter's aesthetic. But a call to paint "life as it is" is somewhat ironic in a novel in which Silas uses his paint to cover the natural landscape with advertisements for itself. Paint can cover up the world as well as accurately imitate it. Granted, Silas's commercial use of paint differs from aesthetic uses of it, such as Bromfield Corey's. For instance, in a statement that Michaels quotes to represent Howells's aesthetic, Corey asserts that "you never hear of values in a picture shrinking; but rents, stocks, real estate—all these shrink abominably" (SL 95–96). Corey does see art as an escape from the speculative fluctuations of the market. But Corey's theory of art is not Howells's.

Causing Corey to respond to a "shrinkage in values" (SL 95) by investing "his values into pictures" (SL 96), Corey's aesthetic contributes to a decline in his family's fortunes. Its concept of imitation also robs him of the originality necessary to develop as a painter. The limits of Corey's classical aesthetic are suggested in the conversation about his house during the book's central dinner scene. Built in "perfect taste" (SL 192) and embodying its architect's "preference for the classic" (SL 187), the house is, according to Silas's architect, neither as "original" (SL 192) nor as well-built as the structure that Silas's "practical sympathy" (SL 191) has allowed him to construct. The point is not that the Corey's house lacks aesthetic value. Howells continues to value taste, just as he continues to value human "character." The house does create a space for impeccable taste and trustworthy character. But in protecting itself from "modern fuss" (SL 191), it shuts out the temporality necessary for the *development* of character.[31]

Corey's classical, "painterly" aesthetic assumes that the real is stable and unchanging. In contrast, Howells's novelistic aesthetic assumes a world in which temporality has become a component part of reality, one in which a future reality is always capable of rendering an existing reality unreal. Incapable of expression by spatial metaphors, this sense of reality plays havoc with balancing efforts that depend on foundational thought.

Michaels argues that Howells's realism rests on the solid foundation of stable values of morality and art. For him Howells dramatizes the moral depravity of speculation through Silas's failed efforts in the stock market. To be sure, both Silas and his wife look down on the "unearned" wealth gained in the market. Mrs. Lapham calls it "gambling" (SL 129); Silas claims that "every cent" of his fortune "was honest money—no speculation—every copper of it for value received" (SL 206). What Michaels overlooks, however, is that Silas loses money in an effort to balance his accounts. Just as Silas tries to balance his accounts with Jim Millon by throwing good money after bad into the bottomless pit of alcoholism, so in trying to recoup his economic losses Silas throws good money after bad in the stock market. Rather than establish a simple opposition between a speculative economy and one based on firm foundations, Howells shows how Silas's speculation is motivated by an impossible dream of establishing a firm foundation for his investments. A case in point is his investment in his paint "farm," which links Silas's economics to the complicated relationship between the chance worlds of humans and God.

Silas certainly believes that he has invested in something with intrinsic value. Harvested, appropriately enough, from the earth, his paint, he believes, "will stand like the everlasting hills, in every climate under the sun" (SL 11). It is, he tells Tom Corey "with the solemnity of prayer" (SL 76), "the best paint in God's universe" (SL 76). Silas makes it, as Mrs. Lapham puts it, his "god" (SL 47). He tells Bartley Hubbard, "I believe in my paint. I believe it's a blessing to the world" (SL 17). But Silas's belief is seriously flawed. He may grant his paint an everlasting value, but, as Tom reminds him, it is merely "the best in the market" (SL 76). When West Virginia paint enters the market, Silas's faith proves to be misplaced.

Silas's problem is that he has invested too much in his paint. That investment has to do with more than its cash value. It is not money, but his paint that is "the poetry of Silas's nature, otherwise so prosaic" (SL 50). "A sentiment, almost a passion" (SL 50), his paint connects him to what he believes is an almost sacred natural order. More than greed, his sentimental attachment to the paint discovered by his father causes Silas to make crucial business mistakes, such as keeping the works open too long. Indeed, it seems that if he would recognize the split between God's order and the humanmade world of the market and see his paint as simply a cash investment, he would be financially better off.

But in Howells's fiction the chance economic world of human beings is never completely divorced from the chance world of God. If Silas's financial rise is enabled by the chance location of mineral paint on his father's land, the chance presence of a "vein of natural gas" (SL 301) close to the West Virginians' paint guarantees his decline by keeping their manufacturing costs below his. What to Silas is a solid investment in a natural substance, rooted in the earth and linked to family values, turns out to be a speculative investment in a hole in the ground, an investment subject to chance. Silas has, according to Tom, "put a great deal of money into his Works" (SL 301), but "the value of his Works" (SL 301) is subject to forces outside of his power. There is, it seems, always an element of economics over which humans have no control.

Another illustration of Silas's failure to establish firm foundations is his house, which would seem to be a stable investment preferable to risky speculation in the stock market. The house is an attempt to establish foundations in a variety of ways. Most obvious is the metaphor of foundation itself. A house is constructed on a foundation rooted in the earth. It is built on a piece of *real* estate. But Silas's investment in his house is also an investment in the social status of his daughters. He first considers building it after Mrs. Corey's visit to their Nankeen Square house and her remark that " 'nearly all our friends are on the

New Land or on the Hill.'" (SL 29). Mrs. Lapham, who at first resists the notion of building on Silas's Back Bay lot, ponders the consequences for her daughters and grants that "'we ought to do the best we can for the children, in every way.'" (SL 29). The Back Bay location will provide the daughters with a social foundation lacking in their Nankeen Square address.

The speculative nature of this investment is dramatized when the house goes up in flames. But even earlier, Howells hints at the investment's shaky foundation. Houses in Back Bay are built on top of a salt marsh, so that "before they began to put in the piles for the foundation they had to pump. The neighborhood smelt like the hold of a ship after a three years' voyage. People who had cast their fortunes with the New Land went by professing not to notice it; people who still 'hung onto the Hill' put their handkerchiefs to their noses, and told each other the old terrible stories of the material used in filling up the Back Bay" (SL 43). As in the case of his paint farm, Silas invests in a piece of land with a hole in it whose value is subject to market fluctuations. Significantly, Silas loses his entire investment because the passage of time causes his insurance policy to lapse.

In dramatizing how seemingly solid investments are themselves a form of speculation, Howells establishes a complicated relation among sentimentalism, realism, and capitalism. Bromfield Corey suggests a link between sentimentalism and capitalism when he complains that sentimental fiction "flatters the reader by painting the characters colossal, but with his limp and stoop, so that he feels himself of their supernatural proportions" (SL 197). Such flattery generates what is known as mimetic desire in the reader. Mimetic desire is generated, on the one hand, by the lack of proportion that so irritates Sewell and, on the other, by a form of imaging that evokes a root meaning of speculation; that of a *speculum* or a mirror. Unleashing a desire in readers to become the flattering image that it constructs of them, sentimental fiction simultaneously makes fulfillment of that desire in the human world of time impossible. As Michaels has argued, this production of endless desire helps to feed a consumer-driven economy.

But for Michaels, Howells's dislike of sentimental writers is not simply caused by the fact that they generate uncontrolled desire. According to him, Howells faults them, not only because they offer unrealistic models, but, more important, because they offer any models at all. "Realism, defined by its fidelity to things as they are, can never in principle serve as a model, good or bad, since only when art is *not* like life can life attempt to be like art. The true scandal of sentimentality is thus its inversion of the proper relation of life to art, an inversion made possible only by the introduction of a discrepancy between the two terms."[32]

What Michaels fails to see is that such a discrepancy exists for Howells as well. "We start in our novels," he argues, "with something we have known of life, that is of life itself; and then we go on and imitate what we have known of life. If we are very skilful and very patient we can *hide the joint.* But the joint is always there, and on the one side of it are the real ground and real grass, and on the other are the painted images of ground and grass."[33] In fact, the discrepancy within *Silas Lapham* is so pervasive that business is not even equivalent to itself. Even so, not all discrepancies are the same. Howells's problem with sentimental fiction is not that it presents us with a discrepancy between life and art and thus offers itself as a model. All fiction, because it will never be completely equivalent to life, has the capacity to do that. What is at stake is the nature of the discrepancy that it presents between itself and life and thus the type of model that it offers.

Howells objects to sentimentalism not because it awakens desire but because it awakens it only to close off possibilities for human development. Sentimental fiction generates endless movement, but that movement takes place within a closed world bounded by its mirror reflections. Rather than generate an open-ended economy, subject to chance, it ultimately rules out the possibility of chance and with it chances for development. Why it does so is suggested by the fact that one of its bounding mirrors offers images of the supernatural. That flattering image causes sentimental fiction to establish a relation between the worlds of God and humankind quite different from that of Howells's realism.

Sentimentalists frequently attribute their "works" to the hand of God. Responsibility for what they write lies with God, and they are no more than passive agents through whom God reveals his Word. This seemingly modest claim is, however, one full of hubris, for it implies that their works reveal the infinite perspective of God necessary to see the ultimate balancing of human accounts. As a vehicle for God's word, their fiction gives us a view of the world as if from a higher perspective, which corresponds to the meaning of speculation that comes from *specere,* or to see and thus *specula,* or a watchtower.

As titles like *Gates Ajar* and *Barriers Burned Away* indicate, the sentimentalists of Howells's day assumed access to a timeless, transcendent world that would balance accounts left uneven in the imperfect world of human history.[34] That balanced economy means that what

Michaels takes to be sentimentalism's production of unregulated desire is, in fact, highly regulated, as it remains subordinate to the supernatural force that first awakens it.[35] By placing human actions in the hands of a transcendental force, sentimental fiction removes the risks of chance—and thus human responsibility—from life. Solving the conflicts that it raises through plot devices similar to a deus ex machina, it produces mechanical, rather than human, agents who model their lives on the supposedly fixed values that govern the contingent world of time. In contrast, Howells does not claim to reveal God's perspective. Acts of human labor constructed out of the materials offered to him, Howells's novels are the responsibility of human, not divine, agency. As such, they serve pragmatically as equipment for living, precisely because they force readers to face the moral complexity of living in a world without fixed principles.[36]

The most important discrepancy between life and art dramatized by Howells's realism is not between a fallen world of history and a transcendental world of permanent values. Resulting in part from the difference between real grass and imitated grass, it also involves what Reinhart Koselleck calls an asymmetry between our space of experience and our horizon of expectations. This asymmetry, according to Koselleck, is constitutive of a modern sense of temporality, one that is future-oriented because the future may always bring about events that present or past experience cannot account for.[37] In such a world people are continually challenged to reconstruct and reorder social arrangements and to reconsider the nature of virtuous action.

Neither painterly nor architectural metaphors can adequately account for this temporal dimension of Howells's fiction. Nonetheless, critics continue to assume that Howells endorses the claim that Corey makes when he says, "You architects and musicians are the true and only artistic creators. All the rest of us, sculptors, painters, novelists, and tailors, deal with forms that we have before us; we try to imitate, we try to represent. But you two sorts of artists create form" (SL 192). Corey, however, neglects an important aspect of a novelist's task. A novelist might work with given forms, but he still needs to place them in relation so as to create "novel" forms. This creative act is crucial for the novelist's fulfillment of his moral responsibility, because by forcing us to revise fixed notions about the nature of what is real it challenges belief in closed systems of morality.

The assessment of responsibility for Howells is a formal one, and his responsibility as a novelist is the formal one of bringing different spheres of action into proportionate relation. But for a novelist to fulfill that responsibility in a temporal world subject to chance, he cannot rest content with finding a form that "captures" reality either through spatial images or a dialectical logic. Instead, starting with existing forms, he must continually work to rearrange and reorder them. If in constructing a form that brings actions into proportionate relation Howells helps us to see how one should act in a given situation, he also knows that the "logic" growing out of that situation is not self-contained. Instead, a responsible action in one situation helps to generate new situations that unbalance whatever tentative balance might have been achieved. "Each novel," Howells wrote, "has a law of its own, which it seems to create for itself."[38]

The need to revise every tentative formal solution helps to account for Howells's Balzacian strategy of interweaving various works. Such interweavings serve both to supplement his balancing efforts in one work with new situations in another and to remind us that, as "novel" as those situations are, they should not be seen in isolation from related ones. Actions in one situation generate actions in another, but precisely because the new situation is a novel one, the solution applied to the previous one cannot be simply translated to the other without some form of revision.

For instance, *The Rise of Silas Lapham* is followed by *The Minister's Charge,* peopled with characters from the previous work who are confronted by another triangular love affair, but one that cannot be solved by Sewell's "economy of pain." In fact, it cannot even be solved by Howells's complicated attitude toward divorce that is partially suggested by *Silas Lapham*'s third plot, for, unlike the third plot, Howells's new novel involves promises made before marriage. Thus Sewell and readers are forced to imagine what would have happened if Tom had promised to marry Irene and then realized that he and Penelope were the ones in love. Although I do not have the time to explore all of the complications that Howells's new novel presents, I do want to look at Sewell's most quoted passage from it because it is so important in assessing Howells's sense of responsibility.

V

Toward the conclusion of *The Minister's Charge* Sewell delivers a sermon on "Complicity." He tells his congregation that "no one for good or for evil, for sorrow or joy, for sickness or health, stood apart from his fellows, but each was bound to the highest and lowest by ties that centered in the hand of God" (MC 341). Although the sermon grows out of Sewell's entanglement in the book's triangular love affair, "it struck one of those popular moods of intelligent sympathy when the failure of a large class of underpaid and worthy workers to assert their right to a living wage against a powerful monopoly had sent a thrill of respectful pity through every generous heart in the country; and it was largely supposed that Sewell's sermon referred indirectly to the telegraphers' strike" (MC 341).

Just as critics take Sewell's comments on the novel as Howells's response to the dangers of sentimental fiction, so they take his sermon as Howells's response to the inequities of capitalism. Howells even suggests a connection between the sermon and novel-writing. Listening once again to her husband blame a woman's false sense of self-sacrifice on novel-reading, Sewell's wife notes his propensity to interrelate everything and exclaims, "What in the world are you talking about, David? I should think *you* are a novelist yourself, by the wild way you go on!" (MC 340). Sewell responds, "Yes, yes! Of course it's absurd. But everybody seems tangled up with everybody else. My dear, will you give me a cup of tea? I think I'll go to my writing at once" (MC 340). What he writes is the sermon that he delivers the next day.

But for Howells a sermon and a novel operate differently.[39] At the end of *The Silent Partner* Sip offers a sermon, whose message about entanglement is similar to Sewell's about complicity. But Howells undercuts the authority of his sermon in a way that Phelps does not. For instance, the comment of Sewell's wife suggests that his propensity to make connections has affinities with the sentimental fiction that he deplores. Indeed, earlier Charles Bellingham mocks sentimentalism when, facing the complications of the triangular love affair, he wonders, "What is the reason these things can't be managed as they are in novels?" (MC 333). In "any well-regulated romance" (MC 333), he concludes, all problems would be solved by a plot that brings everything together by coincidence. Even if Howells agrees with much of Sewell's doctrine of complicity, his suggestion that it shares formal characteristics with the fiction that he condemns deprives it of its transcendental perspective. To be sure, it remains an important point of view within the novel, but only one of many in a world in which there is no regulating hand to guarantee that accounts will come out equal, even if, as in the case of Phelps, their balancing has to wait for death. Ironically, the problems posed by the interconnected action of Howells's fiction expose the limits of Sewell's vision of an interconnected world.

Sewell's doctrine of complicity would seem to challenge boundary theorists' efforts to limit people's responsibility. As such, it has affinities with a challenge to the orthodox method of determining blame in tort cases posed by Nicholas St. John Green, a lawyer who influenced pragmatism's revolt against formalism. At the time, courts would take money from A to give damages to B only if it could be proved objectively that A caused injury to B. Borrowing from current science the notion of "chains of causation," the courts felt that they could trace the line of causation from A to B by distinguishing between remote and proximate causes. Only proximate causes counted as evidence. Green, however, argued that what the courts accepted as scientific proof was actually based on two metaphors, that of a chain and that of the distinction between remote and proximate. "To every event," he claimed, "there are certain antecedents. . . . It is not any one of this set of antecedents taken by itself which is the cause. Not one by itself would produce the effect. The true cause is the whole set of antecedents taken together."[40] A generation later legal realists used this logic to argue that singling out one person to pay damages was not a scientific determination of responsibility but judicial policy as to who should pay for a damage that had an interconnected set of causes.

Similarly, Sewell's doctrine of complicity plays havoc with efforts to use science to fix responsibility by demarcating the natural boundaries between different spheres of action. But if Sewell's stress on complicity challenges boundary thought, it also rules out blaming it alone for the inequities that it supposedly legitimates. Sewell, for instance, argues that "if a community was corrupt, if an age was immoral, it was not because of the vicious, but the virtuous who fancied themselves indifferent spectators. It was not the tyrant who oppressed, it was the wickedness that had made him possible" (MC 341). If the "virtuous" are as responsible as the "vicious," how can we untangle the complicated interweavings that "cause" an action in order to assess blame? Indeed, although Sewell counsels humanistic compassion, the logical consequence of his doctrine is that it too is complicit with the market conditions that it implicitly criticizes, a complicity that confirms Thomas Haskell's argument about the rise of a humanitarian sensibility in the context of the market.[41]

It is certainly plausible to argue that Silas's humanistic concern about how the sale of worthless stock would affect people beyond his immediate circle grows out of the same understanding of the market's complexity that helped him to reap financial gain. In both cases Silas must take into consideration the remote consequences of his actions. To be sure, his sympathy seems to be awakened only when he himself becomes a victim of "business" chances. But without a sense of the market and its consequences, he would not have been able to recognize the similarity of his position to that of complete strangers.

Haskell, however, does not simply argue that a market economy calls attention to people's interdependence. Interdependence, after all, is not a new idea. Medieval thinkers also imagined an interconnected world. Instead, Haskell claims that to an unprecedented extent the market rewarded people for thinking of the future consequences of their actions. This future-orientation contributes to a modern sense of temporality that undercuts what Morton White calls a formalist order to the world.[42] Rather than a medieval interconnectedness in which elements of the system turn back on themselves in resemblance to create a self-contained world, modern interdependence is open-ended. In such a world the medieval solution of determining responsibility according to preordained status sanctioned by God will not do. Neither will the formalist solution of fixing responsibilities through scientifically establishing boundaries. That world also suggests problems with those who, like Green, still caught within the framework of scientific formalism, dismiss metaphors as invalid. "Nothing," Green argues metaphorically, "more imperils the correctness of a train of reasoning than the use of metaphor."[43]

To be sure, metaphors are rhetorical rather than scientific or logical, but without an ability to establish formal principles based on scientific or logical foundations they become useful tools. Is, for instance, the distinction between remote and proximate causes inappropriate because it is metaphoric? It is one thing to argue for an interconnected world. It is another to argue that a situation is affected equally by all others. If the distinction between proximate and remote causes cannot be determined scientifically—even logically—we can still attempt, to use one of Howells's favorite phrases, to place various situations in their "true proportion and relation" (SL 197).

Rather than reject a determination of responsibility because it relies on metaphors, Howells is concerned with the justness of metaphors to bring actions into their proper relation and proportion. Thus, for him, the assessment of responsibility remains a formal question, and his responsibility as a novelist is the formal one of bringing different spheres of human action into proportionate relation to try to reveal the logics of various situations which reliance on transcendental principles would only obscure. Those logics determine who is to blame in an interconnected world in which otherwise we all seem complicit. But because in a temporal world no situation remains constant, Howells's formal solution challenges the premises of formalism by suggesting the need for constant revision of forms. Limited by his temporal perspective, Howells cannot reveal the logic of each situation in supernal clarity. What he can do is sharpen our focus enough to put us in a position in which we have a chance to risk determining the responsibilities of his various characters.

Of course, one formal demand of a novel (and a chapter) is that it must end. To turn to Sewell's doctrine of complicity in *Silas Lapham*'s sequel is to risk using it as an excuse to avoid the difficult task of judging how well Howells solves the problem of ending a book that calls out for endless revision. It is time, therefore, to turn to the conclusion of *Silas Lapham*.

VI

At the end of his novel Howells does not nostalgically return us to a precapitalist, agrarian economy founded on a set of natural values.[44] Not disguised sermons, his novels were condemned by some for not offering models of virtuous action. Howells's failure to prescribe a set code of behavior is not, however, a sign of immorality. It is instead his way of showing that character develops only when tested by experience in a world without fixed values. What Howells does try to imagine are revised institutional structures that allow individuals and the economy better chances to develop responsibly, without stifling, paternalistic control.

One example is the institution of marriage. Andrew Delbanco has argued that a model marriage in Howells "was always, in its rock-bottom meaning, a barricade against the liberated self."[45] On the contrary, as we have seen, Howells advocates neither unrestrained self-assertion in marriage nor rigid institutional restraints on the self. For instance, far from being a barricade against a liberated self, Tom and Penelope's marriage results from acts of self-assertion: Tom's against the wishes of his family; Penelope's against a sentimental code of self-sacrifice. To be sure, their marriage will not work if confronted with unbridled egotism. At the same time, it will work in Howells's eyes only if it allows for further individual growth. Such growth will be unlikely under an inflexible code of behavior, and marriage needs to be imagined more flexibly to allow the development of an immanent logic growing out of the couple's particular mode of relating to one another. Paradoxically, then, Tom and Penelope's marriage is a "model" precisely because its outcome is uncertain.

Although marriage, as Howells imagines it, is subject to the unaccountable, it does not necessarily lead to economic development, which for him is necessary if more people are to have the possibility for individual growth. Nonetheless, Tom and Penelope's marriage is linked to another corporate structure that promises to serve that function. Tom supports his family by going to work for the West Virginia company whose competition contributed to Silas's economic ruin. According to his wife, Silas broke up his partnership with Rogers because he was unwilling "to let anybody else share in [the] blessings" (SL 47) of his paint. That unwillingness illustrates what for many in Howells's day was the problem with an economy dominated by large, individually owned businesses. Their alternative was not limited partnerships, like the one Silas had with Rogers. It was large, jointly owned corporations uniting the interests of a diverse society. For instance, Harvard's President Charles W. Eliot called "incorporation with limited liability . . . the greatest business invention of the nineteenth century," because it responded to the conflict between "collectivism" and "individualism" by providing for structures that "are great diffusers of property among the frugal people of the country."[46] Other reformers, including Christian socialists, like Bellamy, saw corporations as an important step toward a collective community.

Pease claims that the "business corporation that tacitly resulted from Penelope's marriage to Tom Corey" is "Lapham and Son," which is "structured like Lapham's ideal for the family, combining the commercial interests of a growing enterprise with the trustworthy self-reliance of its founder."[47] In fact, Corey works for the Kanawaha Falls Company that started as a family-owned company but is now a large corporation. Presenting a possibility for economic growth without the individualist abuses of laissez-faire capitalism, it even incorporates Lapham's "works," allowing Silas to contribute to its success by manufacturing the Persis Brand of paint whose quality it cannot match but can help market. By allowing his decaying company to be incorporated by the new one, Silas not only has his debts absorbed, he gains "an interest in the vaster enterprise of the younger men, which he had once vainly hoped to grasp all in his own hand" (SL 361).

Silas's vain hope should be read as a prideful as well as an empty hope. He had vainly hoped to control more wealth than any individual should. In contrast, the Kanawaha Falls Company unites the diverse interests (and strengths) of the Corey and Lapham families—and not only by hiring Tom. In *The Minister's Charge* we learn that by taking the risk to invest in the company's stock, Bromfield Corey has restored his family's wealth. (So much for a Howells who fears all forms of speculation in the stock market.)

Through the Kanawaha Falls Company's collectivism Howells imagines how to have it both ways. The dynamics of an unbalanced economy organized along corporate lines seem to provide for individual development while helping to balance competing social interests. Nonetheless, even though this corporation makes possible the increased well-being of more individuals, there is no guarantee that all will do so. In fact, what seems to be Howells's utopian corporate vision contains its own potential for unbalancing. First of all, as Silas's speculation in stocks indicates, the hazards associated with economic development increase, if anything. Second, as the telegrapher's strike alluded to in *The Minister's Charge* indicates, monopolistic corporations can deny "worthy workers" their "right to a living wage" (MC 341). Like the G. L. & P. Railroad, which had rendered Silas's stock in midwestern mills worthless, corporate monopolies can stifle growth.

A crucial difference between the West Virginia corporation and monopolies is that the former opens markets while the latter close them. Opening of markets is important for Howells because it increases opportunities to take advantage of chance. In contrast, the monopolistic closing of markets creates a sense of tragic inevitability in which human beings lose the opportunity to act freely. Silas, for instance, is left with no choice in his battle with the railroad. But his lack of choice does not mean that he is simply a victim of economic law. If the closing of markets eliminates possibilities for responsible human action, for Howells human action is often responsible for the opening or closing of markets. The position in which Silas is placed by the railroad is the same in which he places Rogers when he forces him out of partnership. Both actions may seem to be no more than taking advantage of a "business chance," but, as we saw in the case of Silas, an appeal to a transcendental "logic of the market" is a way to deny responsibility for one's actions.

The fact that Silas's action is repeated by the railroad indicates that for Howells the rise of corporations may complicate, but does not basically alter, questions of responsible human agency.[48]

As I have stressed from the start, Howells's portrayal of different logics growing out of different situations undercuts an economic determinism. Nonetheless, the seepage of the business plot into all areas of the novel indicates that economic structures do affect the possibilities of action in other spheres as well as vice versa. Therefore, for Howells some economic structures help to open up possibilities for responsible human action while others tend to close them off. At the same time, responsible action within the economic sphere cannot be totally divorced from questions of responsible action in other spheres. Indeed, the West Virginia company's opening of markets repeats—with a difference—Howells's efforts to make visible the realistic possibilities for human action that otherwise might seem determined by transcendental forces such as The Market or Fate.

Nonetheless, readers of the late twentieth century might well ask whether Howells's narration of open-ended development is still a responsible one. First of all, to what extent does it depend on a human-centered exploitation of the environment summarized by Silas's "I say the landscape was made for man, and not man for the landscape" (SL 15)? Second, and related, to what extent does it rely on a discredited pattern of American exceptionalism? Hegel argued that the safety valve of the frontier protected the United States from the contradictions of European history.[49] Attempts to balance social interests might always generate something that cannot be accounted for, but so long as the United States possessed a space to accommodate the unaccountable, it could develop without Europe's tragic necessity to resolve contradictions through dialectical confrontation. Rather than follow the exclusive logic of winners and losers, it could provide the best possible, if never perfect, social balance by encouraging the expansion of an unbalanced economy according to a logic of inclusion. With Frederick Jackson Turner about to announce his "frontier thesis," however, the narrative of American history seemed condemned to lose its exceptional character. Even so, Howells's ending suggests that a developmental space remains possible through the opening of foreign markets. Tom's assignment for the West Virginia company is, after all, to open markets in Mexico and Central America.[50]

To members of an interconnected global economy with the limited resources of "Spaceship Earth," the need to maintain a developmental narrative through expansion into third-world markets may seem irresponsibly to open up possibilities for individual growth in developed countries while closing them off for others. Perhaps it is no accident, then, that in our postmodern age developmental narratives and their link to Howells's sense of human agency have come under attack as modernity's belief in a *munda novas* becomes less imaginable. But it is not at all clear that such attacks can fully account for all of the possible ways of reenvisioning Howells's narrative. Indeed, the strikingly similar concerns that he shares with the efforts of Amartya Sen and Martha Nussbaum to formulate a "developmental ethics" for the global distribution of resources raise the question of whether it is possible at this time to imagine a just new world order without retaining at least some aspects of Howells's account of human action within an economy of the unaccountable.[51] If it would be against the thrust of my argument to claim that the "logic" of *The Rise of Silas Lapham* perfectly fits our present situation, it is not inconsistent to claim that its challenge for readers to face the hazards of responsible development remains.

Howells's detractors too often miss his complicated fictional strategies that transfer to readers the task of responsibly judging what constitutes responsible action. One strategy is his self-conscious manipulation of point of view that undermines any illusion of a transcendental perspective that he might have created. If Flaubert begins *Madame Bovary* with a first-person narrator who shortly gives way to third-person omniscience, Howells begins with a third-person narrative only to introduce a first-person narrator late in his novel. One function of Howells's use of a first-person narrator is to displace the authority of any one character—including Sewell—to serve as Howells's spokesperson. Certainly the narrative "I" has more authority than any character. Nonetheless, the "I's" authority is itself limited. Indeed, in his few intrusions the narrator calls attention to his inability to penetrate the interior of characters to report their feelings and intentions (SL 359, 360, 362). Thus, readers are forced, as in Holmes's theory of the law, to make judgments based on the results of actions, not motives. Rather than link an omniscient perspective to God, Howells speaks of a "wicked omniscience in Rogers" (SL 321), whose first name, Milton, recalls *Paradise Lost* and Satan's effort to usurp God's role.[52]

In undermining his narrative omniscience, Howells invites readers to enter a contingent world of chance, in which determination of responsibility is risky business because it can never be made with certainty. For Howells the realm of human agency is precisely this realm in which people, subject to chance, nonetheless, risk taking advantage of it. Such a vision of agency might seem to bring us back to the period's laissez-faire theorists. They too wanted an unregulated economy in which everyone can take advantage of the economic chance world in which we live. Indeed, to identify situations in which people take advantage of chance as those in which human agency is possible does not solve the problem of *responsible* human action. Taking advantage of chance can, as in the case of Silas's exploitation of a "business chance" with Rogers, be an act of selfishness, or it can, as in the case of Penelope and Tom, be a legitimate assertion of self.[53]

Nonetheless, Howells suggests a form of moral accountability different from that of boundary thinkers, with whom, otherwise, he has much in common. That difference has to do with his positionality within history. Laissez-faire thinkers claim to place us in an economic world in which everyone has an equal opportunity to take advantage of chance. But their vision depends on imagining an originary moment outside of history, in which contracting parties enter exchanges with equal standing. Starting instead with the imbalances that he confronts within history, Howells presents a different version of our economic chance world.

The ideal vision of equitable capitalist growth implies that balanced agreements result in mutual profit for all contracting parties. Confronted with the reality of the situations in which one person profits at another's expense, laissez-faire apologists argued that such situations were the natural outcome of economic laws. In contrast, Howells implies that more often than not, profits gained from taking advantage of such business chances result from historically conditioned imbalances among contracting parties. If boundary ideologists assumed that contracting partners have equal standing, Howells's attention to status reminds us that the mere assertion of free will is not enough to put oneself on an equal footing with another. Howells does not, however, assume that an equitable society will result if we simply correct social and economic imbalances. Instead, he offers the disconcerting warning that frequently our balancing efforts, as important as they are, generate yet other imbalances. Subject to, if not completely determined by, a chance that they cannot control, human beings will never balance their accounts within history, although a progressive history is in part generated by attempts to do so.

Because people never perfectly balance their moral accounts, Howells does not offer models of definitively moral behavior. We can never be certain if noble actions result from moral character or chance. Did Jim Millon receive a bullet aimed at Silas because he happened to be standing where he was, or did he self-consciously position himself to save his friend? Did Silas refuse to sell worthless stock back to Rogers because he was "standing firm for right and justice" (SL 332) or because by chance the railroad's offer for the mills came in the next morning's mail?[54] It is no accident that both of these actions concern metaphors of standing, since Howells suggests that responsible action is determined neither solely by one's predetermined standing in society—as in a status-oriented culture—nor by what others think of one's actions—as in a totally commodified culture—but by a combination of where one is placed at birth, where one places oneself in life, and what others think of that placement. What readers think of characters' actions does not totally determine whether or not their actions are responsible, but readers' judgments do play an important part in determining the moral economy of the world Howells presents, a moral economy always subject to revision precisely because our judgments, as important as they are, will never provide a perfectly balanced account of all of the book's actions.

CHAPTER 6

Charles W. Chesnutt: Race and the Re-negotiation of the Federal Contract

I

Attempting a formal balance of diverse interests, Howells's realism demands continual revision because it assumes a world subject to historical change. But the need for revision does not stop with Howells. Our assessment of his formal solutions also requires revision as the importance we grant to the interests that he represents changes over time. An obvious example is *An Imperative Duty* (1892), in which race complicates the plot involving a woman who almost refuses to marry a man she loves because of a false sense of self-sacrifice.[1] Rhoda Aldgate is a beautiful orphan, whose African ancestry has been concealed by her guardian aunt. Facing a bad conscience as her niece contemplates marrying a minister, the aunt tells Rhoda about her mixed blood and promptly dies from an accidental overdose of drugs designed to calm her after the nerve-wracking scene. Dr. Olney, who had known the two in Italy, has, in confidence, learned the secret while treating the aunt and finds himself falling in love with Rhoda. Rhoda refuses to go on with her planned marriage, not only because of her changed sense of identity but, more important, because she realizes that she does not love the minister. When, however, she begins to awaken to her attraction to the doctor, her recently revealed heritage seems to rule out marriage. Instead, she feels that it is her duty to find her unknown black family "to help them and acknowledge them . . . [to] try to educate them and elevate them; give my life to them" (ID 96). Olney responds with logic similar to that generated by the love plot in *Silas Lapham*.

He tells Rhoda that she would have a duty to her relatives "if [she] had voluntarily chosen [her] part with them—if [she] had ever *consented* to be of their kind," but since she has not, "there is no more specific obligation upon [her] to give [her] life to their elevation than there is upon [him]" (ID 96). Reverting to an arithmetic calculation of responsibility, he jokingly asks that she renounce her puritan heritage of "dutiolatry" (ID 89). "No, if you must give your life to the improvement of any particular race, give it to mine. Begin with *me*. You won't find me unreasonable. All that I shall ask of you are the fifteen-sixteenths or so of you that belong to my race by heredity; and I will cheerfully consent to your giving our colored connections their one-sixteenth" (ID 96–97). Married after an exchange of promises—he not to reveal her secret; she to believe that he would not be ashamed to do so—they return to Italy, where Rhoda passes as a dark beauty.

Howells's story illustrates how much our assessment of realism is subject to a revision in attitudes between a work's past moment of production to its present moment of reception. To some of today's readers, by stressing personal gain over racial loyalty, Howells fails in his responsibility to paint "human feelings in their true proportion and relation" (SL 197). Indeed, from their perspective, Howells's devaluation of obligations owed to blacks in post-Reconstruction society limits his vision. A better solution for such readers is found in Francis E. W. Harper's *Iola Leroy* (1892), when a mulatto who can pass for white makes the choice that Rhoda rejects, and devotes her life to the advancement of blacks. But even though Harper's solution might seem more responsible to some today, we should not ignore how Howells's solution reveals his sense of realism's relation to the genre of tragedy.

Rhoda believes that her secret lineage locks her into tragedy. Facing a course of action determined by a racial heritage over which she has no control, she sees no possibility of self-assertion. Whereas Howells does not deny the existence of situations of life and death that are completely out of human control, he insists on using his fiction to help us to recognize chances for human action and development that would otherwise seem tragically and fatally closed off. For instance, in a review he writes that the "higher function" of the novel is "to teach that men are somehow masters of their fate."[2] Thus the narrator mocks Rhoda's tragic reaction with: "As tragedy the whole affair had fallen to ruin. It could be reconstructed, if at all, only upon an octave much below the operatic pitch. It must be treated in no lurid twilight gloom, but in plain, simple, matter-of-fact noonday" (ID 94). As in *The Rise of Silas*

Lapham, Howells offers realism as an antidote to moralistic submissions to "fate."

The aunt is a special target of Howells's attack. She is one of those people "to whom life, in spite of all experience, remains a sealed book, and who are always trying to unlock its mysteries with the keys furnished them by fiction. They judge the world by the novels they have read, and their acquaintance in the flesh by characters in stories, instead of judging these by the real people they have met, and more or less lived with" (ID 24). This tendency makes her not only a poor reader of good literature, but also a potentially dangerous character. For Olney such a woman "would be capable of an atrocious cruelty in speaking or acting the truth, and would consider herself an exemplary person for having done her duty at any cost of suffering to herself and others" (ID 24). Olney unwittingly links her narrow moralism to contemporary views of the color line when he thinks that "the right affected her as a body of positive color, sharply distinguished from wrong, and not shading into and out of it by gradations of tint, as we find it doing in reality" (ID 24). For Howells questions of right and wrong are no more simple questions of black and white than are questions of race in a country where there is a history of racial intermixture. Similarly, the "race question" has no clear-cut and predetermined answers.[3]

If *An Imperative Duty* is Howells's attempt to revise the plot of the tragic mulatto, his revision is in turn revised eight years later by the African-American novelist and lawyer Charles W. Chesnutt. In *The House Behind the Cedars* (1900), Chesnutt self-consciously responds to Howells by insisting on the tragic outcome of a beautiful mulatto's attempt to marry a white man. Molly Walden, a free person of color who mixes mostly European with African and a bit of Indian blood, has two children by her rich, white lover in Patesville, North Carolina. John, who inherits "his father's patrician features and his mother's Indian hair" (HBC 160), leaves Patesville as a young man, passes as white, manages a plantation in South Carolina during the Civil War, and marries the orphaned daughter of its owner, who bears him a son before dying herself. Rich and admitted to the bar, John, in a moment of "sentimental weakness" (HBC 28), returns home for the first time and convinces Rena, his younger sister, to live with him and care for his son. Attracting attention at a medieval tournament inspired by Walter Scott, the beautiful "Rowena Warwick" wins the heart of her brother's trusted friend, George Tryon. Before the two can marry, however, Rena, concerned about her mother's health, sneaks off for a short visit home. As a result of crossed letters and coincidence, Tryon comes to Patesville on business and discovers the secret of his fiancee's identity. Tryon does not betray John by publicizing his black blood, but he does break with Rena, who, as a school teacher, now devotes herself to the education of black children. Tryon plans to marry Blanche Leary, his mother's favorite, but when by chance he sees Rena again his love rekindles, and he inwardly vows to marry her. But the vow comes too late. Rena has been struck ill by the stress and dies at her mother's house, having been brought home by Frank, the loyal black neighbor, who has consistently and unselfishly watched over and loved her.

Part of Chesnutt's response to Howells is to give Olney's logic to John. Commending that logic, William L. Andrews argues that "John Walden is a singular figure in the race literature of post–Civil War America," because "he is perhaps the first character in American fiction who, having been raised 'black,' decides on his own to pass for white and constructs a legal and moral justification for doing so." According to Andrews, when John disappears, the novel "retreats with its still largely unrealized heroine into the sentimental byways of the novel of seduction."[4]

If Andrews is right about the novel's use of sentimentality, he fails to note how it supplements John's pragmatic logic. John's point of view gets human feelings out of proportion. As the narrator says of John, "Men who have elected to govern their lives by principles of abstract right and reason, which happen, perhaps, to be at variance with what society considers equally right and reasonable, should, for fear of complications, be careful about descending from the lofty heights of logic to the common level of impulse and affection" (HBC 28–29).

As contrived as it is, the melodramatic plot of *The House Behind the Cedars* responds to Howells's vision in *An Imperative Duty* by employing the Howellsian strategy of showing how difficult it is to translate the logic of one situation to a comparable, if somewhat different, one. But in this case Chesnutt outdoes his model. Not one of Howells's best works, *An Imperative Duty* falls short in part because it employs the logic of the "economy of pain" that helps to solve the dilemma of the love plot in *The Rise of Silas Lapham,* without complicating that logic by bringing it into contact with something like the business plot in Howells's earlier work. *The House Behind the Cedars* provides such complication by providing not one but two stories of passing, one of

John and one of Rena. Because what works for John does not work for Rena, these two stories complement one another in an almost Howellsian manner. But complications alone do not make a work realistic.

Biographically Howells may have believed in a moral order to the world, but in his best works he refuses to adopt a transcendental perspective that provides a clear standard of judgment. In contrast, Chesnutt not only retains an eighteenth-century vision of a morally principled world in which equitable standards are knowable through reason, he writes his fiction with the didactic purpose of helping his readers see those standards. One symptom of their differences is the third plot of *Silas Lapham,* which generates related but "novel" events that cannot be accounted for by an overarching logic governing all situations. In *House Behind the Cedars* we get the complications of two plots, but in the end both can be judged by the same equitable principle. Indeed, Howells and Chesnutt present different views of principles in their works.

In *A Hazard of New Fortunes* Howells has the business manager of a literary journal contrast principles and convictions. But as the book's dramatic action brings various people's principles into conflict, they become harder and harder to distinguish from convictions. Similarly, in *The Marrow of Tradition* Chesnutt distinguishes principles from prejudice when a Southerner jeopardizes the success of an operation by refusing to allow a black doctor to participate. Evoking his professional code of ethics, the Northern doctor in charge protests. "It is a matter of principle," he proclaims, "which ought not give way to a mere prejudice" (MT 71). As in Howells, the distinction is called into question when another doctor compares the Southerner's stand with the Northern doctor's. The Southerner, he explains, also "has certain principles,—call them prejudices, if you like—certain inflexible rules of conduct by which he regulates his life. One of these, which he shares with all of us in some degree, forbids the recognition of the negro as a social equal" (MT 71). But if Chesnutt points to a structural similarity in how principles and prejudices can regulate people's conduct, he ultimately needs to differentiate between the two.

We can get a sense of how this difference affects Howells's and Chesnutt's presentations of their fictional worlds by comparing two characters sometimes taken as authorial spokesmen: Howells's Reverend Sewell and Chesnutt's Judge Archibald Straight. If Sewell's advocacy of an "economy of pain" is often taken as Howells's own, Howells places it in a dramatic context that questions its universal application.

Indeed, in his next novel, Howells tests Sewell's ideas in circumstances that place the minister in an ironic light. In contrast, Chesnutt's Judge Straight maintains an equitable point of view. From the bench he "dispensed justice tempered with mercy" (HBC 163), going so far as to sentence "a man to be hanged for the murder of his own slave" (HBC 163–64). Although Chesnutt does not mention it, this decision results from Straight's appeal to equity, since it defies the precedent established in *State v. Mann* (1829), a case used to structure Harriet Beecher Stowe's *Dred: A Tale of the Great Dismal Swamp* and cited by Stowe as proof of the horror of slavery in *A Key to Uncle Tom's Cabin*. In it North Carolina's Judge Thomas Ruffin ruled that because "the power of the master must be absolute to render the submission of the slave perfect,"[5] an owner has the right to kill his slave. Straight's ability to overrule the law by an appeal to an equitable sense of justice shows the extent to which Chesnutt clings to a republican vision of a moral universe.

Although Howells's seeming spokesman is a man of God, Howells does not grant him a transcendental perspective. In contrast, Straight is an ideal republican lawyer, a southern version of the type that Howells kills off in *A Modern Instance*. Straight, however, is not naive. He knows that the abolition of slavery is not enough to ensure equality for people of color. Thus, although he feels that "in equity [John] would seem to be entitled to his chance in life" (HBC 35), he worries that John will be denied it. Howells does not abandon the effort to imagine a more equitable balance to social relations, but tries not to impose that balance from a transcendental perspective. In *An Imperative Duty* the result is a pragmatic solution with which he tries to avoid unnecessary tragedy. In contrast, Chesnutt presents a tragedy while measuring the unjust treatment of blacks by a universal standard of equity.

In a review Howells notes this difference when he argues that Chesnutt is not "so inartistic as to play the advocate; . . . but while he recognizes pretty well all the facts in the case, he is too clearly of a judgment that is made up."[6] Chesnutt's clear sense of judgment makes his fiction more didactic and less open than Howells's realism at its best. But, as Howells himself acknowledges in the same review, when the issue is race it is hard to fault Chesnutt on his principled stand. As the title of George Washington Cable's famous "The Freedman's Case in Equity" indicates, in the post-Reconstruction era those concerned about achieving justice for a group denied equal representation had few options other than an appeal to equity.[7] In this chapter I want to explore how Chesnutt's fiction exposes the failure of contract—especially the newly negotiated "contract" between North and South—to generate an equitable situation for people of color. At the same time, I want to draw attention to how Chesnutt's embodiment in fictional form of his belief in a " 'power that works for righteousness,' and that leads men to do justice to one another," distinguishes his work from that of the realists.[8]

Chesnutt's differences from the realists do not, however, cause him to present a morally simplistic world. On the contrary, he is much more attuned to racial complications than Howells. For instance, on the highly charged issue of whether it is right or wrong for a person with African blood to pass as white, Chesnutt seems to adopt a stance of moral relativism. As the narrator notes, commenting on the dilemma, "It was not the first time, nor the last, that right or wrong had been a matter of point of view" (HBC 82). Andrews uses this statement to link Chesnutt to the realists and their challenge to clear-cut moral standards.[9] But for Chesnutt the question of passing is morally uncertain precisely because the United States has failed to live up to its promise to provide equity for its black citizens. People designated white are not confronted with the moral dilemma of passing, because they have nothing to gain by claiming to be black. In contrast, for someone designated black there is a moral dilemma, because to remain black means being denied deserved opportunity, while to pass as white means the loss of connection to family and kin. Because the country has not reached the equitable state in which race is irrelevant, the proper course of action is unclear and Chesnutt has to evoke the equitable solution of judging each decision on a case-by-case basis. Chesnutt's moral uncertainty on specific issues, in other words, grows out of his belief that "the laws of nature are higher and more potent than merely human institutions, and upon anything like a fair field are likely to win in the long run" (HBC 148). Moral dilemmas arise—as today's debates over affirmative action indicate—when a fair field does not exist.

If part of the complexity of Chesnutt's fiction results from a lack of racial equality that creates moral dilemmas demanding equitable consideration, another part of its complexity involves the way in which it complicates standard notions about what constitutes an appeal to equity. Appeals to equity often rely on sentiment, whereas those to law usually rely on logic. But in Chesnutt's world what seems an equitable solution results from John's cool logic, while his sister's reliance on sentiment reinforces the absence of an equitable situation. This complication indicates that for Chesnutt the standard opposition between reason and sentiment does not work. But before we see why, we need to compare the two stories of passing.

II

Rena's story functions by pitting the power of love against the prejudices of custom. Guided by novels that she has read, Rena hopes that love will conquer all, "that neither life nor death, nor creed nor caste, could stay his triumphant course" (HBC 75). Sure enough, in Tryon's case class would have been no barrier to their marriage. "Had her people been simply poor and of low estate, he would have brushed aside mere worldly considerations, and would have bravely sacrificed convention for love" (HBC 146). Race, however, is a different matter. Even though Tryon's love eventually overcomes his prejudice, it does so too late. Love alone, it seems, is not capable of overcoming racial prejudice.

John must also overcome prejudiced custom. But whereas Rena relies on love, he relies on reason. The result is, for the most part, more successful. That success is in part due to reason's power to expose the arbitrary determination of race by custom. As a boy, John, wanting to be a lawyer, visits the law offices of Judge Straight, a friend of his now deceased father. When the Judge finds out the boy's ancestry he tells him that he cannot fulfill his ambition. When John insists that he is white, the Judge responds that appearance doesn't matter because "one drop of black blood makes the whole man black" (HBC 170). To John's question, "Why shouldn't it be the other way, if the white blood is so superior?" the Judge answers, "Because it is more convenient as it is—and more profitable" (HBC 170). Nonetheless, in memory of an old friend, the Judge reconsiders.

Knowing that the determination of race is so arbitrary that it varies from state to state, he looks up the South Carolina law declaring that "mulatto . . . is not invariably applicable to every admixture of African blood with the European, nor is one having all the features of a white to be ranked with the degraded class designated by the laws of this State as persons of color, because of some remote taint of the negro race. Juries would probably be justified in holding a person to be white in whom the admixture of African blood did not exceed one eighth. And even where color or feature are doubtful, it is a question for the jury to decide by reputation, by reception into society, and by their exercise of the privileges of the white man, as well as by admixture of blood" (HBC 171–72). According to this law, the Judge agrees that "away from Patesville" John need not be black. Like Howells's Rhoda, John has the "unusual privilege" of "choosing between two races" (HBC 172). To help him choose, the Judge hires John as his office boy and lets him read his law books to prepare him for a legal career.

Supported by an understanding of existing law, John makes a logical choice and succeeds as a white lawyer. Nonetheless, when the Judge sees him on his secret visit ten years later, he warns him not to stay long. "The people of a small town are inquisitive about strangers, and some of them have long memories. I remember we went over the law, which was in your favor; but custom is stronger than law—in these matters custom *is* law" (HBC 34). When John leaves, Judge Straight muses on custom's power. "Right and wrong . . . must be eternal verities, but our standards for measuring them vary with our latitude and our epoch. We make our customs lightly; once made, like our sins, they grip us in bands of steel; we become the creatures of our creations" (HBC 35).[10] Worried about John, he goes on: "In equity he would seem to be entitled to his chance in life; it might have been wiser, though, for him to seek it farther afield than South Carolina" (HBC 35).

Despite the Judge's concern, John, unlike his sister, seems to have overcome the prejudices of custom by adhering to a strict logic derived from principles of higher law. How he should act was, for him, "in the main a matter of argument of self-conviction. Once persuaded that he had certain rights, or ought to have them, by virtue of the laws of nature, in defiance of the customs of mankind, he had promptly sought to enjoy them. This he had been able to do by simply concealing his antecedents and making the most of his opportunities, with no troublesome qualms of conscience" (HBC 78). What seems to deprive Rena of her equitable chance in life is precisely the troublesome qualms of conscience that her brother's logic has subdued. For instance, she feels that it is her duty to tell Tryon her "secret" before marrying him. John's counterargument sounds as if it were lifted from a Howells novel.

Chiding Rena for taking "too tragic a view of life," he insists that marriage has to do with only the immediately contracting parties. "Marriage is a reciprocal arrangement, by which the contracting parties give love for love, care for keeping, faith for faith. It is a matter of the future, not of the past. . . . We are under no moral obligation . . . to bring out . . . the dusty record of our ancestry. . . . George Tryon loves you for yourself alone; it is not your ancestors that he seeks to marry" (HBC 79). Evoking the logic of an economy of pain, John points out that for Rena to reveal her ancestry would cause unnecessary suffering for George, himself, and his son. What seems to her a noble act would, in fact, be a "bit selfish" (HBC 82), an effort to secure her "own peace of mind" (HBC 82). Convinced that to keep silent is an act of "self-sacrifice" (HBC 82), Rena agrees to her brother's plan. As logical as it is, however, the plan fails. Its failure points to the flaws in John's—and by extension Howells's—logical solution to the dilemma of passing.

The novel of passing was of special interest in an age in which one's duties and responsibilities to others were supposedly determined by contract rather than status, because contract tested people's resolve to accept people for who they were, in the present, without consideration of birth. For instance, Tryon is so convinced of Rena's value that, to overcome his mother's prejudice in favor of Blanche Leary, he plans to present to her Rena herself as his only "argument" (HBC 82). He believes, as Mrs. Burrage did of Verena in *The Bostonians,* that Rena can create her own value. Of course, the belief that Rena's presence alone without any other form of persuasion can overcome prejudice is naive, as indicated by Tryon's own inability to overcome *his* prejudice upon learning of her ancestry. Indeed, despite his protestations to the contrary, Tryon does not fully believe that Rena's ancestry plays no part in her present value. His mistake is to believe that her physical presence makes her value self-evident. Tryon claims not to worry about Rena's family because he believes that "she carries the stamp of her descent upon her face and in her heart" (HBC 84).

If there is such a stamp of descent in terms of race, the novel of passing forces us to realize that it is not necessarily visible.[11] As a result, it seems that either where people come from is more important than who they are, or what people are cannot be defined by their physical presence alone, because where they come from helps to determine who they are. In the first case, we are confronted with a prejudiced society, in the second, one in which status remains important. There is, however, a third possibility. For both Olney and John, people's identities are indeed influenced by where they come from, but their descent should not influence how they are accepted by others. So long as racial prejudice exists, people have every right to conceal their racial descent.

But this logic contradicts itself by ruling out the possibility that someone of mixed blood can ever be accepted for who he or she is, which is not only a self-contained person, but a person with an intricate network of relations. To fulfill one's potential for success means by definition the loss of part of one's self, while to embrace one's partial racial heritage is to deny oneself the success that one deserves. Rena's tragedy results from her inability to sever ties with those who help to define her. As the narrator notes, "Our lives are so bound up with those of fellow men that the slightest departure from the beaten path involves a multiplicity of small adjustments" (HBC 74). Rena easily adjusts "her speech, her manners, and in a measure her modes of thought" (HBC 74). But "when this readjustment [goes] beyond mere externals and concerned the vital issues of life, . . . tragic possibilities" develop (HBC 74). In *An Imperative Duty* Olney mocks Rhoda's tendency to give in to such possibilities. Chesnutt lets us see that Olney's mockery is justified only because Howells creates special circumstances for his heroine.

Olney can dismiss Rhoda's desire to help blacks as sentimental "dutiolatry" because she was raised white and had no contact with the black family she dreams of elevating. Her racial identity is determined solely by blood. In contrast, Rena's is determined by close ties to the black community and a loving relation with her mulatto mother. It is no accident that Rena's identity is revealed to Tryon on a visit to her mother. In addition, Howells concocts a special relation between Rhoda and her possible husband. By manipulating the plot so that Olney already knows Rhoda's "secret," Howells relieves Rhoda of Rena's dilemma of whether or not to conceal her identity from her husband-to-be. As much as John's logic resembles Olney's, it is not certain that Howells's doctor would agree with Chesnutt's lawyer when the lawyer encourages his sister to withhold information from her husband-to-be with: "What a poor soul it is that has not some secret chamber, sacred to itself; where one can file away the things that others have no right to know, as well as things that one himself would fain forget" (HBC 79).

By having John advocate concealment, Chesnutt exposes the most obvious contradiction in both his and Olney's logic. Both see themselves as representatives of enlightened reason against prejudiced custom, but on the issue of race their reasoning leads them to champion concealment not revelation. Enlightened reason might be a force against prejudiced custom, but prejudice—at least in terms of race—has its revenge by forcing reason to advocate repression. This paradox leads us to the way in which Chesnutt complicates the opposition between reason and sentiment.

John's success in passing seems to come from his use of reason to cut off the ties of sentiment that would bind him to past attachments. In contrast, Rena's failure seems due to her inability to sever the sentimental ties that bind. But this contrast doesn't quite work. John may owe his success to reason, but, as we have seen, that success begins with a "moment of sentimental weakness" (HBC 118) on the part of Judge Straight when he helps John because of "quixotic loyalty to the memory of an old friend" (HBC 118–19). And just in case that action tempts us to believe that it is really sentiment rather than reason that is responsible for John's success, Chesnutt reminds us that Judge Straight's sentiment is itself guided by a reasoned judgment that allows him to transcend the prejudices held by most Southerners on issues of race. Furthermore, although Chesnutt makes clear that John's decision to conceal his past is dictated by a reasoned logic that cuts its ties with sentiment, his sister's decision to conceal her identity from Tryon is dictated by sentimental ties to her brother and his son. Her secret, she realizes, is "not hers alone" (HBC 76). To reveal her racial identity is necessarily to reveal that of her blood relatives. In one case logic dictates concealment, in the other sentiment does.

Finally, whereas John seems the one who follows an Olneylike logic, while Rena adopts Rhoda's sentimental position regarding duty to one's black relatives, Rena's own sentimental love for Tryon eventually leads her to adopt Olney's solution, even if it is too late. After her lover has spurned her, she laments to her brother, " 'The law would have let him marry me. I seemed as white as he did. He might have gone anywhere with me, and no one would have stared at us curiously; no one need have known. The world is wide—there must be some place where a man could live happily with the woman he loved' " (HBC 180). Rena may very well have moved to Italy with Tryon, if he had married her.

Although Chesnutt uses John and Rena to present two different stories of passing, by presenting the stories of a brother and a sister he necessarily links them. We could even say that Rena's tragedy results from her brother's sentimental link to her. If he had not wanted to share his good fortune by having her rise with him, she would have been spared her tragic fate.

The interaction between the two plots forces us to reconsider our tendency to think that John succeeds and Rena fails. Whereas John clearly avoids Rena's fate, there is, nonetheless, a tragic component in his success because he achieves it at the price of isolating himself from his loved ones. As a result, rather than conclude that Chesnutt allows John to succeed and condemns Rena to tragedy, we should say that the tragic effect of his novel comes from their combination. There are, Chesnutt confirms, isolated stories of people of color who pass and achieve their deserved success, as in his subplot or Howells's novel. The tragedy is, however, that such success must remain isolated. John's "succeeds" only by cutting himself off from those he loves and relations that help define who he is.[12]

Once again a comparison with Howells is useful. In *The Rise of Silas Lapham* Howells also stresses the interconnectedness of his various plots, but by offering an open-ended narrative economy rather than a closed one he is able to avoid a tragic ending and present an ongoing possibility of development. In *An Imperative Duty* he once again avoids a tragic ending by allowing his newly married couple the space to relocate in Italy. That relocation is, however, Howells's implicit acknowledgment that a solution for Olney and Rhoda does not exist in their home country. The tragic ending in *The House Behind the Cedars* is in part due to Chesnutt's effort to seek a solution within the United States. One result is a difference in the representativeness of the action in the two works, a difference that affects their modes of presentation.

Chesnutt uses the novel of passing as an allegory for the possibility of acknowledged racial intermixture in the United States. In contrast, for Howells, Olney's and Rhoda's dilemma is, quite literally, a novel one. Any solution that it offers is confined to their specific situation. To read it allegorically—as Howells's suggestion that a solution to the race problem in America is that people of color should escape to Italy— would be to misread it. In fact, its inability to find a solution within the United States suggests that it has a more important place in the corpus of Howells's work than normally granted.

An Imperative Duty is not simply Howells' brief foray into the issue of race. It provides insight into *A Hazard of New Fortunes*, which he was working on at almost the same time. If Howells resists the allegorical in *An Imperative Duty*, he succumbs to it in his major work when he uses the marriage of Northerner and Southerner to imagine a unified country after the Civil War and the tensions of Reconstruction. Thus, Howells has Mr. Fulkerson, a representative of Northern business sense, marry Madison Woodburn, whose father is a Southern colonel who defends slavery and Southern honor. By implying that their marriage will work because Miss Woodburn already recognizes the need to adopt Northern habits of industry and because Fulkerson is in need of a sense of honor to temper his business morality, Howells reveals his desire to have the federal family reunite on new terms.[13]

His hope that a new sense of interdependence would replace sectional rivalry was shared by Northerners and Southerners alike. Speaking in Atlanta in 1881 Edward Atkinson, a New England cotton-mill owner, stressed the need for citizens of both sections to "visit each other, learn the respective methods and opportunities of each State, and become convinced that in this mutual inter-dependence is the foundation of their true union."[14] Even the violence of the Civil War was used to stress the bonds between North and South. In the poem "Spring in New England" Thomas Bailey Aldrich, who succeeded Howells as editor of *The Atlantic Monthly* and accepted Chesnutt's first conjure woman story for publication, memorializes the Northern dead buried in Southern soil.

> So let our heroes rest
> Upon your sunny breast:
> Keep them, O South, our tender hearts and true,
> Keep them, O South, and learn to hold them dear
> From year to year!
> Never forget,
> Dying for us, they died for you.
> This hallowed dust should knit us closer yet.[15]

The marriage of Northern and Southern interests was especially important for advocates of the New South, such as Henry W. Grady. In his famous speech to the New England Club of New York, entitled "The New South" (1886), Grady ends with two emotional appeals for the united interests of North and South. The final one draws on the image of the handshake. Asking if the North will "withhold, save in a strained courtesy, the hand which straight from his soldier's heart Grant offered to Lee at Appomattox," he then quotes Daniel Webster from a speech on the North and South made to the same club forty years earlier: "Standing hand to hand and clasping hands, we should remain united as we have been for sixty years, citizens of the same country, members of the same government, united, all united now and united forever."[16]

The image of North and South united through a handshake reinforces an image in the next-to-last paragraph that expands on Aldrich's trope of the Northern dead buried in Southern soil by adding the crucial metaphor of blood. His message, Grady insists, "comes to you from consecrated ground. Every foot of soil about the city in which I live is as sacred as a battle-ground of the republic. Every hill that invests it is hallowed to you by the blood of your brothers who died for your victory, and doubly hallowed to us by the blow of those who died hopeless, but undaunted, in defeat—sacred soil to all of us—rich with memory that makes us purer and stronger and better—silent but staunch witnesses in its red desolation of the matchless valor of American hearts and the deathless glory of American arms—speaking an eloquent witness in its white peace and prosperity to the indissoluble union of American States and the imperishable brotherhood of the American people." By hallowing the Southern soil through spilled blood that has led to "white peace and prosperity," Grady reminds us how much the vision of a reunited North and South depended on the exclusion of blacks. For him the old division marked by "Mason and Dixon's line" could be "wiped out" only if the color line remained in place in the South.[17]

That exclusion points to the importance of seeing *An Imperative Duty* as a supplement to *A Hazard of New Fortunes*. Whereas Howells seeks aesthetic and moral unity, he is also acutely aware of how efforts to balance accounts usually leave something unaccounted for. The something unaccounted for in his effort to imagine a union of Northern and Southern interests in *A Hazard of New Fortunes* is race. Not dealt with in depth in this major work, the problem of race is central to the minor work that he was composing at about the same time. His solution to the problem of race in *An Imperative Duty* may be unsatisfactory because he confines it to an individual level, but at least Howells felt the need explicitly to confront the problem, which is more than we can say of Henry James, whose fiction is virtually silent on the dilemma of blacks in the United States. Nonetheless, whether intended or not, *The Bostonians* was inserted into the context of the debate about race. Both *The Rise of Silas Lapham* and *The Bostonians* were serialized in the volume of *The Century* that published Cable's "The Freedman's Case in Equity" and Grady's response to it. Indeed, even James implicitly links the issues of race and national renewal by having his proposed *unhappy* marriage between a Northerner and Southerner coincide with the death of the abolitionist Miss Birdseye, who had mistakenly hoped that Verena would convert Basil rather than vice versa.[18]

But James's portrayal of a potentially unhappy marriage was not the national norm. Again and again, writers imagined conciliatory marriages between Northerners and Southerners.[19] Their narratives were complemented by new interpretations of the Civil War and Reconstruction that helped to overcome sectional differences.[20] Southern historians conceded that secession was unconstitutional and even proclaimed the war necessary for revitalizing the nation. In return Northern historians wholehearted denounced the outrages of Reconstruction. Equally important, Southerners got virtually unqualified endorsement of their belief that the national character born in the fratricidal struggle was Anglo-Saxon. As a Senator from Virginia put it, stressing sectional unity, "The instinct of race integrity is the most glorious, as it is the predominant characteristic of the Anglo-Saxon race, and the sections have it in common."[21]

Within this context, Chesnutt's stories of the color line make clear what is only suggested by seeing *An Imperative Duty* as a supplement to Howells's vision of a possible North-South marriage in *A Hazard of New Fortunes:* the renegotiation of the federal contract needs to include all of its citizens in the new federal family. Chesnutt makes this point by appropriating the rhetoric of interdependence and interconnectedness but for different purposes. Take, for instance, the narrator's comment: "For connected with our kind we must be; if not by our virtues, then by our vices,—if not by our services, at least by our needs" (HBC 154). This belief in connectedness by kind underlay both Grady's vision of the white peace and prosperity of a new American people and Harper's call for mulattoes to devote their lives to the advancement of "their people." In contrast to both, however, Chesnutt seems to link connectedness, not to a progressive vision, but to tragedy, for it is Rena's inability to break connections with her kind that contributes to her fall. Indeed, Chesnutt recognizes that the image of connectedness lends itself to a traditional trope for Fate, that of an interconnected web woven together. His use of this trope is most obvious in the short story "The Web of Circumstances," but he also refers to Fate frequently in *The House Behind the Cedars,* including a direct reference before the narrator's comment on our inevitable connection to our kind. This apparent fatalism gives his fiction an atmosphere akin to that of the naturalists writing at the same time. Human attempts to break from the web of circumstances, which as Tryon remarks is spun by "nature and society" (HBC 257), seem condemned to fail. But as fatalistically tragic as Chesnutt's vision of interconnectedness seems, it eventually offers hope through an enlightenment belief in the universality of humankind.

Whereas Grady and Harper would limit connectedness by race, Chesnutt ultimately considers "our kind" to be all human beings. In *The Marrow of Tradition,* for instance, Chesnutt's narrator insists that the

"the people" means "the whole people, and not any one class, sought to be built up at the expense of another" (MT 92). To be sure, Chesnutt's stubbornly humanistic vision is open to criticism for its gender politics. Rena's failure to use marriage, as John does, to advance suggests gender imbalances in the marriage contract, which we have explored in earlier chapters. Furthermore, the narrator's remark that the strongest feeling of "universal brotherhood" comes "when one loves some other fellow's sister"(HBC 72) tends to reduce Rena to an object of exchange binding the fraternal bonds of two males.[22] Nonetheless, this binding still establishes connection among the races.

The most obvious way in which the novel of passing demonstrates the interconnectedness between races is through its mixed-blood protagonists. A more subtle way involves the misrecognition at the heart of the genre, a misrecognition that allows connections between people who otherwise would be separated by the color line. If Tryon did not mistake Rena for white, he would never have considered marrying her. But because she can cross over the color line, he establishes a connection with her that eventually allows his love to overcome his prejudices. The tragedy is, of course, that his enlightened act of recognition—which grows out of an initial act of misrecognition—comes too late. Thus, as Aristotle describes in *The Poetics,* Chesnutt uses tragedy mimetically to generate an act of recognition. But Chesnutt does not use tragedy only mimetically. He also uses it rhetorically to bring about an enlightened attitude on issues of race. By presenting a tragic situation he urges readers who share Tryon's recognition of the interconnectedness of all human beings not to come to that recognition too late.

Contemplating a career as a writer, Chesnutt wrote in his journal on May 29, 1880, that the object of his writing would not be "so much the elevation of the colored people as the elevation of whites." For him the "unjust spirit of caste" that whites perpetuate is "a barrier to the moral progress of the American people." Breaking down that barrier requires not force but "a moral revolution." The Negro's role in that revolution is "to prepare himself for social recognition and equality." The "province of literature" is "to open the way for him to get it—to accustom the public mind to the idea; and while amusing them to lead them on, imperceptibly, unconsciously, step by step, to the desired state of feeling."[23]

As a writer, Chesnutt never abandons this didactic purpose, which is linked to his ultimate belief in the possibilities of moral progress. But the fact that he has to present a tragic vision in order to get people to alter their existing state of feeling indicates how for him such progress is connected with a sense of loss. Tryon, for instance, seems most open to transformation when confronted by the loss of a dream of what might have been. But even then an enlightened sense of reason is crucial in guiding him toward "the desired state of feeling." Tryon's love might eventually triumph over his prejudice, but only because he has "a mind by nature reasonable above the average" (HBC 144).

If in his first novel Chesnutt uses tragedy to make a reasoned plea for his audience to recognize, as Tryon does, the interconnectedness of all human beings, in his last novel he insists that only such a recognition will keep people's dreams of a reunited North and South from ending in tragedy.

III

The protagonist of *The Colonel's Dream* is Henry French, a white man who is part owner of a Northern company that manufactures burlap bags. By presenting the book's action through the perspective of a moderate white, as he did in the frame narrative of his conjure woman tales, Chesnutt tries to elicit the sympathy of his predominantly white audience. The book opens on Wall Street with the widower French and his junior partner awaiting the pending sale of their company to a monopolistic corporation. Holding out for terms that will make them and the widow of a former partner rich, the two risk disaster and win when the sale goes through.

This sale is not a naive celebration of Northern capitalism. If the monopoly takes over, "labor" will have to "sweat and the public groan in order that a few captains, or chevaliers of industry, might double their dividends" (CD 5). Nonetheless, the focus of Chesnutt's concern is not the company's workers. Nor is it, as it was with Elizabeth Stuart Phelps, the gendered inequality of the firm's partnership. In fact, for Chesnutt, the chivalrous duty of the two active male partners is to shield their "silent partner" from "needless anxiety" (CD 7) about a risky sale. Instead, Chesnutt uses the sale to give his protagonist enough capital to spend time in the South—a course of action advised by his doctor for his health and that of his young son, Philip.

Once located in Clarendon, French cannot resist getting involved in the local economy, which is small enough for his money to make a difference. In a city his capital "would have been but a slender stream, scarcely felt in the rivers of charity poured into the ocean of want," but in this small Southern town "he could mark with his own eyes the good he might accomplish" (CD 117). To do good French has to fight Bill Fetters, who exploits racial prejudice to control the local economy. Confident of the victory of "forces of enlightenment" over the "retrograde forces represented by Fetters," French dreams of a town, a "few years hence, a busy hive of industry, where no man, and no woman obliged to work, need be without employment at fair wages; where the trinity of peace, prosperity and progress would reign supreme; where men like Fetters and methods like his would no longer be tolerated" (CD 118). That dream is supported by Laura Treadwell, who embodies the cultivation and generosity of the Old South. Their shared goals lead French to ask Laura to marry him and serve as mother to Phil. But the proposed marriage never comes off, falling victim to a failed dream. Returning North, French ends up marrying the silent partner of his firm.

The colonel's failed dream not only challenges the standard plot that signals the reconciliation of the federal family through the marriage of a Northerner and a Southerner, it also complicates it by having French embody Northern and Southern characteristics. Born into one of Clarendon's first families, French fought for the South, receiving a colonelcy at nineteen. After the War he sought his fortune in the North, and he had not been to the South for thirty years. A true Southern colonel, who has internalized Northern commercial values, French is ideally suited to reconcile sectional differences. As Laura tells him, he "will do more for the town than if [he] had remained here all [his] life," because he has "acquired a broader view" without losing his "love for the old" (CD 85). French's potential for doing good makes his return to the North at the end of the book even more bleak, for he abandons not only his dreams of reform but also a woman who represents all that he loves about the South.

If Chesnutt uses the colonel's unfulfilled marriage contract to undercut visions of Northern and Southern reconciliation, he uses the South's appropriation of Northern contract ideology in the realm of business and labor to show why the promise of that vision goes unrealized. Fetters, after all, controls the population by keeping large farmers in his debt, while "the small farmers, many of whom were coloured, were practically tied to the soil by ropes of debt and chains of contract" (CD 78). A character similar to the uncouth Captain McBane in *The Marrow of Tradition,* this son of a speculator and slave catcher uses contracts to perpetuate a system more ruthless at times than the Old South's slavery.

As we have seen, the belief that every adult male had the right to contract his labor for wages took on almost sacred status after the Civil War because it distinguished the Northern social and economic system from the depraved Southern system of slavery. If the 13th Amendment abolished slavery, the much more complicated 14th Amendment was evoked in the period to protect the "freedom of contract." Contrary to Northern expectations, however, the introduction of a contractual labor system in the South did not transform long-standing Southern institutions that had developed under slavery. In fact, the South, having waged an ideological battle with the North over the relative merits of wage and chattel slavery, was fully aware of how contracts exploit as well as emancipate.[24] Thus, after Reconstruction some Southern states adopted "Black Codes" that used the logic of contract to institute a new form of "slavery." For instance, Albion W. Tourgée cites a Louisiana law in which "all agricultural laborers were compelled to make labor contracts during the first ten days of January, for the next year. The contract once made, the laborer was not allowed to leave his place of employment during the year except on conditions not likely to happen and easily prevented. The master was allowed to make deductions of the servants' wages for 'injuries done to animals and agricultural implements committed to his care,' thus making negroes responsible for wear and tear. Deductions were to be made for 'bad or negligent work,' the master being the judge" (IE 56–57).

Another ploy was to sell the labor of vagrants at public auction to pay off high vagrancy fines while setting wages as low as two dollars a month. In the year that Chesnutt published *A Colonel's Dream*, Florida passed a law subjecting vagrants to a $250 fine or six months on the chain gang. Included were "persons who neglect their calling" and "all able-bodied male persons over eighteen years of age who are without means of support," such as a labor contract.[25]

To link criminality with breach of contract and the failure to be contractually employed was especially repressive because of the nature of the convict-lease system in many Southern states where fortunes were made off convict labor. The system even encouraged arrests, since more convicts meant more cheap labor for the state and private industry. In his *Report on Peonage* (1908) Assistant United States Attorney General Charles W. Russell, a native of Virginia, described the system as "largely a system of involuntary servitude." He added that "if a State can make a crime . . . whatever it chooses to call a crime, it can nullify the [13th] amendment and establish all the involuntary servitude it may see fit."[26]

Peonage and convict-leasing raise two questions about contract's promise to produce liberty. First, can freedom of contract go so far as to allow people to contract away their freedom?[27] Second, are not laws enforcing contractual promises themselves a denial of liberty? John Stuart Mill confronted the first question and concluded that there were limits to one's freedom to contract. For Mill someone who sells himself into slavery abdicates his liberty. "The principle of freedom cannot require that he should be free not to be free. It is not freedom to be allowed to alienate his freedom."[28] Mill also implies that without limits to the enforcement of promises, the freedom to contract will result in the slavery that it claims to avoid. Mill, however, provides no means to determine precisely when people's freedom to alienate their labor needs to be limited in order to preserve their inalienable right to life and liberty. Since it is absurd to argue that such a limit can be determined by contract, the answer seems to lie in some form of legal paternalism.

The contract-oriented Supreme Court, however, only reluctantly acknowledged that it in fact perpetuated paternalism. Instead, it found a way to limit contractual abuses while claiming to uphold the freedom of contract.[29] It did so by drawing on the precedents of an Anglo-American legal system that had managed to avoid facing contradictions that arose from putting the claims of personal autonomy against those of freedom of contract. For instance, there was a long tradition opposed to making breaches of contract criminal. Breaches were considered violations of *private* obligations not violations of duties owed to the public. In addition, the common law had resisted prescribing the specific performance of a task as a remedy for someone's failure to maintain contractual promises. One reason for that reluctance, as Frederick Maitland put it in his *Lectures on Equity* (1910), was that to make employees perform personal services as compensation for an unfulfilled agreement in a labor contract was to risk having them "in effect sell themselves into slavery."[30] Provisions for specific performance were usually linked to equity, not common law. Drawing on common law precedent, the Court made two important decisions. In *Bailey v. Alabama* (1911) it struck down a law that declared it an act of criminal fraud to receive an advance loan based on a promise of future labor and then to breach the agreement. In *United States v. Reynolds* (1914) it invalidated laws under which indigent convicts contracted themselves into servitude for employers who would pay their fines.

These decisions helped economic conditions for Southern blacks. Nonetheless, they made no connection between race and the abuses in question. Indeed, the Court's contractual assumptions encouraged it to believe that it was simply creating conditions so that all citizens, black and white, had equal opportunity. For instance, in *Hodges v. United States* (1906) Justice Brewer writes, "When the problem of the emancipated slave was before the Nation," it "declined to constitute them wards of the Nation or leave them in a condition of alienage where they would be subject to the jurisdiction of Congress." They were given citizenship, because the nation "doubtless believed that in the long run their best interests would be subserved, they taking their chances with other citizens in the States they should make their homes."[31] In *Bailey* Justice Hughes begins, "We at once dismiss from consideration the fact that the plaintiff in error is a black man." He adds, "No question of a sectional character is presented, and we may view the legislation in the same manner as if it had been enacted in New York or in Idaho."[32]

Claiming to decide the cases on the basis of a race-neutral right guaranteed by freedom of contract, the Court avoided charges that it was providing for paternalistic, equitable relief against racial discrimination in the South.[33] In contrast, Chesnutt makes clear why a solution blind to the issue of race is not enough. If the Court thought that guaranteeing color-blind rights based on freedom of contract would solve problems of racial discrimination, Chesnutt demonstrates that contract's promise will be fulfilled in the South only if racial equality is guaranteed.[34]

Shortly after he arrives in Clarendon, the colonel witnesses a sale of vagrant labor. He is personally shocked when he recognizes one of the victims as Peter, formerly a loyal slave belonging to his family. Finding no other solution, French buys Peter's labor for life. In forcing the colonel to revert to his role as a slave owner to help Peter, Chesnutt shows how the new form of contractual slavery can be even harsher than the older variety, which at least occasionally tempered its cruelty through an owner's paternalistic sense of responsibility.[35] In contrast, the new system was devoid of paternal appeals to sentiment. In the New South the entire criminal law system was marshaled to enforce obligations derived from labor contracts. Indeed, Fetters leases convicts to provide labor for his agricultural and industrial investments.

Chesnutt exposes the horrors of the convict-lease system to induce moral shock in his readers, but he realizes that moral outrage is not enough. Thus he links his moral argument to an economic one. Critics of the Old South had insisted that slavery was not only morally but economically wrong. In *The Colonel's Dream* Chesnutt makes the same point about racial prejudice in the post-Reconstruction South by evoking the image of a revitalized Southern economy promised by advocates of the New South. Chesnutt may not share New Southerners's views on race, but he does demonstrate, as the racist newspaper the *Anglo-Saxon* puts it, that the South's "vast undeveloped resources needed only the fructifying flow of abundant capital to make it blossom like the rose" (CD 86–87). The source of that capital was, of course, the North, and when the colonel begins to invest in the local economy "the stream of ready money" that he puts "into circulation . . . soon permeated all the channels of local enterprise" (CD 88).

The resulting prosperity makes the colonel a popular man. One action, however, drives a "thin entering wedge" (CD 192) between him and his popularity. Buying a factory that hires local people to make bricks rather than import them from the North, the colonel replaces his foreman with the most efficient of his remaining workers, "George Brown, a coloured man" (CD 191). When whites protest, the colonel explains that his action is based on a proposition that is at "the very root of his reform" (CD 192). He respects someone's "right to choose one's own associates" (CD 192), but "the right to work and to do one's best work was fundamental, as was the right to have one's work done by those who could do it best" (CD 192). If Southerners cannot overcome "an unhealthy and unjust prejudice" (CD 192), they will undermine the efficiency of a labor system based on contract by allowing status to overrule merit. "These people," he argues, "have got to learn that we live in an industrial age, and success demands of an employer that he utilise the most available labour" (CD 192).

For Chesnutt North and South differed on the labor question. In "The Averted Strike," an unpublished short story set in the Middle West, "not far from the old line that in former years had separated free labor from labor enslaved," a factory owner born in New England considers promoting to foreman a man named Walker, the "only colored man employed in the factory" and the best qualified worker. The other workers object and threaten to strike. To the workers, who are thinking of unionizing, the owner responds, "You talk of the rights of labor, and yet you come and ask me to deprive an industrious and faithful man of the highest right of labor—the right to an opportunity to do the best he is capable of, and to obtain the proper reward for it."[36] Soon thereafter the factory bursts into flames, catching in a tower the owner's daughter and a friend who were touring the building. A former seaman, Walker scales the tower, rescues the women, and saves the factory by setting off the fire-extinguishing system. After Walker's display of courage, the workers quietly withdraw their objections, and he is promoted and given five thousand dollars' worth of stock in the company.

Because the Southern whites refuse to learn the lesson that the workers in the North did, the colonel's attempt to establish an efficient system based on the promise of contract cannot compete with Fetters' system based on the exploitative possibilities of contract. With Fetters in control the New South will not blossom, but slowly deplete its resources, just as Fetters exhausts a large stretch of land after working it for turpentine. "He had left his mark, thought the colonel. Like the plague of locusts, he had settled and devoured and then moved on, leaving a barren waste behind him" (CD 216). For Chesnutt the South's economic barrenness is linked to its moral barrenness. People complain about Fetters's control over them, but their prejudices support his corrupt system.

In exposing the abuses of contract in the South, Chesnutt points to the limits of the Republican Party's faith that moral and economic progress would follow once the South abandoned a slave economy for a contractual one. Southern institutions take over contract rather than vice versa. Nonetheless, by attributing contract's failure to "unnatural" racial prejudice, Chesnutt continues to support the Republican Party's link between moral progress and a particular economic system. But to show that linkage he has to demonstrate the superiority of the colonel's system over the system that defeats it. Because this point cannot be made by plot alone, Chesnutt evokes organic metaphors to suggest how a contractual economy devoid of racism's unnatural effects can cultivate life.

"Communities, like men," he tells us, "must either grow or decay, advance or decline; they could not stand still. Clarendon was decaying" (CD 118). Clarendon's decay cannot be attributed solely to the lack of capital. After all, Fetters has lots of money. What matters is not money itself but how it is used. Of the colonel, the narrator writes, "The love of money might be the root of all evil, but its control was certainly a means of great good" (CD 211). In contrast, Fetters's control of money leads to decay. "Fetters was the parasite which, by sending out its roots toward rich and poor alike, struck at both extremes of society, and was choking the life of the town like a rank and deadly vine" (CD 118).

A parasite chokes life because it lives at another's expense without making proper return. The colonel, however, reinvests his money so that it circulates throughout the economy. For instance, when he offers money to help blacks found an industrial school, "the result was the setting in motion of a stagnant pool" (CD 161). Crucial to Chesnutt's moral economy, therefore, is the contrast between circulation, which brings life and growth, and stagnation, which brings death and decay. Like Henry Carey, the prominent nineteenth-century American political economist, Chesnutt believes that the barrier to development is not lack of land but lack of investment. When enough capital circulates through the land, it will blossom. When its circulation is blocked, it dries up.[37]

By linking the circulation of capital and life for a community, Chesnutt might seem to advocate a completely unregulated economy. But the free circulation of capital is not enough to bring about "the trinity of peace, prosperity, and progress" (CD 118) that the colonel envisions. Chesnutt's is a *moral* economy because society is best served when the circulation of capital is controlled by progressive ideas. At the same time, free economic exchange facilitates the development of progressive ideas.

Chesnutt does not believe that Southerners are constitutionally incapable of improvement. Despite noting their laziness and "quixotic devotion to lost causes and vanished ideals" (CD 89), the colonel is "glad to find that this was the mere froth upon the surface, and that underneath it, deep down in the hearts of the people, the currents of life flowed, if less swiftly, not less purely than in more favoured places" (CD 90). To activate those currents of life, Southerners need "some point of contact with the outer world and its more advanced thought" (CD 90). Railroads, for instance, "while they bring in supplies and take out produce, also bring in light and take out information, both of which are fatal to certain fungus growths, social as well as vegetable, which flourish best in the dark" (CD 215). Fetters's plantation, we learn, is remote from any railroad connection.

Fetters's control has national as well as local implications. The South's stagnant economy makes it a virtual colony of the North. "There were no mills or mines in the neighborhood, except a few grist mills, and a sawmill. The bulk of the business consisted in supplying the needs of an agricultural population, and trading in their products. The cotton was baled and shipped to the North, and reimported for domestic use, in the shape of sheeting and other stuffs. The corn was shipped to the North, and came back in the shape of corn meal and salt pork, the staple articles of diet" (CD 77–78). This imbalance of trade might seem to benefit the North, which, like Fetters, can reap a profit by extracting wealth from the South. But in Chesnutt's moral economy, the South rather than the North is the parasite. If the South had a vital economy, its wealth would circulate throughout the nation, contributing to increased prosperity for everyone. As it is, the South is a drain on the nation's wealth. By insisting on the interdependence of the Northern and Southern economies Chesnutt also suggests an interconnection between social, economic, and political realms that the period's boundary ideologists would deny.

In renegotiating its relationship with the North at the end of Reconstruction, the South demanded control over race relations in the social sphere. Replying to Cable's "The Freedman's Case in Equity," Grady insists, "The South must be allowed to settle the social relations of races according to her own views of what is right and best. There has never been a moment when she could have submitted to have the social status of her citizens fixed by an outside power. She accepted the emancipation and the enfranchisement of her slaves as the legitimate results of war that had been fought to a conclusion. These once accomplished, nothing more was possible."[38] Reasons why the North went along are complicated, but boundary thought made its capitulation easier by assuming that different spheres of action followed different natural laws.

According to the premises of boundary thought, blacks' lower social status should not affect their political and economic rights. As Grady puts it, "The races meet in the exchange of labor in perfect amity and understanding. Together they carry on the concerns of the day, knowing little or nothing of the fierce hostility that divides labor and capital in other sections. When they turn to social life they separate. Each race obeys its instinct and congregates about its own centers."[39] In contrast, *The Colonel's Dream* shows that the inferior social status granted to blacks stagnates the Southern economy by disrupting the natural efficiency of a labor force based on contract. As an old Southern general tells the colonel, "It's a social matter down here, rather than a political one. . . . We had to preserve our institutions, if our finances went to smash" (CD 166–167). Seeing no economic prospects in the South until it changes its sentiments about race, the colonel, disillusioned, returns to the North.

IV

In linking the prospects for progress in the South to a change in its sentiment about race, Chesnutt resembles Harriet Beecher Stowe. Indeed, like Stowe, he sees the function of his fiction to help effect that change. But if Chesnutt's desire to alter what Raymond Williams calls an audience's "structures of feeling"[40] links his fiction to sentimentalists like Stowe, his relationship to the sentimentalists is complex. Like the realists, he mocks the romantic view of the world perpetuated by writers like Scott, and unlike most sentimentalists of the period, he makes virtually no appeal to religion. Furthermore, although he tries to alter people's feelings, he relies as much on logos as pathos to do so. Howells notes this appeal and argues that the case Chesnutt makes for his people "has more justice than mercy in it."[41] As important as a "desired state of feeling" is for Chesnutt, it is achieved when feelings are guided by enlightened ideas. In positing an enlightenment view of a moral universe, Chesnutt's fiction is ultimately closer to that of staunch Republican John Hay than that of either the realists or the sentimentalists.

Chesnutt, like Hay, stresses justice more than mercy precisely because he believes in the possibility of achieving an equitable moral economy. For both, the barrier to its realization is unenlightened ideas. Nonetheless, a crucial difference remains between Hay and Chesnutt on the degree of moral progress in the United States at the turn of the century.

In 1869 Hay wrote "The Foster Brothers," a short story set on the banks of the Mississippi River between Missouri and Illinois in the antebellum period. In it Clarence Brydges, a Southern white, falls in love with Marie Des Ponts, a woman who, unknown to her, has inherited black blood from her father, now passing as a white lawyer, but who turns out to be an ex-slave—and half-brother—of Clarence's father. Traveling North for the wedding, Clarence's father meets and recognizes his brother who helps rescue him after a shipwreck. Marie's father refuses to let his ex-master stop his daughter's wedding, and the two fight, sinking to death at the bottom of the river. When their intertwined bodies are recovered, the newly wed couple assumes that they died trying to save one another from drowning. Commenting on the fraternal violence of the recent war, "The Foster-Brothers" implies that the only hope for racial mixture in the United States is an act of re-

pression, an apocalyptic moment of forgetting in which an older generation must be sacrificed for the future of the new.[42]

By the end of the century Hay had joined most members of the
Republican Party in their own act of forgetting. But the terms of the
plot had dramatically changed. No longer was the Civil War's conflict
between North and South seen as a sacrifice necessary for the birth of
a new generation of Americans mixing the interests of blacks and whites.
Instead, the common sacrifice of the Civil War was memorialized as the
basis for a new federal family that married the interests of Northern and
Southern whites, while forgetting those of blacks. The terms of this
family romance allowed Hay, as secretary of state, to forge an Anglo-
Saxon alliance with England that for him stood for the "triumphant
march of progress."[43]

Insisting that the moral and economic progress of the country will be
stunted until an equitable remedy is found for forgotten people of color,
Chesnutt cannot join in Hay's end-of-the-century optimism. The result
is Chesnutt's presentation of a tragic plot. Nonetheless, as we saw in *The
House Behind the Cedars,* Chesnutt can use tragedy as didactically as Hay
uses his happy ending in *The Bread-Winners.* Chesnutt's combination of
tragedy and didacticism contributes to his presentation of allegorical
rather than individualized characters and raises technical problems that
he does not always successfully overcome.

For instance, having used the marriage plot to represent the union of
Northern and Southern interests, Chesnutt is faced with the possibility
that the colonel's symbolic act of giving up on the South at the end of
the book will force the colonel to refuse to honor the promise he made
to marry Laura Treadwell. That, of course, will not do for such an
honorable man. Thus, Chesnutt has Laura refuse to accept the colonel's
offer because she fears that his love for her was linked to a false dream
he had of the South. A part of the colonel's memory of a lost past, Laura,
like the South, seems "too old to learn new ways" (CD 284), and in a
moment of sentimental sacrifice she declares, "My duty holds me here!
God would not forgive me if I abandoned it. Go your way; live your life.
Marry some other woman, if you must, who will make you happy. But
I shall keep, Henry—nothing can ever take away from me—the memory
of one happy summer" (CD 285).

As much as this romantic sacrifice would have irritated Howells, it is
complicated. First of all, it is not only the colonel but Chesnutt himself
who sees Laura as a type who takes meaning from her role in an imaginary scheme. Furthermore, there is an element of psychological realism

in the scene that helps to give power to Chesnutt's fiction. As Chesnutt knew—it was hard for anyone of color not to know—people are rarely seen as individuals. Laura, for instance, is right about the colonel. His love for her *is* linked to an unrealistic dream. As such, it has little chance of surviving. Indeed, one point that Chesnutt wants to drive home is that dreams influence personal relations and that the false dream of the New South is as destructive of relations as false dreams of the Old South. He makes this point in a contrived subplot that, nonetheless, contains some of the book's most interesting suggestions about the role of blacks in the Southern economy.

V

Lifted from the unpublished short story "The Dumb Witness" and grafted onto the main plot, the subplot offers a postbellum version of Hawthorne's "Peter Goldwaithe's Treasure" or *The House of the Seven Gables*. It involves Malcolm Dudley, an old Southerner, and his ex-slave and lover Viney.[44] Dudley is from a North Carolina family that includes a Revolutionary War general and a distinguished judge. The family's estate began to decline while in the hands of Malcolm's bachelor uncle Ralph, who lived a life of pleasure and left management of the property to his nephew. During the Civil War, Ralph worked for the Confederate government in Richmond. Meanwhile, Malcolm courted a rich Southern war widow, who accepted his offer of marriage. When told to prepare the house that she had run for ten years, for a new mistress, Viney intervened and caused the widow to cancel the engagement. Enraged, Malcolm had her whipped but later regretted his cruelty, especially when he found a letter from his uncle saying that on a short trip home he hid fifty thousand dollars in gold in the house and confided its whereabouts to Viney. Because the uncle has died, Viney is Malcolm's sole access to the unsolved mystery. Viney, however, has been rendered speechless by her beating, and for twenty-five years Malcolm seeks in vain to get her to reveal the secret that he hopes will make him a rich man.

During this time the Dudley estate lies in neglect, as Malcolm dreams about a lost treasure rather than devote his energy to productive farming. At the time of the main plot Ben Dudley, Malcolm's nephew, runs the decaying estate. But, although gifted, he too, much to the dismay of his ambitious girlfriend, dreams of finding the long lost treasure. Finally, on his deathbed, Malcolm learns from Viney that she has been faking for all these years, that she could indeed talk, and that the real secret that she kept from him was that there was no hidden gold, the uncle having removed it an hour after he wrote the letter indicating its presence. Thus, Dudley had truly wasted his life in a vain dream, which is, as Viney makes clear, her revenge. "You had me whipped—whipped—whipped—by a poor white dog I had despised and spurned! You had said that you loved me, and you had promised to free me—and you had me whipped! But I have had my revenge!" (CD 273). Nonetheless, Viney still loves Malcolm, and when he dies, she kisses him passionately and dies herself.

The importance of this subplot is indicated by changes between the unpublished story and the novel. The major difference is that in the unpublished version a "treasure" exists, and Viney reveals its whereabouts to the young nephew, but only after Malcolm dies. Not gold, "the treasure" consists of several promissory notes and mortgages on neighboring plantations plus the old uncle's will leaving the estate to Malcolm. Although many of these papers can no longer help accumulate or protect property, their existence does lend some legitimacy to Malcolm's dreams. In contrast, the nonexistence of a treasure in the novel powerfully exposes the debilitating effects of Southerners's dreams of romance buried in the past, thus allowing the subplot to complement the main plot's demystified dream of the New South by adding one of the Old South. The novel also undercuts the unpublished version's suggestion of renewal in the South. In the short story the nephew, carrying his great-uncle's name, restores the estate. In the novel the nephew, like the colonel, sees no hope in the South as it exists. At the end of the book he and his new bride follow the colonel North where he can use his imagination to invent new machinery for industry.

The bleakness of the novel's ending is intensified by another change. In the story Malcolm courts not a Southern war widow but a rich Pennsylvania widow who recently moved South. By having Viney stop their marriage Chesnutt undercuts the standard plot of Northern and Southern marriage, reminding us that a history of abuse to blacks can disrupt that attempted union. Nonetheless, the failed marriage is at cross-purposes with the resulting Southern renewal. The novel eliminates this inconsistency. Furthermore, the unpublished version's themes of inheritance and North/South marriage are not lost. They are transferred to the main plot where they receive fuller development.

The marriage theme is, of course, dramatized through the colonel and Laura. The theme of inheritance through long lost documents occurs when the colonel finds some old papers in a desk that Laura insists on giving him because it had once belonged to both his father and hers. Unexamined, the papers are misplaced until late in the book when the colonel discovers that one is a promissory note, about to expire, requiring Fetters to pay considerable money to Laura's father. This note makes it easier to accept the colonel's failure to marry, since it leaves Laura and her mother financially secure—financially secure, but not restored to power. Though forced to pay this debt, Fetters remains in power in the South.

Fetters remains in power, and yet another change between story and novel suggests that his rule will be uneasy. In a deathbed confrontation added to the novel Malcolm accuses Viney of failing to forgive even in the face of death. Through this scene Chesnutt warns his white readers about blacks' capacity for revenge.

Tourgée wrote that people were mistaken when they assumed that "in the course of a generation or so the descendants of the American slave will have forgotten all about slavery." On the contrary, he asserts, citing history and the Old Testament, "a hundred years hence the hardships and wrongs of slavery will constitute a stronger impulse to united action on the part of the colored race than they do to-day." Sounding prophetic, he predicts that "even with the lapse of centuries, the colored orator and poet" will likely "dwell upon the wrongs of their forefathers with a fervor and intensity that would surprise the recipient of the wrongs described" (ATC 103–4). Viney's obsession with revenge for an action long past makes a similar point. After witnessing the final scene between his uncle and Viney, young Ben "thanked God that he lived in another age, and had escaped this sin" (CD 274). But Viney's response suggests that the present may not escape the effects of past sins, even when it no longer sins itself. Chesnutt's subplot reinforces that suggestion by using the old-fashioned romantic device of lost and mysterious letters to complicate Chesnutt's life-giving metaphor of circulation, a complication that has important consequences for the effort to introduce a contractual economy into the South after the Civil War.

One of the dangers of Chesnutt's use of the metaphor of circulation is that it can create the illusion that the flow of either capital or ideas is self-generating. But circulation can occur only through a series of exchanges, exchanges that in the case of ideas involve communication and in the case of capital involve contracts. Tourgée, for instance, describes

Wall Street as "a contract-machine" (GS 11). We have already seen that in the main plot Chesnutt shows how racial prejudice can block the natural circulation of capital, which contributes to the free trade of ideas necessary to overcome unenlightened prejudice. The subplot suggests another way in which racial prejudice can disrupt the exchange of ideas and capital. The handing over of gold from uncle to nephew, if it had happened, would not have been direct, but dependent on a letter. And not a letter alone, but on someone reading and interpreting it. By drawing on the convention of a mysterious letter in the subplot, Chesnutt reminds us of the mediations that occur in any exchange. It is not an accident that when letters play an important part in the action of both *The House Behind the Cedars* and *The Colonel's Dream*, Chesnutt often entrusts their delivery or the delivery of their message to blacks.

In *The House Behind the Cedars* Judge Straight senses potential disaster when he sees Tryon in town, so he sends a letter to Rena's mother warning her not to let her daughter out of the house for a day or two. But the black boy paid ten cents to deliver the letter dawdles and arrives too late. As a result, Rena wanders into town, where Tryon discovers her secret identity. If in *The House Behind the Cedars* a black boy's late delivery of a letter results in an unintended revelation leading to a personal tragedy, in *The Colonel's Dream* a black woman, whose trust in her lover had been violated, intentionally withholds information that she has been entrusted dutifully to deliver. Both of these incidents suggest difficulties that the South will have in maintaining a productive economy that by necessity involves neglected blacks in the circulation of its capital.

In the first case the late delivery of the message is due to the boy's unexpected delight at receiving money that he does not know how to use wisely. As the narrator puts it, upon receiving his ten cents, our young "capitalist" heads to "the grocery store and invested his unearned increment in gingerbread" (HBC 122), which he consumes before accomplishing the task for which he is paid. A labor force made up of people like this well-intentioned but undisciplined boy does not make for an efficient system of exchange. Judge Straight may be Chesnutt's figure for equity, but when the Judge attempts to ensure an equitable outcome through the delivery of his letter, the letter hardly takes a straight path. Its path is diverted and delayed by the young boy's desire to reward himself with some long-deferred pleasure.

In the second, and more telling case, Chesnutt implies that even though denying blacks a position as free and equal bargaining partners places them at an economic and social disadvantage, they still have the power to disrupt the exchanges necessary for the development of a productive economy. This example has emotional appeal because it involves a couple whose "natural" exchange of love has been distorted by socially condoned racial prejudice. Thus the failed trust between lovers in the subplot supplements the failed promise of marriage in the main plot, a reminder that the marriage of Northern and Southern interests will not be fully possible until there is also recognition of the marriage between the interests of whites and blacks. Without harmonization of those interests, Southern whites will face black revenge that causes economic as well as moral deprivation.

That for Chesnutt such revenge results from more than a betrayal of trust between lovers is signaled by the similarity between Viney's response of silence and that of the black laborer Bud Johnson, who like Peter is sold under the convict-lease system but, unlike Peter, does not have a paternalistic protector like the colonel to buy him. Instead, he is sold back to Fetters, from whose service he had previously escaped. Asked to defend himself, he has nothing to say because he feels that nothing he says will be listened to. Chained, Johnson looks at his captors with an expression of "fierce hatred, as of some wild thing of the woods, which finding itself trapped and betrayed, would go to any length to injure its captor" (CD 69). Then, "he threw toward the colonel a look which resembled an appeal; but it was involuntary, and lasted but a moment, and, when the prisoner became conscious of it, and realized its uselessness, it faded into the former expression" (CD 69). Indeed, Johnson later escapes and gains revenge by shooting Fetters's son, rendering him permanently blind in one eye and dedicated to racial hatred. Captured, Johnson is lynched, his earlier silent appeal to the colonel hauntingly raising the question of who is responsible for the book's bloody violence.

Johnson's unanswered appeal for help from the colonel is paralleled by the 1903 Supreme Court case of *Giles v. Harris,* which Chesnutt discusses at the conclusion of a unpublished speech he wrote, entitled "The Courts and the Negro."[45] On behalf of himself "and on behalf of more than five thousand negroes, citizens of the county of Montgomery, Alabama, similarly situated and circumstanced as himself," Giles brought forth a bill in equity demanding relief for being denied the right to register to vote on the arbitrary basis of color. Speaking for the Court, Justice Holmes denied the request, noting that "equity cannot undertake now, any more than it has in the past, to enforce political rights."

If the conspiracy to keep blacks from voting is as powerful as alleged, Holmes concludes, "unless we are prepared to supervise the voting in that state by officers of the Court, it seems to us that all that the plaintiff could get from equity would be an empty form. Apart from damages to the individual, relief from a great political wrong, if done, as assigned by the people of the state itself, must be given to them or by the legislative and political department of the government of the United States."[46] Refusing a paternalistic role for the Court, Holmes signals the legal system's unwillingness, for the most part, to entertain the freedman's case in equity.

The public's unsympathetic response to *A Colonel's Dream* also indicated that it was not willing to listen to Chesnutt's equitable appeal in fiction. When Chesnutt began his career as a writer, he shared the classical republican belief of the antebellum lawyer Rufus Choate, who argued that literature, even more than law, could move the nation by speaking "directly to the heart and affection and imagination of the whole people" and instruct them in right reason. Elaborating, Choate adds, "A keen, well-instructed judge of such things said if he might write the ballads of a people, he cared little who made its laws."[47] But in his next-to-last novel Chesnutt has a character proclaim, "The man who would govern a nation by writing its songs was a blethering idiot beside the fellow who can edit its news dispatches" (MT 83). With his final novel and the poignant image of Bud Johnson's silent, unanswered appeal, Chesnutt himself moves into silence as far as published fiction is concerned.

He did not, however, retire into silence. He continued to make appeals for racial justice in his community activities and essays. In his speech "The Courts and the Negro," he identifies the "separate but equal" decision of *Plessy v. Ferguson* (1896) as the most important case restricting the rights of African-Americans. Chesnutt even gives us a glimpse of the consequences of that decision in *The Colonel's Dream*, when the colonel witnesses a young mulatto being kicked off a train for having "presumed on his complexion to ride in the white people's car" (CD 109), a reminder that in the South even the railroads that facilitate the exchange of ideas and goods carry evidence of unenlightened prejudice.[48] It is to *Plessy v. Ferguson* and its relation to the promise of contract in the fiction of Mark Twain and Tourgée that I now want to turn. But before doing so, I need to call attention to my use of a contemporary label that does not quite do justice to Chesnutt's fictional world.

Frequently, I have referred to Chesnutt's advocacy of the rights of blacks. But Chesnutt, himself a mixture of African and European blood, fought against seeing race solely in black-and-white terms. To do so was to fall prey to terms adopted in Grady's "In Plain Black and White." Chesnutt's stories of the color line complicate that simplistic opposition. As Judge Straight knows, "the two races had not dwelt together, side by side, for nearly three hundred years, without mingling their blood in greater or less degree" and "that in their mingling the current had not always flowed in one direction" (HBC 117).[49] One implication of Chesnutt's life-giving metaphor of circulation is that the free exchange of racial blood is a natural and healthy component of a progressive moral economy. But for him to advocate that exchange too openly was to guarantee that the ideas embodied in his works would find very little circulation with the public. Thus, whereas he uses his fiction to present to the public his arguments, which, like the colonel's, "avoided the stirring up of prejudice" by being directed "to the higher motives and deeper principles which underlie society, in light of which humanity is more than race" (CD 195), his advocacy of racial mixing in his fiction is usually indirect.

Nonetheless, reminders of an already existing racial mixture are present in even its tiniest detail. For instance, when sight of the uncle's letter convinces Ben's lover of the reality of Dudley's buried treasure, the narrator remarks that, after all, "it was there in black and white, or rather brown and yellow" (CD 127).[50] A black-and-white division of races, Chesnutt suggests, is as nonexistent as the buried treasure, even if legal documents try to establish its existence. The fiction of such a division is central to Homer Plessy's case against Jim Crow laws as well as to Twain's *Pudd'nhead Wilson* and Tourgée's *Pactolus Prime*.

CHAPTER 7

Twain, Tourgée, and the Logic of "Separate but Equal"

I

On June 7, 1892, Homer Plessy was arrested for violating Section 2 of Act 111 passed by the Louisiana legislature in 1890. The law called for "equal but separate accommodations for the white and colored races" on all passenger railways within the state. Plessy's arrest was part of a planned challenge to the law by New Orleans blacks. In September 1891 they contacted the white lawyer Albion Winegar Tourgée. Living in New York state, Tourgée was perhaps the most famous living white spokesman for blacks. After serving in the Union army, he became a carpetbagger judge in North Carolina. Returning to New York, he chronicled his experiences in *A Fool's Errand by One of the Fools* (1879), which was a novelistic success. Exposing the Ku Klux Klan, he used literary and legal means to improve conditions for freedmen. He agreed to work for the New Orleans committee at a distance for no fee.

Homer Plessy had been born free in 1862. His family was French-speaking. Only one-eighth of his blood was African and, according to his counsel, "the mixture [was] not discernible."[1] Most likely he could have passed and ridden in the white car without trouble, but Tourgée's strategy was to have someone of mixed blood violate the law. By pre-arrangement the railroad conductor detained Plessy when he sat in the forbidden coach.

A month after his arrest Plessy came before the court of John Howard Ferguson. A native of Massachusetts, Ferguson was a carpetbagger who stayed in the South, marrying the daughter of a prominent New Orleans attorney. Between Plessy's arrest and his trial, Ferguson had ruled that the law was unconstitutional on interstate trains because of the federal government's power to regulate interstate commerce. Plessy, however, was traveling on an intrastate train, and at his trial Ferguson upheld the law, arguing that a state had the power to regulate railroad companies operating solely within its borders. The constitutional challenge was under way, as (apparently with some help from Ferguson in the process) the decision was appealed to the State Supreme Court and eventually the United States Supreme Court.

The Louisiana Jim Crow law threatened to undermine much of the work of Reconstruction, whose legal foundation was the three Civil War amendments, which granted freedmen economic and political rights. Also important were the three civil rights bills of 1866, 1870, and 1875. The Act of 1875 was especially important, because the controversial election of 1876 led to the compromise that ended Reconstruction in March 1877. With federal troops returned to their posts and no longer governing the South, rights of the freedmen were now in the hands of Southerners. Thus it was a major defeat when in 1883 the Supreme Court declared much of the Act of 1875 unconstitutional. The next year the first Democrat since before the Civil War was elected president.

Some of the mugwumps whose defection from the Republican Party helped elect Cleveland warned him to guarantee the rights of Southern blacks.[2] At stake was the determination of which rights should be protected. Because the Supreme Court had undermined the effort to extend the civil rights of freedmen, George Washington Cable, a novelist and friend of Mark Twain, as well as someone who shared mugwump concerns, was forced to appeal to a standard of equity rather than positive law. The question, he declares, "is no longer whether constitutional amendments, but whether the eternal principles of justice, are violated."[3] In response Henry W. Grady, a spokesperson for the New South, agrees, but differs on what equity demands. Assuring his readers that no one in the New South wants a return to the economic system of slavery, he also claims that the South will, reluctantly, abide by protections of political rights. But it will not tolerate efforts to guarantee civil rights that violate natural social differences between blacks and whites.[4] The issue in the *Plessy* case was whether or not states had the right to pass laws maintaining the color line socially.

At the beginning Tourgée was confident that Plessy's challenge would succeed. But between 1892 and 1896 the climate for victory got worse rather than better. Even an event considered a triumph for blacks tended to work against Plessy. Invited to address the 1895 Atlanta Exposition, Booker T. Washington argued for the mutual dependence of blacks and whites in the South by employing the metaphor of a hand. "In all things that are purely social we can be as separate as the fingers, yet one as the hand in all things essential to mutual progress."[5] Washington's metaphor helped to confirm arguments, such as Grady's, for segregation.

May 18, 1896, the *Plessy* court handed down its decision that laws requiring the social separation of the races on intrastate railroads were constitutional, so long as facilities were equal. Seven of the eight judges who sat on the case denied Tourgée's claim that the Louisiana law violated both the 13th and 14th Amendments. Writing for the majority, Justice Henry Billings Brown quickly disposed of the 13th Amendment claim. He cites Justice Bradley in the *Civil Rights Cases* to rule that "it would be running the slavery argument into the ground"[6] to claim that a law that implies a legal distinction between races based on color reestablishes a state of involuntary servitude. The 14th Amendment claim, he admitted, was more complicated.

The intention of the 14th Amendment, he writes, "was undoubtedly to enforce the absolute equality of the two races before the law" (P 544). But he adds a qualification that relies on logic very similar to Grady's. "In the nature of things," he asserts, the amendment "could not have been intended to abolish distinctions based upon color or to enforce social, as distinguished from political equality, or a commingling of the two races upon terms unsatisfactory to either" (P 544). To demonstrate that states have a right to use their police powers to enforce social separation of the races, he cites the antebellum Massachusetts case of *Roberts v. City of Boston* (1849). Speaking for the court, Lemuel Shaw, Herman Melville's famous father-in-law, declared that segregated schools did not violate the Massachusetts constitution's guarantee of equality before the law.[7] The crucial issue in the *Plessy* case according to Brown is whether the Louisiana law provides for the reasonable use of police powers.[8] Granting the state legislature "large discretion," Brown rules that "in determining the question of reasonableness it is at liberty to act with reference to the established usages, customs and traditions of the people, and with a view to the promotion of their comfort, and the preservation of the public peace and good order" (P 550). According to this standard the Louisiana law is not unreasonable. Indeed, Brown declares that the "underlying fallacy" in Plessy's argument is to assume that the "enforced separation of the two races stamps the colored race with a badge of inferiority. If this be so, it is not by reason of anything found in the act, but solely because the colored race chooses to put that construction upon it" (P 551).

From a strictly logical point of view Brown is correct to point out a fallacy in Plessy's argument. The Louisiana law demanded separate but *equal* facilities. Thus, as written, it did apply equally to whites and blacks.[9] A white person, for instance, was as subject to arrest for sitting in a car designated for blacks as a black for sitting in a car designated for whites. But Brown's logic falls prey to the abstracting tendency of the period's contractual thought, which neglected the concrete social and historical conditions in which people lived. Both Tourgée and Justice Harlan, the lone dissenter, recognized that the effect of the law could not be measured by logic alone.[10]

Harlan's dissent relied on many points made by Tourgée. For instance, he argued that the 13th Amendment did apply since the Louisiana law could be explained by the history of slavery. Thus enforced separation of the races marked blacks with "badges of slavery or servitude" (P 555). Furthermore, the 14th Amendment issue for Harlan was whether the law was constitutional, not whether it was reasonable. For Harlan the intention of the Civil War amendments was not to defer to the established usages, customs, and traditions of the people on issues of race but to alter them by creating a "color-blind" (P 559) Constitution. Jim Crow laws were not color-blind. In fact, if the Court relied on the abstracting logic of the period's contractual thought to justify the Louisiana law, the law failed to measure up to the promise of contract, which is not only about exchanges but also about exchangeability.

By their very nature Jim Crow laws denied whites and blacks the right to change places. The reason why was clear to both Tourgée and Harlan: such laws maintained a system of status based on race. Relying on boundary ideology, the Court claimed that, although the Louisiana law recognized "natural" social differences between the races, it did not affect the political and civil rights of blacks. Harlan knew better. Intended to degrade blacks, the law, he argued, affected both the political and civil standing of blacks by perpetuating a caste system at odds with constitutional principles.

Harlan, of course, was a dissenter, and for the most part the country ignored his argument. Nonetheless, a year later W. E. B. Du Bois published an essay that, while not explicitly citing the *Plessy* case, explained why the majority's appeal to logic was inadequate to describe the effect of "separate but equal" laws. Defining the condition of "double-consciousness," Du Bois argued that when it is assumed that to be American is to be white, a black becomes an African-American rather than simply an American. For the Negro the American world is a "world which yields him no self-consciousness, but only lets him see himself through the revelation of the other world. It is a peculiar sensation, this double-consciousness, this sense of always looking at one's self through the eyes of others, of measuring one's soul by the tape of a world that looks on in amused contempt and pity. One ever feels his two-ness,—an American, a Negro; two souls, two thoughts, two unreconciled strivings; two warring ideals in one dark body, whose dogged strength alone keeps it from being torn asunder."[11]

The *Plessy* court reasoned that the "separate but equal" law did not itself stamp the black race with a badge of inferiority. Du Bois's account of double-consciousness explains why blacks almost inevitably interpreted it as doing so. Condemned to see themselves through the eyes of whites, blacks interiorized a standard that marked them as inherently inferior, a standard established by attitudes of both contempt *and* pity. Given the history of racial relations in the country and the political and economic realities of late nineteenth-century America, when the white race passed a law demanding the social segregation of races, blacks could not help but see it as an attempt to avoid contact with people judged inferior.

Significantly, Du Bois first experiences double-consciousness during an exchange of visiting cards with a white schoolmate. Indeed, exchanges involving race are an excellent way to test the Court's claim that the Jim Crow law applied equally to blacks and whites. For instance, novels of passing explore whether someone can live the same life as a black and a white. They also challenge the logic of separate but equal by focusing on characters with mixed blood. As Tourgée argued, the assortment of races into two self-contained categories assumed an absolute division between races. The actuality of widespread mixture of blood prompted him to test the Louisiana law with someone of mixed blood, since a mulatto demonstrated the folly of dividing people between black and white. To be sure, most Southern states had laws specifying how much African blood was necessary to make one black. But because they varied from state to state Tourgée used them to point out the arbitrariness of racial divisions. Furthermore, since only the heritage of slavery could explain why a small amount of African blood could "brand" someone as black, these laws violated the 13th Amendment by marking blacks with a badge of servitude.

The Court refused to accept Tourgée's arguments. For instance, even though it admitted that race was defined differently from state to state, it ruled that in the federal system definitions of race remained a matter for the states. But Tourgée's failure to convince the Court does not negate the challenge that novels of passing posed to the *Plessy* logic. The rest of this chapter will examine two more novels of passing: Mark Twain's *Pudd'nhead Wilson* (1894) and Tourgée's own *Pactolus Prime* (1890).[12] Both were written before the *Plessy* decision. Nonetheless, to place them in conjunction with it should not only help us better understand the logic legitimating segregation, it will also help to distinguish between the aesthetic practices and politics of one of the most important practitioners of realism and an important literary lawyer who attacked a realist aesthetic.

II

Pudd'nhead grew out of an abandoned comic story about Siamese twins called *Those Extraordinary Twins*. Faced with what he called the "most embarrassing circumstance" that the story he was writing "changed itself from a farce to a tragedy while [he] was going along with it" (PW 119), Twain "pulled out the farce and left the tragedy" (PW 122). Twain's experience of having the genre of a story change without his control is shared by his mulatto heroine Roxy. As Roxy contemplates a cradle exchange of her son for her master's, she justifies her act by recalling a tale about a similar exchange—servant for heir—in England. "'Tain't no sin," she reasons with herself, "*white* folks has done it" (PW 15). Roxy, however, entangles herself in a tragic, not comic, plot.

For both Twain and Roxy, tragedy replaces comedy/farce because of cultural circumstances beyond their control. The traditional plot of European comedy in which confusion over identity disrupts a hierarchical order that is restored when true identity is revealed does not seem to work in democratic America—at least not when the confusion of identity involves race. For instance, if Ben Jonson's *Volpone* is a comedy even though its trial scene punishes Mosca's impostures by condemning him to life as a galley slave, *Pudd'nhead,* which also concludes by selling an impostor into slavery, is tragic, as it confirms the impotency of Roxy's "rage against the fates" (PW 22). The effort of a mother to have her son defy the fate allotted a slave in America ends in futility.

Tourgée also presents a tragic story. The publisher's introduction goes so far as to call Pactolus Prime, the title character, "the Edipus of American fiction." Observing the three unities, the book takes place on Christmas day in Washington, D.C. Prime is a bootblack at the "Best Hotel." So black that he appears of pure African blood, he has a light-skinned mulatto assistant named Benny, who is reading law with a white lawyer named Phelps. Using Phelps as an agent, Prime has amassed a fortune in real estate under the assumed name of P. P. Smith. Living modestly, he supports a beautiful, young white woman named Eva Collins, who does not know the identity of her benefactor, although she does love her "Uncle Pac," who raised her as a child, claiming to be fulfilling a promise to his lost master, her father. Through Phelps, Prime tries to give a huge Christmas gift to Eva, who refuses until she knows more about the identity of the donor. Struck down in an accident, Prime is taken to Eva's where he is nursed by her and her white maid, Mrs. Macey, only to die. A doctor seems to solve the mystery of Prime's relation to Eva when he confides to Phelps that from medical literature he recognizes Prime as a rare victim of argyria in which his white skin was permanently discolored by treatments with a silver preparation. Phelps, however, knows better, and the reader is presented with a four-chapter memoir Prime left with him.

Born a slave, a son of his master, with so much white blood that he was sometimes mistaken for his master's white son, Prime was sent to school and then university with his half brother, to help him in his studies. His half brother, a Collins, inherits him when their father dies. As the Civil War begins, Prime falls in love with Mazy, a mulatto slave, whom he later discovers in his master's arms. Betrayed, he strikes Collins and flees, eventually joining the Union army as a color-bearer (!), under the name of P. P. Smith. Advised by the regiment's colonel, a lawyer, Prime passes as a white man. After the war he reunites with Mazy and marries her. Both passing as white, they buy a plantation in South Carolina and raise their daughter, Eva. Collins, however, surprises Prime, shoots him, leaves him for dead, and moves in with Mazy. Nursed back to life by a black conjure woman in the swamp, Prime receives his silver treatment, turns completely black, steals his daughter, and heads north. Prime and Eva settle in Washington, D.C., where he starts his double life, later meeting and employing Benny, his wife's son by Collins. Hiring him to keep track of Mazy, whom he fears will betray him, Prime admires Benny's skill and plans to leave him the business. In the meantime, Mazy, passing again as white, ends up as the maid for her blue-eyed, fair-haired daughter. Shown this memoir after Prime's death, Eva joins the Sisters of Mercy, vowing to work for the colored race as Sister Pactola.

Critics have not been convinced by this bizarre story. For instance, the noted African-American critic Sterling Brown complains that it "is not completely convincing" because it has "more argument than characters in action,"[13] and Theodore L. Gross dismisses it as "the product of an author whose literary voice has lost its range and flexibility and power and has become a screeching monotone."[14] But despite such harsh criticism, *Pactolus* deserves closer attention. Even if it subordinates dramatic action to argument, the argument is worth remembering since, as Brown notes, it is "too easily forgotten today."[15] Tourgée's novel also plays an important role in the history of the novel of passing.

If Chesnutt's *House Behind the Cedars* self-consciously responds to Howells's *An Imperative Duty*, it is likely that both respond in part to *Pactolus Prime*. Chesnutt's reading of Tourgée's novel is clearly documented. In a June 5, 1890, letter to Cable about *The Century*'s response to "Rena Walden," the early version of *House,* Chesnutt notes that an English writer need not "immerse" characters having mixed blood "in convents, as Tourgée does his latest heroine, to save them from a fate worse than death, i.e., the confession of inferiority by reason of color."[16] Evidence of Howells's response is circumstantial, but convincing.

In December 1888 Tourgée published an essay entitled "The South as a Field for Fiction." In it he proclaims that "American fiction of to-day, whatever may be its origin, is predominantly Southern in type and character." "Hardly a novelist of prominence," he adds, "except Mr. Howells and Mr. James, but has found it necessary to yield to the prevailing demand and identify himself with Southern types." One of the types they fail to portray is the freedman. To be sure, existing portrayals are themselves flawed. "The traditions of the freedman's fireside are richer and far more tragic than the folk-lore which genius has recently put into his quaint vernacular." The realists, Tourgée claims, although technically capable of portraying such richness, will probable not do so because the type evokes the pathos that their fiction tries to avoid. "Pathos lies at the bottom of all enduring fiction. Agony is the key of immortality. The ills of fate, irreparable misfortune, untoward but unavoidable destiny: these are the things that make for enduring fame. The 'realists' profess to be truth-tellers, but are in fact the worst of falsifiers, since they tell only the weakest and meanest part of the grand truth which makes up the continued story of every life."[17]

As if to show the realists what he means, Tourgée produces *Pactolus,* conceived as a Christmas story and then expanded as it was serialized in the *Advance* from December 13, 1888, to March 14, 1889. Tourgée's wife recorded receiving the first bound copies of the book March 27, 1890. On August 27, 1890, Howells wrote Hamlin Garland that he was at work on *An Imperative Duty.*[18] "The Letters of Olney" had been in Howells's mind since 1886, but very likely Tourgée's attack on him and Tourgée's novel played a role in his return to this project, which, in contrast to Tourgée's aesthetic, shows how belief in unavoidable destiny perpetuates unnecessary racial tragedy.

On the issue of racial destiny Twain seems closer to Tourgée and his sense of tragedy than Howells and his limited optimism. If Howells self-consciously offers an ending that combats the standard fate of the "tragic mulatto," Twain refuses to imagine a way out for his characters of mixed blood. One reason for this difference is that Howells creates a plot in which his heroine can choose between being black or white. Her liminal status allows her free exchange. In contrast, the cradle exchange that Twain imagines invites readers to compare the fates of a white boy raised as black and a "black" boy raised as white. That comparison has comic possibilities, but the outcome is tragic.

The differences and similarities among the endings of Twain's, Tourgée's, and Howells's novels indicate that a realist aesthetic cannot be distinguished simply at the level of plot. A closer look at Tourgée's and Twain's works in conjunction with the *Plessy* decision can move us toward such a distinction. Before turning to that distinction, however, I first want to use similarities between the novels to shed light on debates among Twain's critics about his racial politics. I then want to explore how, despite many similarities, the two novels imply different senses of individuals' duties and obligations, with Twain's closer, if not identical, to those associated with the promise of contract.

III

Liberal and radical critics have both praised and condemned Twain's portrayal of race in *Pudd'nhead.* A debated passage is one in which Roxy mocks her son's cowardice for refusing to accept the challenge of a duel. "It's de nigger in you," she cries, "dat's what it is. Thirty-one parts o' you is white, en on'y one part nigger, en dat po' little one part is yo' *soul*" (PW 70). For some this passage proves Twain's belief in the shaping power of blood. But the passage can also dramatize Twain's awareness of Roxy's double-consciousness. Not only has she internalized the whites' false code of honor that values duels over rule of law; she also has internalized a sense of black inferiority. If so, the passage illustrates the linguistic construction of race in Twain's world. For instance, Roxy later calls attention to the extent to which "nigger" is linguistically determined. "I is a nigger, en nobody ain't gwyne te doubt it dat hears me talk" (PW 80).

Those critical of Twain can grant such readings and still argue that his trading-places plot leads to problems. The thrust of Twain's brief against racism, so the argument runs, depends on his belief that, as one of Pudd'nhead's calendar entries puts it, "training is everything" (PW 23). By having Roxy switch Chambers and Tom in the cradle, he demonstrates the power of nurture over nature in constituting identity. But when the plot unravels to reveal the false Tom as the murderer, Twain nonetheless gives his villain black blood. Lee Clark Mitchell summarizes this point of view: "*Pudd'nhead Wilson* derides the belief in innate racial capacities, and exposes the absurdity of assumptions that arbitrarily separate black from white. Yet the novel resorts to a logic of inheritance that seems at the same time to legitimate belief in racial distinctions. What makes it difficult to sort out the claims of nature from those of nurture is that the latter inevitably alters whatever understanding we have in the former."[19]

What then are we to think of the racial politics of Twain's work? Comparison with *Pactolus* can help us to answer that question. Let's turn first to the argument that Twain reveals the cultural and linguistic construction of race. There is much evidence to support this claim. For instance, when the narrator reminds us that Roxy and her son are black only by a "fiction of law and custom" (PW 9), he clearly challenges the essentialist thinking that helped to legitimate segregation. Nonetheless, when Evan Carton claims that Twain's occasional use of quotation marks around "nigger" calls attention to the term's status as sign (PW 89), we should not forget that Tourgée also places quotation marks around "nigger" and calls the term "expressive of the concentrated contempt of centuries" (PP 44).[20] In fact, Tourgée's attention to linguistic indicators of race begins with his first novel, when a mulatto woman passing as white during the war comes upon her wounded master and lover in a prison camp. She nurses him to health, only to have him betray her, when in front of others he adopts the voice of master, which she answers "instantly, with the inimitable and indescribable intonation of the slave: 'Sir?' That was all she said. It was enough. It revealed all. The brand showed" (RG 78). In *Pactolus Prime* Phelps rebukes Prime for adopting the voice of a slave. "You ought not to perpetuate even the language of slavery—much less its spirit" (PP 156).

Tourgée may have even seen a legal possibility in exposing the language of slavery as a sign of subserviency. If a black's language constituted a "badge of servitude," he could argue that there was a constitutional obligation to provide blacks with an education that could remove that badge. Prime, for instance, having attended college, is bilingual, able to switch from dialect to standard English at will. Knowing how to play "nigger" to provoke the consciences of his prestigious customers, he can also argue with the best lawyer in the lawyer's own language.

Seven years before Du Bois identified double-consciousness and four before Twain wrote *Pudd'nhead,* Tourgée uses Prime's two voices to mark his split identity and express ambivalence toward his black blood. Mixing pride and self-loathing, Pactolus counsels Benny, as he had been counseled by the colonel, to pass as white. Doubleness of this sort structures the book. Tourgée, a white lawyer, speaks out on race by adopting the voice of a black man, who in the novel needs a white lawyer to act as his agent. Trained in the law by this same white lawyer, Benny is told by Prime that, because the world is ruled by whites, he can do more for his race as a white lawyer than as a black. Such advice implies that the only way for a black to succeed in a white man's world is to lie and be a divided self, a possibility that motivates Eva's final act of committed withdrawal, "for she saw no other way to avoid either deception or the confession of inferiority" (PP 358).

Pac's advice to Benny is important for another reason. Much work in law and literature explores how literary texts respond to legal decisions. But for Tourgée, fiction served as a testing ground where he could rehearse legal arguments that sometimes made their way into court. The Louisiana law, Tourgée claimed in *Plessy,* conferred upon the conductor of a train "the power to deprive one of the reputation of being a white man, or at least to impair that reputation." In turn, reputation is a form of property because it can affect earning power. "How much," Tourgée goes on, "would it be worth to a young man entering upon the practice of law, to be regarded as a white man rather than a colored one? Six-sevenths of the population are white. Nineteen-twentieths of the property of the country is owned by white people."[21] Tourgée first worked out this imaginative argument in his portrayal of Benny. Of course, Twain also knew that reputation was a form of property, as evidenced not only by Pudd'nhead's failure to attract clients once he is branded a fool, but also by the status accorded to the two Toms.

The similarities between *Pactolus* and *Pudd'nhead* suggest that, although Twain's exposure of linguistic elements in the construction of race challenges the logic of the *Plessy* decision, it is not necessarily aesthetically innovative. At the same time, other similarities between Tourgée and Twain suggest that the problems that Twain's novel encounters with the nature/nurture opposition might reveal more about the assumptions of contemporary critics than reactionary racial politics on Twain's part. Concerned that he take the correct stand on race, we insist that he demonstrate the power of training. But within Twain's world the phrase "training is everything" has repressive, not liberating, connotations. In *A Connecticut Yankee* Hank Morgan asserts, "Training—training is everything: training is all there is to a person. We speak of nature; it is folly; there is no such thing as nature; what we call by that misleading name is merely heredity and training. We have no thoughts of our own, no opinions of our own; they are transmitted to us, trained into us" (CY 208).

Morgan's fear would seem to be confirmed in *Pudd'nhead Wilson,* which dramatizes what Earl F. Briden calls the "enslaving effects of communal opinion upon the individual."[22] Not immune to these enslaving effects, some contemporary critics have been so trained to evoke the powers of training on issues of race that they ignore the way in which *Pudd'nhead* is a tragedy *because* of the powers of training. No one in the novel seems free from the enslaving effect of existing cultural narratives, including Roxy with her double-consciousness. Thus, in our demand that Twain remain consistent on the issue of training, we reveal our own inconsistencies. The consequences of that inconsistency are made more poignant when we remember that the *Plessy* court allowed state legislatures to defer to communal opinion on race to pass laws for the public good. To abandon judgment of Twain long enough to try to understand his position might put critics in a better position to understand the circumstances in which inconsistencies in contemporary opinions arose.

Prospero's judgment in *The Tempest* that Caliban is "a born devil, on whose nature / Nurture can never stick" (iv. i. 188–89) could tempt us to assume that our present formulation of the nature/nurture opposition was always already there. But both "nature" and "nurture" have complicated histories in themselves. Furthermore, nineteenth-century theories of evolution altered their relation. For evidence that Twain was not operating within the opposition as we see it at present, we can look more closely at Morgan's passage on training. For us nature versus nurture means heredity versus environment, but this is not the case for Morgan. "There is no such thing as nature," he says; "what we call by that name is merely heredity and training." What is nature for us is not nature for Morgan. For him, heredity is not opposed to training but lumped with it in joint opposition to what he calls nature. Seemingly inconsistent from our present perspective, Morgan's statement would have made perfect sense within late nineteenth-century thought that linked, rather than opposed, environmental training and hereditary transmission.

Although Darwin's nonteleological theory of natural selection was common knowledge, the experimental work necessary to confirm it was not available until the 1890s or later. For instance, Gregor Mendel's work on genetics in the 1860s was not disseminated until 1900. As a result, most scientists in America clung to a neo-Lamarckian view of evolution in which acquired characteristics could be inherited. Neo-Lamarckianism suited nineteenth-century notions of teleological progress because it allowed people to believe that the adaptive learning of one generation was passed on to the next. Morgan's comment that "training is everything," followed by the grouping of heredity and training, makes perfect neo-Lamarckian sense.

To identify Morgan's comment as neo-Lamarckian does not resolve the debate over Twain's racial politics, since neo-Lamarckianism underlay nineteenth-century scientific racism by implying that different races had different behaviors, temperaments, and levels of intelligence. In conjunction with a Eurocentric view of teleological progress, it enabled the common belief that Africans were "outcasts from evolution."[23] For instance, in the 1895 presidential address to the American Association for the Advancement of Science, Daniel G. Brinton correlated the mental and physical structures of races and argued that some, especially among the "black, brown, and red races," manifested "a peculiar mental temperament which has become hereditary and general, of a nature to disqualify them for the atmosphere of modern enlightenment." Also, in 1896, Frederick Hoffman published a book with the assistance of the American Economic Association editorial staff, which used the racial situation in the United States to prove the inferiority of the African race. Influenced by the widespread link between race and country, as well as by the fact that blacks had been free for a generation (and thus able to transmit adaptive characteristics), Hoffman noted that the "natural bond of sympathy [typically] existing between people of the same country, no matter how widely separated by language and nationality, cannot be proved to exist between the white and colored races of the United States." Good citizens, these experts used their science to advise the country on racial laws. Brinton, for instance, concluded that the "only sure foundation for legislation" was scientific evidence about racial difference, "not *a priori* notions of the rights of man."[24]

Twain's neo-Lamarckianism would, therefore, seem to confirm a latent racism. But the situation is complicated. One of the targets of scientific racists was Tourgée. Hoffman, for instance, questioned the shaky foundation for "the many foolish utterances" on race made by people like Tourgée.[25] Yet Tourgée, whose credentials as a defender of blacks are hard to question, seems himself to have been a neo-Lamarckian. The prefaces to both *Pactolus* and *Murvale Eastman: Christian Socialist,* also published in 1890, declare that inheritance and environment shape character. Often Tourgée calls attention to the influence of blood. Benny, Pac insists, will be a smarter man for having Collins blood in his veins. "The fact that you've got that blood in your veins makes it certain that you'll succeed, if you don't let the stubbornness you inherit with it, spoil your chances" (PP 138). As Prime puts it, "no human law can prevent the transmission of qualities" (PP 140.)

Tourgée shows how racial injustice could be challenged even within a neo-Lamarckian framework, which is not to say that Tourgée was free of nineteenth-century racial prejudices any more than we are from twentieth-century ones. But refusing to believe that Africans were outcasts from evolution, he turned neo-Lamarckianism into an argument to improve conditions for blacks. "One who has been a slave can never be made wholly free," Pac writes. "Liberty is a growth—an evolution—not an instantaneous fact" (PP 311–12). Raised in the environment of slavery, blacks will transmit slavelike characteristics. Provided with a proper environment, however, they would acquire different characteristics to pass on to future generations. Within a neo-Lamarckian framework, what today we call the cultural construction of identity was merely part of the combined force of nature and nurture. Thus, Tourgée was devoted to providing blacks with equal conditions, especially education.

An Appeal to Caesar (1884) spelled out his argument for federal support to wipe out illiteracy, especially in the South. *Pactolus* returns to the issues that he raises in that work.[26]

Tourgée's neo-Lamarckian argument suggests that Twain too combats racism from within a neo-Lamarckian framework. *Pudd'nhead,* we can conclude, is a tragedy of both heredity and training. Roxy's attempt to defy the socially constructed fate of her son as a slave ends up producing two "niggers." "Tom" is born a "nigger" because he has black blood, while the real Tom is condemned to remain one because of acculturation. As Tourgée writes, "There ain't ever any good comes of tryin' to make white folks out of niggers. White folks may git to be niggers, but niggers can't ever git to be white folks" (PP 223).

If neither Twain's nor Tourgée's works oppose heredity and training, they do, however, as the last quotation indicates, distinguish between the two. A white person can be made a "nigger" only through training, whereas heredity makes it impossible for training to make a "nigger" white. This distinction is linguistically available in Morgan's 1889 passage on training. If, as the passage begins, "training is everything," then training must also include hereditary transmission. But not quite, for why else would Twain need to write both "heredity" and "training," both "transmitted" and "trained"? Clearly, for Morgan there is a distinction, if not necessarily an opposition, between heredity and training. What links the two is not identity, but a common opposition to a "nature" that is not what we mean by nature today.

Morgan does not define what he means by nature, but he offers a suggestion when he concludes his passage vowing to "save that one microscopic atom in me that is truly *me*" (CY 208). The way in which that microscopic atom qualifies the power of training is important for understanding *Pudd'nhead.*

As we have seen, critics concerned with the issue of race read the phrase "training is everything" positively, whereas those concerned with the tyranny of communal opinion read it negatively. But since part of the tyranny of communal opinion in Twain's fictional Dawson's Landing concerns race, neither of these readings is satisfactory. Indeed, the immediate context in *Pudd'nhead Wilson* invites an ironic reading. In the very chapter to which the entry is appended, Judge Driscoll offers some of Pudd'nhead's "quips and fancies" to a few of the town's "chief citizens." "Irony," however, "was not for these people; their mental vision was not focused for it. They read those playful trifles in solid earnest . . ." (PW 25). Earnestly concerned, on the one hand, to demonstrate the bleak consequences of the fact that Pudd'nhead's "dictum" on training, unlike Hank Morgan's, "no longer admits qualifications or exceptions,"[27] and, on the other, to argue that it should not admit qualifications or exceptions, contemporary critics resemble the community of readers in Dawson's Landing whose mental vision rules out a playful reading of his calendar entries.

That "training is everything" should not be read purely negatively is suggested by the sentence that follows it: "The peach was once a bitter almond; cauliflower is nothing but cabbage with a college education" (PW 23). Not only is the tone here far removed from Morgan's despair, the promise of a college education suggests that the effects of training are not all bad. Twain demonstrated his belief in education by supporting a black student through Yale law school. But Pudd'nhead's quip also points to education's limits. As Sherwood Cummings has pointed out, the remark about the peach echoes a sentence in Darwin.[28] After all, few would argue that education could transform a cabbage into a cauliflower. Indeed, if the student Twain supported eventually helped Thurgood Marshall in his early legal career, "Tom" has his manners changed by two years at Yale, but not his character.[29]

Many critics assume that Tom resists training because of black blood. In fact, for Twain resistance comes from that microscopic atom of a self that is determined by neither training nor heredity. For him that atom is not linked to color. Tom may be a rascal, but he was a rascal in early drafts when he was all white. Because there are black, white, and mulatto rascals, on the issue of rascality Twain is neutral.

Neutrality, however, may not be as neutral as it seems. After all, the *Plessy* majority also claimed to maintain a stance of neutrality on issues of race. But Twain's neutrality is not the Court's. If the Court felt that under the "separate but equal" law the position of blacks and whites was equal, Twain's novel, with its portrayal of double-consciousness, challenges the Court's logic. In fact, Twain does not confine his portrayal of double-consciousness to Roxy. When "Tom" first discovers that he has black blood, Twain dramatizes how someone defined as black interiorizes a sense of inferiority. After Tom's revelation, Twain writes, "the 'nigger' in him was surprised when the white friend put out his hand for a shake with him. He found the 'nigger' in him involuntarily giving the road, on the sidewalk, to the white rowdy and loafer" (PW 45). The list goes on for two paragraphs.

In other words, Twain's neutrality is not the neutrality claimed by the *Plessy* majority. Nonetheless, it still makes sense to evoke the criterion of neutrality for him. Not neutral in the sense that he has no position on racial issues, but neutral in the sense that "black" and "white" characters in his work are, if not absolutely exchangeable, more exchangeable than in many other novels of passing. There are, for example, those unchanged passages in the final text that were written before "Tom" acquired black blood in Twain's imagination. Herschel Parker points to them and calls criticism on the theme of slavery in *Pudd'nhead Wilson* an "exercise in futility."[30] Trained as a textual critic, Parker demands some material indication that for Twain the meaning of the passages changed from the time that Tom was white to the time that he is black. But Parker fails to consider the possibility that Twain would have enjoyed the irony that passages written while Tom was all white continue to work once Tom has acquired black blood. It is certainly consistent with Twain's views of race that, like Tom, the passages retain the same surface appearance but their identity has been dramatically transformed. In refusing to acknowledge this possibility Parker is like the townspeople who miss the irony of Pudd'nhead's joke about the dog because they demand a visible sign of his intention.

Twain's neutrality in terms of race is closer to the color-blind standard evoked by Justice Harlan in his *Plessy* dissent. Because Harlan borrows his metaphor from Tourgée, it might seem that Tourgée shares Twain's sense of neutrality.[31] But Tourgée is also aware that color blindness can be a defect that keeps people from seeing the actual conditions of freedmen. In *Bricks without Straw* (1880) Tourgée's narrator describes how the freedman had been granted rights, and he complains: "Right he had, in the abstract; in the concrete, none. Justice would not hear his voice. The law was still color-blinded by the past."[32] Appearing in a chapter entitled "Nunc Pro Tunc," a legal phrase meaning "now for then" that describes acts with a retroactive effect allowed to be done after the time when they should have been done, Tourgée's literary use of the metaphor indicates that he recognized how color blindness could become myopia, keeping the law from acting affirmatively to help improve the concrete conditions of freedmen. That recognition helps to distinguish the duties and obligations that Tourgée imagines for his characters from those imagined by Twain.

Like most novels of passing, Twain's contrasts the interests of self with those of family. To save his inheritance Tom murders the uncle who has adopted him. Even worse, to save his skin he sells his mother down the river. But Twain does not link familial loyalty with racial loyalty, while Tourgée does, even if, as we shall see, he complicates that standard linkage.[33] This difference results in some conventional beliefs of Twain's, especially on gender, and some innovative beliefs of Tourgée's, especially on the condition of black Americans. Nonetheless, if Twain's blindness to the historical need for racial loyalty points to limits of his realism, Tourgée's awareness of it does not redeem his outmoded aesthetic. Whereas Tourgée claims to untangle the complications of late nineteenth-century society so as to free readers to think properly on racial issues, Twain uses them to entangle his readers, past and present, in the community that he constructs, a community, according to Carton, of "disingenuousness and guilt."[34]

IV

Twain's sense of responsibility grows out of his belief in human sympathy. As we have seen, universal human sympathy is closely related to the promise of contract and helps to explain the popularity of Smith's *The Theory of Moral Sentiments* in the period. Belief in racial affinities presents a problem for that promise. Indeed, by the end of the century people began to argue that sympathy could draw groups apart as much as draw individuals together.[35] By not stressing racial loyalty, Twain, like Howells, retains remnants of the ideal of universal human sympathy. In contrast, Tourgée, while deploring racial prejudice, encourages blacks to maintain a sense of racial loyalty. If the two realists' sense of universal sympathy challenges the logic of segregation, it also leads to some fairly conventional portrayals.

Twain's realism would seem to oppose the sentimentality of a writer such as Harriet Beecher Stowe.[36] But both attack slavery by dramatizing how it violates bonds of sentiment by reducing human beings to pieces of property.[37] In Twain the icon of such violations is a contractually agreed upon bill of sale for a human being. If it seems inconsistent for Twain, who supported liberal economics, to expose damaging effects of contractual exchanges, he, like Stowe, did not attack the market itself, only its disruption of the ties that bind.[38] Indeed, a comparison of the roles played by bills of sale in *Huckleberry Finn* and *Pudd'nhead* reveals distinctions even within exchanges of sentiment themselves.

In both works the bills are counterfeit. Allowing Huck to prove ownership of Jim, the one in *Huckleberry Finn* raises perplexing questions about the possible counterfeit nature of the documents that form the foundation of market exchanges. In fact, when it is later used to sell Jim back into slavery, it illustrates how commerce can disrupt the fraternal bond established between Huck and Jim. Nonetheless, for Twain their bond is constructed. The bond that Tom violates by selling his mother down the river is not. For Twain this bond is natural, more natural than the one between a father and his children.

Fathers are everywhere absent in *Pudd'nhead*. The father of Roxy's child never acknowledges his son and dies when the son is still a boy. The father of the true "heir" also dies early, leaving a worthless inheritance as the result of unwise speculation in real estate. The "father" murdered by Tom is a father by adoption.[39] In contrast, Tom's mother is very much in evidence. Her attempt to save her son generates the plot of the novel, and his lack of gratitude makes him seem a naturally depraved villain.

A mother's natural relation to her child also helps drive the plot in *Huckleberry Finn,* even if through its absence. Huck, of course, starts the book without a mother and with an irresponsible father, who soon dies, leaving Huck an orphan. What needs to be emphasized, however, is that the book's attack on domesticity almost demands that Huck be motherless. The reader and Twain have no problem when Huck rebels against the civilizing efforts of the widow and Aunt Sally. But the sympathies of both would have been complicated if Huck's rebellion had been directed against his mother. Twain may not recognize natural bonds of race, but he does recognize one between mother and child.[40]

Tom's betrayal of his mother allows Twain to show that under slavery, when the work of motherhood was often done by slaves, the bond between mother and child was threatened. The death of the real heir's mother does not alter the fact that Roxy would have been the surrogate mother of a white child anyway. What Roxy's exchange of infants does is turn her surrogate motherhood into a seemingly real motherhood. Nonetheless, she retains secret affections for her son by birth, a son who has no knowledge of his relationship to his mother even though she mothers him, just as she would have had to mother any white child in his position. In one sense, then, Tom's lack of gratitude is Twain's comment on the lack of gratitude that so many masters displayed to the black women who raised them. Tom, however, is in fact Roxy's real son, and his lack of gratitude seems even worse. Thus, as much as Twain recognizes the importance of acknowledging the work of surrogate mothers, he continues to privilege the ties of blood through the mother, whether that blood be black or white. The world of commerce threatens those ties because its bonds are not natural, but constructed. And in Twain's world no invisible hand or higher moral order presides over their construction.

The ties that bind and their relationship to the world of commerce is quite different in Tourgée. Like John Hay, Tourgée retains classical republicanism's patriarchal principle of moral order. Indeed, of the works of passing that I have examined, only Hay's "The Foster Brothers" and *Pactolus* focus on a father/daughter rather than a mother/daughter or a mother/son relation. Like Hay, Tourgée also adheres to an American version of republicanism in which commerce can lead to virtue rather than threaten it, so long as the commercial world is governed by the same patriarchal moral order that governs the family.

Even so, Tourgée's republicanism was much less influenced by liberalism than Hay's was. One result is different views on race and labor. For instance, Tourgée disliked *The Bread-Winners* and sympathized with wage earners. "Wage-earning is not slavery," Tourgée writes in the preface to *Murvale Eastman,* "but when it becomes a fixed condition it is one of sheer dependence" (ME iv). That dependency creates new social conditions. In the "new feudalism" (ME iii) of the present, "the 'wealth of nations' has proved a delusion" (ME v). Previously, the battle for freedom had been one of rights, as both serfs and slaves struggled for the rights of citizenship. But the subjection of the wage earner "does not trench upon the domain of personal right. No individual laborer has a right to demand work and wages of an individual employer" (ME iv). Restoring workers' independence is not a question of personal rights. "It is a question between society and the employer as to the control of opportunity" (ME iv). Recognizing that relations between employers and workers are not providing promised opportunities, Tourgée evokes a societal obligation. In doing so he separates himself from the mainstream of the Republican Party, which continued to conceive of duties and obligations in terms of contracting individuals. In 1890, in *Murvale Eastman,* he works out the consequences of his position for the "Labor Question"; in *Pactolus Prime,* for the "Negro Question."

If the question facing society is one of opportunity, merely granting former slaves rights is not enough. They also need commercial opportunity. If for Twain and Stowe slavery illustrates the potentially damaging effects of commercial logic intruding into the domestic circle, Tourgée, like Chesnutt, shows how racism can undermine the potentially positive effects of commerce. In *Pactolus* commercial enterprise more often than not serves the interests of family. The propensity to accumulate wealth that Pac and Benny inherit from their Collins blood allows Pac to provide unselfishly for his daughter. She, unlike the greedy Tom, does not pursue her inheritance at the expense of family members. She even refuses the gift offered her until she clears up the mystery of her relation to its donor. But a racist society makes it necessary for her father to conceal his role as patriarchal protector.

By linking Pac's commercial prowess with the fulfillment of his role as a patriarchal protector of his daughter, Tourgée creates an impossible dilemma. The lawyer Phelps wants Pac to get rid of his disguise and become a public model to combat the prejudice that blacks lack business sense. But publicly acknowledging himself as the person who has amassed the fortune to pass onto his daughter is precisely what Pac cannot do, since to do so would be to reveal himself as Eva's father and thus to brand her black and taint her life forever. The same sense of duty that motivates Pac to accumulate wealth makes it impossible for him to reveal to the world how much he has embodied the commercial virtue recognized by American society. Unable to acknowledge himself to his daughter, he must play the role of a servant, while a white lawyer acts as the agent for a fictional father named P. P. Smith.

In trying to elicit public sympathy for an argument based on opportunity as well as rights, Tourgée needed to revise the standard account about the horrors of slavery. In "The South as a Field for Fiction," he writes: "About the Negro as a man, with hopes, fears and aspirations like other men, our literature is very nearly silent. Much has been written of the slave and something of the freedman, but thus far no one has been found able to weld the new life to the old. This indeed is the great difficulty to be overcome. As soon as the American Negro seeks to rise above the level of the former time, he finds himself confronted with the past of his race and the woes of his kindred."[41] In making the reduction of human beings to pieces of property the major evil of slavery, Twain, like Stowe, could tap into the widespread belief that all humans had a right to freedom. He could also elicit a powerful emotional reaction by showing how such a system allowed family relations to be violated by the logic of the market. But his focus severely limited his ability to face the "great difficulty" of welding the life of the freedman to that of the slave. After all, once the freedman is no longer a piece of property, the emotional force of Twain's plot disappears.

This limitation may help to account for why Twain sets his two most important works dealing with race, in the era of slavery. It may also explain Steven Mailloux's remarkable discovery that, despite the publication of part of *Huckleberry Finn* in the issue of *The Century* containing "The Freedman's Case in Equity," there is no contemporary commentary linking Twain's novel to debates over the "Negro Question."[42] Indeed, insofar as Grady makes clear that those in the New South do not want a return to slavery, it could even be argued that Twain's portrayal of the inhumanity of slavery does not explicitly take sides in the post-Reconstruction debate. The same could not be said of Tourgée's works.

The worst evil of slavery in *Pactolus Prime* is not the reduction of human beings to property. It is the production of a racism that continues to brand even freedmen with a badge of inferiority. According to Pac, "Slavery was never half so great a curse as that brand of infamy which stamps the soul at its birth with ineradicable inferiority" (PP 45). The end of slavery does not mean an end to this infamy. Persisting in the postbellum period, it undermines the moral order that should govern both the domestic and commercial worlds. The lack of such order forces Pac to face a conflict between his personal interests and the duty to serve as a model for his race.

Standard as that conflict is in the novel of passing, Tourgée complicates it in a number of fascinating ways. First, Pac's personal interest is not for himself but a duty that he feels for his daughter. Second, Pac serves that interest as a "white" man while still remaining black. Third, and perhaps most important, Pac recognizes that the circumscribed role allotted blacks in the public sphere creates conditions in which someone who can pass is able to accomplish more for his race by choosing to be white. At the book's end Eva recognizes this irony, and earlier Pac responds to Benny's question, "But can't I do something for the race?" with: "As a white man you can do more than a thousand colored men" (PP 140).

Pac's insistence that Benny will be able to help his race more as a white lawyer than a black one calls attention to how much Tourgée remains focused on the public sphere. As a black lawyer Benny could certainly help members of the black community in their private affairs, but he would have little power in the public sphere of politics. Without that power he could do little to guarantee just treatment for the entire black race. For Tourgée the central issue remains achieving justice for the freedmen. If justice remains a question of what is right, it can no longer be satisfied only in terms of rights.

Through a discussion that Benny has with a customer, Tourgée, like so many others, makes a case for the freedman in terms of equity, which a judge listening to the exchange defines as " 'what the common reason of mankind approves as just and true' " (PP 87).[43] Nonetheless, the judge calls attention to difficulties that occur "when one tries to apply the rules of equity to the practice of peoples and nations" (PP 87). For instance, how could a distinction be made between former slaveholders or their descendants and those who opposed slavery? Benny's response is: "It is the duty of *all* the people to see that the law wrongs no man, is it not" (PP 88)? The slave's labor, after all, "has gone into the national wealth—that immense aggregate that we have recently seen paraded before the world's eyes with so much boastfulness" (PP 87). Admitting the power of Benny's argument, the judge ends by referring to "Heavenly Chancery" (PP 92), which operates with a steadier hand than equity presided over by human beings. "God," he declares, "has a strange way of keeping his accounts—the debit and credit of right and wrong between races and peoples—and settling them according to His own notions" (PP 91).

Tourgée's appeal to equity distinguishes his moral economy from Twain's. First, there is his faith in the "common reason of mankind," a faith that Twain calls into question with his portrayal of communal opinion in Dawson's Landing. Indeed, given the *Plessy* court's deference to communal opinion to define reasonableness, Tourgée's faith seems misplaced. Of course, when he evokes the common reason of mankind he is not referring simply to public opinion. He has in mind a higher notion of right reason. But his belief in right reason serves to distinguish him further from Twain, for faith in a higher source of justice is not embodied in the structure of Twain's novel.

Another difference is Tourgée's desire to balance accounts between races and peoples. Pac, for instance, demonstrates to a businessman that for whites to have their financial "account squared" with blacks so as to "start afresh" (PP 73), they would have to pay at least ten billion 1890 dollars for uncompensated labor. To be sure, Twain also believed that whites owed blacks a debt. But in the dramatic working out of his novel Twain focuses on debts owed on an individual level. One of the aesthetic problems with Tourgée's novel is that it can find no way to dramatize his fascinating idea that equity needs to be applied to nations and peoples, not just individuals.

But, as important as equity is for Tourgée, it is not his final word on the issue of race. Despite his calculations to balance accounts, Pac declares, "It is not recompense that we seek, but right. Justice to-day, pays all the debts of yesterday, and nothing else will" (PP 94). In fact,

Pac does not even insist on strict justice, if it means "to make compensation for the past." All he really asks for is an end to injustice, which "pertains only to the future and is always possible" (PP 117). The entire discussion of credit and debit, he asserts, was in response to someone "who believes that political society is merely a business association for business purposes" (PP 117). Not opposed to commerce but lodged within the republican tradition, Tourgée has a different sense of political society. His means of avoiding further injustice within it is education.

As Pac shines the shoes of a senator, he argues for Tourgée's plan to eliminate illiteracy. When the senator expresses doubt about such a "great National charity" (PP 129), Pac admits that the charity of the North has been "as boundless as its faith" (PP 128), but insists that his plan is a matter of justice not charity. Furthermore, wiping out illiteracy is in the national welfare, since the "ignorant voter is a source of actual peril" (PP 120). His plan, therefore, is a "great defensive policy on which the peace and welfare of the United States are certain some time to depend" (PP 130).[44]

Like sentimentalists, Tourgée believes in a controlling higher moral order, but his order is one governed by right reason, not sentiment. Pac, for instance, claims that his policies are a "matter of right rather than one of sentiment" (PP 126). Devoted to the enlightenment project of educating the public on the dictates of right reason, especially on issues of race, Tourgée saw prejudice and custom as barriers in his way. Yet he was not naive about how to deal with prejudice. For instance, he has Prime echo Lemuel Shaw in *Roberts v. City of Boston*. "Prejudice," Prime admits, "whether right or wrong, can rarely be legislated out of existence, and the schools of the South would be valueless to the colored people if they were opened by compulsion to them" (PP 118). Tourgée also knew that the Supreme Court was not free from prejudice. The Court, he wrote, "has always been the foe of liberty until forced to move on by public opinion."[45]

As part of what Prime calls "this coming warfare of opinion" (PP 141), Tourgée wrote newspaper columns and founded his own journal. He also expressed a belief shared by a number of recent critics that fiction could accomplish important cultural work by fixing public opinion.[46] A necessary supplement to his legal activities, Tourgée's literary activities were devoted to a campaign "to reach and awaken public sentiment."[47]

Tourgée's use of literature to advocate his views on race led to attacks by those believing that to subordinate literature to politics is to ruin it.

For instance, the editor of *The Century* who refused an essay of Chesnutt's because of its politics, wrote to George Washington Cable that his manuscript of *John March, Southerner* had "gleams of the delightful old art." But, he complained, it was "a tract, not a story. . . . Instead of a return *to* literature; an attempt to fetch everything into literature save & except literature itself. . . . Shades of Tourgée!"[48]

The contempt addressed toward Tourgée for defending the novel of purpose has led Kenneth Warren to take seriously his attack on realism. For Warren American realism in general "must be read against a backdrop of the North's retreat from a commitment to securing freedom and equal rights for black Americans—a retreat that moved the body of Northern opinion to an acceptance of policies and decisions mandating the social, political, and economic subordination of the nation's freedmen."[49] There is, without a doubt, truth to the argument that Howells and James tried to avoid the partisan politics between North and South in their fiction.[50] It is important to remember, however, that attempts to avoid partisan politics are not necessarily apolitical. If political rhetoric is, as Aristotle defines it, linked to questions of the social good, there are times when not taking part in partisan squabbles can be an important political move. Not abandoning belief in universal human sympathy, the realists remained more focused on imagining possibilities for the entire population than advocating the position of one party or group. To be sure, insofar as the defense of black rights came to be seen as a sign of partisanship, Warren's complaint about realism is an important one, although, as we have seen, the realists were not all alike on racial issues. Part of the function of this chapter is to distinguish Twain's portrayal of race from James's and Howells's. It is also to distinguish his literary practice from Tourgée's. What Warren does not consider in his analysis of the realists is Tourgée's alternative aesthetic.

V

Tourgée grants that Howells and James are masters in fiction. For instance, calling the courtroom scene in *A Modern Instance* one of "immense vigor and dramatic effect," he declares that "no more scathing words on certain divorce laws have ever been spoken."[51] Nonetheless, he expresses concern over both the content and method of realism. The preface to *Pactolus* has the realists in mind when it states that Tourgée's method "is not only original, but almost unique. He does not develope [*sic*] his characters by self-analytic monologue or the unnatural expedient of making them constant seekers for advice." Elsewhere Tourgée complains that realists exalt "accuracy of detail . . . almost to the exclusion of other artistic qualities. It mattered little what was the subject, save that it must have no historical or emotional significance." Tourgée was especially upset with how, according to him, realists sneered at attempts to show how lives were influenced by "the rise and fall of empires, the movements of races and peoples, the conflict of jarring civilizations." Sneering himself, he claims that instead realists focused on "the littlest and meanest characteristics of the lives [they seek] to portray."[52]

Tourgée's complaint that the realists focused on the accuracy of details at the expense of their historical significance is similar to Lukàcs's years later about the naturalists.[53] Like Lukàcs, he insists on a higher significance for the details of life, and he disputes the notion that life, even if common, can be commonplace. "Life, whether of low or high degree, is never commonplace if we reach its core. The depiction of the mere commonplace, therefore, however accurate, is not a true portraiture of life. The commonplaces of emotion, sentiment, and aspiration, are only incidents which sometimes reveal and sometimes hide the real life. One might as well recall Washington's account of his expenses a history of the Revolution. It is part of that history, but only the meanest part."[54] If for Lukàcs Marxist history makes life significant, for Tourgée spirituality does. In *Murvale Eastman* he faults realism for assuming that human character is a result of natural law. "So it is; but those laws are not all physical, nor purely mental. The soul must be taken into account if we would comprehend humanity or truly portray character" (ME 113). "Till some gleam of spirituality is added" to James's work, Tourgée warns, "he must remain artist, but can never become creator."[55]

For Tourgée, who supported a campaign to remove books from the Boston Public Library that were "objectionable from any rational standpoint" and "unfit for decent people to read,"[56] the realists lacked moral purpose and unfairly mocked traditional values. To his insistence that "love, and honor, and self-sacrifice remain, despite the flood of unhealthy caricature that comes from the press of to-day," he adds: "In his desire to avoid unreal sentimentality, the modern American novelist has gone to the other extreme of a more unreal and unnatural cynicism."[57] That cynicism is especially apparent in the treatment of love.

Writing shortly after the publication of *The Rise of Silas Lapham* and *The Bostonians,* and very likely alluding to them, Tourgée complains that, in satirizing sentimental love and presenting a "stage on which a pair of self-conscious actors perform a miserable comedy of self-deception," the realist novel has eliminated the idea of love itself and "substituted a poor, petulant, selfish desire for possession." "Surprised glances, analytic agony, and morbid self-anatomy have taken the place of honest love-making. No man woos in true manly fashion, no woman yields with tender truthfulness, in the modern realistic novel. Courtship has come to be a war of wits. The wooer is transformed into a pursuer. . . . He frets, and worries, and persecutes, until the overwrought sensibility of the poor creature gives way, and she spitefully or tearfully capitulates, apparently for the mere sake of peace."[58]

In contrast, Tourgée praises Helen Hunt Jackson's *Ramona* because it recognizes that love is not dead. Although he knows that *Ramona* will be attacked for advocating the cause of Indians, Tourgée calls it "unquestionably the best novel yet produced by an American woman."[59] He also publishes Elizabeth Stuart Phelps and celebrates E. P. Roe, the sentimental author of the religious novel *Barriers Burned Away.* "Few men have extended a healthier influence upon the life of today than Mr. Roe. In these times when the novel of purpose is made a matter of artistic ridicule by our over-refined dilettanti, and the novel without a purpose is corrupting the heart and brain of the rising generation . . . the very large scales which his works have had disclose to us the pleasing fact that our American reading public is not yet entirely given over to the worship of realism which insists that fiction shall be given up to the painting of life as it is, dirt and all."[60]

Tourgée, whose favorite author was the literary lawyer Walter Scott deplored by Twain, belonged more to the tradition of legal men of letters who dominated the political and literary scene in the first years of the republic than to the tradition of sentimental fiction. But his attack on the realists and his praise of sentimentalists indicate that for many contemporaries republicanism and sentimentalism had more in common with one another than either had in common with the practice of realism.

One area of the country where the traditions of both republicanism and sentimentalism were more successful in resisting the rise of realism was the South. In singling out the South as the most promising field for American fiction, Tourgée adhered to the widespread belief that it retained a sense of honor and virtue undermined in the North by forces of modernity. In fact, Tourgée's aesthetic practice had more in common with Southern writers of the plantation school, such as the lawyer-novelist Thomas Nelson Page, who openly fought against the political, social, and civil rights of blacks, than with the realists who at their worst may have been complicit with the Northern retreat from rights for freedmen, but who, nonetheless, advocated an aesthetic that undercut the increasingly sentimentalized view of the slaveholding South. As Howells's Basil March puts it in *Their Wedding Journey*, "I suppose that almost any evil commends itself by its ruin; the wrecks of slavery are fast growing a fungus crop of sentiment, and they may yet outflourish the remains of the feudal system in the kind of poetry they produce" (WJ 95).[61] To base an aesthetic practice on right reason, as Tourgée did, did not guarantee agreement on what was right. Tourgée and Page might have shared one another's beliefs in honor, self-sacrifice, and love, but they had very different notions as to what right reason dictated on race.

The problem with Tourgée's attempt to use fiction to fix the public's opinion on racial matters was that the public adhered more to Page's views than his own. As a result, Tourgée's cultural work stopped working. If Benny and Prime win every argument in a work of fiction, the public was no more swayed by *Pactolus Prime* than the Court would be by his argument in *Plessy*. In contrast, Page's fiction along with work by revisionist historians helped to establish in the public's mind a view of the antebellum South in which race relations were not tense and blacks were often better off than in their freed condition.

The failure of Tourgée's fiction points to the limits of his literary project. A child of the enlightenment, Tourgée believed that by embodying right reason in his fiction he could educate public opinion and eliminate prejudice. The problem with that goal is similar to the one he himself noted in the Court's interpretation of the "equal but separate" law. The works that he hoped would alter racial prejudice could not be interpreted free from the history of prejudice that he would alter. Whereas Tourgée thought that he had expressed right reason in *Pactolus Prime,* even his "moderate" critics declared the book fanatical.[62]

To recognize the limits of Tourgée's literary project is not to claim that realism has none, but it can help us better understand the realists' options within their historical context. Not directly related to racial politics, part of that context was the rise of a professional middle class. Twain's and Tourgée's responses to it affect their aesthetics.

VI

Tourgée never mentions Twain in his criticism. Of course, he could not fault Twain for neglecting the South in his fiction. He might even have seen Twain as an ally in demystifying false images of Southern society.[63] Nonetheless, as we have seen, Twain did not take up the difficult task of explicitly linking the condition of the freedman to slavery. Twain was also a mugwump. Tourgée had more against mugwumps than their disloyalty to the Republican Party. He opposed their proposals for civil service reform.

His opposition was linked to racial politics. For Richard Watson Gilder and E. L. Godkin, a terrible example of corruption was Reconstruction and carpetbaggers' use of spoils to buy the votes of uneducated freedmen.[64] They feared that dependent wage laborers in Northern cities would be as vulnerable to corruption as former slaves. But Tourgée's opposition was also related to his classical republicanism. Recognizing the need to do something about the spoils system, he nonetheless warned that a system of state examinations and life tenure would undermine citizens' active participation in governance by creating a permanent class of professional bureaucrats. The United States, he noted, liked to think of itself as superior to China, yet as China opened its borders, the United States took over two distinctive features of Chinese life. "We have built a wall to prevent foreigners from entering our territories and have adopted the principle of scholastic examination and life-tenure in office." Local acts of individual corruption should not prompt the adoption of "reforms" that would corrupt the virtue of the republican system.[65]

If Tourgée clung to the traditional notion of republican virtue, the mugwumps attempted to update it through reform. For them, the spoils system was a perfect example of the corruption that followed from people's refusal to sacrifice self-interest and partisan politics to the public good. Civil service reformers assumed that the professionalization feared by Tourgée was the best answer to self-interested partisanship. Even so, the mugwumps' sense of self did not allow them to be perfectly comfortable with the implications of professionalism.

Antebellum America tended to grant authority for knowledge to either intuitive individuals in touch with higher laws or a moral standard of right reason associated with republicanism. But the rise of professionalism in postbellum society meant that it was increasingly granted to communities of trained specialists. As Thomas Haskell has observed, the ascendancy of professionalism received philosophical legitimation from the rise of pragmatism, especially C. S. Peirce's notion of scientifically trained communities of the competent.[66] In contrast, as the mugwump origins of the right to privacy indicate, the mugwumps remained individualists. To be sure, the philosophical school of pragmatism and the political alliance of mugwumps were not mutually exclusive. Nonetheless, the pragmatic redefinition of truth and selfhood helped to transform the reformist tendencies of the mugwumps into the early twentieth-century movement of progressivism. If the individualism of many mugwumps was not quite compatible with professionalism, progressivism depended on it.

In law pragmatism had an important influence on Oliver Wendell Holmes Jr. In the 1870s Holmes, Peirce, and William James were members of an informal Metaphysical Club whose meetings led to pragmatism's formulation. In turn, Holmes's pragmatically inspired aphorism that the life of the law has been experience, not logic, contributed to the rise of legal realism, which is associated with progressive reform.[67] Against laissez-faire theories of legal neutrality, legal realists argued that law was an active force in shaping public policy. If their emphasis on law's affirmative role helped to revitalize aspects of the republican tradition, they transformed republicanism as they revitalized it, making it incompatible with both Tourgée's classical version and mugwump gentility. Following Holmes, legal realists anchored law in felt necessities of the time, not right reason. For them law served the public interest by balancing the demands of competing interest groups.[68] Unable to find the principles needed to achieve their goal of efficient management in either a virtuous, if nonexistent, right reason or a neutral, if impossible to achieve, legal science, they increasingly turned elsewhere, especially to the newly established professional social sciences, which pragmatism had helped to legitimate philosophically.

The authority that Peirce gave to professionally trained communities of the competent seems to give progressives a solution to a problem that our comparison of Twain and Tourgée has raised. Tourgée places great faith in the power of education to make people see right reason. Skeptical about the transcendental governance of right reason, Twain calls attention to the power of training to reinforce prejudiced communal opinion and places his hope for resistance in an undefined "natural" self. From a Peircean perspective Tourgée's error is to believe in right reason, whereas Twain's is to rely on the "microscopic atom" of a resisting self. Rather than work to keep that microscopic atom visible, Peirce denied its existence altogether. For him no ideas or beliefs originate with one person. Instead, "every cognition, every awareness, conscious sensation or reasoning, was determined by previous cognitions. There were no 'simple' ideas determined by their object alone that could be built by the gentle force of association into a static web of knowledge. Instead, every act of knowing was a moment in a continuous stream of experience, a moment irrevocably conditioned by previous moments."[69]

If, as Peirce writes, "belief is of the nature of habit," the Emersonian hope of seeing with new eyes is impossible, and Peirce's account of the self would seem to confirm the Connecticut Yankee's fear that training is everything. But Peirce does not despair, because to say that belief is of the nature of habit is not to say that belief cannot change, only that individuals cannot be the generating force in changing their beliefs. Thus for Peirce the question becomes, "how to fix belief, not in the individual merely, but in the community."[70] Reviewing various methods of fixing belief, Peirce concludes that the superior one is science with its ideal model of a community in which the individual is subordinated to a group's shared quest for truth.

Peirce's faith in scientifically trained communities of the competent allows him to retain Tourgée's enlightenment faith in education without positing the existence of right reason. The absence of right reason is not a problem because professional communities of the competent can provide reliable knowledge for the entire society. Thus, even though the community as a whole might seem enslaved to prejudiced and false beliefs, those properly trained could provide training that would fix proper belief. This belief was taken over by progressivism and also influenced the New Deal and its "brain trust" of professionally trained experts that could engineer the good society. The *Plessy* decision suggests a limitation to this solution.

For the most part the *Plessy* decision conforms to the premises of boundary theory, not pragmatism. Nonetheless, as we saw in chapter 2, whereas legal scholars praise Holmes's *Lochner* dissent and condemn the *Plessy* majority, both depend on the test of reasonableness. Furthermore, when Justice Brown defers to the "established usages, customs, and traditions of the people," he allows the prejudices of Southern whites to define reason and thus confirms Holmes's realistic argument that law is determined by the "felt necessities of the time, the prevalent moral and political theories, intuitions of public policy, avowed or unconscious, even the prejudices which judges share with their fellow men."[71] To be sure, Peirce's communities of the competent should correct the prejudices of custom. In the *Plessy* case, however, they proved no safeguard. The scientific community might have believed in the quest for truth, but the truth that it produced in the late nineteenth century was a "scientific racism" that supported the reasonableness of Jim Crow laws.[72]

In such a situation Twain and Tourgée imagine very different narratives. Tourgée recognizes new problems posed by the late nineteenth century, but clings to old-fashioned republican ideas, especially the republican notion of selfhood, to solve them. Twain makes no explicit effort to solve problems. Instead, his narrative exposes limitations to liberal, republican, and progressive solutions.

VII

Tourgée continues to imagine a world in which right reason exists and is guarded by the moral intelligence of gentlemen lawyers and judges devoted to proper government and justice. Thus, when a judge takes the bootblack's chair in *Pactolus Prime,* silence overcomes the assembled group, a silence "not so much due to the exalted position which he held, as to that innate respect for his moral and intellectual qualities which has been the bulwark of the American judiciary" (PP 92). The authority of the legal profession in Tourgée's world is further illustrated by the disagreement between the lawyer Phelps and his medical friend over Prime's racial identity. The two represent different versions of professionalism. Phelps's professional standard is a moral one traditionally associated with the bar. The doctor's is scientific. For Tourgée, it is the gentleman lawyer, not the scientific expert, who knows the truth about racial identity, the representative of morally right reason who has the knowledge to combat community standards of reason regarding race. In contrast, Pudd'nhead's role in Twain's tragedy registers the displacement of right reason by the authority of scientific professionalism.

Pudd'nhead's role has often been debated. For some, his final success exempts him from the tragic conclusion. For others, he remains a heroic outsider who offers an alternative to the community's prejudiced beliefs.

Still others see his final success as part of Twain's tragedy, since it causes him to lose his status as outsider and succumb to communal opinion.

Whereas this pessimistic view seems closest to the mark, it is not quite accurate to say that Pudd'nhead succumbs to communal opinion. On the contrary, by the end of the novel he has assumed the role of leadership previously occupied by Judge Driscoll, the only other member of the Freethinker's Society. He does not simply conform to communal opinion, he at least in part alters it. That he does so through the use of science distinguishes him from fellow lawyer Driscoll and the lawyer in Tourgée's work.

In *Pudd'nhead* Twain combines the scientist and the lawyer that Tourgée presents as two characters. Discussing Prime's identity in a chapter entitled "The Feat of Science," Tourgée's doctor does a "bit of detective analysis" (PP 241) that draws on scientific evidence to construct a "chain of evidence" (PP 246) that for him solves the mystery. Although impressed by the display, Phelps skeptically responds, "You see, doctor, my profession has learned by sad experience not to put entire reliance upon flesh-marks and—experts!" (PP 244). But if in Tourgée's novel the lawyer overrules science, in Twain's the lawyer's authority depends on it. Destroying the "indestructible chain of evidence" (PW 107) incorrectly used to identify the murderer, Pudd'nhead accomplishes his own bit of detective work by producing another chain based on the scientific evidence of flesh marks.[73] Science, as Peirce argued, does have the power to alter communal opinion, but in this case it confirms rather than challenges prejudices about race, just as the majority of the scientific community would have supported the reasonableness of *Plessy v. Ferguson*.

Unlike Tourgée, Twain avoids making explicit comment on the condition of the freedman by setting his work in the era of slavery. Nonetheless, Pudd'nhead's role in the tragedy suggests that Twain's story does make an indirect comment on its moment of production as well as its moment of representation.[74] First of all, "college bred" and a recent graduate of a "post-college course in an eastern law school" (PW 5), Pudd'nhead represents the new brand of professionalism. Second, entering the South from New York, he might well have evoked fears and memories of meddlesome carpetbaggers, like Tourgée, who also lived in New York. His nickname even recalls *A Fool's Errand*, which is about a Northern lawyer in the South. By the novel's end, however, Pudd'nhead loses his status as a fool and becomes a leader accepted by the Southern community. Marking the ascendancy of a new class of scientific professionals, Pudd'nhead's triumph also signals the formation of a larger community of fools, Northern and Southern, who united after the war by collectively selling down the river blacks' efforts to integrate into the national community.[75] Try as Northerners might to blame Jim Crow legislation on Southern prejudice, the Supreme Court decision upholding such laws was authored by a judge born in Massachusetts, who prominently cited another Massachusetts judge, whereas the lone dissenter was an ex-slaveholder from the South.

Mocking community standards of reasonableness regarding race, Tourgée's and Twain's works are cultural tragedies because racial inequality continues to prevail. Tourgée, however, counters faulty standards of reason with an explicit argument based on right reason, whereas Twain offers no explicit alternative. The supposedly naturally good self of someone like Huck has no force, and the class of gentleman lawyers, who supposedly embody moral right reason, has produced the decaying code of the First Families of Virginia and been replaced by a representative of new communities of the competent, a transformation that has the potential to alter communal opinion but does little to alter the inequitable social order. Thus, Pudd'nhead, Twain's vehicle for criticizing prejudice, becomes himself open to criticism when after, his use of science gains him acceptance into the community, we learn that "his long fight against hard luck and prejudice was ended" (PW 114).

Potentially meaning both that Pudd'nhead's scientific attitude has prevailed over prejudice and that Pudd'nhead himself has succumbed to prejudice, this phrase suggests Twain's divided attitude toward science. On the one hand, he, like Pudd'nhead, believes in the superiority of science over prejudice. On the other, if science, our most effective weapon against prejudice, is no more than a prejudice, the fight against one prejudice has ended with the victory of another.

This dilemma is suggested by Pudd'nhead's combined interests in fingerprinting and palmistry. Distinctions between the two might seem to establish the authority of science. Fingerprinting works; palmistry doesn't; and Twain uses the difference to set up dramatic irony when Tom mocks the fingerprinting that eventually convicts him. " 'But look here, Dave,' said Tom, 'you used to tell people's fortunes too, when you took their finger-marks. Dave's just an all-around genius. A genius of the first water, gentlemen, a great scientist running to seed here in this village, a prophet with the kind of honor that prophets generally get at home—for here they don't give shucks for his scientifics, and they call his skull a notion-factory' " (PW 49). If, however, we laugh at "Tom" as he laughs at Pudd'nhead, we share his skepticism when he responds to the claims made for palmistry with: "That jugglery a science? But really, you ain't serious are you?" (PW 50). Our split response to "Tom's" mockery raises the question of what makes one way of reading a hand a science and another "rank sorcery" (PW 50), a question even more poignant for Twain's contemporary audience, for whom finger-printing was a new discovery, and even more so for the fictional audi-ence in Dawson's Landing, for whom fingerprinting would have been virtually indistinguishable from palmistry. The question becomes even more complicated when we remember that one reason that Twain used fingerprinting was to have a gimmick whose novelty would increase sales.

Pudd'nhead's legal authority to challenge prevailing community be-liefs might depend on the authority of science, but the criteria consti-tuting a science seem to depend on prevailing community beliefs. In a way that Tourgée never does, Twain questions the very notion of rea-sonableness that not only justifies the decision in *Plessy v. Ferguson* but also the final action of *Pudd'nhead Wilson,* for when Judge Driscoll's murder is blamed on the erroneous inventory that overlooked "Tom's" existence as a slave, "everyone saw that there was reason in this" (PW 115).

Even if it is too simple to say that reason and science are products of prejudice rather than correctives to it, rationality never seems quite able to break from the prejudice to which it claims superiority. As John Carlos Rowe has reasonably argued, citing a passage from *A Connect-icut Yankee* in which one of Hank Morgan's rational plans is brought low by a "near-sighted, cross-eyed, pudd'nheaded clown" (CY 315), "every apparently rational intention has something 'pudd'nheaded' about it."[76] That pudd'nheadedness affects Twain's aesthetic. If the natural self no longer exists to resist repressive communal standards, the only disruptive force left may be unpredictable pudd'nheadedness.

Tourgée's aesthetic is based on the enlightenment ideal of public debate fostered by republicanism. According to that ideal, so long as all parties have an equal hearing, the proper argument will prevail, as it does in Prime's public debate with prominent citizens. In a racist society, however, all parties do not have an equal hearing, and, as Prime remarks to a senator, "You have the *Record* and the press to give circulation to your ideas. I have only the men who sit in my chairs or who are waiting for places in them to talk to" (PP 114). To combat this inequitable constraint on the free circulation of ideas in the marketplace, Tourgée proposed national ownership of the communications system, a proposal that indicates how similar Tourgée's ideal of public debate is to Jürgen Habermas's ideal of unconstrained communication, which, not surprisingly, owes a debt to Peirce's notion of the scientific community's quest after truth—which in turn is a pragmatic variation on the ideal of republican right reason. Since the conditions for Tourgée's ideal have never been established, it is impossible to test whether it would work. It is certainly a reasonable goal to work for.

But even as we work for it, its limitations are suggested by the notion of a rationality inhabited by pudd'nheadedness. Tourgée's ideal of right reason assumes that given a level playing field, an argument based on proper assumptions and logic will prevail. But arguments are won by rhetoric as well as logic. Inhabited by pudd'nheaded rhetoric, rational logic does not hold sovereign sway, and the unreasonableness of prevailing community standards of reason cannot be exposed merely by presenting an argument that adheres to right reason, since there is no purely rational argument devoid of rhetoric. The only way to proceed seems to be to deflate existing codes of reasonableness by inhabiting them in such a way as to expose their rhetorical component, a way of proceeding that admits its complicity with that which it would deflate by calling attention to its own rhetoricity.

VIII

Twain's and Tourgée's differences on rhetoric can be highlighted by looking at how they use law to help structure their novels. Tourgée's work is often simply an arena in which to voice legal arguments. In fact, *Pactolus Prime* is structured as a legal brief for blacks. Chapter titles include "An Assessment of Damages," "Some Expert Testimony," "Counterclaim and Set-Off," "An Unsatisfactory Client," "A Puzzled Counsellor," "The Boundary of Right," and "Penalties." The legal structure especially dominates the first half, when Benny and Prime interrogate prominent citizens occupying the shoeshine chair as if it were the witness chair in court. Faced with questions, these expert witnesses inevitably testify, if often unwillingly, to past injustice to blacks and the need to prevent further injustice in the present and future. In contrast, Twain is more intent on exploiting dramatic possibilities in the law. As the final courtroom scene reveals, the law for him is both spectacle and theater. If Tourgée subordinates the form of his novel to its legal argument, Twain uses law to advance his aesthetic purposes.

This neat contrast demands qualification, however, because Twain's aesthetic purposes are not completely separate from an argument he at least implies about the desirability of having the legal system serve the ends of justice. For Twain this implied argument depends on a realistic presentation of experience. To be sure, in his prefatory "Whisper to the Reader" he mocks the attempt to achieve an authentic recreation of a trial scene in fiction. Nonetheless, the theatricality that he exploits in rendering his final scene is not opposed to his realism but a vital part of it.

No writer in the American tradition has better captured voices and dialects than Twain. For instance, Hay praised Twain's "1601" as "a serious effort to bring back our literature and philosophy to the sober and chaste Elizabethan standard." Twain, however, denied any such moral intention. The piece was written, he claims, while "saturating myself with archaic English to a degree which would enable me to do plausible imitations of it in a fairly easy and unlabored way." It was inspired by a passage "which commended itself to me as being absolutely real, and as being the kind of talk which ladies and gentlemen did actually indulge." Testing himself, he tried to "contrive one of those stirring passages out of my own head."[77]

Twain knew that his ability to create dialogue was like an actor's ability to "get into" a character. Indeed, Twain was a success on the lecture circuit in part because of his acting abilities. Upstaging Charles Dickens and his popular reading tours, Twain did not simply read from his books, he performed them. Similarly, his best books were created by his ability to let his characters speak in their own voices. His first story published in a widely respected journal was, appropriately, "A True Story, Repeated Word for Word as I Heard It."

Twain's obsession with letting characters speak for themselves rather than subordinate them to a preexisting design or argument grows out of an obligation that he felt toward them as unique individuals. That obligation contributed to his abandonment of *Those Extraordinary Twins*. As he was writing that story, "other people got to intruding themselves and taking up more room with their talk and their affairs. Among them came a stranger named Pudd'nhead Wilson, and a woman named Roxana; and presently the doings of these two pushed up into prominence a young fellow named Tom Driscoll, whose proper place was away in the obscure background. Before the book was half finished those three were taking things almost entirely into their own hands and working the whole tale as a private venture of their own—a tale which they had nothing at all to do with, by rights" (PW 120). By listening to the voices of these characters who continued to assert themselves, Twain altered the order of the world he was creating.

In allowing himself to be the medium through whom his characters speak, Twain would seem to have affinities with spiritualists. Indeed, although he mocked mediumship, he was also fascinated with its possibilities.[78] Nonetheless, Twain differs from writers like Elizabeth Stuart Phelps and E. P. Roe. The latter two claimed to be mediums through whom God spoke. Twain serves as a medium for individual characters. The evangelical Christians presented a vertically ordered world governed by God. Twain presents a horizontally ordered one constructed by the "private venture" (PW 120) of characters interacting on their own. That interaction allows characters to escape the "proper place" (PW 120) assigned them in a fictional hierarchy.

Even so, the origin of his characters' diverse voices remains in question. Carton has argued that in exposing racial categories as fictions of law and custom, Twain calls attention to our role as the authors of social forms. But Twain's account of the authorship of his story seems to confirm the structuralist notion about the death of the author. Transforming itself beyond Twain's control, the story seems to be produced by an autonomous writing machine. Indeed, although characters take "things almost entirely into their own hands" (PW 120), eventually their lives seem controlled by the cultural narratives into which they are born. Since the book's realism seems to depend on conforming to the logic of those narratives, Twain too would seem to be controlled by them. Thus his role is close to Pudd'nhead's, which he describes as merely "a button or a crank or a lever, with a useful function to perform in a machine" (LL 291). Just as Twain claims not to have created the tragedy that he wrote, but merely to have made it visible as it grew out of his attempt to write a farce, so Pudd'nhead merely makes visible the evidence provided by his fingerprinting. Not free agents controlling the terms of the action, Twain and Pudd'nhead seem to serve as agents through which a mechanistic fate accomplishes its dirty work of perpetuating a cultural tragedy.

As similar as the roles of character and author are, however, they are not identical. If Pudd'nhead makes fingerprints legible, Twain makes visible the cultural narrative in which Pudd'nhead's scientific professionalism helps to restore order temporarily disrupted by a black woman's attempt to advance her son. Twain's role as an author may seem to be no more than that of a crank in a machine, but this particular crank makes a difference. First, even though Twain seems to let characters speak through him, they in fact are his creations. The process by which they come into existence is similar to the one by which Twain produced "1601." He so saturates himself in the voices that he hears around him that he acquires the ability to create them out of his own head. Second, Twain does not simply record the interaction of his characters. Their actions generate a plot by being filtered through his imagination. Twain offers, to use Wolfgang Iser's distinction, an active presentation of reality not a passive representation of it, an act of *Darstellung* not mimesis.[79]

Not a closed society, the world that Twain presents continues to perform itself by involving readers, past and present, within it. By not dictating a particular set of beliefs, it nonetheless tested past readers' relations to the communal and scientific beliefs that two years later supported the *Plessy* decision. Even though most present-day readers are confident that such beliefs are a thing of the past, *Pudd'nhead* poses a test or two to us as well by inviting us to scrutinize standards of reasonableness constructed by our communities of scientifically trained professionals.

For example, we can examine the common assumption that *Plessy* was overruled by *Brown v. Board of Education* (1954) or, if not by *Brown,* by *Gayle v. Browder* (1956), which, appealing to *Brown,* forbids segregated transportation facilities. Nonetheless, *Brown* never explicitly claims to overrule *Plessy* on a question of law. Instead, it focuses on the evidence that was available to the *Plessy* court about the effect of segregated facilities. Citing recent evidence from the social sciences in footnote 11, Chief Justice Earl Warren concludes that segregation has a detrimental effect on black children because it imparts a sense of inferiority that affects their motivation to learn. "Whatever may have been the extent of psychological knowledge at the time of *Plessy v. Ferguson,*" he declares, "this finding is amply supported by modern authority."[80] Rather than make Harlan's "color-blind" Constitution the law of the land, *Brown* more explicitly than *Plessy* rests on the authority of our communities of the competent. In fact, if it had declared the Constitution color-blind, it would have ruled out affirmative action programs that try to guarantee professional training for minorities, as evidenced by the *Bakke* case (1978).

What supporters of *Brown* too rarely ask is, what will happen if in the future the "modern authority" of social science evidence shows that separate but equal schools do not necessarily have a detrimental effect? Should *Brown* then be overruled? The answer to that question is not an easy one because *Brown* does not rest solely on social science evidence. Certainly, the answer will not be found by reading Twain's *Pudd'nhead Wilson*. Nonetheless, Twain's book continues to force us to raise such difficult questions.

Describing his composition process, Twain distinguishes himself from a "born-and-trained novelist" and refers to the pulling out of his tragedy from his farce as the operation of a "jack-leg" (PW 119). But for the author of a work about the tragedies of birth and training, the epithet "jack-leg" may not be completely pejorative. Indeed, in a culture of professionalism, in which racism persists, the tragedy that this incompetent pudd'nhead pulled out continues to have the capacity to produce "most embarrassing circumstance[s]" (PW 119) for those who read it, despite, or at times because of, their cultural and professional training and birth.

CHAPTER 8

Corporate Liberalism, the Politics of Character, and Professional Management in Phillips's *The Cost* and Lynde's *The Grafters*

I

In *Those Extraordinary Twins,* the work from which *Pudd'nhead Wilson* grew, David Wilson also shines in court, even if in a different manner. In *Pudd'nhead* he wins his case by clearing up confusion over identity caused by the exchange of babies; in *Twins* he wins by relying on the confusion of identity caused by merging two people into a corporate body. Wilson defends Siamese twins who are on trial for kicking Tom Driscoll at an antitemperance meeting. The witnesses called by Tom's attorney all testify that the twins kicked Tom. Nonetheless, when pressed by Wilson they cannot say who delivered the kick. Tom's attorney protests that the issue is "an irrelevant triviality. Necessarily they both kicked him, for they have but one pair of legs, and both are responsible for them" (ET 145).[1] His protest fails, however, when the jury concludes that, although an assault was committed by one of the twins, it cannot identify the guilty party. As a result, the jury laments, "We cannot convict both, for only one is guilty. We cannot acquit both, for only one is innocent. Our verdict is that justice has been defeated by the dispensation of God, and ask to be discharged from further duty" (ET 153).

As humorous as this scene is, the judge suggests serious possibilities when earlier he remarks, "There is no doubt whatever that an assault has been committed. The attempt to show that both of the accused committed it has failed. Are they both to escape justice on that account? Not in this court, if I can prevent it. It appears to have been a mistake to bring the charge against them as a corporation; each should have been charged in his capacity as an individual . . ." (ET 148–49). How is a legal system that assigns guilt and blame on an individual basis to deal with corporate acts? Can individuals escape responsibility by hiding behind a corporate identity? Or should the legal system change in order to accommodate the reality of corporate identity?

Twain, who for financial reasons incorporated himself, certainly knew that one advantage of incorporation was that it limited the financial liability of individual shareholders.[2] In contrast, in a standard partnership the liability of individual partners is not limited. The difference results because in a corporation people lose their identities to the corporate body, whereas in a partnership they maintain separate identities while entering into a contractual agreement. Thus, when a corporation goes bankrupt, shareholders are not liable for its debts, whereas when a partnership goes bankrupt general partners are. Complicated by the development of limited partnerships, this distinction, nonetheless, draws attention to the challenge that corporate forms of association pose to those who think of society as being held together by contractual agreements among discrete individuals. How far-reaching those challenges could be are suggested by the turn-of-the-century German legal historian Otto Gierke.

II

Today we normally think of corporations as private businesses. But the commercial use of the corporate form is fairly recent, having been developed primarily in seventeenth- and eighteenth-century Britain. Gierke traced early legal uses of the corporate form to Roman law, which recognized two forms of associations. The *universitas* corresponded to the corporation; the *societas* to the partnership. The two have had very different legal histories, however, ever since Pope Innocent IV declared the *universitas* a fictional person. The need to grant a corporate body a legal personality, even if a fictional one, is fairly obvious. If a corporation is to be brought to court by, for instance, creditors, or if it is to bring debtors to court, it must be given the status of a person. The problem with Innocent's solution, as far as Gierke was concerned, was that in declaring a corporate personality a legal fiction it caused people to dismiss corporate forms of organization as artificial creations of the law. For Gierke it was a mistake to assume that the law preexists corporate bodies. A strong advocate of the German *Rechtsstaat,* he was at pains to counter, on the one hand, legal positivism, in which all law emanates from the sovereign state, and, on the other, natural law theory, in which a universal, natural law precedes the formation of social organizations. In contrast, he argues that the existence of law and social organizations are mutually dependent on one another. To assume that corporate bodies are the artificial creations of the law is to ignore the fact that the "inner content of the law" is a "historical manifestation of human corporate spirit."[3]

Gierke bolstered his argument by turning to the medieval German system of *Genossenschaftrecht,* or the law of associations. Under it, associations such as guilds and boroughs clearly preceded the establishment of a centralized state. Having their own form of organization and identity that could not be attributed to a higher sovereign, they retained an independent life even when they became units of a larger composite structure. As capable of bearing rights as individuals, these associations did not derive their rights from the state, nor were they formed to guarantee the pre-social rights of individuals. Indeed, for Gierke such corporate bodies are as natural to human existence as the individual. Thus, he urged legal recognition of a *Gesammtperson,* or a group personality, one that as much as an individual is a rights-bearing person.

Intent on freeing German legal thought from the Roman influence that had reigned since Napoleon, Gierke used *Genossenschaftrecht* to challenge the privileged position that the *societas* had gained in modern political and legal thought. If after Innocent IV the *universitas* had been reduced to an artificial creation of the law, when political thinkers sought a model to describe the modern state arising in the Renaissance, they turned, according to Gierke, to the legal concept of *societas.* In doing so, they had mistakenly posited a state of nature inhabited by discrete individuals who then joined together to form a social contract establishing the sovereignty of the state. Some consequences of their model are obvious. First, it assumes that for human beings a state of discrete individuals is more natural than a collective one. Second, it grants extraordinary authority to the sovereign state. By declaring the state the exclusive representative of the common interest and by granting it the power to maintain order and justice, theories of social contract risk dismissing as illegitimate all rival centers of authority between the state and the individual. As a result, the social contract model lends itself to narratives framed by conflicts between the lone individual and an all-inclusive, totalized concept of society.

Gierke's insistence on the *Gesammtperson* of corporate bodies challenged this contractual model of society. Whereas he recognized that the state is the normal body through which a social conviction of right is transformed into law, he demonstrated how other groups, such as the church, family, and *Gemeinde,* are also formative organs of law. He did not, therefore, have to posit pre-social natural rights to question the sovereign authority of a centralized state. He looked instead to the intermediary groups who rivaled the state for individuals' loyalty. As he puts it, "We proceed from the firmly established historical fact that man everywhere and at all times bears within himself the double character of existing as an individual in himself and as a member of a collective or association."[4]

Gierke was clearly interested in more than legitimating business corporations. Nonetheless, his argument for a *Gesammtperson* had the potential to aid corporations in their battle for legal rights in the United States. Like Innocent IV, Anglo-American law considered corporations fictional persons that owed their existence to the state. Orthodox legal doctrine concerning corporations in the United States was formulated in *Dartmouth College v. Woodward* (1819), when Chief Justice John Marshall drew on common law tradition to define a corporation as "an artificial being, invisible, intangible, and existing only in contemplation of law. Being the mere creature of law, it possesses only those properties which the charter of its creation confers upon it, either expressly or as incidental to its very existence."[5]

If Marshall's definition granted a corporation legal status different from that of the people who comprise it, by calling a corporation an artificial creation of the state it continued to assume that contracting individuals form its real basis. Marshall's decision also furthered the primacy of contract by holding that legislative charters creating corporations were themselves contracts that cannot be impaired. Furthermore, although *Dartmouth College* prevented state legislatures from altering the terms of corporations' charters, it also confirmed a state's sovereignty over corporations. Nonetheless, Marshall's doctrine was gradually altered when, with limited success, corporate advocates in the late nineteenth and early twentieth centuries put forth arguments similar to Gierke's granting corporations an existence independent of the state.[6]

Walter Benn Michaels uses such arguments to assert that in the philosophy of Josiah Royce and in Frank Norris's *The Octopus,* the notion of corporate personality renders problematic the anticorporate rhetoric that appeals to the rights of "natural" persons.[7] Elsewhere I have argued that, whereas Michaels's reading draws on a logical possibility, it is historically inaccurate. Even though some pro-corporate thinkers in the United States did use continental theories of a *Gesammt-person* like Gierke's, they never totally embraced it. Far more individualistic, they never went so far as to argue for the ontological equality of individual and group personalities. Attracted to the notion that corporations did not owe their existence to the state, they nonetheless continued to think of them as fictional personalities different in kind from the human beings whose association created them.[8]

Even so, pro-corporate forces did make significant legal gains during the nineteenth century. In the antebellum period most states replaced special legislative charters of incorporation with laws that made incorporation available to anyone following proper procedures. After the Civil War, pro-corporate forces also won certain 14th Amendment protections in *Santa Clara v. Southern Pacific Railroad Company* (1886), when a unanimous court ruled that both its equal protection and due process clauses applied to all "persons," including the legal fiction of corporate personalities.[9] By 1911, six hundred and seven 14th Amendment cases had reached the Supreme Court. Three hundred and twelve involved corporations. Only thirty, including the failed effort of Homer Plessy, involved rights of minority groups.[10]

As extensive as these victories were, however, courts continued to distinguish between human beings and the legal fiction of a corporate person. For instance, even as corporations were granted 4th Amendment protections in *Hale v. Henkel* (1905), they were denied 5th Amendment ones. Similarly, corporate personalities never achieved the right to marry, and they have been denied the tort right to privacy.[11] Even so, the "incorporation of America" did call into question the sense of agency at the heart of contractual thinking.[12] Threatened was contract's vision of equal opportunity generated by a society composed of individuals whose responsibilities and duties are defined by their promises.

Corporations rose in part because they efficiently pooled the capital needed to develop an expanding economy. An obvious example is railroad companies. Helping to create an interconnected market, railroads amassed such vast resources that individuals could rarely compete with them. Nonetheless, through a fiction of the law a contract between an individual and a major corporation was considered to be one between equal bargaining powers. Even advocates of laissez-faire capitalism, who thought that labor contracts between individual employers and employees were conducted on a level playing field, were reluctant to consider fair the ones between a human being and a fictional corporate personality.

Indeed, the relationship between laissez-faire and corporate advocates was extremely complicated. Because robber barons controlled highly visible corporations, it is easy to assume that corporate apologists advocated rugged individualism. In fact, a number of laissez-faire thinkers feared that corporations would destroy individual autonomy. For those who pitted the forces of individualism against the forces of collectivism, corporations were on the side of socialism against a virtuous capitalist republicanism based on the responsible actions of autonomous individuals. Socialists reinforced such thinking when they concluded that the corporate concentration of capital was a stage in the ultimate triumph of socialism. In contrast, Christopher G. Tiedeman, whose *Treatise on the Limitations of Police Power* (1886) attacked socialist evils while articulating laissez-faire legal principles, declared in a second edition (1900): "I advocate, as a return to a uniform recognition of the constitutional guaranty of equality before the law, the repeal of the statutes which provide for the creation of private corporations."[13]

But if laissez-faire and corporate advocates disagreed about a contractual or corporate distribution of capital, they agreed that governments should not interfere into business affairs. They did not, however, agree on the definition of governmental interference. Whereas pro-corporate forces viewed proposals such as Tiedeman's as examples of governmental interference into corporate affairs, he argued that what he proposed would simply take away the state's power to *create* organizations that interfered with the "natural" economic relations among contracting individuals. These and other complications are illustrated by a case decided in the federal circuit court in California in 1880.

III

In re Tiburcio Parrott involved a challenge to a state law based on Section 2 of Article 19 of the 1879 California Constitution.

Entitled "Chinese," the article listed various anti-Chinese measures. The one in question stated: "No corporation now existing, or here after formed under the laws of this state, shall, after the adoption of this constitution, employ, directly or indirectly in any capacity, any Chinese or Mongolians. The legislature shall pass such laws as may be necessary to enforce this provision."[14] This provision followed one that allowed the removal of "aliens who are or may become vagrants, paupers, mendicants, criminals, or invalids, afflicted with contagious or infectious diseases, and . . . aliens otherwise dangerous or detrimental to the wellbeing or peace of the state" (494). Like the Black Codes in the South, these two sections declared people without contracts of employment to be vagrants. But whereas most blacks in the South were citizens, most Chinese in California were not. As aliens, they faced deportation. Indeed, the provisions were aimed at purging California of a Chinese presence.

That goal could have been furthered by forbidding individual persons as well as corporations from employing Chinese. But doing so would have been an obvious violation of the 14th Amendment's implied guarantee of "freedom of contract." In 1880, however, the Supreme Court had not yet ruled that the amendment's use of "person" applied to corporations as well as individuals. As a result, the California measures focused on corporations, assuming, as was argued in court, that, since corporations were creations of the state, it had an unlimited right to impose upon them "laws for the conduct of their business, and restrictions upon the use and enjoyment of their property, which would be unconstitutional and void if applied to private persons" (486).

Based on the assumption that the state had the right to do precisely what Tiedeman twenty years later would advocate—repeal its general laws of incorporation—Section 2 was as anticorporate as it was anti-Chinese. Recognizing the important implications of the section's anticorporate assumptions, Justice Hoffman addressed them, even though he could have decided the case by noting that the Burlingame Treaty of 1868 guaranteed Chinese the right of employment. Admitting that the state has a right to repeal or alter its general laws of incorporation, Hoffman left open the thorny question of what effect a repeal would have on already existing corporations. But he forcefully denied that this right implied the right "to impair the obligation of any contract made by a corporation, or to deprive the corporation of any vested property *or rights of property* lawfully acquired" (493). To the objection that these were rights that belong to individuals not artificial creations of the state, he replied that the state's absolute power over corporations could be maintained only by ignoring the rights of stockholders. "Behind the artificial or ideal being created by the statute and called a corporation, are the corporators—natural persons who have conveyed their property to the corporation, or contributed to it their money, and received, as evidence of their interest, shares in its capital stock. The corporation, though it holds the title, is the trustee, agent, and representative of the shareholders, who are the real owners. And it seems to me that their right to use and enjoy their property is as secure under constitutional guarantees as are the rights of private persons to the property they own" (491–92).

The corporate form of organization may theoretically threaten a contractual conception of social relations, but in his decision Hoffman, as did many justices of the period, combated an anticorporate measure by relying on essentially contractual assumptions. The rights he protected were not those of a fictional corporate personality, but the rights of the "natural persons," the "corporators." Hoffman was especially at pains to defend the right to contract one's labor. The "right to labor for a living," he asserted, is "as inviolable as the right of property, for property is the offspring of labor. It is as sacred as the right to life, for life is taken if the means whereby we live be taken" (498). In short, Hoffman's decision helped to illustrate the extent to which corporate capitalism in the United States operated—as it still does—within a legal system devoted to the notion of individual rights. Even though historians concerned with establishing tidy categories of periodization are prone to announce the "death of contract," the rise of corporate capitalism did completely knock contractual relations from the field of play. As Martin J. Sklar points out, the "modern capitalist system is a realm of contracts and property rights." At the same time, the "corporate liberalism" that arose altered the economic role of contract.[15] It also, as I will argue, had the power to appeal to the "promise of contract" while making realization of that promise even more distant.

In re Tiburcio Parrott illustrates how "corporate liberalism" can complicate issues that still concern us. Corporations may threaten the individualistic assumptions that Hoffman adopted to combat anticorporate sentiment, but they were often the allies of Chinese seeking legal protections. To be sure, they were in part serving their own interests, just as the Louisiana railroad did in lending limited support in Homer Plessy's fight against Jim Crow laws. Corporate exploitation of Chinese labor is well-documented. Nonetheless, we should not forget that it was labor unions, not corporations, that supported anti-Chinese measures.

Granted, labor had ample reasons to identify corporate interests as counter to those of the "people." A California case decided two years later, *Mrs. David Colton v. Leland Stanford, et al.* (1882), confirmed the public's suspicion that many legislators, railroad commissioners, and judges were controlled by the Southern Pacific Railroad. It also confirmed the public's belief that the Southern Pacific was merely a front for California's notorious Big Four: Leland Stanford, Collis Huntington, Mark Hopkins, and Charles Crocker.[16] As a result, anticorporate forces drew on rhetoric similar to that used by Judge Hoffman to defend corporate rights in the name of the individuals "behind the artificial or ideal being created by statute and called a corporation" (491). Intent on assigning individual responsibility for corporate abuses, anticorporate forces insisted on "piercing the corporate veil" in order to find the real people behind the fictional corporate personality. Indeed, the metaphor of "piercing the corporate veil" is used in the law when courts feel that justice demands dissolving the legal fiction of a corporate personality. For instance, if a corporation is so dominated by an individual that it serves as his alter ego, courts feel free to identify the two. As the court in *Bartle v. Home Owners Cooperative* (1955) puts it, "Generally speaking, the doctrine of 'piercing the corporate veil' is invoked 'to prevent fraud or to achieve equity.'"[17]

Legal fictions have traditionally been used to achieve equity.[18] But in this case, equity seems to demand a fiction's unveiling, for, as *Those Extraordinary Twins* illustrates, there are cases in which the corporate fiction can cover up individual responsibility for unjust acts. Twain, however, does not develop that possibility. Milking his scene, instead, for its humorous possibilities, he suggests the link between the twins' act and that of corporations only through an offhand remark by the judge. Indeed, the best works of Twain, James, and Howells offer little insight into corporate affairs. To be sure, corporations occasionally appear, as in *The Rise of Silas Lapham*. But the role that they play is usually subordinated to those of other interests.

There is no simple answer for this neglect. It can be attributed in part to the demands of the novel, which was the realists' preferred genre.[19] Focusing on the social interaction of individualized characters, the novel has to stretch its generic limits to represent the dynamics of collective forms of organization.[20] Granted, generic demands have not kept all novelists from writing about corporations. Nonetheless, those who do almost always offer individualized narratives of corporate intrigue. Indeed, it was with equitable purposes in mind that writers of the period used literary fictions to unmask a legal fiction and reveal individuals behind the corporate veil. The lack of realism in two such novels published by Bobbs-Merrill in 1904, David Graham Phillips's *The Cost* and Francis Lynde's *The Grafters,* allows us to explore two prominent imaginary responses to the threat that corporations posed to the promise of contract.

IV

Both Phillips's and Lynde's novels were part of a public fascination with the workings of Wall Street in the first years of this century. For instance, in the April 1903 *Literary Digest* the J. A. Hill Company advertised their Wall Street Library, which promised to reveal the "influence of this gigantic money-making machine."[21] Their strategy of piercing the corporate veil was also part of a larger fascination with what was favorably called the "literature of exposure" and unfavorably called muckraking.[22] It is generally accepted that Theodore Roosevelt drew on John Bunyan's *Pilgrim's Progress* to popularize the term "muckraker" in response to Phillips's *The Treason of the Senate* series, his notorious exposé of corporate influence in the Senate.[23] Works that promised to pierce the corporate veil responded to people's interest in, as Richard Hofstadter puts it, "throwing the light of publicity on hidden horrors of life, especially if they could be regarded as anachronisms outside the mainstream."[24]

In the wake of recent fascinations with the workings of Wall Street, it is easy for us today to understand why the public would crave works revealing individuals responsible for corporate power and abuse. It is less clear why corporate horrors would be regarded as anachronisms. After all, today both corporate apologists and critics tend to agree that corporations are a modern force. But many turn-of-the-century Americans continued to adhere to Henry Sumner Maine's argument that the movement in progressive societies had been from status to contract. From this perspective, concentrated corporate power threatened progress by returning to earlier forms of organization that undermined an important achievement of modernity—individual autonomy. Furthermore, individual autonomy was often associated with Anglo-Saxon culture. In contrast, collectivism was most poignantly associated with Asiatic or Eastern cultures, which had not advanced beyond a feudal mode of social organization. For instance, anti-Chinese rhetoric frequently denounced the collectivism of "coolie" labor. To many businessmen and laborers, Asiatic collectivism combined with corporate feudalism was contrary to the progressive individualism on which the United States was based.

These advocates of progress found little comfort in arguments such as Gierke's which stated that the corporate form justified recognition of a medieval form of a *Gesammtperson*. For instance, in his first installment of *The Treason of the Senate* Phillips warned that the Senate had become the "agent of interests as hostile to the American people as any invading army could be, and vastly more dangerous; interests that manipulate the prosperity produced by all, so that it heaps up riches for the few, interests whose growth and power can only mean the degradation of the people, of the uneducated into sycophants, of the masses toward serfdom." Senator Chauncey Mitchell Depew, a corporate lawyer and social acquaintance of Mark Twain, was branded Vanderbilt's "butler" and "soul-vassal Depew."[25] Works that pierced the corporate veil promised both to throw light on the hidden horrors of quasi-feudal forms of organization and make those horrors understandable by explaining them in terms of individual actors.

In themselves neither Phillips nor Lynde represents the period's varied fictional response to corporate power.[26] Their responses have significant differences, with Lynde expressing more sympathy for corporate structures than Phillips does. Nonetheless, even in their differences both react to two perceived threats: the loss of individual autonomy and an imbalance of power in the public sphere. These threats were often linked.

C. Wright Mills, for instance, distinguishes between an older middle class consisting mainly of independent entrepreneurs and professionals and a new middle class mainly in the employ of corporations.[27] For middle class observers already frightened by the control that political machines supposedly had over the working class, the increased economic dependence of their own class threatened its proud tradition of moral and political independence. Thus, a writer for the journal *Independent* feared in 1903 that this corporate dependence "already partly realized, is likely to be more fully achieved in the near future. The middle class is becoming a salaried class, and rapidly losing the economic and moral independence of former days."[28] At the same time, in *The Treason of the Senate* series Phillips attributes the loss of autonomy to corporate control of the Senate. Its "treason" had contributed to an "unnatural descent of the masses, despite skill and industry . . . toward the dependence of wages and salaries."[29]

Phillips and Lynde respond to these perceived threats by imagining narratives in which the interests of the people are guarded by that traditional, yet paradoxical, figure: the independent politician who stands above the political arena in which various interests are played against one another. Standing above such partisan politics, both Phillips's and Lynde's heroes preside over their novels' sentimental moral economies, whose foundations in traditional values are revealed in romantic love plots that both authors interweave with tales of corporate wheeling and dealing. I call their moral economies sentimental not because the values on which they are based are necessarily unworthy— often they are well worth defending—but because they assume the inevitable triumph of certain values. It is precisely in presenting fictional worlds governed by a sentimental moral economy that Phillips and Lynde most clearly abandon the promise of contract still evoked by the realists. That abandonment makes their works historically interesting, because it corresponds with a similar abandonment of the promise of contract by reformers intent on containing the increasing power of corporate influence.

Whereas various reforms did provide some control, they also helped to legitimate the rise of corporate liberalism. By examining the moments of aesthetic weakness in these two novels, when various aspects of corporate influence can be contained only through the contrived, mechanical operations of the authors' moral economies, we get insight into the inadequacy of such reforms. At the same time, the sentimental appeal of the novelists' imaginary solutions helps to reveal why the historical solutions that were adopted seemed attractive.

But these works do more. They also allow us to explore the paradoxical sense of what constitutes "modernity." On the one hand, corporations seem a force of modernity, opposed by a nostalgic vision of individual autonomy that belongs to an outmoded tradition of republican virtue. For instance, Phillips's "progressive" attack on corporate influence as a form of modern feudalism extends criticism by the traditional republican Tourgée, who argued that corporations must be controlled in order to "relieve our civilization of the peril of a feudalism based on wealth."[30] On the other hand, the appeal to a corporate mode of organization seems itself to be part of the period's nostalgic medi-evalism as it searches for order in response to the sense of individual alienation brought about by the modern breakup of community. Cor-porate liberalism appeals simultaneously to the period's—and our—individualistic and communal nostalgias.

But if it appeals to those nostalgias, it in fact accompanies the rise of two new senses of agency. One is linked to what I call Phillips's "politics of character," a politics celebrating those whose character guarantees their independence. The other is linked to Lynde's association of po-litical independence with professionally trained managers. Historians generally agree on the rise of the second, but the first seems to be a throwback to an older sense of autonomy. Indeed, an emphasis on character would seem to contradict Warren Susman's argument that in this period personality started to be emphasized over character.[31] What Susman's account leaves out, however, is how the perceived disappear-ance of character actually created a nostalgia for it. Phillips's novel dramatizes how the desire to combat corporate power fostered con-struction of a new, ideal vision of autonomy, just as Warren and Bran-deis constructed a new notion of privacy.

V

Because neither Phillips's nor Lynde's novel is well known I will provide a brief summary of their plots. *The Cost* is Phillips's first of three novels exposing corporate and Wall Street corruption published from 1904 to 1905. It is in part a tribute to Phillips's friend Indiana Senator Albert J. Beveridge, most remembered for his famous "Follow the Flag" speech in defense of turn-of-the-century American imperialism. Beveridge and Phillips had been roommates at Asbury University (now Depauw University and the *alma mater* of both Dan Quayle and Charles A. Beard). Hamden Scarborough, a self-made re-formist politician from an Indiana farm, is the protagonist, supposedly modeled on Beveridge, although it is impossible to imagine any real person as noble as Scarborough. The plot is framed as a battle between Scarborough and John Dumont, also from Indiana, who becomes the ruthless head of a corporation that corners the market on woolens and thus can dictate whether or not people go cold in the winter. Their battle is waged over Pauline Gardiner, Dumont's childhood sweetheart.

Scarborough meets her during their first year at Battle Field University and falls in love. Pauline, however, had secretly married Dumont at seventeen, partly as an act of rebellion against her father, who had forbidden her to see him because of Dumont's questionable character, a character that Pauline is not yet able to see through. After their marriage and the birth of their son, she discovers his infidelity and egotism. Living in luxury supported by his wealth, she spends much of her time with her son on an estate in her hometown, while Dumont runs the Woolens Trust in New York City.

In Indiana she meets Scarborough again. A successful lawyer, Scarborough runs for governor and wins, partially through the help of Pauline, who is able to keep from circulation money that her husband sent to bribe the nominating convention. Scarborough's election poses a particular problem for Dumont because Indiana is the state where his corporation has its charter. Threatened from the outside and facing an internal rebellion of two associates within the Woolens hierarchy, Dumont, after a courageous struggle that occupies the last third of the book, finally succumbs. In the last chapter, Scarborough and Pauline marry, consecrating the values of Scarborough's farm-raised and fiercely independent mother and father.

Lynde, who once worked for the railroads, also interweaves a story about corporate intrigue and a love story. The protagonist of *The Grafters* is David Kent, who, after graduation from law school, gives up the legal practice that he inherits from his father in a small New Hampshire town and heads west, to Gaston, where he is the local attorney for the Western Pacific Railroad, "the best-hated corporation this side of the Mississippi" (G 13). In choosing as his protagonist a corporate lawyer who also serves as a lobbyist in the state legislature, Lynde immediately challenges some of the stereotypes of anticorporate fiction. His love story, however, remains predictably sentimental.

Kent moves west because of his love for the rich Elinor Brentwood, who with her widowed mother and younger sister had spent a summer in New Hampshire. Sensing the social inequality "between a young woman who is an heiress in her own right, and a briefless lawyer" (G 28), Kent tries to accumulate enough money to place himself on an equal footing with his lover. But his attempt to strike it rich in the railroad-driven Gaston real estate market goes bust. Then, on a visit from his college friend Loring, secretary of the Western Pacific Advisory Board in Boston, he learns that the Brentwoods are planning a western trip because of the mother's health. Loring also informs him that Elinor's financial status has been put at risk by bad advice on investments, and that it now depends on the value of Western Pacific stock, in which the family has tied up its remaining fortune.

That fortune is threatened along with the railroad when Jasper G. Bucks is elected governor on an anticorporate, People's Party platform. Bucks's threat allows Kent to use his position as a minor corporate lawyer to play the role of a modern knight and save the fortune of his lover. The plot is complicated, however, because Elinor is already being courted by Brookes Ormsby, "club-man, gentleman of aesthetic leisure, and inheritor of Ormsby millions" (G 32). It is complicated even further because Bucks's populist rhetoric is a sham.

Bucks is in the pay of the Plantagould interests, whose legal genius, Semple Falkland, devises an elaborate plot by which the Western Pacific will be thrown into receivership and then brought under control of the massive National Oil company. Bucks, however, has committed a fatal error. While on a secret journey in another state, he killed a man. With the help of Portia van Brock, the political hostess of Gaston, and Ormsby, who out of a sense of fairness has released Elinor from her engagement, Kent manages to save the railroad—and Elinor's fortune. Through a series of intrigues, including a thrilling ride along the rails, Kent brings Bucks across the state line and to justice. The book ends with Elinor and Kent planning to marry and the former corporate lobbyist embarking on a career as a reformist politician.

VI

As different as these two plots are, both are examples of what a reviewer for *The Outlook,* quoted in an advertisement for *The Grafters* in *The Cost,* calls "a new and distinctly American class of fiction—the kind which finds romance and even sensational excitement in business, politics, finance, and law." Both pierce the corporate veil by revealing figures behind the fictional corporate personality, although significantly Phillips pits a reformist politician against a corrupt corporate giant, whereas Lynde pits a corporate lawyer aspiring to politics against a politician masquerading as a reformer. Finally, in both, true reform depends on politicians who cannot be bought. Scarborough tells Pauline how moneyed interests "took me onto a high mountain and showed me all the kingdoms of the earth, as it were. I could be governor, senator, they said, could probably have the nomination for president even,—not if I would fall down and worship them, but if I would let them alone. I could accomplish nearly all that I've worked so long to accomplish if I would only concede a few things to them" (C 218). Christlike, he refuses because, even though he would be "almost free," almost is "not free at all" (C 218). Kent too, although not so self-assuredly, refuses to be bribed. As he tells Portia, "They say every man has his price: mine is higher than any bid they have yet made—or can make, I hope" (G 278). Later he proves his character by refusing to be "in the market" (G 301).

If both authors imagine figures who stand above the peddling of influence, Phillips structures his narrative by setting up a conflict between the interests of "the people" and those of "bigness." The conflict is a familiar one because it has been passed on to us by historians of the period, who from various perspectives have told the story of how "the people" lost, whether it be to the powerful and manipulative forces of capital or to irresistible technological and bureaucratic forces of modernity.[32] In advocating "the people" Phillips felt that he was a voice for democracy. But his need to imagine a story in which the interests of the people triumph, raises problems about his democratic vision, since he needs to imagine a hero of the people as powerful as the forces of bigness. Thus Scarborough, who seems so at odds with his corporate rival, has many qualities in common with him. We can start our examination of *The Cost*'s moral economy by looking at the similarities between Phillips's reformist politician and his corporate scoundrel. Those similarities help to highlight the extent to which Phillips's solution to corporate influence is what we can call the "politics of character," a politics in which a politician's character is more important than specific programs that he advocates, a politics that is very much alive today.

Looking at a portrait of Dumont, Pauline's friend Olivia thinks, "He's of the same type as Scarborough" (C 159). Pauline also notes the resemblance and blames it for her failure to recognize Dumont's faults while she was at college. Receiving letters from Dumont, she had mistakenly read the "present Scarborough" (C 151) into the "absent Dumont" (C 151). "Yes, and—the answers she addressed and mailed to Dumont had really been written to Scarborough" (C 151). If Pauline can now see the difference between the two, their resemblance, which is one "found in all men of strong and tenacious will" (C 151), is as important to Phillips's vision as their differences.

Pauline is not alone in her infatuation with Dumont. It is shared by her creator, who is especially fascinated by his villain's power. Dumont is acutely aware of the new force fields in the modern world. According to Phillips, "the discoveries of steam and electricity" established "inexorably and permanently" the "principles of concentration and combination" making the "whole human race more and more like one community of interdependent neighbors."[33] Attuned to changed conditions, Dumont announces, "Time and space used to be the big elements. We practically disregard them" (C 170). To his lawyer's objection that their merger with another company is "our private business" and not fit for newspaper stories, he responds, " 'There's no such thing as a private business nowadays. . . . Besides don't we want the public to take part of our stock?' " (C 165). He is also part of a new order on Wall Street that consists of coyotes, wolves, and lions. If coyotes are the hacks and wolves the speculators, "Dumont became less of a wolf and more of a lion, less of a speculator and more of a financier" (C 268). As a financier he controls the speculators of Wall Street rather than be controlled by them.

Dumont's power to control and manipulate might seem to mark the difference between him and Scarborough, who after all represents the interests of the people. But Phillips is quite frank about Scarborough's ability to control and manipulate. In his speech at the nominating convention, "delegates and spectators" were his "captives" after five minutes. "Fifteen minutes, and he was riding a storm such as comes only when the fountains of the human deeps are broken up. Thirty minutes and he was riding it as its master, guiding it where he willed" (C 254). As Dumont acknowledges, Scarborough could use his brain to "make millions" (C 276). The difference between the corporate giant and the reformist politician is not an ability to control and guide events and people, it is, as Pauline knows, their character.

Dumont can control others, but he lacks Scarborough's virtuous self-control. Olivia sees him "not as an ambition but as an appetite, or rather a bundle of appetites" (C 169). Lacking an ideal to direct his boundless energy, Dumont awakens the appetites and self-interest in those he controls, although because of his power their interest usually lies in remaining loyal to him. At one point Pauline asks her husband why he can't use his power for good. "When a doctor or a man of science or a philosopher makes a discovery that'll be a benefit to the world . . . he gives it freely. . . . Why shouldn't a man with financial

genius be like men with other kinds of genius? . . . Just think, John, how
the world would honor you and how you would feel, if you used your
genius to make the necessaries cheap for all these fellow-beings of ours
who have such a hard time getting on" (C 198–99). Dumont responds
by dismissing her suggestion as "sentimentalism" (C 201).

This exchange reveals two important aspects of Phillips's response to
corporate influence. First, Phillips grants Dumont financial genius. His
"great combine" is so efficient that it employs "more men," pays
"higher wages," and makes "the goods better than ever, and at less
cost" (C 197). As Beveridge argued, "better products at cheaper prices
to the consumer is the only justification for trusts."[34] Second, Phillips
never contradicts Dumont's claim that Pauline's plan to use his corporate genius is sentimental. Instead, he embraces what Dumont rejects as
the "preposterous project" of a "good, sentimental woman" (C 200),
placing his hopes for realizing it in Scarborough.

But Scarborough can preside over Pauline's ideal vision only because
he is equal to the powers that control the mighty corporations. He too
has a "genius for organization" (C 156). Furthermore, if Phillips praises
Dumont's lawyer Herron for his brilliant "legal piloting" (C 270), with
Scarborough the "people had in their service a lawyer equal in ability to
the best monopolies could buy, and one who understood human nature
and political machinery to boot" (C 276). They also have in their service
a man of impeccable private character who shares Pauline's sentimental
idealism. As Dumont's sister Gladys remarks to Scarborough, "You are
a strange combination, aren't you? In one way you're so very practical—
with your politics and all that. And in another way—I suspect you of
being sentimental—almost romantic" (C 286).

It is important to note that Dumont cannot be distinguished from
Scarborough in terms of *commercial* honesty. To be sure, Dumont feels
that he is above the morality of ordinary people. A lion, he need not live
by a sheep's code. "He had made his own code—not by special revelation from the Almighty, as did some of his fellow practitioners of high
finance, but by especial command of his imperial 'destiny'" (C 372).
But this code "was a strict code—it had earned him his unblemished
reputation for inflexible *commercial* honesty and *commercial* truthfulness" (C 372–73).

In portraying his villain as a man who scrupulously keeps his commercial promises, Phillips recognizes, as more and more in his generation did, that maintaining them is not enough, that such inflexible

commercial honesty and truthfulness does not guarantee equity. But because he attempts to explain that lack of social equity in terms of the qualities of the individual who rules the commercial world, Phillips is forced to find another flaw in Dumont's character. He finds it in Dumont's domestic relations.

Dumont may keep his commercial promises, but he does not honor the sacred promise of marriage. In contrast, Scarborough stays true to Pauline even while she is married to Dumont. When Dumont's sister finds herself attracted to the handsome politician, she actively pursues him. But although Scarborough momentarily lets down his guard and gives Gladys a kiss that she invites, he immediately apologizes and retains his devotion to Pauline.[35] In Phillips's world only someone who is as efficient and powerful as Dumont *and* whose character is informed by the domestic values that he rejects can guarantee an equitable social order.

The nature of Phillips's politics of character comes into focus when we compare Scarborough with the traditional hero of republican civic virtue and the laissez-faire Man of Principle, discussed in chapter 2. As self-contained as the republican hero is, his independence cannot be imagined outside the polis. First of all, in republicanism, as in Plato's *Republic,* the state plays a crucial role in the construction of virtuous character. Second, although virtue is related to a capacity for self-governance necessary for independence and self-sufficiency, self-governance is impossible without knowledge of one's social status, which in part determines the identity of the self to be governed. Finally, one achieves true virtue only by displaying it in the public sphere where private and class interests are sacrificed to the general public good. As a result, the traditional republican hero, like Shakespeare's Brutus, often faces a conflict between his role as a private citizen and his duty to serve the public.

Significantly, Scarborough never faces that conflict. On the contrary, he acquires the ideals lacking in Dumont from his private relationship with Pauline. As he tells Gladys, "I began really to live when I began to love her. And—everyone must have a—a pole-star. And she's mine—the star I sail by, and always must" (C 293). To be sure, this neo-Platonic vision of a lover inspiring the idealism of a hero has a long history of its own. But Phillips's use of it indicates that Scarborough's virtue preexists the state and the public sphere. Furthermore, Scarborough has no use for status. Staying true to his ancestors, who include a "leveler" who was a "Dutch-bred pioneer of Dutch-bred democracy" (C 33), Scarborough does not want to be valued "for any other reason than what I myself am" (C 54).

Scarborough's distrust of status would seem to appeal to the promise of contract. Indeed, just as lawyers pierce the corporate veil in order to reveal individuals behind the legal fiction of a corporate personality, so Phillips reveals the drama of human characters behind a powerful trust. By now, however, it should be clear that simply to imply that society is organized by relations among individuals is not enough to evoke contract's promise. Indeed, Phillips's vision is not even that of classical liberalism as evidenced by the difference between Phillips's Man of Character and the Man of Principle. The Man of Principle is normally a private citizen who remains true to universal values while negotiating for his interests within a system of market exchanges, which, without him, would lose its claim to justice. Phillips holds on to an individualized explanation of society and belief in universal values, but faced with a world in which corporate influence is everywhere, he cannot imagine an equitable order resulting from the existing system of exchanges. Thus he needs someone like the republican figure of virtue to guarantee social justice for the collective "people." But whereas in the republican tradition virtue is achieved and maintained by private citizens submitting to the public good, in *The Cost* the public good is guaranteed by an individual displaying private virtue.

There is nothing new about combining elements of the republican and liberal traditions to create a figure different in kind from the figures representing both. For instance, we saw a similar combination in Hay's *The Bread-Winners* where virtue has also been privatized. But there is a crucial difference between Hay's and Phillips's sense of virtuous character. In Hay's world social status is a birthright, but virtue and the independence of character that accompany it are not. Indeed, Hay maintains a republican notion of equality, which results not from equality of status or condition, but from the equal opportunity of people from all classes to achieve virtue by submitting to the public good. If Hay values independent and self-governing individuals, for him they are never autonomously produced. Thus in *The Bread-Winners,* proper self-regulation still results from a combination of external discipline and traits that one is born with. Maud, we remember, goes astray because of lax discipline at home and because her high school education feeds her ambitions to be someone she is not. In contrast, in *The Cost* Pauline's early marriage to Dumont is blamed on too much paternal regulation.

In Phillips the character growing out of self-reliance cannot be imposed from without; it must come from within. Seemingly more democratic because it discounts social status, Phillips's vision in fact makes it impossible for some to achieve virtue because autonomy is itself autonomously produced. Some people are born with the capacity for it; others are not. To be sure, improper training can block the potential one is born with, but proper training cannot produce independence and virtue in those lacking the potential for both. Scarborough, for instance, is reported to believe that "character isn't a development it's a disclosure. He thinks one is born a certain kind of person and that one's life simply either gives it a chance to show or fails to give it a chance. He says the boy isn't father to the man, but the miniature of the man" (C 174–75).

In a sketch of Beveridge, Phillips insists that his friend is "typically American" (B 122), "simply first among equals" (B 124). At the same time, he exalts his "superiority," attributing it to "possession of the combination of qualities—energy, tenacity, and intelligent plan,—that make hard work bear a rich harvest" (B 126). In *The Cost* those qualities are as much in the possession of Dumont as of Scarborough. What finally distinguishes the two is their character, a character that seems to have been mysteriously imparted to Scarborough at birth from his status-hating ancestors. Ironically, however, in the world that Phillips presents, such character itself becomes a sign of status. In fact, it becomes the new ordering principle of the world.

What ultimately contains Dumont's corporate threat is not a political program advocated by Scarborough but a moral economy implied by Phillips's "politics of character." Despite the threat that they pose to Dumont's designs, Scarborough's policies, which are never specified, play a minor role in Dumont's demise. Instead, Dumont's downfall is set in motion by his treatment of subordinates, which sets off a rebellion within the corporate hierarchy. By having an affair with the wife of one of his coyotes and by insulting his lawyer, Dumont creates an alliance intent on bringing him "to an accounting for his depravity" (C 272). That alliance almost succeeds. But even it is not powerful enough to bring down Phillips's corporate giant. Dumont rallies from his deathbed and, with a remarkable effort "directed by a single mind to a single purpose," (C 390) regains control. Indeed, his final defeat has no empirical explanation. It does, however, conform to the demands of poetic justice. Shortly after his final victory, Dumont meets his end, choked to death by the Wall Street ticker tape that he keeps in his bedroom.

The deus ex machina scene of Dumont's death reveals the moral economy that governs Phillips's fictional world. First, the ticker tape in Dumont's bedroom calls attention to his violation of domestic values. Second, Dumont's execution by a machine registering the transactions of Wall Street emphasizes his failure to achieve self-governing autonomy.

Power in Phillips's world is marked by an ability to stand above chance and to control the operations of fate. Dumont, for instance, is a financier not a mere speculator. Furthermore, Dumont and his executives are the "holders and manipulators of the secret strings whereto were attached puppet peoples and puppet politicians," while Dumont himself is the "master, at the innermost wheels, deep at the heart of the intricate mechanism" (C 241). A trust, Beveridge claimed, is a tool, a "labor-saving machine" in the service of people.[36] In the end the machinery of Wall Street that Dumont seems to control destroys him.

In contrast, by not having a price, Scarborough stands above the machinery of Wall Street that brings Dumont to his end. Indeed, Scarborough stands above all mechanical forces of fate. On the page after Dumont is described as the master of the "intricate mechanism," we are told how Scarborough, in a "moral victory," "wrested away from the machine" (C 241) nearly three hundred delegates. Dumont's cronies believe that politics is a "mere game of chance—you won or you didn't win; and principles and oratory and likes and dislikes and resentments were so much 'hot air'" (C 238). Scarborough shows that more than bribes can influence that game of chance.

Scarborough's victory would seem to show that principles and oratory can triumph over the machine. In fact, a more powerful force is at work. When Scarborough expresses joy at seeing "so many young men in arms for a principle," the patriarchal ex-judge to whom he goes to seek advice responds, "Principles without leaders go begging. . . . If the moment should come for you to think of [running for governor], do not forget that the leader is the principle" (C 233). More than any set of principles, it is Scarborough's character that gives him the power to control Dumont, whom otherwise he so resembles.

Scarborough's political victory is remarkable because "everything" was "against him—money and machine and the skilful confusing of the issues by his crafty opponents" (C 242). We are, however, never confronted with specific examples of that "skilful confusing of the issues." If we were, we might mistakenly side with Scarborough's opponents. What we are presented with is a leader whom we can trust always to serve the interests of the people. That trust comes, not so much from the particular programs that he advocates, but from his character.

In his sketch of Beveridge, Phillips admits that he may not share "details of [Beveridge's] political beliefs" (B 123). But "at bottom, all Americans—all honest Americans,—are heartily agreed in matters political. We want to do all we can to insure that 'government of the people, by the people, and for the people, shall not perish; [*sic*]' we differ only as to how to bring about that result" (B 123). So long as a leader is committed to serve the interests of the people, he will inevitably abandon a policy once he recognizes that it doesn't serve them and adopt one that does. The questions to ask therefore are " 'Is he honest? Is he intelligent? Is he open-minded'" (B 123)?

Phillips believes that policies truly representing the interests of the people will—despite the tendency of interest politics to obscure them—be easily recognized. Indeed, the "literature of exposure" itself assumes that a process of unmasking will reveal the simple truth behind attempts to cover it up. Piercing the corporate veil to show us the truth behind the corporate corruption, Phillips presents his fictional world from a transcendental perspective that, like that of his hero, can readily distinguish what serves the interests of "the people" from what doesn't. Yet if we stay true to the aims of the literature of exposure and identify the real characters behind the images that Phillips constructs, we find an Indiana senator whose career was promoted by an author who wrote his famous *The Treason of the Senate* series for William Randolph Hearst, a newspaper mogul unsuccessfully seeking the governorship of New York as a stepping stone toward the presidency. We also find an author who contributed to confusion over the issue of corporate influence by reducing it to a question of character.

Phillips's celebration of character coincides with the demise of transcendental standards used to judge it. Indeed, even in *The Cost* there are moments when character seems to be a pure product of reputation. A major factor in Dumont's initial downfall is the public revelation of his affair, for it "tore away the foundation of reputation—private character" (C 316). Why it should do so is puzzling since, "in the newspaper exposure there was no fact of importance that was not known to the entire Street" (C 322). Nonetheless, as the narrator remarks, "there is an abysmal difference between everybody knowing a thing privately and everybody knowing precisely the same thing publicly" (C 322). On Wall Street the public's image of character counts more than real character. Indeed, Dumont's "chief asset" is "his reputation" (C 326).

Thus Dumont respects Scarborough, "not for his character, which made him impregnable with the people, but for his intellect, which showed him how to convince the people of his character and keep them convinced" (C 276).

The politics of character thrives in a world in which it is more and more difficult to distinguish between authentic and inauthentic character, a world in which authenticity of character has been severed from the status of one's birth so that everyone seems capable of manufacturing one's own status. The link between such politics and sentimentality is indicated in Phillips's novel by the fact that Scarborough's triumph would have been impossible without Pauline's help. At the nominating convention she keeps Dumont's money from bribing delegates, thus allowing Scarborough to win while remaining completely independent and above the messy compromises necessitated by partisan politics.

In *The Grafters*, Lynde, like Phillips, presents us with a political reformer whose promise to represent the interests of the people is guaranteed by his fidelity to values that others in the book dismiss as sentimental. But Lynde at least forces his hero to prove his character by wrestling with the moral dilemmas that the rise of corporate influence presents. As a result, we get a more complicated sense of how corporate influence altered the public realm of interest politics, one that challenges the simple opposition between the people and the forces of bigness.

VII

Lynde invites complication by making his hero a lawyer representing corporate interests. For instance, whereas many in Gaston are furious because Kent's railroad lives up to the motto "All the tariff the traffic will stand" (G 25), Kent argues that corporations are not primarily to blame. "Corporations here, as elsewhere, are looking out for the present dollar, but if the country were generally prosperous, the people would pay the tax carelessly" (G 63). In addition, when the grafters place the Western Pacific in receivership, Lynde suggests that too much governmental interference can result in disaster. For instance, the first act of the receiver is to replace trained railroad managers with "political troughsmen" (G 153), an act guaranteed to ruin the company's efficiency and its service to its customers.

The internal perspective that Kent offers into corporate affairs helps to reinforce the work of recent historians intent on combating the assumption that "the people" were simply helpless victims in the face of corporate power. For instance, Lynde, like Phillips, associates corporations with feudal modes of governance, but he does not necessarily condemn that association. Instead, he is much closer to W. J. Ghent, who in 1902 predicted that "the next distinct stage in the socioeconomic evolution of America, . . . the next status of society . . . will be Benevolent Feudalism."[37] Lynde foreshadows such benevolence in the American railroad, which "in its unconsolidated stage is a modern feudalism. Its suzerains are the president and board of directors; its chiefs are the men who have built it and fought for its footing in the sharply contested field of competition. To these leaders the rank and file is loyal, as loyalty is accorded to the men who build and do, rather than to their successors who inherit and tear down" (G 283).

Viewed from the perspective of Maine's contrast between status and contract, a corporation does indeed have feudal elements. Most notably, each person within the organization must first and foremost know his place, a place that defines and limits his responsibilities and duties, responsibilities and duties that each must fulfill for the efficient operation of the corporate whole. Nonetheless, each employee's role is contractually agreed upon.[38] For Lynde this contractual agreement indicates that corporate agency does not, as it does for Phillips, result in a total loss of freedom. On the contrary, he suggests that the rank and file willingly assent to their position so long as managers are competent in both the "science of railroading" and the "sub-science of industrial manhandling" (G 283).

If Lynde's portrayal of worker loyalty is in part ideological distortion, it at least grants workers limited, if not boundless, agency. Indeed, they play an important role in winning back the corporation. A major mistake of the Plantagould people is to underestimate the rank and file's agency and loyalty. Their loyalty expresses itself in the workers' support of Kent and Loring. Their agency expresses itself in their courageous and highly skilled efforts to deliver Bucks to justice in the book's action-filled climax. For Lynde, workers are not mere cogs in the corporate machinery; without them the machinery does not operate. To be sure, their agency is circumscribed by the role granted them within the corporate whole. But so too is the agency of managers. Contrary to the direction of much recent labor history, however, Lynde's portrayal of worker agency suggests that it was not necessarily directed *against* the forces of corporate capitalism. Indeed, if Lynde does not indulge in pure ideological distortion, his book suggests that the rank and file often felt that their interests lay in remaining loyal to an efficiently run company. And if the rank and file often felt a sense of corporate loyalty, white collar workers, like Kent, felt it even more.[39]

To be sure, Kent is loyal not only to his corporation. In defending its interests he also defends those of his lover. But by linking those two interests, Lynde once again complicates the opposition of "the people" against the forces of corporate bigness. Corporate interests can't be against those of all the people because some people have interests in corporations. Not all, however, have interests in the same ones. What anticorporate rhetoric too often forgets is that not all corporations are the same. Thus, whereas one measure might aid all corporations, another can aid some and hurt others.

The most effective way that Lynde complicates the opposition between the interests of the people and those of corporations is by putting anticorporate, populist rhetoric in the mouth of a politician serving the interests of one corporation over another. Similar to Dumont, Bucks is described as "a man of titanic strength, of tremendous possibilities for good or evil" (G 24). Nonetheless, his campaign rhetoric sounds more like that of Scarborough than Dumont. Expressing belief in the ultimate victory of the people through the law, his campaign pits "plain, honest justice" and the "will of the people" against "the money of the Harrimans and the Goulds and the Vanderbilts and all the rest of 'em" (G 24–25). To underscore his honesty, Bucks emphasizes that all of his reforms will be accomplished lawfully. Law in his administration, he warns, will place corporations under control of the sovereign state, which "will stand out glorious and triumphant as a monument against oppression" (G 25).

Bucks's rhetoric is not empty. When elected he stays true to his word by advocating a bill requiring foreign corporations, that is, those with charters in other states, to acquire the standing of local corporations. Under this new law the state asserts its power "to deal only with creatures of its own creation" (G 72).

Admitting that the law is "equitable enough on its face," Kent worries that it can be "made an engine of extortion" (G 97). Indeed, shocked by this "tinkering with corporate rights" (G 83), he learns from other lobbyists that they plan to bribe the governor in order to have him make the law inconsequential through its administration. What they don't know is that Bucks is already in the pay of the Plantagould people, whose lawyer, Falkland, has masterminded Buck's entire campaign as a way to force the Western Pacific into receivership and have it taken over by a corporation controlled by the huge National Oil trust.

Kent, of course, is on the side of the "good" corporation in its fight against the "bad" corporate giant and its corrupt politicians. Nonetheless, by structuring his narrative as a battle between competing corporate interests, Lynde poses a dilemma for his would-be reformist politician: how can he represent the interests of *all* the people so long as he represents the interests of one corporation? That dilemma in turn is related to a question at the center of Lynde's novel, one raised by corporations' increased influence in the arena of interest politics: what constitutes graft?

The answer to that question seems clear-cut. Graft is acquired through illegally peddling influence. But a 1903 lecture delivered by a Tammany Hall favorite, entitled "Honest Graft and Dishonest Graft," indicates that for Lynde's and Phillips's generation the answer was not so clear-cut.[40] Corporations, for instance, recognized that it was in their interests to wield influence inside rather than outside the law. Corporations may have urged the government to keep its hands out of their business, but they desired as much predictability as possible for their investments. That predictability, they knew, was best guaranteed by a consistent and universally applicable legal system. This corporate desire for predictability is registered by Phillips in Dumont's code of strict commercial honesty and by Lynde in the "aphorism that capital can never afford to be otherwise than strictly law-abiding" (G 108). Thus in *The Grafters* every exchange that buys influence can be accounted for legally. Furthermore, even the judge in the pay of the Plantagould interests is instructed to deliver an opinion with "some formal compliance with the letter of the law" (G 348).

The acknowledged power of corporations to benefit from the legal system helped contribute to the demise of legal formalism in this period by suggesting that formal compliance with the law was less important than its effects. The corporate control of judges also contributed to lessened faith in the paternal function of the judiciary. To be sure, in both *The Cost* and *The Grafters* a patriarchal judge appears. Significantly, however, in both cases he is an ex-judge, who accomplishes his most important work in the executive branch. The judges in both books who actually deliver opinions are in the pay of corporations.[41] Unable to turn to the judiciary to find a realm that transcends interest politics, both

Phillips and Lynde turn to a figure who promises to do so through equitable *administration* of the laws.

Phillips's Scarborough faces no dilemma over graft because he adheres to an absolute standard. For him *any* acceptance of influence is too high a cost to pay because it threatens his independence. He hopes "never to 'belong' to anything or anybody" (C 54), and with Pauline's help he doesn't. Phillips's belief in the existence of such a disinterested position allows him to reassert formalist doctrine in the face of threats posed to it. Legal interpretations favoring corporations are for Phillips simply misinterpretations. Thus he condemns the "legal pilots" (R 136) of corporate interests for construing the Constitution so as to make the plutocracy's "needs seem sound law and the rights and needs of the people 'unconstitutional'" (R 143). Serving the interests of the people, "The Constitution is a common-sense document" (R 141). What we need to interpret it is, "not craft, for we have too much of that, but common democratic honesty and common-sense; not searching after strained readings of fundamental law, but straight away obedience to the law as it plainly reads" (R 143–44).

True to the premises of the "literature of exposure," Phillips insists that truth is self-evident once we clear away the obfuscations caused by the crafty manipulations of those in the service of special interests. For Lynde, however, the problem is more complicated, for what is he to do with someone aspiring to be a reformist politician, who is by profession a corporate lobbyist? It would seem impossible for Lynde to claim a disinterested position for his corporate lawyer. Indeed, if we adopt the pragmatic approach of measuring an act by its effects, it is difficult to distinguish Kent's lobbying activities from the bribery of the grafters. Both are effective when they buy influence.

Despite this complication, Lynde finds a solution. He finds it, just as Phillips does in his sentimental love plot. The love plot in *The Grafters,* like that in *The Cost,* is structured by two triangular relations. The first one in *The Cost* involves Scarborough and Dumont's battle for Pauline; the second, Pauline and Gladys's battle for Scarborough. The pairing of Pauline and Scarborough serves the cathartic function of eliminating the book's representatives of corruption, who are also brother and sister. The first relation in *The Grafters* involves Kent and Ormsby's battle for Elinor's affections; the second, Elinor and Portia's hope to capture Kent's. But the pairing of Elinor and Kent is complicated. If in *The Cost* Phillips eliminates barriers to Scarborough's success, in *The Grafters* Lynde is forced to eliminate two sympathetic figures, both of whom are necessary for Kent's success. Ormsby provides needed financial support in the fight against Bucks and the Plantagould interests; Portia lends Kent invaluable advice. As he admits, she is the "head," and he is only the "hand" (G 490). Kent's victory over Ormsby signals, however, a victory of the professional middle class over the idle rich. Elinor's over Portia guarantees that the representative of the professional middle class will hold on to values that his drive for success imperils. It is the latter victory that helps to transform Kent from a corporate lobbyist to a man of the people.

Recognizing that "the sentimental young woman went out some time ago," Elinor doesn't want to be an "anachronism" (G 34). Nonetheless, late in the novel she realizes that she can't help her "foolish, romantic sentiment" (G 334) that is linked to an uncompromising moral standard that she inherited from the "Grimkie blood" (G 40) of her Puritan ancestors. In contrast, Portia is the "only child of a somewhat ill-considered match between a young California lawyer, wire-pulling in the national capitol in the interest of the Central Pacific Railroad, and a Virginia belle tasting the delights of her first winter in Washington" (G 79). Financially independent as the result of lucky investments, Portia combines the talents of both parents (now dead) in her role as political hostess in Gaston. A political pragmatist, Portia urges Kent to cast off his "Jonathan Edwardsy notions" (G 315) and discover his manhood "deep down under the rubbish of ill-temper and hesitancy and—yes, I will say it—of sentiment" (G 205–6).

The conflicting claims that the two women have on Kent reach a crisis when he has to decide whether to use the information that he has gathered about the Plantagould plot to bribe Bucks. Told by Elinor that to give a bribe is as bad as taking one, Kent struggles for a week with his "Puritan virus of overrighteousness" (G 279). Nonetheless, he finally decides that he has no "moral right to use the weapon he had so skilfully forged." If his decision forces him to face Portia's "scornful disappointment" (G 296), his discovery of "such an out-of-date thing" as a "conscience" in this "nation of successfulists" (G 38) qualifies him as a reformist politician. As Ormsby puts it, "a little conscience—of the right old Pilgrim Fathers' brand—goes a long way in politics" (G 336). Kent refuses to rely on graft of his own to defeat the grafters.

In having Elinor lead Kent to the values that qualify him as a man of the people, Lynde structures his plot as a modern day version of the *scalus amoras*. As the narrator puts it, "From looking forward to success in the narrow field of professional advancement, or in the scarcely broader one of the righting of one's woman's financial wrongs, he was coming to crave it in the name of manhood; to burn with an eager desire to see justice done for its own sake" (G 182). At first Kent felt that he had to win Elinor's love by becoming rich, then by protecting her fortune. In fact, those goals are simply stages of his growth into a manhood truly worthy of her love, since what she admires most are those with the "gift of true leadership and a love of pure justice in their hearts" (G 98). Like a chivalric knight, Kent proves himself by saving the woman he loves from hostile forces.[42] Marrying her, he is ready to do battle for the people as he ventures into the world from the new home that he and Elinor have bought, the repository, as the last words of the book describe it, of all of their "ideals," and Kent's "haven when the storms beat" (G 408).

The restoration of order signaled by Kent and Elinor moving into their new home of domestic tranquillity is reinforced by the patriarchal Judge Marston's ascent to the governorship, a man who reminds Kent of his father (a small-town New England lawyer of the type that Howells leaves paralyzed at the end of *A Modern Instance*). But the restoration of order is not contrived simply because of its sentiment. Portia is such a powerful figure that Kent's choice of Elinor over her is as aesthetically unsatisfactory as Phillips's mechanical elimination of Dumont. Lynde seems to sense this problem and even has Kent offer to marry Portia, only to have her refuse, when she recognizes that his sense of duty alone makes him ask. Lynde's decision to couple his reformist politician with Elinor rather than Portia has a number of implications.

Most obviously, it shows how the book's restoration of moral order depends on the hierarchical status of gender difference. Quite self-consciously, Lynde opts for a woman whose "soul harks back to the eternal-womanly" over the "most modern of girl bachelors" (G 43). As Kent puts it while courting Elinor, the "most hardened criminal in the dock was less dangerous to humanity than the woman who had forgotten how to cry" (G 327). Evoking Shakespeare's heroine in *Merchant of Venice*, Portia is a threat because she is given "masculine" qualities of reasoning. For instance, as she and Kent plot a new scheme, she conducts herself in a manner "almost man-like," even if she was "dangerously beautiful" (G 297). Attracted to the beauty but intimidated by the brainpower, Kent imagines a "frank, sexless friendship" (G 180) between the two. In a revealing moment he blurts out, "You ought to be a man. If you were, I should never give you a moment's peace until you consented to take a partnership with me" (G 188). Kent can imagine Portia in the contractual relationship of an equal partnership, but he prefers entering into a marriage contract with Elinor.

Kent's choice of Elinor over Portia, like Scarborough's idealization of Pauline as his "pole-star," indicates that much reformist thought of the period depended on a vision of female virtue, as Hay did in *The Bread-Winners*. For instance, Charles Edward Russell, Phillips's friend and former editor, told the American Woman Suffrage Association that "if the 'eternal feminine' should cease to lead us upward forever, if the idealism and loftier impulses that a woman furnishes in the world, were to be crushed out of it, I cannot see wherein would lie the least chance for progress."[43] Nonetheless, Portia is an interesting case because, while she challenges images of the "eternal feminine," she, like James's Verena, is sympathetically portrayed. As a result, her unfixing of traditionally established gender hierarchies poses a more serious threat to the book's moral economy than an obviously corrupt figure might.

Chiding Kent for his narrowness, Portia asks, "Is there then no other code of morals in the round world save that which the accident of birth has interleaved with your New England Bible? What is conscience? Is it an absolute standard of right and wrong? Or is it merely your ideal or mine, or Shafiz Ullah Khan's" (G 316)? Just as Phillips offers no counter to Dumont's charge that Pauline's view of the world is sentimental, so Lynde offers no answer to Portia's questions. Instead, like Phillips, he simply chooses to hold on to the moral code that his most interesting fictional creation calls into question. He does so because, without that code, he has no answer to the problem of corporate graft that the book raises. Nonetheless, in contrast to Phillips's moral economy in which Dumont represents an actively evil threat, in Lynde's the major threat comes from the serious possibility of moral relativism as raised by Portia.

Portia is above all concerned with questions of "ways and means" (G 204). That concern links her to one of the most interesting aspects of the novel—one that lends energy and suspense to its plot. So far I've emphasized how the ending promises to restore moral order, but I haven't pointed to its most contrived element. Kent may win his battle without a bribe, but only because Bucks, like Dumont, contributes to his own undoing through a flaw in his private character. The intricate plans of the Plantagould interests fail because Bucks's primitive nature causes him to kill a man. In a chapter entitled "The Relentless Wheels" he is transported against his will across the state line to waiting law enforcement officers. Thus, in another example of a deus ex machina resolution, a villain is brought to justice through a turn in the wheel of fortune.

As contrived as this scene is, Lynde pulls it off with great skill. Bringing into play many technological devices—telegraphs, telephones, automobiles, and of course the railroad itself—he generates suspense through the split-second timing necessary to maneuver the train along tracks controlled by hostile switchmen. As well as any novel in the period, Lynde's registers how technology altered networks of exchange and the conveyance of information. It is new technologies that make possible the rise of intricate corporate networks given visual embodiment in the system of railroad lines stretching across the nation. Connecting all parts of the country, these new networks emphasize the interdependence rather than independence of those they affect.

Portia is linked to them because her role in the plot is foremost that of a conveyor of information. Her parties are notorious for exchanges of political information. Those exchanges and the conveyance of information through new technologies are morally neutral. What counts, as the chase scene makes clear, is who controls networks of exchange.

The importance of controlling those networks seems to divide society into two classes of people: those who control the flow of information and capital and those who serve as simple mechanical agents helping to convey the flow. This distinction helps to explain both Phillips's and Lynde's admiration for what Phillips calls "legal piloting" (C 270). For instance, Portia and Kent marvel at the "skilful bit of engineering" and "artistic skill" (G 188–89) of the lawyer Falkland, who masterminds the takeover of the Western Pacific. Such mental activity distinguishes the new middle class described by C. Wright Mills. But as Mills points out, members of the middle class were rarely independent engineers or artists. More often than not, large corporations controlled the flow of information and capital, and the mental work of middle-class workers was subordinated to an overall corporate design. Indeed, new technologies made for closer supervision of corporate employees. Even though Kent is thousands of miles from Boston, the telegram keeps him in close contact with corporate headquarters.

Corporate control of technologically advanced networks of exchange may increase corporations' efficiency and power, but it creates a moral dilemma even for Lynde who does not demonize corporations. As he admits, corporations look "only to their own interests, as they're duty bound to do" (G 22). For Kent to become a representative of "the people," he needs to transcend his loyalty to a single corporation. He needs to direct the flow of information and capital along morally neutral networks of exchange in such a way that it will serve a higher moral purpose—the public interest rather than private corporate interests. For instance, explaining to a friend why he did not bribe Bucks with the information that he so skillfully gathered, he says, "I couldn't traffic with it" (G 309). Or as the friend puts it, indicating that he understands Kent's logic, "It is public property and you couldn't divert it into private channels" (G 309).

Nonetheless, although Elinor is behind Kent's effort to serve the public interest by adopting a moral code above the trafficking of private interests, it is, significantly, Portia who tells him how to resolve the conflict between his loyalty to his employers and the public he aspires to serve. He must, Portia insists, "be free to deal with Boston as an outsider" (G 321). Thus she urges him to resign his position with the railroad and act as an independent agent, negotiating his own terms, if he succeeds in saving the line. To his objection that the terms she names for his service are too high, she responds, "Not when you consider it a surgeon's risk. You happen to be the one man who has the idea, and if it isn't carried out, the patient is going to die to-morrow night, permanently. You are the specialist in this case, and specialists come high" (G 323).

Portia's solution frees Kent from his legal obligation to the railroad at the same time as it allows him to serve the cause of justice—as well as Elinor—by saving it. It also moves him one rung closer to his role as an independent voice of the people. In linking roles of independent, professional specialists and reformist politicians, Portia's solution also suggests an answer to a question that historians of progressive reform have wrestled with. Accepting Mills's definition of a new middle class, two of the best historians of the period—Hofstadter and Robert Wiebe—disagree on its relation to reform. Hofstadter argues that the middle class' transformation corresponded with the late nineteenth century's "status rebellion," in which a cultured elite of the past was replaced by a new uncultured, business elite. For him progressive reformers are members of the old middle class who try to impose social justice by reasserting the status and influence that they were losing to corporate interests.[44] In contrast, Wiebe argues that the "heart of progressivism was the ambition of the *new* middle class to fulfill its destiny through bureaucratic means."[45] Far from producing a Kafkalike state, those bureaucratic means were deemed necessary to increase efficiency. For instance, Olivier Zunz describes how Louis Brandeis combined forces with the efficiency expert Frederick Winslow Taylor to "reassert the primacy of technical over financial control" in the 1910 freight rate cases.[46] The figure represented by Kent suggests that some progressives could have seen themselves maintaining the autonomous moral judgment of Hofstadter's older, independent middle class while fostering the professional and bureaucratic efficiency of Wiebe's newer, corporate middle class. Having experienced Hofstadter's "status rebellion," such reformers didn't merely look backward. Instead, they found a solution to what Wiebe characterizes as the period's "search for order" by imparting a new *status* on professionally trained specialists whose task it was to move society forward while safeguarding traditional values.

Dewey Grantham has described Southern Progressivism as a "reconciliation of progress and tradition."[47] His description applies to Kent as well. Although Kent's New England tradition was not the operative tradition in the South, he too looks forward by holding on to seemingly outmoded values. If the reconciliation of progress and tradition creates what David Noble calls the "paradox of progressivism,"[48] it also allows Kent, like Scarborough, to become a politician who stands above politics in order to represent the public interest. Kent needs professional expertise to avoid defeat by the greater efficiency of corporate forces. But he also needs values to ensure that efficient ways and means are put to proper ends. The society over which he will preside is, however, one that has moved one step further from the promise of contract, since it is organized according to a corporate, not contractual, model of efficiency. Indeed, when Elinor describes the relationship of her ideal politician to the people, her description sounds most of all like the "modern feudalism" of an efficiently run, hierarchically organized railroad company. "The great heart of the people," she says, "is honest and well-meaning: I think we all admit that. And there is intelligence, too. But human nature is the same as it used to be when they set up a man who *could* and called him a king. Gentle or simple, it must be led" (G 98). If Phillips's "king of the new democracy" is a self-sufficient and independent figure from the "free West" (C 31), Lynde's is an independent, professionally trained specialist.

VIII

By presenting us with such heroes, Phillips's and Lynde's novels help us to understand the mode of thinking that caused many progressive-era reformers to respond to the influence of corporate power by matching their concentration of power with more concentration and imagining as a solution a centralized governmental agency, staffed by a disinterested elite, whose responsibility was to manage the economy efficiently and equitably. They also help us to pinpoint limitations to that solution.

The most famous effort at corporate reform was the Sherman Antitrust Act of 1890. There was, however, a long debate over how to interpret and administer that act. Until 1911 it was interpreted as providing greater restrictions on corporate control of markets than under common law. Adhering to the "Harlan construction," the Supreme Court tried to promote unrestricted competition by limiting mergers and cartels. Paradoxically, however, unrestricted competition could be guaranteed only by government regulation. As Brandeis put it, "The right of competition must be limited in order to preserve it. For excesses of competition lead to monopoly, as excesses of liberty lead to absolutism."[49] Opposed to such regulation, pro-corporate forces won an important victory in 1911 when the so-called rule of reason prevailed and the Court interpreted the Sherman Act as simply reinforcing common law standards under which a reasonable amount of restraint on trade was allowed. The debate over how to control corporate influence was resolved in 1914 by creation of the Federal Trade Commission (FTC).

The FTC was a victory for the New Freedom of Woodrow Wilson, whose position on corporate control should be distinguished from that of Theodore Roosevelt and William Taft. Roosevelt viewed corporations as creatures of the state that, like public utilities, were subject to strict regulation by the state. In contrast, Taft restricted the government's regulative powers to modified antitrust laws, because for him corporations were not simply artificial creations of the state. Staking out a middle position, Wilson advocated more control than Taft but without Roosevelt's direct interference by the state. The FTC served Wilson's needs because, according to Sklar, it provided for market regulation at the same time that it removed it from "determination by electoral politics or by the exclusive or paramount power of the state."[50]

Of these positions Phillips's is closest to Roosevelt's (even though Roosevelt did not personally like the "muckraker's" anticorporate novels). Phillips suggests that corporations will be controlled only by placing them under the supreme authority of a sovereign state run by a powerful and fair executive. In contrast, by using Bucks to call into question such a solution while simultaneously recognizing the need to control the efforts of corporate monopolies, Lynde comes closest to Wilson's position. In *The Grafters* corporations violate the public interest only when one gains too much control or takes unfair advantage of others. Furthermore, whereas Lynde's solution of sending Kent into politics might seem at odds with Wilson's solution, which separated market regulation from electoral politics, it actually helps to confirm it. Kent may become a politician, but he is a politician whose independent professionalism allows him, like Scarborough, to stand above the play of electoral politics. As such, Lynde's solution has important similarities with Wilson's solution of placing responsibility for regulation in the hands of non-elected, supposedly nonpartisan, bureaucrats.

Sklar and other left-wing historians have, with justification, criticized the form of corporate liberalism that Wilson's solution institutionalized. Far from adhering to classical liberal notions of the free play of the market, it allowed a corporate reorganization of American society that emphasized cooperative management of the market, administered through the FTC, which responded to the various interests of large corporations. Indeed, Lynde's novel anticipates this victory of corporate interests.

Kent's disinterested position is supposedly signaled by his resignation from his job as a corporate lawyer. But, as we have seen, when Portia suggests that solution, Kent at first hesitates, concerned that the fee he will demand from the railroad is too high. "It looks," he revealingly protests, "like extortion; like another graft" (G 322). Losing patience, Portia convinces him by responding, "Of all the Puritan fanatics! . . . If it were a simple commercial transaction by which you would save your clients a round seventy million dollars, which would otherwise be lost, would you scruple to take a proportionate fee" (G 322)? In *The Cost* Pauline tells Dumont that a doctor or man of science gives his discovery "freely" to the world. Portia, however, knows differently. Rather than stand above the "traffic," in which "public property" is diverted into "private channels" (G 309), the specialist is very much within it. Kent's role as a professional specialist—suggested by the morally ambiguous Portia, not Elinor—may not be as disinterested as it seems. Indeed, Kent's first action as a supposedly independent operator is, in the process of controlling corporate abuse, to save a corporation. Similarly, the FTC, by promising independent bureaucratic control of the unfair deployment of corporate interests, in effect legitimates the continued existence and influence of corporations.

But if Lynde's novel confirms Sklar's analysis of Wilson's solution, both Lynde's and Phillips's idealization of a politician who can stand above politics complicates Sklar's criticism of it for "depoliticizing" market regulation. Lynde and Phillips turn to idealized figures because corporate influence made it increasingly difficult to imagine someone within the field of interest politics representing the public interest. To be sure, the desire to find politicians who stand above interest politics is not new, as *The Federalist* 10 by Madison makes clear. But if Madison worried that elected officials would represent the interests of the district or state that elected them over the public interest, the corporate control of electoral politics created a situation in which those elected would represent corporate interests over both. Thus the first installment of *The Treason of the Senate* is revealingly entitled "New York's Misrepresentatives."

On the surface Phillips solves this threat by trusting the people to elect responsible representatives. For instance, he argues that "however imperfectly the laws, so often the product of plutocratic intrigue, may express the popular will they are nonetheless the only definite expression of it" (R 143). We should, he implies, trust the electoral process. His writings are even given credit for hastening the passage of the 17th Amendment, which provides for the direct election of senators. For him, however, only someone whose character allows him to transcend the realm of interest politics can truly represent the public.

In contrast, Lynde, more realistic about the play of interest politics, suggests a solution closer to that adopted by Wilsonian reformers. That solution was to add another level to the governmental apparatus, one staffed by supposedly disinterested, professionally trained bureaucrats responsive to the interests of the people at large. As such, Wilson's solution is very similar to the previous generation's attempt to control the spoils system through civil service reform.[51] But it also anticipates the "New Deal" and its "brain trust," for Wilsonian bureaucrats were not simply specially trained, lifelong governmental employees. They were specialists who supposedly could manage the economy and society in the interests of the entire people, just as corporate officials managed their business in the interests of the entire corporation.

When Sklar criticizes Wilson's solution for "depoliticizing" corporate regulation, he fails squarely to confront the political dilemma facing reformers both then and now. How can we trust the electoral process to control corporations, when that process is partially controlled by corporate influence? Wilson's solution was not so much a "depoliticization" of market regulation as part of a redefinition of the political sphere in light of its partial control by corporate interests.

The dilemma that corporate influence poses for the political system is another manifestation of what throughout this book I have called the failed promise of contract. The promise in this instance would be that the play of individual interests in the political sphere would generate an immanent self-regulation resulting in an equitable system that incorporates the interests of the whole. If delivery of that promise was always problematic, it was rendered more so by the rise of corporate influence. Despite their claims to defend individual autonomy against the forces of "bigness," progressive reformers abandoned contract's promise by relying on a partially corporate model of government in which non-elected bureaucrats were given the political role of taking on the sacred trust of representing the interests of the people.

Both Phillips and Lynde register that abandonment by imagining a figure who represents the interests of the people by standing above the play of interest politics. Not accidentally, the role they imply for literary authors shares similarities with the role they advocate for reformist politicians. If, for Phillips, contemporary politicians are guilty of misrepresenting the interests of the people, he presumably gives them proper representation in his novel. But he can become a voice of the democracy only by claiming to see through the confusion of interest politics to the true interests of the people.

Less paternalistic, Lynde implies an author more immersed in the complicated world of corporate affairs. As a result, his point of view is closer to that of the corporate lawyer whose "skilful bit of engineering" and admirable "artistic work" brought "into line" every loose end to construct a plot in which "there was no hitch, no slip, and nothing was overlooked" (G 188–89). But if Lynde shares the lawyer's technical skills, he still has to establish his lawyer's independence before he can confidently speak for the people's interests. He suggests such independence by having Kent restore order, not while working for the railroad, but as a free agent. Indeed, what unites Phillips's and Lynde's implied images of authorship is belief in the possibility of professional, writerly independence.

Christopher Wilson has shown how Phillips contributed to the professional image of authorship by highlighting the importance of hard work and discipline for success.[52] But we should also stress that for Phillips a writer earned the independence necessary to restore virtue to the political sphere only if he were a professional "free lancer," not a dependent, salaried writer. Similarly, Kent's hero gains his independence only when he removes himself from the railroad's salary. If a "free lancer" evokes an image of independence, it also has medieval origins. Those origins remind us of the extent to which Phillips's and especially Lynde's responses to the rise of corporations are drawn to both a corporate and a contractual model for society. In such a society most individuals subordinate their interests to the whole by finding their proper place—contractually agreed upon—within its organic structure. At the same time, people of character or independent, professionally trained specialists supposedly safeguard the virtue of the whole. At the end of the twentieth century, voters continue to seek in politicians that elusive combination of virtuous character and managerial efficiency. Lynde's and Phillips's novels help us to reconstruct the conditions that made that search a crucial part of corporate liberalism's efficient operation rather than a barrier to its rise.

CHAPTER 9

The Question of Agency and Delivering the Promise

I

P. S. Atiyah repeats a commonplace assumption when he asserts that in contract law, promise-based liability "rests upon a belief in the traditional liberal value of free choice."[1] In turn, free choice is possible only if the self is conceived of as a "free agent." So long as people entering into contracts do so willingly and are capable of acting on their intentions, they incur a responsibility to deliver their side of the bargain. In this chapter I will argue that works of literary realism, while not denying the value of free choice, complicate what most take to be free agency. In doing so, they force a reevaluation of the commonplace link between contract and traditional liberalism while also dramatizing difficulties with delivery of contract's promise.

A number of well-meaning critics have assumed that to attack free agency is to help undermine liberal ideology. Distinctions between liberalism and republicanism indicate problems with that assumption. Classical republicanism, as we have seen, shares liberalism's belief in free agency. Both consider agents free when individuals have sovereign control over themselves and their actions. They disagree, however, on the origin of individuals' duties and responsibilities. Whereas classical republicans would not deny the duty to deliver on one's promises, they do not think of contract as the source of almost all political and economic obligations. Instead, for them, many such obligations continue to derive from one's standing in society. In contrast, for classical liberals most political and economic obligations are conceived of contractually. These differences result in different notions of freedom. Freedom for republicans is impossible without self-control and discipline. People are free only when they have enough control of their faculties to submit individual desires to the demands of the public good. In contrast, classical liberals are more prone to see freedom as the pursuit of self-interest. Indeed, the public good is best served by allowing people to pursue their interests, within limits that correspond with various natural laws.

Both the liberal and republican senses of self are at odds with the corporate sense of self, which we explored last chapter. Not an initiator of actions freely chosen, the corporate self acts within the design of a larger body of which it is a part. To be sure, classical republicanism also stresses individual submission to the body politic. But for republicans, that submission is the responsibility of a freely acting individual, whereas in corporate thought the individual's submission is not a question of individual will. From both a liberal and republican perspective, therefore, the corporate self lacks sovereignty over itself and is not free. If differences among liberal, republican, and corporate senses of self challenge the assumption that free agency is a unique property of liberalism, those differences are themselves complicated, because few thinkers in the late nineteenth century perfectly represent one type of thought. In addition to these three ways of thinking, we have corporate liberalism and various combinations of liberalism and republicanism. Within this complicated field, where can we locate the realists' sense of agency?

In asking that question I am not primarily concerned with discovering the realists' stated beliefs, as important as they might be. Instead, my focus is on what their literary productions imply. The realists, I have shown, bring us to the limits of a contractual sense of agency. They do not, however, close off possibilities of free agency. Instead, their works suggest an alternative to seeing freedom as individuals' sovereign control over their actions. This alternative calls for a reconsideration of links usually drawn between freedom and autonomy, between the liberal value of free choice and the promise of contract.

Since an agent is an actor, any account of agency depends on a theory of action. The realists' sense of action is illuminated by the work of Hannah Arendt. For Arendt, human action is inherently paradoxical. On the one hand, it allows us to have new beginnings and thus avoid complete control by external forces, whether they be fate or the laws of a mechanical universe. On the other hand, action thrusts us into a world of unpredictability since the consequences of an act cannot be controlled. As Arendt puts it, "The reason why we are never able to foretell with certainty the outcome and end of any action is simply that action has no end."[2] Action has no end because any "spontaneous beginning of something new" (HC 234) initiated by one actor gets entangled in a "web of human relations" (HC 233) produced by many actors. Caught within this "predetermined net of relationships," an agent seems to forfeit "his freedom the very moment he makes use of it" (HC 234). "Nowhere does man appear to be less free than in those capacities whose very essence is freedom and in that realm which owes its existence to nobody and nothing but man" (HC 234).

Arendt might seem to be restating the paradox of free will and determinism. Indeed, that paradox has allowed those who continue to believe that the universe is governed by a moral or supernatural force to conceive of human beings as free agents. But whereas Arendt does not deny people the capacity to will, she does argue that theories of free will, "born of a religious predicament and formulated in philosophical language" (PF 160), result in a misleading notion of freedom. The will, which involves the power to dictate and control, is "not a matter of freedom but a question of strength or weakness" (PF 152). To link the capacity for freedom with the will is mistakenly to equate freedom with sovereignty.[3] For instance, at one point Arendt defines sovereignty as "the ideal of a free will, independent from others and eventually prevailing against them" (PF 163). Freedom, however, resides not in control over action but in action itself. Freedom "is not an attribute of the will but an accessory of doing and acting" (PF 165). As a result, "if men wish to be free, it is precisely sovereignty they must renounce" (PF 165).

For Arendt, "freedom as inherent in action is perhaps best illustrated by Machiavelli's concept of *virtù*, the excellence with which man answers the opportunities the world opens before him in the guise of *fortunata*," and "its meaning is best rendered by 'virtuosity,' that is, an excellence we attribute to the performing arts . . . where the accomplishment lies in the performance itself and not in an end product which outlasts the activity that brought it into existence and becomes independent of it" (PF 153). Freedom conceived as sovereignty asserts the will as a way to control action. It is, in other words, an effort to combat action's inherent unpredictability. But since the consequences of action can never be totally controlled, the equation of freedom with sovereignty breeds a tradition in which freedom lies in one's retreat into the self and one's refusal to indulge in actions that cannot be controlled.

Rousseau, "the most consistent representative of the theory of sovereignty" (PF 163), exposes the limits of this concept of freedom when he argues that for the will to remain free it cannot bind itself to the future. As a result, to depend on a willing agent is not to control the future but to cut oneself off from it by isolating oneself in endless present moments.

This problem is recognized by Machiavelli, which is why the transatlantic tradition of republicanism that develops from his work emphasizes what Pocock calls the "Machiavelli moment," in which the initial act of seizing power is always threatened by decline.[4] But if for Machiavelli the art of politics is asserting the will so as to delay the fall into corruption as long as possible, for Arendt the "fall" is itself the realm of politics, a realm in which actions get entangled in a web of human relations. It is this realm of human plurality that those who adhere to theories of sovereignty maintained by a singular will try to avoid.

Whether the will is defined as an inner space of freedom or the general will of the people, it is designed to control the plurality of existence that is a precondition of freedom. Rousseau, for instance, believes that a divided will is inconceivable. This belief affects his sense of the self and his sense of the state, both of which he derives from Plato. "For Plato rulership, whose legitimacy rested upon the domination of the self, draws its guiding principles . . . from a relationship established between me and myself, so that the right and wrong relationships with others are determined by attitudes toward one's self, until the whole of the public realm is seen in the image of 'man writ large,' of the right order between man's individual capacities of mind, soul, and body" (HC 237–38). But since there is no singular body politic, the realm of politics "rests on experiences which nobody could have ever made with himself, which, on the contrary, are entirely based on the presence of others" (HC 238). "No man can be sovereign because not one man, but men, inhabit the earth" (HC 234).

For Arendt freedom is not the possession of a sovereign self that exists prior to the political. It is the product of a particular form of the political. In a passage that recalls the construction of privacy in James, but adds a role for law, Arendt claims that "to abolish the fences of laws between men—as a tyranny does—means to take away man's liberties and destroy freedom as a living political reality; for the space between men as it is hedged in by laws, is the living space of freedom" (OT 446). If a politics of plurality makes freedom possible, it is plurality that makes control of our actions impossible.

"The simultaneous presence of freedom and non-sovereignty, of being able to begin something new and of not being able to control or even foretell its consequences" (HC 235) may seem absurd from the perspective of those who identify freedom with sovereignty. But the potential to act contains two faculties that allow human beings to "survive the disabilities of non-sovereignty" (HC 236). They are the intersubjective capacities to forgive and to promise. The faculty to forgive confronts the irreversibility of action; the faculty to promise, its unpredictability. Since we cannot undo past actions, forgiveness is the only way to avoid being forever trapped by their consequences. Without forgiveness, in other words, it would be impossible to begin anew. Similarly, promising "at least partially dispels" the twofold nature of unpredictability, "that is, the basic unreliability of men who can never guarantee today what they will be tomorrow, and . . . the impossibility of foretelling the consequences of an act within a community of equals where everybody has the same capacity to act" (HC 244). Although promises cannot guarantee certainty, they provide "islands of predictability" and "guideposts of reliability" (HC 244). For Arendt, "all political business" derives "in the last instance from the faculty to promise and to keep promises in the face of the essential uncertainties of the future" (PF 164). Political business is so important for Arendt because it can produce actions that help human beings combat the natural tendency toward fatality.

"If left to themselves, human affairs can only follow the law of mortality, which is the most certain and the only reliable law of a life spent between birth and death. It is the faculty of action that interferes with this law because it interrupts the inexorable automatic course of daily life, which in its turn . . . interrupted and interfered with the cycle of the biological life process. The life span of man running toward death would inevitably carry everything human to ruin and destruction if it were not for the faculty of interrupting it and beginning anew, a faculty which is inherent in action like an ever-present reminder that men, though they must die, are not born in order to die but in order to begin" (HC 246). The intersubjective faculties of forgiving and promising, not a singular, sovereign will, make beginning anew possible.

I have spent considerable time on Arendt because she demonstrates how free agency can be opposed to the notion of an autonomous, self-contained individual rather than dependent on it. Furthermore, she points out that such agency relies on promising, which is a faculty that depends on "plurality, on the presence and acting of others" since "no one can feel bound by a promise made only to himself" (HC 237). The sense of agency outlined by Arendt is, I argue, very close to that implied by the works of realism that I have discussed in this book. I can begin to give substance to that claim by using Arendt to distinguish the realists' sense of agency from that of the literary naturalists.

In the introduction I argued that the realists and naturalists ordered the details of their worlds quite differently. When Richard Chase claims that naturalism is simply realism with a "necessitarian ideology," he ignores how that ideology causes naturalists to subordinate details to a governing ordering principle.[5] The realists, in contrast, work to find a form that will be true to the contingency of events. Albion W. Tourgée senses this distinction when he complains about the realists' interest in the "every-day and insignificant happenings of uneventful life." In contrast, the naturalists treat both the highs and lows of life without abandoning attention to issues of vice and virtue. For Tourgée, "so far as truth-telling is concerned, the argument lies rather with the 'naturalist' than the 'realist.'"[6] Tourgée's preference for the naturalists is influenced by his belief in a governing moral order. But he also recognizes that the naturalists present worlds quite different from his. A crucial difference is Tourgée's continued belief in the human soul and humanity's capacity for free will. In contrast, for the naturalists the distinction between humans and machines is problematic. As Walter Benn Michaels puts it, paraphrasing Mark Seltzer, "The point is not simply that human agents are less powerful than nature but that reduced to the 'forces' that they really are, human agents are not agents at all."[7] Or, as Seltzer puts it, human agents become no more than mechanical agents or "middlemen, equally subject to or carriers of uncontrollable forces."[8] The naturalist sense of agency, in other words, betrays a similarity with the corporate sense of agency, although it lacks its organicism. Both are at odds with the promise of contract and the sense of agency suggested by the realists.

In a world in which mechanization seemed more and more to take command, the realists too sensed the threat to free agency. Like the naturalists, they dramatize human beings' inability to maintain sovereign control over their actions. Nonetheless, whereas the realists' works question a strict opposition between human and mechanical agency, they do not collapse the distinction. An example of a character who tries to maintain the opposition is Basil March in Howells's *The Hazard of New Fortunes*. At a pivotal moment March has been asked by Dryfoos, the owner of the magazine he edits, to fire Lindau, a longtime friend

March has employed to translate various literary pieces from Europe. At a dinner the socialist Lindau had insulted his host, Dryfoos, by declaring his hatred of capitalism. March does not so much object to the firing as to Dryfoos's attempt to do it through him. Asked by his wife why, he responds that "if it had been a question of making [the journal] the vehicle of Lindau's peculiar opinions— . . . I shouldn't have a ground to stand on" (HNF 357). But, even though the journal has just printed an article defending the dead institution of chattel slavery, it has not— for prudent business reasons—printed one against the slavery that Lindau claims still exists—the wage slavery of capitalism. "But that isn't the point," March goes on. "Lindau's connection with [the journal] is almost purely mechanical; he's merely a translator of such stories and sketches as he first submits to me, and it isn't at all a question of his opinions hurting us, but of my becoming the agent to punish him for his opinions. That is what I wouldn't do; that's what I will never do" (HNF 357).

For March to fire Lindau would be to prove his German-American friend right, showing that even editors of magazines are little more than slaves to the will of capital. Indeed, March's friend Fulkerson has already sided with Dryfoos because his "standards are low; they're merely business standards" (HNF 357). But when Fulkerson reminds March that "Dryfoos owns the magazine," March responds, "He doesn't own *me*" (HNF 352). When March decides that it is his "duty—in a matter of principle" not to submit to Dryfoos's command, Fulkerson, "with a dazed look and a mechanical movement" (HNF 352), lets him act alone. By resisting Dryfoos's order, March demonstrates his independence, thus becoming a moral rather than merely a mechanical agent. Shortly thereafter, he even dreams of resigning his post to become a "free lance" so that he could fight in "whatever cause he thought just," without "ties," without "chains" (HNF 359).

March, then, seems to present us with clear oppositions. On the one hand, there is the slave to forces of the market; on the other, someone free of chains and ties. On the one, the mere translator; on the other, the freelance. The mechanical agent controlled by forces outside himself versus the independent agent able to steer his or her own course. Someone willing to take a principled stand versus someone lacking the courage to do so.

At the end of the novel, when Dryfoos offers March and Fulkerson ownership of the journal and apparent control over its content, Howells might seem to endorse the republican virtues of an artisanal economy in which laborers have ownership of their means of production. But if Howells is attracted to that vision (just as he is attracted to the republican world of Equity in *A Modern Instance* and an agrarian economy in *The Rise of Silas Lapham*), the dramatic action of his novel undercuts it and thereby complicates, without collapsing, March's clear-cut oppositions. Indeed, they depend on the identification of freedom with sovereignty that the dramatic action of works of realism challenges.

As always, Howells presents March somewhat ironically. For instance, March's sense of republican superiority surfaces when he tells Fulkerson, "I'm not used to being spoken to as if I were the foreman of a shop, and told to dismiss a sensitive and cultured man like Lindau, as if he were a drunken mechanic" (351 HNF). March may not want to treat Lindau as if he were a drunken mechanic, but he himself claims to have hired him to do nothing more than the "mechanical" work of translation. March's comment, therefore, raises questions about both the distinction that he draws between an independent magazine editor and a dependent shop foreman as well as the one between mechanical and original writing.

Literary authorship would seem to allow people to retain ownership over their means of production. After all, authors rely on their imaginations, which they alone seem to control. The independence that writing promises is one reason why March dismisses Lindau's job as a translator as "almost purely mechanical" (HNF 357). In contrast, a freelance seems to be in total control over what he produces. But the relation is more complicated. As Howells well knew, translation can be more than mechanical work. It can also alter meaning. At the end of the novel we are told how in Europe, "where society has them, as it were, in a translation" (HNF 495), the Dryfooses meet with social success denied them in New York. Likewise, the book's many reflections on the artistic process suggest that artistic creation involves translation. March, for instance, works diligently at descriptions of New York life. Those descriptions would fail if he did not give himself up to his subject matter and attempt to translate it for his readers. For Howells the need of artists to translate their material is linked to the question of what constitutes responsible moral agency.

Commenting on his New York sketches March admits, "If I went to work at those things with an ethical intention I should ruin them" (HNF 149). This comment could be read as emphasizing a divide between aesthetics and ethics. Good art, we might conclude, does not necessarily do good. But in a world in which absolute knowledge of the good is impossible, the comment's significance is more nuanced. Ethics and aesthetics are not identical; nonetheless, it is as true in everyday actions as in artistic creation that ethical intentions do not necessarily produce ethical results. In fact, those who act with too secure a knowledge of what is good can often generate harm. In Howells's world neither responsible moral action nor responsible aesthetic creation results from following preconceived principles. Thus we can see why someone like Tourgée felt that the realists' aesthetic was unreceptive to novels with a purpose. As Twain wrote Howells about *A Hazard*, "It is a great book; but of course what I prefer about it is the high art by which it is made to preach its great sermon without seeming to take sides or preach at all."[9]

Twain's comment demands close attention. Howells, Twain seems to imply, has abandoned belief in preconceived moral principles only to adopt the principle of aesthetic independence that refuses to take a particular side on an issue. Indeed, March's principled stand against Dryfoos is linked to his belief in the value of aesthetic independence for the journal he edits. But Twain does not say that *A Hazard* lacks a point of view, only that it has the art to hide it. Aesthetic independence is not a principle standing above all others. It too is committed to a point of view, a point of view that Howells presents in the novel through March.[10]

Nonetheless, Twain's praise of Howells's novel suggests that such a point of view can be different in kind from one based on a belief in set moral guidelines. The only action that the aesthetic point of view prescribes is the act of presenting to readers differing points of view and the web of interconnected actions that make it impossible to achieve sovereign control over our actions. If that presentation is not completely neutral, since it still places points of view and actions in formal relation with one another, it is not based on a set of first principles that will help readers adjudicate among competing points of view. It also has the advantage—if we can call it that—of dramatizing the limits of its own point of view, as Howells does so poignantly by indicating the inadequacy of March's point of view to give guidelines for preventing the violence of the book's strike. In pointing to the limits of the point of view that generated his own novel, Howells reminds us that even his artistic principles are not absolute principles but what Fulkerson calls "convictions" (HNF 441) subject to revision. Howells also complicates any distinction that we may be tempted to draw between the freedom that March will have when he owns his journal and the constraints he faces working for Dryfoos.

To be sure, March will no longer have to answer directly to Dryfoos. Nonetheless, unless he wants the journal to fail, he will still have to take into consideration economic constraints. Indeed, Fulkerson first sought Dryfoos's money with the hopes that it would give the journal *more* freedom. New ownership changes the types of relations that the journal has with market forces, but the journal continues to aspire to be what the illustrator Beaton calls, "the missing link; the long-felt want of a tie between the Arts and the Dollars" (HNF 177).

People often assume that free agents must originate their actions. But the journal's position as a link between two entities reminds us, as a common usage of the word implies, that an agent is someone or something who acts for someone or something else. March, for instance, objects to becoming Dryfoos's "agent" to punish Lindau. For Howells moral agency, like artistic creation, involves an act of translation. March does not originate his moral stand; instead it results from his refusal to "submit to the dictation of a man like Dryfoos" (HNF 352). In case the reader misses the linguistic metaphor of this phrase, Howells repeats it a few pages later. For him the refusal to submit to dictation describes the conditions of both realistic art and free agency.

Working with given material, realistic artists are not original creators. Nor, however, are they simply passive recorders of already existing discursive systems. Rather than mechanically submit to dictation, they actively translate the material that they are given to work with by giving it a formal structure. Similarly, free agents are not in sovereign control over their actions. As historical beings, human beings are not originators but agents, or middlemen, positioned in a present between the past and the future. Whether or not those agents are free depends on whether they occupy that position as active or mechanical translators. In a deterministic world they are simply agents through whom larger forces move from the past to the future. Free agents do not reverse that situation and take total control over their actions. Instead, they retain the capacity to produce actions that are not totally controlled by the forces that create the conditions in which action occurs.

Arendt offers an example of how subtle the distinction between free and mechanical agency can be. In Hitler's Germany, she notes, the Nazis changed the military's "recipient of orders," a *Befehlsempfänger*, to a "bearer of orders," a *Befehlsträger* (EJ 24). At first glance a bearer of orders might seem to be someone with a more active role than that of a receiver of orders. To be sure, the change was supposed to impress upon people their responsibility to execute orders. Without each person in the chain of command carrying out his duty, the will of the corporate body of the German people would not be fulfilled. Nonetheless, the responsibility that bearing an order creates undercuts free agency as I am defining it. The responsibility of a *Befehlsträger* is to be a passive medium through which a larger entity carries out its will. If a *Befehlsempfänger* also seems to involve a passive role, it, in fact, draws attention to the activity involved in the passing along of any order. A received order stops unless it is re-sent. Furthermore, a receiver can cause interference in the sending of an order. A *Befehlsträger* occupies a purely transitional position along a chain of command. A *Befehlsempfänger* occupies that of a potential translator of the order received. If a *Befehlsträger* occupies a space through which an order is borne, a *Befehlsempfänger* occupies a potential space of disruption out of which a new or altered order might be born.

This distinction helps to clarify some usages of mechanical imagery by Twain and James. For example, as we have seen, Twain described Pudd'nhead's role in his story as merely "a button or a crank or a lever, with a useful function to perform in a machine."[11] In his role as author Twain too might seem to be no more than a passive agent recording the outcome of a mechanistic fate. But, even though Twain works with material and voices made available to him by his culture, when that material passes through his imagination it is translated into a different form.

James once remarked, "I regard the march of history very much as a man placed astride of a locomotive, without knowledge or help, would regard the progress of that vehicle."[12] This passage certainly conveys a lack of control over the forces of history. But it does not necessarily imply that human beings are mechanical agents. For demonstration we can turn to *The Golden Bowl*, which was published in 1904 as other writers struggled with the increased power of corporations. At one point Charlotte comes close to expressing the ideal of corporate agency, "The great thing is," she declares, "to 'know' one's place" (GB 23, 259).[13] Later we are told that "the fulness of one's measure amounted to no more than the equal use of one's faculties or the proper playing of one's part" (GB 24, 8). Occupying this world, Maggie evokes the mechanical image of a family coach as she contemplates the complicated network of relations that were established when she married the Prince. If it "lumbered and stuck," she thinks, "the fault was in its lacking its complement of wheels. Having but three, as they might say, it wanted another" (GB 24, 23). When Charlotte married Maggie's father, her friend immediately acted as a fourth, allowing the coach to move with marvelous grace. "So far as *she* was one of the wheels," Maggie thinks, referring to herself, "she had but to keep in her place" (GB 24, 23). If she does, she will do her part in maintaining the "precious condition" of "equilibrium" (GB 24, 73) that their life together had created. Eventually, however, in an almost undetectable manner Maggie refuses to play the part allotted to her. Though she is uncertain about the consequences of her actions and even what the other players know and think, Maggie through her improvisations alters the equilibrium of the group.[14]

Actions like Maggie's do not depend on the presence of an autonomous self, but instead a self inhabited by a space of emptiness that keeps it from being identical with its social roles. That sense of selfhood is also dramatized by *Adventures of Huckleberry Finn*. A commonplace of Twain criticism is to assume that the naturally good heart and conscience of Huck are threatened by a corrupt society.[15] According to this reading, Huck can get in touch with his true self only on the river, while on the world of the shore he is contaminated by the perverted values of a slaveholding society. But as much we imagine that Huck has a true self, that self is never named. During the course of his journey, Huck adopts role after role. At one point he is a slave owner; at another a young British servant; at another a girl; toward the end of the book he is even Tom Sawyer. But in each case he casts off the role that he plays. We get to know Huck, in other words, by who he is not, not who he is. Huck's identity depends, therefore, on whatever it is that keeps those adopted roles from sticking. The Connecticut Yankee might call whatever it is, the microscopic atom that constitutes his true self. My point is, however, that it is a space of vacancy, not a definable essence. Furthermore, it is not a space inevitably given, but one, such as that of privacy in James, that is constructed through intersubjective exchanges. Huck is Huck because he is not somebody else. This vacancy, not a positive presence, makes free agency possible.

Possible, but not inevitable. It is not inevitable because a space of emptiness within the self is neutral. Viewed by some as a hollowness at the core of the self, it leads some to despair. For others, it is proof of people's infinite malleability, since it seems to allow us to be filled by whatever social role is available. For others, it indicates that human beings are not free agents but simply empty vessels through whom forces larger than themselves are transmitted. Filled by many roles and functions, it gives human identity a fundamental plasticity.

Nonetheless, it is important to remember that once a space has been filled, it is no longer empty. What distinguishes the realists' sense of agency is how their techniques of presenting the self tend to call attention to a vacancy that other writers of the period (and at times they themselves) fill with metaphors of sovereignty or mechanism. Those techniques suggest that human identity is constituted by a structure of doubleness in which there is an built-in discrepancy between the bearer of a social role and the role itself. As Helmuth Plessner puts it, "The role-player or bearer of the social figure is not the same as that figure, and yet cannot be thought of separately from it without being deprived of its humanity. . . . Only by means of the other of itself does it have— itself."[16] The notion of a bearer of a social figure might seem to bring us back to a *Befehlsträger,* but it is wrong to equate the self with the bearer alone. There is no self without a role, which is why human identity is always historically constituted. But it is not completely determined. The discrepancy between bearer and role (which, as Plessner warns, can always be forgotten) makes possible action that is not completely controlled.[17]

This structure is related to, but not the same as, Du Bois's definition of double-consciousness. Not resulting from a discrepancy between the bearer of the role and the role itself, double-consciousness results from two seemingly contradictory social roles that blacks in America are forced to adopt: that of an American, which is assumed to be a white role, and that of an African, which is a role reserved for blacks. Still within a tradition that considers a unified consciousness the only authentic consciousness, Du Bois laments this division, especially because it invites blacks to internalize a sense of their own inferiority. Indeed, in his 1897 version Du Bois had written that the American situation yields blacks "no self-consciousness."[18] In *The Souls of Black Folk* he amends this to: "no true self-consciousness."[19]

In both passages Du Bois desires a unified self, but in the second he acknowledges that a double-consciousness is at least some form of consciousness. In fact, in the second he recognizes that the consequences of double-consciousness are not all bad. For instance, it gives blacks a critical perspective on both American and African culture that they would not have if they were completely immersed in one or the other. Although Du Bois would not put it this way, that critical perspective is linked to the structure of doubleness that I have described.

The incommensurate roles allotted to blacks make them aware of something within themselves that cannot be filled by either role. Not a space of fulfilled, authentic consciousness, this structure of doubleness nonetheless allows the possibility for a reflective self-consciousness too easily obscured by those who feel at one with their given social role.

Of course, many who, like Du Bois, assume the existence of an autonomous self also feel at odds with their social role or roles and experience a split within the self. But they think that the split is between an authentic and an inauthentic self. Since for them an action is free only when it is controlled by the will of the authentic self, they continue to see free agency in terms of a unified self. In works of realism, however, resistance to the self's total identification with its roles comes not from an authentic, interior self, but from a space of emptiness.

I am, to be sure, exaggerating somewhat in order to spell out distinctions. The realists have not completely broken with belief in an authentic self that lies buried beneath a socially constructed one. Twain and Howells cling to it more than James. For instance, Twain most likely shared the Connecticut Yankee's belief in an atom of the self that was truly him. Or to be more accurate, when in his later years Twain lost faith in its existence, he despaired and succumbed to a mechanical view of human beings, a view that undermined his aesthetic effectiveness. His best works are those in which there is a division in the selves of his protagonists. And, as we have seen, even if he believes that that division is caused by repression of a "true" self, his techniques of presentation do not allow him to name it. Just as Du Bois, in struggling with the phenomenon of double-consciousness, gives us a formulation that calls attention to an aspect of the self that cannot be filled by either role, so Twain's works dramatize a doubleness that he is not fully aware of.

Similarly, in *Silas Lapham* Howells may suggest the existence of a private, interior self for his characters, but he self-consciously avoids representing it. We are never told Silas's exact motives for his actions, and when a narrator begins to intrude by the end of the book it acknowledges its inability to know characters' feelings. We are told, for instance, "Whether Penelope, on her side, found it more difficult to harmonize, I cannot say" (SL 360). Through this strategy Howells demonstrates more respect for the "privacy" of his characters than does James, who, while seeming to decry the intrusions into people's privacy, became famous for his artistic explorations of characters' interiority. What those explorations reveal, however, is not the presence of a "true" self but how interiority itself is constructed in interpersonal exchanges enabled, not by a positive willing agent, but by a vacancy constitutive of selfhood.

These differences emphasize an important point. If I am correct in my claim that identity is constituted in part by a vacancy, our task is not simply to expose aporias within the self through a deconstructive reading, since they become our only anthropological constant. As Hans Blumenberg puts it, "What remains as the subject matter of anthropology is a 'human nature' that has never been 'nature' and never will be. . . . Man comprehends himself only by way of what he is not. It is not only his situation that is potentially metaphorical; his constitution already is."[20] What is important, therefore, is to analyze the metaphors used to fill aporias, metaphors that help to determine our sense of the possibilities of human action. The realists do not present the same metaphoric constitution of identity. But in the works that I have examined, they do present ones that suggest a structure of doubleness that has the capacity to generate freedom of action while being generated by it in turn.

In *The Bostonians* Verena's privacy, constructed through her relations with others, gives her the power to resist those who would totally possess her, a power that she loses when that space is effaced at the end of the book. In *The Aspern Papers* Miss Tina achieves a moment of dignity when she burns Aspern's letters. The "new" self that she achieves does not result from asserting a true self that has been hidden so far in the book. Instead, through the space of vacancy that she creates by destroying the only thing that gives her value in the narrator's eyes, she demonstrates that there is something more to her than an exchangeable commodity.

Of the three authors, Howells offers the most positive vision of the possibilities of free agency. Although he is not as naively optimistic as some of his detractors claim, through Silas he illustrates Arendt's description of Machiavelli's concept of *virtù* as "the excellence with which man answers the opportunities the world opens up before him in the guise of *fortunata*" (PF 153). Silas's "rise" does not correspond with his return to a true, agrarian self of virtuous self-control that he has abandoned in his drive for economic success. On the contrary, it results from him learning to confront the hazards of acting in a world in which he cannot control the consequences of his actions. Not a retreat to the past, his "rise" allows him to begin anew. His new beginning does not guarantee a happy ending, but it does avoid a tragic one. Indeed, *Silas Lapham* has markings of classic tragedy: its rising and falling action, its hero with a fatal flaw. But Howells does not present a fatalistic world. Instead, his book ends with an image of a new beginning. When Sewell asks Silas if he regrets contributing to his own financial demise by refusing to sell worthless stock to Rogers, he replies, "Well, it don't always seem as I done it. . . . Seems sometimes as if a hole opened for me, and I crept out of it. I don't know" (SL 365). Not made on the basis of sovereign control over himself, Silas's act results from hesitantly taking advantage of holes opened in what seems to be a course of action closed off by fate.

"The miracle that saves the world, the realm of human affairs, from its normal 'natural' ruin," writes Arendt, "is ultimately the fact of natality, in which the faculty of action is ontologically rooted. It is, in other words, the birth of new men and the new beginning, the action they are capable of by virtue of being born. Only the full experience of this capacity can bestow upon human affairs faith and hope, those two essential characteristics of human existence which Greek antiquity ignored altogether, discounting the keeping of faith as a very uncommon and not too important virtue and counting hope among the evils of illusion in Pandora's box" (HC 247).

Worsening social conditions made maintaining faith and hope difficult for Howells. Unlike writers in the tradition of republican virtue (including Chesnutt), he did not attempt to embody in fictional form a higher standard of equity to regulate the moral economy of his works. Instead, he tried to imagine how a more equitable social order could be achieved through immanent exchanges within a heterogeneous society made up of competing interests. Invested in a vision of social harmony, he saw his role not as an imposer of order, but as a translator facilitating communication among various social groups. In *A Hazard,* however, it is ironically a successful act of translation that helps drive the novel to its bleak conclusion. At the dinner party bringing together representatives of different points of view, Lindau insults Dryfoos in German, not thinking that he understands. But he does. Rather than leading to communicative harmony, Dryfoos's successful translation increases conflict. Nonetheless, even as Howells questions his faith that social communication can deliver its promise of an equitable order, he still places responsibility squarely in the realm of human action.

Twain had even more difficulty than his friend Howells in maintaining faith and hope. But even in the tragic world of *Pudd'nhead Wilson,* where the microscopic atom of a true self that helped to sustain Twain's faith seems to have disappeared, agency has not been completely mechanized. Not positively dramatized, resistance to total mechanization is suggested by the doubleness that pervades the structure of the entire work, from the doubling of characters' identities to the way that readers are entangled in the world of its actions. As different as it is from works by James and Howells, *Pudd'nhead,* like the other works of realism that I have treated, does not impose a unified will on its readers, dictating how they should act. Instead, offering a network of interacting voices, none of which has ultimate authority, it leaves open a space for readerly interaction.

Readerly interaction is possible because textual identity, like individual identity, is constituted by a structure of doubleness. Whereas a text bears a representational relation to the discourses of its day, it is not identical with them. If this double structure constitutes all texts, realists' techniques work to keep it from being effaced, thus giving to their works the plasticity that James so admired about the novel.[21] A work's plasticity does not mean that readerly participation is unconstrained. Every work, after all, bears specific historical representations that determine readers' textual positions. But there is a crucial difference between determining the position that readers occupy and predetermining their responses. Like the opportunities opened by *fortunata,* the empty spaces within texts offer readers possibilities for action.

The readerly contract implied by works of realism is quite different from Georges Poulet's description of readers mysteriously merging their consciousnesses with that of the author through the text.[22] Similarly, its implied sense of agency challenges that assumed by those who see a contract as evidence that contracting parties have had a "meeting of the minds." It also suggests the inadequacy of Holmes's influential attack on this subjective theory of contractual obligation.

As Yosal Rogat puts it, "By Holmes' time jurisprudence had gone as far as possible, and sometimes farther, in relating legal rules to voluntary individual choice, in attempting to state the entire law in terms of willed intentions." The law of contracts, for instance, was seen as "enforcing actual willed intentions and a literal consensus."[23] For Holmes, to understand contractual liability in terms of the subjective agreement reached by contracting parties smacked of metaphysics.[24] To put law on a firmer foundation, he determined contractual obligation through clearly designated formalities that could be objectively determined and measured. But to do so, as we saw in the second chapter, he felt that he had to separate contract from promising. The result was what Lawrence Friedman calls contract law's blindness to "subject matter and person."[25]

If the realists, like Holmes, challenge the sense of agency implied by the subjective theory of contractual obligation, they do not need to abandon promising to do so. Instead, by implying that promising is by nature intersubjective, they help us reconsider what is entailed in the "promise" of contract. The subjective theory of contract assumes that a promise is made the moment there is a meeting of the minds of two already-formed individuals. Once a promise is made it creates a future obligation, but that obligation does not affect the identities of the contracting parties. The only question that remains is whether or not they choose to live up to its terms or not. In contrast, works of realism imply that a promise is a performative act, establishing a relationship that in part constructs the subjects participating within it. Promising so conceived becomes a moral act itself rather than one simply recording an obligation created by the mysterious merger of two autonomous wills. As Arendt argues, the moral precepts that grow out of the faculties of promising and forgiving are the only ones "that are not applied to action from the outside, from some supposedly higher faculty or from experiences outside action's own reach" (HC 246). Instead, arising directly out of the effort "to live together with others in the mode of acting and speaking," they are "like control mechanisms built into the very faculty to start new and unending processes" (HC 246). Not the fusion of autonomous wills into a Rousseaulike general will, promising is an activity that allows people to "act in concert" without effacing plurality.

To perform an intersubjective relationship without a complete loss of identity, a self must retain a space that cannot be totally defined by its social role. Wanting to free contract law from a metaphysical tradition in which that space is identified as the soul or the will, Holmes denies the importance of subjective intention and separates contract from its moral associations with promising. In doing so, however, he condemns the law of contract to working with a one-dimensional self.[26] Works of realism offer an alternative to Holmes's reasoning by suggesting how, through promising, people can act in concert while maintaining the plurality effaced in theories of sovereignty and corporatism.

But the realists' sense of agency raises an important dilemma. If, on the one hand, a space of emptiness makes intersubjective relations possible, on the other, it seems to present an insurmountable barrier to the delivery of a promise. The problem of delivering a contract is poignantly illustrated when Chesnutt has blacks, as deliverers of messages, either intentionally or unintentionally disrupt the system of exchanges in the South. For Chesnutt, however, the problem grows out of inequitable relations of race. As his organic metaphors imply, that imbalance leads to an unnatural disruption of the natural circulation of exchanges. The agency implied by works of realism builds disruption into the system. Such disruption is not simply the result of an agent's power to refuse, through the assertion of its will, to pass on a command or to enter into a contract. Whereas it would be naive to discount that power, the dilemma that I am focusing on involves the structure of promising itself, for how are the gaps between people and their promises and actions to be overcome without some fusion of subjectivities?

While creating a dilemma, that structure also implies an answer. Promising, as we have seen, is future-oriented. One enters into a promise because its terms cannot be immediately fulfilled. A promise's delivery is, in other words, by nature deferred. Indeed, once the promise has been delivered, the parties involved are no longer in the act of promising. To be in the act of promising is, as Hume argues, to participate in an exchange that places one's reputation in the hands of another. That exchange does more than create future obligations for sovereign individuals. As an interpersonal exchange, a promise is not simply made and then delivered or not delivered. Instead, contracting parties remain bound together, suspended in the act of promising, until the promise is delivered. That binding has the capacity to alter the subjectivities of the contracting parties by giving a future projection to the space of emptiness that both makes promising possible and contributes to its deferred delivery.

If a self constituted by a space of emptiness has an inherently plastic identity, participation in the act of promising grants it a relative stability that is, nonetheless, future-oriented. As Arendt puts it, "Without being bound to the fulfillment of promises, we would never be able to keep our identities; we would be condemned to wander helplessly and without direction in the darkness of each man's lonely heart, caught in its contradictions and equivocalities" (HC 237). Arendt's description has particular relevance for analysis of Edna Pontellier in Kate Chopin's *The Awakening*. This study ends by looking at how Chopin's remarkable work of realism dramatizes the problems of identifying freedom with individual sovereignty at the same time that it questions whether contract's promise for future generations must always be deferred.

II

A dilemma facing readers of *The Awakening* is what to do with the spectacle of Edna "daily casting aside that fictitious self which we assume like a garment with which to appear before the world" (A 57). The most common response has been to assume that Edna's socially constructed self hides what Cynthia Griffin Wolff calls her buried, "true self."[27] At the same time, most feminist readings critics assume that her fictional self has been imposed upon her by an inequitable patriarchal society. As Jules Chametzky puts it, "The struggle is for the woman to free herself from being an object or possession defined in her functions or owned by others." Awakened by "a glimpse of life as an autonomous self," she gains increased "self-awareness" as she searches for a more authentic life.[28] The failure of her quest demonstrates the power of the constraints that oppress her.

Critics have recently challenged the association that such readings draw between freedom and the autonomous self. Margit Stange, for instance, draws on C. B. Macpherson's claim that a theory of possessive individualism is the basis of contractual ideology and argues that Edna's quest needs to be seen as an effort to achieve the self-ownership advocated by feminists like Elizabeth Cady Stanton. Self-ownership for Edna manifests itself in the right to withhold herself sexually from her husband. But, if that right seems to give Edna the autonomy to resist the system of exchanges that constitute the contractual economy, it in fact affirms it, for "the freedom to withhold oneself has its complement in the freedom to give oneself."[29]

Read this way Edna's quest for freedom feeds the logic of the market rather than resists social constraints. This is especially the case since, at this time, the United States developed an economy in which questions of consumption began to take priority over questions of production. Economists influenced by Malthus assumed that growth was limited because production could never keep up with demand. But, as Albion W. Tourgée argued in 1896, increased efficiency in agriculture and industry brought about "The Reversal of Malthus." According to Tourgée, economic problems in the future will not be caused by underproduction but overproduction, "with its naturally depressing effects on prices and inevitable over-supply of labor." Based on his belief in a sovereign self in control of its appetites, Tourgée's solution called for restriction of production and employment of excess labor in activities that have been dismissed as "silly, unprofitable and unpractical sentiment," such as "pride of home, of family, of ancestral honor and hopeful anticipation of regard by posterity." "The permanent beautifying of homes and country estates, and the preservation of woods, is not only a debt we owe to the future but one we owe to the past as well."[30]

Tourgée knew that his proposal had little chance of being adopted. In fact, what had already begun was the production of increased demand for consumption. Dependent on producing subjects with unquenchable desire, consumer society benefits from a belief, like Edna's, in a nonexistent authentic self, since the unsuccessful attempt to find it generates endless desire. It is, therefore, no surprise that Edna's quest for freedom, generated by the circular logic of the market, ends in suicide.

Even so, there is more to *The Awakening* than the self-defeating logic of Edna's possessive individualism. Whereas a reading like Stange's seems to recognize a vacancy within the self rather than an authentic presence, it in fact effaces the double structure that such a vacancy can produce by assuming that a self is identical with the social roles that it bears. In doing so, it flattens both Edna's identity and that of the text that she inhabits. By suggesting a vacancy within Edna, Chopin's text is not, like its heroine, completely caught within the logic of consumer capitalism.

A way to restore perspective to the text is to see Edna as a turn-of-the-century Madame Bovary.[31] To be sure, that comparison is not flattering. Like Stange's reading, it reminds us that Edna casts off one fictional self for another, not for an authentic one. At the same time, it calls attention to an emptiness within Edna that cannot be completely filled by the roles that she adopts. How that emptiness, not an authentic self, provides textual perspective is illustrated by a short exchange between Edna and the doctor late in the book.

When the doctor asks whether Edna is going abroad, as her husband has suggested, she responds, " 'Perhaps—no, I am not going. I'm not going to be forced into doing things. I don't want to go abroad. I want to be let alone. Nobody has any right—except children, perhaps—and then even then, it seems to me—or did seem—' She felt that her speech was voicing the incoherency of her thoughts, and stopped abruptly" (A 109). Demonstrating Edna's confusion, this passage reinforces affinities between Edna and Emma Bovary, as well as the need to view her with ironic distance. That irony is largely directed at Edna's deluded notion of freedom. Even so—and this is a crucial point—the passage's irony does not undercut the importance of Edna's desire for freedom and her questions about duties and responsibilities that she owes to her children.

Edna's conception of freedom is confused even without the complications of motherhood. To think of freedom as she does is to invite isolation, since, as we have seen, it is the nature of action to entangle us in relations that cannot be totally controlled. Within this context, Edna's desire to be let alone is an appropriate prelude to her suicide since, as Arendt points out, the only way completely to control one's actions is not to act. Suicide, after all, leads to the ultimate state of nonaction: death. But suicide is also an act. While allowing Edna her final solitude, even it has consequences that cannot be controlled, as evidenced by the critical controversy over the novel's ending.

There is, however, an irony to this irony, since uncertainty over the motive of Edna's suicide is perhaps linked to her final effort at control. Leaving no note and drowning while swimming in the sea, Edna allows her death to be interpreted as an accident. Such an interpretation would both save her reputation and relieve her children of the stain of having a mother who committed suicide. Thus even in her final act, in which she would seem to take responsibility for at least her death, Edna, claiming to seek freedom, abdicates responsibility. Rather than develop during the course of the book, Edna becomes more and more childlike. "I don't want anything," she tells the doctor, "but my own way. . . . Don't blame me for anything" (A 110).

Soon after her talk with the doctor, Edna experiences her only awakening in the novel. She returns home expecting Robert, whom she wants to be her lover, to be waiting, hoping that he will be asleep so that she can "awaken him with a kiss" (A 110). "She could picture at that moment no greater bliss on earth than possession of the beloved one" (A 110). Edna, a woman who claims to want to escape the possessive domination of her husband, wants to possess in turn. But the object of her desire is not there to be possessed. Instead, Robert has left a note, "I love you. Good-by—because I love you" (A 111). Interpreted by some as proof that Robert too is a slave to convention and does not have the courage to ruin Edna's marriage by matching her passion, this note can also be seen as Robert's way of letting Edna down easily when he realizes what a possessive lover she would be. In any case, after reading the note, Edna does not, as she has in many scenes before, fall asleep. Instead, she stays awake the entire night. Awakened to the dead end of her feelings and the emptiness within herself, she commits suicide that very day.

Edna's failure stems from her inability to answer what Chametzky calls the question of "how to be free in one's and for one's self but still meaningfully connected to others."[32] Lodged within the logic of possessive individualism, Edna has no answer to that question, since any connection with others imposes constraints and thus limits freedom. Edna is so caught within those assumptions that she, who complains that her husband treats her as a possession, desires to possess her lover. As a result, she refuses to accept responsibilities created by the mutual agreements of promising and must face the emptiness of a self lacking a direction for the future.

But even though the book exposes as fictional Edna's quest for autonomous freedom, its complexity lies in the fact that its irony does not undermine our sense that she is unfairly confined by the role allotted to married women. For instance, Edna's desire to be let alone echoes the sentiment that Warren and Brandeis appealed to in arguing for a right to privacy. Nonetheless, it takes on a different significance. In fact, rather than use it as ammunition to advance claims for what her husband calls her notion "concerning the eternal rights of women" (A 65), it confuses her sense of rights, as she adds, "Nobody has any right— except children, perhaps—and then even then, it seems to me—or did seem—" (A 109).[33] That confusion stems in part from the different significance that privacy had for men and women in late nineteenth-century culture. As we have seen, for Warren and Brandeis the right to be let alone meant protection against intrusions into the domestic sphere. But it is precisely confinement within the domestic sphere that concerns Edna. To be sure, she does not think through her dilemma with any clarity, and her abrupt silence when frustrated by confusion dramatizes her immature behavior. Nonetheless, her dilemma is real.

Readers are invited to wrestle with Edna's dilemma because of the vacancy created in the text by her suicide, which is not the exchange of one fictional self for another, but the exchange of a fictional self for nothingness. Created by Edna's failure to solve her problems, that vacancy provides readers who occupy it no clear-cut moral guidelines. As Edna says the night before she kills herself, "Perhaps it is better to wake up, . . . even to suffer, rather than remain a dupe to illusions all one's life" (A 110). Given Edna's sense of freedom, death is her only alternative to entrapment by illusions. That the specific illusion to which Edna refers is what the doctor calls nature's "decoy to secure mothers for the race" (A 110) reminds us how central the responsibilities of motherhood are to the book. Those responsibilities may be, to use the doctor's phrase, the creation of "arbitrary conditions" (A 110), but they nonetheless point to one of the most powerful challenges to the promise of contract: the responsibility that an older generation has to a younger.

The act of promising offers Edna an alternative for her dealings with adults, but it does not work in her relationship with her children, for her duties as a mother do not derive from a mutual agreement negotiated with them. Instead, her duties seem arbitrarily thrust upon her. Thus Edna's dilemma forces us to face what Carole Pateman in her criticism of the gender inequities of contract calls "part of the general problem of contractarianism." "Would an 'individual' ever enter into a contract to be a parent?" she asks. "A contract for mutual sexual use can accommodate physical genesis without difficulty. The problem arises with the long-term commitment as a parent required for human development." Having raised this crucial question, Pateman, who is otherwise scrupulous in her analysis, unfortunately drops it. "I am," she concludes, "concerned with adult heterosexual relations not parent-child relations, so I shall merely raise and not pursue such questions."[34] Edna does not have that luxury.

To be sure, her dilemma can be addressed at least in part by contractual thinking. Motherhood is related to "arbitrary" conditions because women in Edna's society are disproportionately burdened with the responsibilities of child-raising. Much of our sympathy for Edna comes from our sense that they do not seem open for negotiation. But even if they were, problems would remain. First, the responsibilities of child-raising might be open for negotiation between men and women, but the responsibilities of child-bearing do not seem to be.[35] Second, negotiations between men and women do not solve the problem that the relationship between adults and children presents to contractual thinking.

Both of these problems suggest the difficulty that contract has dealing with the question of inheritance. An important part of the promise of contract is not to base a person's worth on descent. The year before the appearance of *The Awakening*, the Supreme Court expressed that ideal in *United States v. Wong Kim Ark* (1898) when it ruled against the government's refusal to grant citizenship to someone of Chinese ancestry born in the United States. Interpreting the 14th Amendment's citizenship clause to mean that citizenship is never a question of descent, it implies that, regardless of their "inherited legal statuses," people "within a given territory must inevitably and intensively interact with and affect one another, thereby creating a common life that ordinarily shapes their interests."[36] Yet, as Chesnutt illustrates, this ideal risks neglecting problems raised by inheritances from the past and, as Chopin suggests, the question of what we owe future generations.

The Awakening especially points to a paradox in Arendt's claim that "the fact of natality" saves "the world of human affairs" from its "normal 'natural' ruin." (HC 247). For Edna, the means by which a new generation is delivered into the world marks a woman's enslavement to nature, not her liberation from its cycles. A crucial moment in the book occurs when Edna watches Madame Ratignolle give birth. She "witnessed the scene [of] torture," we are told, with "an inward agony, with a flaming, outspoken revolt against the ways of Nature" (A 109).[37] Only by avoiding the burdens of birth does it seem possible for a woman to resist the ways of nature. The relationship between mother and child during the labor of birth is not a form of labor that can be accounted for by contractual thought—even the revised version made possible by Arendt's notion of promising.

If the labor of birth creates a particular paradox for women, the child that is delivered into the world creates one for all adults. The birth of a child holds out promise for new beginnings, yet in "The Crisis in Education" even Arendt admits that the act of promising that is so crucial for new beginnings does not work for the relationship between adults and children. The education of children, she argues, requires that we "take toward them an attitude radically different from the one we take toward one another" (PF 195). Paradoxically, then, an older generation can deliver on its promise to provide a better future for a younger one only by not relating to it through contractual promises. In a controversial argument, Arendt contends that in education adults must apply "a concept of authority and an attitude toward the past which are appropriate to it but have no general validity and must not claim a general validity in the world of grown-ups" (PF 195). Only then, she argues, will we live up to our responsibilities to the young. "Education is the point at which we decide whether we love the world enough to assume responsibility for it and by the same token save it from that ruin which, except for renewal, except for the coming of the new and the young would be inevitable. And education, too, is where we decide whether we love our children enough not to expel them from our world and leave them to their own devices, nor to strike from their hands their chance of undertaking something new, something unforeseen by us, but to prepare them in advance for the task of renewing a common world" (PF 196).

Arendt offers a valuable perspective on Edna, who expels her children from her world through an act of suicide that signals her refusal to assume responsibility for the world she inhabits. But that perspective is achieved by reinscribing status into the very human relation that allows the survival of the species. Arendt may be right. Given my generation's abysmal record of living up to its responsibilities to its children, she certainly deserves a hearing. Nonetheless, her writings indicate that she does not successfully confine relations of status to the sphere of education alone.

About the time that she was working on her essay on education, Arendt published another in which she questioned the strategy of forced integration in Little Rock, Arkansas, in 1957.[38] She starts by criticizing black and white adults, who placed the burden of integration on children while leaving unchallenged the laws that denied grown-ups the right to marry across racial lines. But in a related argument she also defends the right of private individuals and groups to discriminate when it comes to freedom of association in the social, not political, realm.[39] Indeed, Arendt's sense of duties and responsibilities depends on a complicated, but problematic, division between public and private spheres that has uneasy parallels with the logic of the *Plessy* majority.

The Awakening dramatizes the issues raised by Arendt. Taking place in the New Orleans that produced the *Plessy* case, it even raises questions about intersections between racial and gender identity.[40] It does not, however, provide solutions to the questions that it raises. Instead, our need to rely on the language of paradox to describe its actions indicates that it brings us to the limits of the assumptions that generate its world. Nonetheless, those paradoxes create spaces of emptiness in which, as in other works of realism, readers are invited to wrestle with the questions that the book leaves unanswered. How readers in the present occupy those spaces is also a question of inheritance and the possibility it allows for new beginnings.

The Awakening points to the limits of the ability of even a reconstructed sense of the promise of contract to deal with an older generation's duties to a younger one. As a number of works treated in this book illustrate, contractual obligations cannot completely replace various forms of noncontractual interpersonal commitments. Nonetheless, they can and do add to those commitments in significant ways. For instance, if the promise of contract alone is not adequate to deal with an older generation's duties to a younger one, it can help to fulfill them by providing for children what Arendt calls "islands of predictability" and "guideposts of reliability" (HC 244) in what would otherwise be an overwhelmingly uncertain future. The creation of such limited reliability through promising is, as Arendt argues, the most important of political business.

One of the great political failures of the late nineteenth century was the way in which the legal system made future generations so vulnerable to the unpredictability of a economic chance world. It did so in part by using contract to limit the liability of the powerful rather than, as Arendt urges, using the faculty of promising to create a future of limited reliability. To be sure, as various works of realism show, not to limit liability in some way is to make everyone equally responsible for everything and thus to undercut the assessments of individual responsibility that are so crucial to the very sense of human agency on which the possibilities of promising depend. Nonetheless, in dramatizing the failure of contract to deliver on its promise of a more equitable society, these works also invite us to take on the responsibility of determining more responsible limits to liability, ones that have a better chance of creating a future world of limited reliability for the next generation.

But these works can have future effects only if readers in the present retain a sense of responsibility to the past. The reading of past texts poignantly raises this question of responsibility because they can speak to us only if we give them renewed birth. It is, therefore, all too easy to adopt a paternalistic attitude toward them and judge them harshly for not living up to our preconceived standards. But to impose our wills on texts from the past rules out the possibility of learning from them. To keep that possibility open for works of American realism, we need to relate to them on the terms that they offer us, which is not to provide definitive answers, but to engage the dilemmas that they raise. That involves the aleatory contract that I described in the introduction.[41]

Most contracts spell out the specific terms of what is to be exchanged. The implied contract with the realists' texts is, however, to enter into an exchange that keeps our acts of reading free, if we agree with Arendt that "action, to be free, must be free from motive on one side, from its intended goal on the other" (PF 151). That contract asks, in other words, for the virtuosity that Arendt associates with *virtù*, so that reading becomes a performative activity rather than one that judges works against already existing standards. The point is not that motive and concern with pragmatic goals are unimportant. They are important. The point is that, so long as one of our goals is to keep open the possibility for new beginnings, we must continually work to create limited spaces in our society for such open-ended exchanges.

In this book I have examined how various realistic novels attempt to create such spaces. Their attempts might be doomed to failure, but those failures are not all in vain. To be sure, failures offer no models to live by. But works of realism remain an important part of our cultural inheritance precisely because they do not impose a preconceived model on us. Instead, through dramatizing the failed promise of contract, they create vacancies that challenge future generations willing to occupy them "to call something into being which did not exist before, which was not given, not even as an object of cognition or imagination, and which strictly speaking, could not be known" (PF 151). Our contract with works of American literary realism is still open.

Notes

Chapter 1. Introduction

1. Owen Fiss, *Troubled Beginnings of the Modern State, 1888–1910,* vol. 8 of *The Oliver Wendell Holmes Devise: History of the Supreme Court of the United States* (New York: Macmillan, 1993). A remarkable effort to get beyond the progressive and New Deal view that the Court simply used its power to advance class interests, Fiss's book confirms much of my argument about the promise of contract. On Fiss's and my differences, see chapter 2, n. 34 of my book.

2. Sir Henry Sumner Maine, *Ancient Law: Its Connection with the Early History of Society and Its Relation to Modern Ideas,* 10th ed. (1861; reprint, New York: Dorset, 1986), p. 141.

3. William Graham Sumner, *What Social Classes Owe to Each Other* (New York: Harper & Brother, 1883), pp. 24–25.

4. William Graham Sumner, p. 26.

5. William Graham Sumner, p. 25.

6. Karl Polanyi, *The Great Transformation* (New York: Farrar & Rinehart, 1944), p. 153.

7. William E. Forbath, "The Ambiguities of Free Labor: Labor and Law in the Gilded Age," *Wisconsin Law Review* (1985): 767–817.

8. The status of controlling one's means of production, more than the possibilities of earning power, helps to explain the attraction of a career as an artist in books as different as Elizabeth Stuart Phelps's *The Story of Avis* and Kate Chopin's *The Awakening.*

9. Howells, for instance, tried to get out of a long-term contract that he signed in 1885, in which he agreed "not to write for any other person or firm, and not to act on or allow his name to be used in any editorial relation by any other person or firm during the agreement." Quoted by Daniel H. Borus, *Writing Realism* (Chapel Hill: Univ. of North Carolina Press, 1989), p. 49.

10. Richard Hofstadter, *The Age of Reform* (New York: Alfred A. Knopf, 1955).

11. Alan Trachtenberg, *The Incorporation of America* (New York: Hill and Wang, 1982).

12. "Corporate liberalism" was coined by Martin Sklar in "Woodrow Wilson and the Political Economy of Modern United States Liberalism," *Studies on the Left* 1 (1960): 17–47.

13. Peter Gabel and Jay M. Feinman, "Contract Law and Ideology," in *The Politics of Law,* ed. David Kairys (New York: Pantheon Books, 1982), pp. 172–84.

14. Henry James, *The American* (Boston: Houghton Mifflin, 1962), p. 163. Established by Matthew J. Bruccoli, this text is based on the first authorized English edition, published in 1879 by Macmillan. For a different reading, see Mark Seltzer, *Bodies and Machines* (New York: Routledge, 1992). Seltzer acknowledges that "From one point of view, the conflict in *The American* is the conflict between status and contract." But, he hastens to add, "From another, neither status nor contract, nor their conflict provides the model for understanding the economic and effective 'conditions of identity' or individuality at the turn of the century" (73). For him, more important is the distinction between bodies and machines. Whereas I acknowledge the period's fascination with bodies and machines, I disagree with Seltzer's implication that this fascination provides the key to unlock the period's complexity. My point is not that the conflict between status and contract is the real key, but instead that we need to explore the relations among various conflicts, not seek metaexplanations.

15. Charles Fried, *Contract as Promise* (Cambridge: Harvard Univ. Press, 1981).

16. For an analysis of the "Contract" in terms of contract law, see Stephen L. Carter, "[Breach of] Contract with [Part of] America," *The New York Times Magazine* (9 April 1995), pp. 62–63.

17. Albion W. Tourgée, "The Claim of Realism," *North American Review* 148 (1889): 388.

18. Ian Watt, *The Rise of the Novel* (Berkeley: Univ. of California Press, 1957).

19. Linda Nochlin, *Realism* (Baltimore: Penguin, 1971), p. 45.

20. David Shi, *Facing Facts* (New York: Oxford Univ. Press, 1994).

21. Fredric Jameson notes that "genres are essentially literary *institutions,* or social contracts between a writer and a specific public, whose function it is to specify the proper use of a particular cultural artifact." *The Political Unconscious* (Ithaca: Cornell Univ. Press, 1981) p. 106. For more on readerly contracts, see Northrop Frye, *The Anatomy of Criticism* (Princeton: Princeton Univ. Press, 1957), p. 76; Jonathan Culler, *Structuralist Poetics* (Ithaca: Cornell Univ. Press, 1975), pp. 193, 195–96, 214 (on Greimas's *syntagmes contractuels*); Philippe Lejune, *Le Pacte Autobiographique* (Paris: Edition de Seuil, 1975); and "The Autobiographical Contract," in *French Literary History Today,* ed. Tzetan Todorov, (New York: Cambridge Univ. Press, 1982), pp. 196–222; Tony Tanner, *Adultery in the Novel: Contract and Transgression* (Baltimore: Johns Hopkins Univ. Press, 1979); Ross Chambers, *Story and Situation* (Minneapolis: Univ. of Minnesota Press, 1984); and Carla Kaplan, "Narrative Contracts and Emancipatory Readers," *The Yale Journal of Criticism* 6 (1993): 93–120.

22. Winfried Fluck, *Inszenierte Wirklichkeit* (Munich: Wilhelm Fink Verlag, 1992), p. 362. See also Heinz Ickstadt, "Concepts of Society and the Practice of Fiction: Symbolic Responses to the Experience of Change in Late Nineteenth-Century America," in *Impressions of a Gilded Age,* eds. Marc Chenétier and Rob Kroes (Amsterdam: Univ. of Amsterdam Press, 1983), pp. 77–95.

23. Edith Wharton, "Fiction and Criticism," Beinecke Library, Yale Univ., quoted in Shi, *Facing Facts,* p. 123.

24. Erich Auerbach, *Mimesis* (Princeton: Princeton Univ. Press, 1953), p. 552. Amy Kaplan notes that Howells "anticipates Erich Auerbach's well-known definition of nineteenth-century realism as the breakdown of neoclassical styles," but she also links Howells's efforts to class conflict. *The Social Construction of American Realism* (Chicago: Univ. of Chicago Press, 1988), p. 22.

25. Georges Poulet compares James to a "disciple of Copernicus" who "felt himself to be without a landmark in the vastness of cosmic space." *The Metamorphosis of the Circle* (Baltimore: Johns Hopkins Univ. Press, 1966), p. 308. See also Robert C. Post, "A Theory of Genre: Romance, Realism, and Moral Reality," *American Quarterly* 33 (1981): 367–90 and Winfried Fluck, *Inszenierte Wirklichkeit* (Munich: Wilhelm Fink Verlag, 1992).

26. Ross Posnock, *The Trial of Curiosity* (New York: Oxford Univ. Press, 1991), p. 91.

27. Tony Tanner, *Henry James* (Amherst: Univ. of Massachusetts Press, 1985), pp. 107–8.

28. William Dean Howells, "Review," *Atlantic Monthly* 25 (1870): 124. See also Walter Blair, *Mark Twain and Huck Finn* (Berkeley: Univ. of California Press, 1960), p. 64; Anne Trensky, "The Bad Boy in Nineteenth-Century American Fiction," *Georgia Review* 27 (1973): 503–17; John Crowley, "*Little Women* and the Boy-Book," *New England Quarterly* 58 (1985): 384–99; and Steve Mailloux, *Rhetorical Power* (Ithaca: Cornell Univ. Press, 1989), pp. 111–13.

29. Hans Blumenberg helps with such discriminations by describing four concepts of reality that have appeared in the West. One is self-evidence. Within this concept reality might be obscured by historical contingencies or the inability of people to see it, but an act of mimesis can make it visible by creating a moment of re-cognition. Another concept is that of a guaranteed reality. Descartes expresses this view through his faith in a God who will not deceive and thus guarantees trust in our senses. A third concept is reality as the actualization of a context. Close to the idea of reality as a social construction, this concept assumes the existence of realities rather than one Reality. Finally, there is reality defined by its resistance to efforts to represent it.

By my definition, works of realism operate within three of these concepts. Reality in them almost always involves the construction of social conventions. At times they also reveal a truth obscured by false conventions. At others reality resists agreement with their efforts to represent it. But the one concept that they call into question, and in doing so distinguish themselves from other works at the time, is a guaranteed sense of reality. "The Concept of Reality and the Possibility of the Novel," *New Perspectives in German Literary Criticism,* eds.

Richard E. Amacher and Victor Lange (Princeton: Princeton Univ. Press, 1979), pp. 29–48.

30. On the realists' response to the sentimental tradition, see Alfred Habegger, *Gender, Fantasy, and Realism in American Literature* (New York: Columbia Univ. Press, 1982), and Michael D. Bell, "The Sin of Art and the Problem of American Realism: William Dean Howells," *Prospects* 9 (1984): 115–42.

31. Richard Chase, *The American Novel and Its Tradition* (Garden City, N.Y.: Anchor Books, 1957), p. 186 n, and George J. Becker, "Modern Realism as a Literary Movement," in *Documents of Modern Literary Realism*, ed. George J. Becker (Princeton: Princeton Univ. Press, 1963), p. 35. See also Shi, *Facing Facts.*

32. Sandy Petrey, "The Language of Realism, the Language of False Consciousness: A Reading of *Sister Carrie*," *Novel* 10 (1977): 103.

33. Robert A. Ferguson, *Law and Letters in American Culture* (Cambridge: Harvard Univ. Press, 1984).

34. Michael Paul Rogin, *Subversive Genealogy* (New York: Knopf, 1983), p. 302. For a very different account, see Richard A. Hocks, "Melville and 'The Rise of Realism': The Dilemma of History in *Billy Budd*," *American Literary Realism* 26 (1994): 60–81.

35. Georg Lukàcs, "The Ideology of Modernism," *Realism in Our Time*, trans. John and Necke Mander (New York: Harper & Row, 1962), pp. 17–46.

36. Chase; Eric Sundquist, "Introduction: The Country of the Blue," in *American Realism*, ed. Eric Sundquist (Baltimore: Johns Hopkins Univ. Press, 1982), pp. 3–24. Ortega y Gassett argues that the romance inhabits the entire genre of the novel. *Meditations on Quixote*, trans. Evelyn Rugg and Diego Marín (New York: W. W. Norton & Co., 1961). On Twain's ridicule and use of romanticism, see Edgar M. Branch, "Samuel Clemens: Learning to Venture a Miracle," *American Literary Realism* 8 (1975): 91–9. Trachtenberg argues that "Howells resorted often to 'romance' to preserve the moral assurances of his 'realism.' " *The Incorporation of America*, p. 192. Michael Davitt Bell, in *The Problem of American Realism* (Chicago: Univ. of Chicago Press, 1993), claims that the problem of American realism is its theory of literature based on a radical desire to suppress the "literary." Drawing on Howells's criticism to define realism according to this naive opposition between life and literature, Bell contends that no one except Howells and Norris adhered to the definition. In contrast to Bell, I look not to critical statements about realism, but to its practice. As Bell himself notes, Howells was "no Auerbach, no Lukàcs" (5). Neither was Balzac nor Flaubert. Howells's practice (along with James's and Twain's) does not conform to a naive view of reality.

37. Brook Thomas, "Language and Identity in *Adventures of Huckleberry Finn*," *Mark Twain Journal* 20 (1980–1981): 17–21.

38. Walter Benn Michaels was one of the first to point out the infinite repeatability of "deconstructive" readings. He does so by comparing them to pragmatic ones. "The Interpreter's Self: Peirce on the Cartesian Subject," *Georgia Review* 31 (1977): 383–402.

39. Jean-François Lyotard, *The Postmodern Condition* (Minneapolis: Univ. of Minnesota Press, 1984), p. 82.

40. Hilary Putnam, *The Many Faces of Realism* (La Salle, Ill.: Open Court, 1987), p. 30.

41. In a recent exception, Bruce Robbins proposes reconceiving realism as a "continuing social project that (in some form) one might still want to sign on to." "Modernism and Literary Realism," in *Realism and Representation,* ed. George Levine (Madison: Univ. of Wisconsin Press, 1993), p. 225.

42. Laurence B. Holland, *The Expense of Vision* (Baltimore: Johns Hopkins Univ. Press, 1964), p. ix.

43. *Darstellung* is a crucial concept for Hegel and Marx. Wolfgang Iser relies on it in "Feigning in Fiction," in *Identity of the Literary Texts,* eds. Mario J. Valdés and Owen Miller (Toronto: Univ. of Toronto Press, 1985), pp. 204–28, and "Representation: A Performative Act," in *The Aims of Representation,* ed. Murray Krieger (New York: Columbia Univ. Press, 1987), pp. 217–32. Iser influenced Fluck's discussion of American realism in *Inszenierte Wirklichkeit.* See also my discussion of *Darstellung* and representation in *The New Historicism and Other Old-Fashioned Topics* (Princeton: Princeton Univ. Press, 1991), pp. 177–218.

44. Both Edwin H. Cady, in *The Common Light of Day* (Bloomington: Indiana Univ. Press, 1971), and Everett Carter, in *Howells and the Age of Realism* (Philadelphia: J. B. Lippincott Co., 1954), propose a pragmatic understanding of realism. Cady describes reality as a "socially agreed upon 'common vision' which permits ordinary processes of law and society to succeed, creates the possibilities of games, [and] makes most technical, economic, and even educational processes possible" (19). Carter has a section on "Pragmatism and Realism" (152–56). Both, however, underplay the way in which the realists' technical innovations can transform our common vision.

45. For example, Albion W. Tourgée criticizes literary realists for abandoning the reality of principles, ideals, and hope. Tourgée's objections will be examined at length in chapter 7.

46. Van Wyck Brooks, *The Ordeal of Mark Twain* (New York: Dutton, 1920).

47. Roland Barthes, *S/Z,* trans. Richard Miller (New York: Hill and Wang, 1974). For Foucault the novel is "part of that great system of constraint by which the West compelled the everyday to bring itself into discourse." "The Life of Infamous Men," in *Power, Truth, Strategy* (Sydney: Feral Publications, 1979). See also Leo Bersani, *A Future for Astyanax* (Boston: Little, Brown, 1976).

48. Nancy Armstrong and Leonard Tennenhouse, *The Violence of Representation* (London: Routledge, 1989), p. 2.

49. Philip Fisher, "Democratic Social Space: Whitman, Melville, and the Promise of Transparency," *Representations* 24 (1988): 82. Followers of Foucault often use literary works to explore decentralized, "private" deployments of power. See, for instance, Leo Bersani's discussion of James in "The Subject of Power," *Diacritics* 7 (1975): 2–21. To reconnect such deployments of power

with a police state is to fall prey to paranoid fantasies about the ubiquitous nature of governmental power.

50. Mark Seltzer, *Henry James and the Art of Power* (Ithaca: Cornell Univ. Press, 1984), p. 54. Seltzer's work has strong affinities with D. A. Miller's *The Novel and the Police* (Berkeley: Univ. of California Press, 1987).

51. Kaplan, *The Social Construction of American Realism*, p. 10.

52. Walter Benn Michaels, *The Gold Standard and the Logic of Naturalism* (Berkeley: Univ. of California Press, 1987), and James Livingston, *Pragmatism and the Political Economy of Cultural Revolution, 1850–1940* (Chapel Hill: Univ. of North Carolina Press, 1994). I treat Michaels's argument about corporations at length in "Walter Benn Michaels and Cultural Poetics: Where's the Difference?" in *The New Historicism*, pp. 117–50. I come back to his argument about realism in the chapter on Howells in this book. See also chapter 2, n. 39 of this book.

Livingston links proprietary capitalism with the "rational, autonomous, individual required" by "liberal political theory" and its "indispensable assumption of . . . the ontological priority of the pure self" (125). In contrast he champions a "discursive self" that is appropriate to the "age of surplus" in consumer and corporate capitalism. He finds it in Whitman, the literary naturalists, and pragmatism, whereas the realists (with the possible exception of James) cling to possessive individualism. The "discursive self" he argues, "goes underground after the Civil War, as the realism of Howells and Twain carries the day. But it erupts from the exhausted soil of American letters in the 1890s, in the form of literary naturalism" (137). Livingston is, I believe, correct to see an affinity (if not identity) between the corporate self and pragmatism. But his account of the realists, which depends on equating Howells's point of view with Ben Halleck's in *A Modern Instance*, is far too simple. Indeed, I will argue that the realists challenge Livingston's assumption that the only alternative to a discursive, "postmodern" subjectivity is the autonomous self of possessive individualism.

53. Robert William Fogel, *Without Consent or Contract* (New York: Norton, 1989).

54. Martin Luther King Jr., "Speech at Civil Rights March," Washington D.C., 28 August 1963, in *Martin Luther King, Jr.*, ed. Flip Schulke (New York: Norton, 1976), p. 218.

55. Roscoe Pound, *An Introduction to the Philosophy of Law* (New Haven: Yale Univ. Press, 1922), p. 236.

56. Hugh Collins, *The Law of Contract* (London: Weidenfield and Nicolson, 1986), p. 9.

57. Hannah Arendt, *The Human Condition* (Chicago: Univ. of Chicago Press, 1958), p. 209.

58. William Dean Howells, "A Psychological Counter-Current in Recent Fiction," *North American Review* 172 (1901): 882.

59. *Lynch v. Donnelly*, 465 U.S. 668 at 687 (1984).

60. Michael Walzer, "The Concept of Civil Society," in *Toward a Global Civil Society*, ed. Michael Walzer (Providence: Berghahn Books, 1995), p. 7.

Chapter 2. Contract and the Road from Equity

1. William Dean Howells, *A Modern Instance,* eds. David J. Nordloh and David Kleinman (Bloomington: Indiana Univ. Press, 1977), p. 4. Future references to this text will be cited parenthetically, as MI.

2. Aristotle, *The Rhetoric and Poetics of Aristotle,* bk. 1 (New York: Modern Library, 1954), p. 80. The translation is W. Rhys Roberts's.

3. Joseph Story, *Commentaries on Equity Jurisprudence as Administered in England and America,* vol. 1 (Boston: Hilliard, Gray & Co., 1835), p. 8.

4. Aristotle, *Rhetoric,* p. 81.

5. Story, *Equity Jurisprudence,* vol. 1, p. 12.

6. See, for instance, William Lambarde, *Archeion,* eds. Charles H. McIlwain and Paul L. Ward (Cambridge: Harvard Univ. Press, 1957)—completed 1591, published 1635—and Edward Hake, *Epieikeia,* ed. D. E. C. Yale (London: Oxford Univ. Press, 1953), also written in the 1590s.

7. Sir William Blackstone, *Commentaries on the Laws of England,* ed. Thomas M. Cooley, vol. 2, 3rd ed., rev. (Chicago: Callaghan & Co., 1884), p. 433. Cooley's edition is appropriate for the period about which I am writing.

8. Charges of paternalism do not necessarily disappear when equity is denied a separate institutional structure. For instance, Richard Posner argues that every legal system provides space for equitable relief through the discretionary power of judges: *Law and Literature: A Misunderstood Relation* (Cambridge: Harvard Univ. Press, 1988), pp. 112–13. In Roman law the *jus praetorium,* or discretion of the praetor, was distinct from the *leyes,* or standing law. Nonetheless, both powers were granted to the same magistrate. Similarly, Grotius recognizes the power of judges' discretionary interpretation when a law is too general: "*Lex non exacte definit, sed arbitrio boni viri permittit*" ("Indefinite statutes allow the judgment of good men," quoted in Blackstone, vol. 2, p. 431). But as the fate of the Latin word *arbitrio* in English reminds us, judgment or arbitration left up to one person always raises the specter of arbitrariness. Judges are granted discretionary power only because of the institutional position that they occupy, an institutional position that makes them paternal guardians of the law and justice. Outside of that institutional position, a person exercising discretionary judgment is prone to charges of selective interpretation. Within it, a judge is assumed to have the power to distinguish between the spirit and the letter of the law so as to temper his justice with mercy.

The connection between equity and mercy is a traditional one. In addition to Shakespeare's *The Merchant of Venice,* see St. Germain's claim that "Equity is a righteousness, that considereth all the particular circumstances of the deed, which is also tempered with the sweetness of mercy" (quoted in Story, *Equity Jurisprudence,* vol. 1, p. 11). Howells, who according to Edwin H. Cady refers to the need for a "law of mercy," would seem to be influenced by this notion of equity: see "Introduction," *A Modern Instance* (New York: Penguin Books, 1984), p. xxiii. Nonetheless, at the end of the novel, Ben Halleck, who has presided over the burial of the Squire, writes to his lawyer friend Eustace Atherton asking for "your judgment without mercy" (MI 451).

9. Val Nolan Jr., "Indiana: Birthplace of Migratory Divorce," *Indiana Law Journal* 26 (1951): 515–27. The Squire notes, "Bartley must have been disappointed when he found divorce so hard to get in Indiana. He must have thought that the old law is still in force there" (MI 408). Laura Korobkin offered this reference.

10. On Tönnies's debt to Maine, see George Feaver, *From Status to Contract* (London: Longmans, 1969), pp. 58, 282 n. 51. Maine influenced Holmes's *The Common Law* and Henry Adams. (See Feaver, pp. 132–33, 147–48). Drawing much of his anthropological data from his experience in colonial India, Maine would be a fascinating figure for postcolonial critics to study. Maine's advocacy of contract by no means made him a democratic thinker. On Maine and Howells see, George R. Uba, "Status and Contract: The Divorce Dispute of the 'Eighties and Howells' *A Modern Instance*," *Colby Library Quarterly* 19 (1983): 78–89. On the transition in American society from small communities to a modern society, see Robert H. Wiebe, *The Search for Order, 1877–1920* (New York: Hill and Wang, 1967), Jean B. Quandt, *From the Small Town to the Great Community* (New Brunswick: Rutgers Univ. Press, 1970), and Thomas Bender, *Community and Social Change in America* (New Brunswick: Rutgers Univ. Press, 1978).

11. Bartley is not the only character who does not stay true to his word. The Squire warns his daughter, "Don't keep making promises and breaking them" (MI 165).

12. Stanley Cavell, *The Claim of Reason* (New York: Oxford Univ. Press, 1979), pp. 247–73, 292–312. For Cavell's debt to the "distinction between *Gemeinschaft* and *Gesellschaft*," see p. 299.

13. See Annette Baier, "Promises, Promises, Promises," in *Postures of the Mind* (Minneapolis: Univ. of Minnesota Press, 1985), pp. 174–206.

14. David Hume, *A Treatise of Human Nature,* eds. L. A. Selby-Bigge and P. H. Nidditch (Oxford: Clarendon Press, 1978), p. 522.

15. Sir Frederick Pollock notes that Maine shows the "huge anachronism" involved in "those political theories which seek to make contract the foundation of all positive law and even of government itself." Sir Henry Sumner Maine, *Ancient Law: Its Connection with the Early History of Society and Its Relation to Modern Ideas,* 10th ed. (1906; reprint, Boston: Beacon Press, 1963), p. 444. See also Michael Rosenfeld, "Contract and Justice: The Relation between Classical Contract Law and Social Contract Theory," *Iowa Law Review* 70 (1985): 769–885.

16. For a critical look at the notion of both individual and political sovereignty, see the final chapter.

17. Thomas L. Haskell, "Capitalism and the Humanitarian Sensibility, Part 2," in *The Antislavery Debate*, ed. Thomas Bender, (Berkeley: Univ. of California, Press, 1992), pp. 141–44.

18. Haskell, pp. 146, 151. On Maine and Haskell's argument, see Morton J. Horwitz, "Reconstructing Historical Theory from the Debris of the Cold War," *Yale Law Journal* 102 (1993): 1287–92.

19. Emile Durkheim, "Individualism and the Intellectuals," in *On Morality and Society,* ed. Robert N. Bellah (Chicago: Univ. of Chicago Press, 1973), pp.

48–49. In a note Durkheim adds, "This is how it is possible, without contradiction, to be an individualist, all the while saying that the individual is more a product of society than its cause. It is because individualism itself is a social product like all moralities and religions" (231 n. 4).

20. See Sacvan Bercovitch's fascinating discussion of individualism in "Emerson, Individualism, and Liberal Dissent," in *The Rites of Assent* (New York: Routledge, 1993), pp. 307–52. When Emerson died, Maine was elected in May 1883 to the Academie des Sciences Morales et Politiques in France to fill his vacancy.

21. For Durkheim's views on contract, see Dominick LaCapra, *Emile Durkheim* (Ithaca: Cornell Univ. Press, 1972), pp. 129–33.

22. Thomas L. Haskell, pp. 145, 146. In *Hawkes v. Saunders* (1782), Mansfield is reported to have said, "Where a man is under a moral obligation, which no Court of Law or Equity can enforce, and promises, the honesty and rectitude of the thing is a consideration. . . . [T]he ties of conscience upon an upright mind are sufficient consideration." Quoted in Grant Gilmore, *The Death of Contract* (Columbus: Ohio State Univ. Press, 1974), p. 110 n. 32. My discussion of contract law, especially Oliver Wendell Holmes Jr.'s contribution to it, is heavily indebted to Gilmore. See also the essays collected in *Law, Economy and the Power of Contract,* ed. Kermit L. Hall (New York: Garland, 1987).

23. C. H. S. Fifoot, *Lord Mansfield* (Oxford: Clarendon Press, 1936) and James Oldham, *The Mansfield Manuscripts and the Growth of English Law in the Eighteenth Century* (Chapel Hill: Univ. of North Carolina Press, 1992).

24. P. S. Atiyah, *The Rise and Fall of Freedom of Contract* (Oxford: Oxford Univ. Press, 1979), p. 345.

25. Haskell, p. 152.

26. Story, *Equity Jurisprudence,* vol. 1, p. 9.

27. P. S. Atiyah, pp. 388–97. See also the detailed argument in Morton J. Horwitz, *The Transformation of American Law, 1780–1860* (Cambridge: Harvard Univ. Press, 1977), pp. 256–66. Exaggerating somewhat, Horwitz describes how in the United States equity was either abolished or subordinated to the legal system. For criticism, see A. W. B. Simpson, "The Horwitz Thesis and the History of Contracts," *The University of Chicago Law Review* 46 (1979): 533–601.

28. Quoted in Istvan Hont and Michael Ignatieff, "Needs and Justice in the *Wealth of Nations,*" in *Wealth and Virtue,* eds. Hont and Ignatieff (Cambridge: Cambridge Univ. Press, 1983), pp. 3–4.

29. Quoted in Adam Smith, *An Inquiry into the Nature and Causes of the Wealth of Nations,* eds. R. H. Campbell, A. S. Skinner, and W. B. Todd, vol. 2 (Oxford: Oxford Univ. Press, 1975), p. 9.

30. Hont and Ignatieff, p. 44.

31. David Liedeman, "The Legal Needs of a Commercial Society: The Jurisprudence of Lord Kames," in *Wealth and Virtue,* pp. 203–34.

32. Adam Smith, *Wealth of Nations,* vol. 1, p. 11.

33. Lawrence Friedman, *Contract Law in America* (Madison: Univ. of Wisconsin Press, 1965), pp. 20–21.

34. See Al Katz, "Studies in Boundary Ideology: Three Essays in Adjudication and Politics," *Buffalo Law Review* 28 (1979): 383–435, and Robert Gordon, "Legal Thought and Legal Practice in the Age of American Enterprise, 1870–1920," in *Professions and Professional Ideologies in America,* ed. Gerald L. Geison (Chapel Hill: Univ. of North Carolina Press, 1983), pp. 70–110.

On the Constitution as a self-perpetuating machine, see Michael Kammen, *A Machine That Would Go of Itself* (New York: Knopf, 1986). Kammen's title comes from an 1889 work by A. Lawrence Lowell. A commonplace progressive criticism of late nineteenth-century legal thought (made by, among others, Woodrow Wilson and John Dewey) was its acceptance of a Newtonian universe. Today we should interrogate the organic metaphors that progressives used, and continue to use, to replace mechanical ones.

Boundary thought points to a limitation to Owen Fiss's remarkable effort to understand the Supreme Court in this period according to contractarianism. If contract ruled in the political and economic realms, it did not in the domestic sphere. Fiss's neglect of boundary theory's grounding in nature also causes him to miss its failure to live up to the interpersonal promise of contract. For instance, he argues that the Court "advanced the idea that the traditional government was a constituted authority with no existence outside, or beyond, the Constitution" (252). For many, the superiority of the Constitution lay in its "realistic" grounding in natural laws or reason.

Belief in the superiority of the United States Constitution complicates Fiss's claim that the Court adheres to a social contract model. To be sure, Locke was influential. But, for the most part, social contract theory is universalist, positing a state of nature applicable to all people. As I have pointed out, the argument that progressive societies have moved from status to contract calls into question an original contract. (See this chapter, n. 15.) It also raises a crucial question that members of the Court answered differently: what makes some societies more progressive than others? Is the cause institutional, in which case less progressive societies simply need to adopt a contractual model? Or is it racial, in which some societies would be incapable of living contractually? The latter point of view governs the opinions of some justices in the *Insular Cases*. Justice Brown, for instance, writes, "There are certain principles of justice inherent in the Anglo-Saxon character which need no expression in constitution or statute to give them effect" *Downes v. Bidwell,* 182 U.S. 244 at 280 (1901). *Troubled Beginnings of the Modern State, 1880–1901,* vol. 8 of *The Oliver Wendell Holmes Devise: History of the Supreme Court of the United States* (New York: Macmillan, 1993).

35. Friedman, *Contract Law,* p. 20.

36. LaCapra, *Emile Durkheim,* pp. 108–9.

37. Eric Foner, "The Meaning of Emancipation in the Age of Freedom," *The Journal of American History* 80 (1994): 435–60.

38. *Lochner v. New York,* 198 U.S. 45, 61 (1905).

39. C. B. Macpherson, *The Political Theory of Possessive Individualism* (New York: Oxford Univ. Press, 1962). On republicanism and liberalism, see J. G. A. Pocock, *The Machiavellian Moment* (Princeton: Princeton Univ. Press, 1975), and, among many others, Bernard Bailyn, *The Ideological Origins of the Amer-*

ican Revolution (Cambridge: Harvard Univ. Press, 1967); Gordon Wood, *The Creation of the American Republic, 1776–1787* (New York: Oxford Univ. Press, 1969); John Ashworth, "The Jeffersonians: Classical Republicans or Liberal Capitalists?" *Journal of American Studies* 18 (1984): 425–35; James T. Kloppenberg, "The Virtues of Liberalism: Christianity, Republicanism, and Ethics in Early American Political Discourse," *Journal of American History* 74 (1987): 9–33; "Symposium: The Republican Civic Tradition," *Yale Law Journal* 97 (1988): 1493–723; and Dorothy Ross, *The Origins of American Social Science* (New York: Cambridge Univ. Press, 1991). On republicanism in American law, see R. Kent Newmyer, *Supreme Court Justice Joseph Story* (Chapel Hill: Univ. of North Carolina Press, 1985) and G. Edward White, *The Marshall Court and Cultural Change, 1815–1835* (New York: Macmillan, 1988). For literature, see *Republicanism in the Gilded Age,* ed. Robert Shulman, a special issue of *American Transcendental Quarterly* 4 (1990).

Macpherson's description of classical liberalism's amoral account of market relations leads to the strengths and weaknesses of Walter Benn Michaels, the most provocative new historicist writing on the period's literature. Michaels recognizes the extent to which progressive accounts of the period often remain lodged within a tradition of genteel moralism. Nonetheless, while challenging this moralistic interpretation, he continues to accept its assumption of an amoral, economic realm. Accepting a Macphersonlike account of classical liberalism, he frequently evokes what he calls the "logic of the market," thus ignoring the extent to which laissez-faire theorists were themselves moralists at heart. As a result, Michaels neglects the important role that status played in laissez-faire thought. Seeing all relations as being governed by the "logic of the market," he pays little attention to how laissez-faire thinkers distinguished among social, economic, and political realms. *The Gold Standard and the Logic of Naturalism* (Berkeley: Univ. of California Press, 1987).

Howard Horwitz, Michaels's student, also remains caught within Macpherson's description of liberalism. His neglect of the republican tradition weakens his fascinating argument in *By the Law of Nature* (New York: Oxford Univ. Press, 1991). For instance, Horwitz occasionally refers to the work of Pocock without engaging or even citing *The Machiavellian Moment,* which challenges Horwitz's Louis Hartz–derived assumption that nineteenth-century America is a site of pure liberalism. My own work in *Cross-examinations of Law and Literature* (New York: Cambridge Univ. Press, 1987) was written under the sway of Macpherson, and it occasionally suffers as a result.

40. Herbert Hovenkamp, *Enterprise and American Law, 1836–1937* (Cambridge: Harvard Univ. Press, 1991), p. 94. His narrow definition relies on Herman Belz, *Emancipation and Equal Rights* (New York: W. W. Norton & Co., 1978) and supports Raoul Berger, *Government by Judiciary* (Cambridge: Harvard Univ. Press, 1977). See contrary interpretations in Harold M. Hyman and William M. Wiecek, *Equal Justice Under Law* (New York: Harper and Row, 1982); Aviam Soifer, "Protecting Civil Rights: A Critique of Raoul Berger's History," *New York University Law Review* 54 (1979): 651–706; and "Status, Contract, and Promises Unkept," *Yale Law Journal* 96 (1987): 1916–59.

41. Justice Harlan dissents with an argument for a more expansive reading of protections provided by the 13th and 14th Amendments.

42. See Robert J. Kaczorowski, "To Begin the Nation Anew: Congress, Citizenship, and Civil Rights after the Civil War," *The American Historical Review* 92 (1987): 45–68 (quotation on p. 59). The federal authority behind The Fugitive Slave Act of 1850 derived from Joseph Story's decision in *Prigg v. Pennsylvania*, 16 Pet. (41 U.S.) 539 (1842).

43. Charles Sumner, quoted in Albion W. Tourgée, *An Appeal to Caesar* (New York: Fords, Howard & Hulbert, 1884), p. 72.

44. Quoted in Hovenkamp, *Enterprise in American Law,* p. 95.

45. *Bradwell v. State,* 83 U.S. 130, 141–2 (1872).

46. In 1892 the Illinois court on its own directed that Bradwell be issued a license to practice law. But if the status of women was changing in the eyes of the law, it continued to influence judicial decisions. In *Muller v. Oregon* (1908) the Supreme Court, persuaded in part by Justice Brandeis's use of social science evidence, ruled that a state could regulate working hours of women, even though in *Lochner* it forbade such regulation for men.

47. *Plessy v. Ferguson,* 163 U.S. 537, 551 (1896).

48. *Plessy v. Ferguson,* 163 U.S. 537, 544, 551 (1896).

49. Oliver Wendell Holmes Jr., *The Common Law* (1881; reprint, Cambridge: Harvard Univ. Press, 1963), p. 5, and *Southern Pacific R.R. Co. v. Jensen,* 244 U.S. 205, 222 (1917).

50. Morton G. White, *Social Thought in America* (New York: Viking, 1949). For an argument against White's description of Holmes, see Yosal Rogat, "The Judge as Spectator," *The University of Chicago Law Review* 31 (1964): 251–53, n. 194. See also chapter 7, n. 67 of this book.

51. On similarities between legal and literary realism, see John P. McWilliams Jr., "Innocent Criminal or Criminal Innocence: The Trial in American Fiction," in Carl S. Smith, John P. McWilliams Jr., and Maxwell Bloomfield, *Law and American Literature,* (New York: Knopf, 1983), pp. 45–124. My discussion of Holmes, who influenced the legal realists, suggests differences as well.

52. Roscoe Pound, "Law in Books and Law in Action," *American Law Review* 44 (1910): 12–13.

53. Oliver Wendell Holmes Jr., *Louisville Gas & Co. v. Coleman,* 277 U.S. 32, 41 (1928) (dissenting), and *Schlesinger v. Wisconsin,* 270 U.S. 230, 241 (1926) (dissenting).

54. Oliver Wendell Holmes Jr., "The Path of the Law," *Harvard Law Review* 10 (1897): 462.

55. Thomas M. Cooley, *A Treatise on the Law of Torts, or the Wrongs which Arise Independently of Contract* (Chicago: Callahan and Co., 1880).

56. Holmes, *The Common Law,* p. 242.

57. Holmes's handwritten annotation in his copy of *The Common Law,* reproduced in the 1963 edition, p. 230. Noted in Gilmore, p. 21.

58. Holmes, *The Common Law,* p. 236. By insisting that someone is "free to break his contract, if he chooses," Holmes clearly wants to distinguish contract from slavery. Contractual liability for him is not a form of limited

slavery. Indeed, he opposed the equitable remedy of specific performance, in which someone who breaches a contract is placed in temporary servitude to the contracting party. Holmes agreed with Lord Coke in *Brommage v. Genning,* 1 Rolle 368 (K.B. 1616) that specific performance subverts the freedom implied by contractual agreements. Nonetheless, Holmes dissented in 1911 when the Supreme Court overturned an Alabama law that in effect used contract to bind mostly African-Americans to a form of involuntary servitude. On Holmes's response to that case, see Benno C. Schmidt Jr., "Principle and Prejudice: The Supreme Court and Race in the Progressive Era. Part 2: The *Peonage Cases,*" *Columbia Law Review* 82 (1982): 684–88 and my chapter 6, n. 32.

59. *Lochner v. New York,* 198 U.S. 45, 75, 76 (1905). For another argument stating that in order to understand *Lochner* we need to get out from under the progressive, New Deal reading of it, see Bruce Ackerman, *We the People* (Cambridge: Harvard Univ. Press, 1991), pp. 63–67.

60. See Aviam Soifer, "The Paradox of Paternalism and Laissez-Faire Constitutionalism: United States Supreme Court, 1888–1921," *Law and History Review* 5 (1987): 249–79. Soifer concentrates on 13th Amendment cases in which the Court's paternalism toward women, Native Americans, and sailors is more obvious. Charles Wallace Collins claims that the 14th Amendment is the "introduction of the principle of paternalism among a people whose genius is foreign to such a political ideal." *The Fourteenth Amendment and the States* (Boston: Little, Brown, 1912), pp. 149–50.

61. Ben Palmer, "Hobbes, Holmes, and Hitler," *American Bar Association* 31 (1945): 569.

62. On the notion of historical reoccupation, see Hans Blumenberg, *The Legitimacy of the Modern Age,* trans. Robert Wallace (Cambridge: MIT Press, 1983). "Reoccupation," unfortunately, has connotations that make it much more passive than the German *Umbesetzung,* which implies a reordering as well as a reoccupation.

63. Ralph A. Newman, *Equity and Law* (New York: Oceana Publishing, 1961), pp. 11, 12.

64. Morton J. Horwitz, "Supreme Court: 1992 Term," *Harvard Law Review* 107 (1993): 34.

65. Horwitz, "1992 Term": 34.

66. Horwitz, "1992 Term": 81. For evidence that at the time of *Lochner* Holmes did not believe in the fundamentality of the 1st Amendment, see David M. Rabban, "The First Amendment in Its Forgotten Years, *The Yale Law Journal* 90 (1981), 514–95, and "The Emergence of Modern First Amendment Doctrine," *The University of Chicago Law Review* 50 (1983): 1205–355.

67. 163 U.S. 537 at 550 (1896). Horwitz's oversight causes him mistakenly to assume that *Plessy,* like *Lochner,* went against "a social reality that was already . . . perceived by the rest of the country" ("1992 Term": 92). If *Lochner* brought immediate protests, *Plessy* raised few outside the black community. The *Plessy* decision might have been wrong the "day it was decided," but not because it went against the reigning construction of social reality or even fundamental traditions of United States law as understood by most "rational and fair" men of the time. Better than Holmes, Justice Harlan provides consistent

opposition to *Plessy* and *Lochner*, since he dissented in both. He also opposed the "rule of reason" for corporate regulation.

68. Influenced by Holmes and in turn influenced him, Roscoe Pound makes an appeal to equity without natural-law principles. Recognizing that the diverse interests of the American people could not be reflected in a unified sovereign will, Pound saw "jury lawlessness" as a potential equitable corrective to "law in its actual administration." Although Pound evokes Aristotle, the basis of his equitable correction is not higher law, but the varying points of view that he finds in a "diversified industrial society." As Gary J. Jacobsohn puts it, "Pound's appeal to Aristotle . . . did not eventuate in an Aristotelian solution. For in Aristotle 'equity embodies a moral ideal and is constant and immutable.' Whereas for the Greeks the end of law was perceived in terms of the unity of the whole, for [Pound] the goal was the protection of group diversity and integrity." Pound's equitable correction works from the bottom up rather than the top down.

Holmes said of juries that they "will [and should] introduce into their verdict a certain amount—a very large amount, so far as I have observed—of popular prejudice, and thus keep the administration of the law in accord with the wishes and feelings of the community." Holmes's stress on prejudice contrasts a classical notion that correctives to written law should be based in right reason. It is revealing that, in an essay written only three years after *Plessy,* he demonstrates approval of law expressing the prejudiced wishes and feelings of the community. Holmes does not evoke the idea of equity. Quotations from Jacobsohn, *The Supreme Court and the Decline of Constitutional Aspiration,* (Totowa, N.J.: Rowan & Littlefield, 1986), pp. 29–33.

69. On "thick description," see Clifford Geertz, "Thick Description: Toward an Interpretive Theory of Culture," *The Interpretations of Culture* (New York: Basic Books, 1973), pp. 3–30. On its importance for legal history see Robert Gordon, "Critical Legal Histories," *Stanford Law Review* 36 (1984): 57–126. On the uses of James's novelistic thick description for cultural analysis, see Jean-Christophe Agnew, "The Consuming Vision of Henry James" in *The Cultures of Consumption,* eds. Richard Wightman Fox and T. J. Jackson Lears (New York: Pantheon, 1983), pp. 65–100.

70. Holmes, "The Path of the Law," 457–58.

71. Quoted in Virginia G. Drachman, "Women Lawyers and the Quest for Professional Identity in Late Nineteenth-Century America," *University of Michigan Law Review* 88 (1990): 2414.

72. Henry James, *Literary Criticism: American and English Writers,* vol. 1, (New York: Library of America, 1984), p. 690.

73. Walter F. Pratt Jr., "American Contract Law at the Turn of the Century," *South Carolina Law Review* 39 (1988): 415–63.

74. William Dean Howells, "Henry James Jr.," *Selected Literary Criticism,* ed. Ulrich Halfmann, vol. 1 (Bloomington: Indiana Univ. Press, 1993), p. 320.

75. James's analysis of motive keeps open a hidden affinity between contract and equity that Holmes closes off. According to Aristotle, equity bids us "not to consider the actions of the accused so much as his intentions." Aristotle, *Rhetoric,* p. 81.

76. See Drachman, "Women Lawyers," 2414–43 and *Women Lawyers and the Origins of Professional Identity in America: The Letters of the Equity Club 1887 to 1890* (Ann Arbor: Univ. of Michigan Press, 1993).

77. George Washington Cable, "The Freedman's Case in Equity," *The Century Magazine* 29 (1885): 418.

Chapter 3. Henry James and the Construction of Privacy

1. Henry James, *The Aspern Papers*, vol. 12 of *The Novels and Tales of Henry James* (New York: Scribner's, 1908), p. 12. Future references to this work will be cited parenthetically within the text, designated as AP. The other works cited parenthetically in the text will be *The Bostonians* (New York: Macmillan and Co., 1886) and *The Reverberator*, vol. 13 of *The Novels and Tales of Henry James* (New York: Scribner's 1908), designated as B and R respectively.

2. J. Thomas McCarthy, *The Rights of Publicity and Privacy* (New York: C. Boardman, 1987), pp. 1–3.

3. Morris L. Ernst and Alan U. Schwartz, *Privacy: The Right to Be Let Alone* (New York: Macmillan, 1962), p. 1.

4. *Griswold v. Connecticut*, 381 U.S. 479 at 484 (1965).

5. Alpheus Mason, *Brandeis: A Free Man's Life* (New York: Viking, 1946), p. 70.

6. Samuel Warren and Louis Brandeis, "The Right to Privacy," *Harvard Law Review* 4 (1890): 196. The most influential account of the tort law of privacy since Warren and Brandeis is William L. Prosser, "Privacy," 48 *California Law Review* 383 (1960).

7. Charles Callan Tansill, *The Foreign Policy of Thomas F. Bayard, 1885–1897* (New York: Fordham Univ. Press, 1940).

8. Henry James, *The Letters of Henry James*, ed. Leon Edel, vol. 1 (Cambridge, Mass.: Harvard Univ. Press, 1974), p. 408.

9. Mason, *Brandeis*, p. 46.

10. Ernst and Schwartz, *Privacy*, p. 47.

11. James H. Barron, "Warren and Brandeis, *The Right to Privacy*, 4 Harvard L. Rev. 193 (1890): Demystifying a Landmark Citation," *Suffolk University Law Review* 13 (1979): 875–922; Lewis J. Paper, *Brandeis* (Englewood Cliffs, N.J.: Prentice-Hall, 1983).

12. E. L. Godkin, "The Rights of the Citizen: IV. To His Own Reputation," *Scribner's Magazine* 8 (1890): 66.

13. France levied a fine of 500 francs on every publication of a fact of private life. Warren and Brandeis cite its law in "The Right to Privacy." Whether James was aware of it or not is unclear from the action of *The Reverberator*. On the one hand, the French papers planning to reproduce *The Reverberator* article must be more careful than their American counterpart about what they print. On the other, abuses open them to a "suit for defamation" (R 170).

14. Warren and Brandeis, "The Right to Privacy," 195. They cite Thomas M. Cooley, *Treatise on the Law of Torts*, 2d ed. Brandeis reuses the phrase thirty eight years later in his famous dissent in a governmental wiretapping case,

indicating that, for him at least, intrusions by government and private parties violate the same right. The "right to be let alone," he asserts, is "the most comprehensive of rights and the right most valued by civilized men." *Olmstead v. United States,* 277 U.S. 438 at 478 (1928). James frequently describes characters who seek this right. In *The Reverberator* three different people or groups of people are described as wanting to be left alone. The American girl, Miss Francie, "who had not even the merit of knowing how to flirt," only "asked to be let alone" (R 58); the French-American family thinks of itself as "quiet people who only want to be left alone" (R 197); and the son is told by his artist friend that it would be fair play for the family itself to "let [him] alone" (R 203).

15. "The Right to Privacy," *The Nation,* Dec. 25, 1890: 496–97.

16. "The Point of View," *Scribner's Magazine,* 9 (1891): 261.

17. John Dewey, *The Public and Its Problems: An Essay in Political Inquiry* (Chicago: Gateway Books, 1946), pp. 12–13. The book was first published in 1927.

18. Andrea Dworkin, "The Third Rape," *Los Angeles Times,* April 28, 1991, p. M6.

19. Richard A. Posner, "The Right to Privacy," *Georgia Law Review* 12 (1978): 400, 408. Posner levels another attack against the right to privacy in the introduction to his book on law and literature. See *Law and Literature: A Misunderstood Relation* (Cambridge, Mass.: Harvard Univ. Press, 1988), pp. 4–5.

20. Walter Benn Michaels argues that "the explicit attempt to shift privacy away from property nonetheless produced a dramatic extension of property rights, produced, in effect, new property." "The Contracted Heart," *New Literary History* 21 (1990): 526 n. 13.

21. Quoted in Godkin, "Reputation," 59.

22. Philip Fisher, "Appearing and Disappearing in Public: Social Space in Late-Nineteenth Century Literature and Culture," in *Reconstructing American Literary History,* ed. Sacvan Bercovitch (Cambridge, Mass.: Harvard Univ. Press, 1986), pp. 180, 178. For an overlapping, but different, view, see Ian F. A. Bell, "The Personal, the Private, and the Public in *The Bostonians,*" *Texas Studies in Literature and Language* 32 (Summer 1990): 240–56. For an argument that Verena is a "pure token of publicity, a figure to be used in an infinity of promotions," see Jennifer Wicke, *Advertising Fictions* (New York: Columbia Univ. Press, 1988), p. 99.

23. Godkin, "Reputation," 65.

24. Robert C. Post, "Rereading Warren and Brandeis: Privacy, Property, and Appropriation," *Case Western Law Review* 41 (1991): 663.

25. Fisher, "Appearing and Disappearing," pp. 179, 180.

26. A major complication for laissez-faire thinkers was the rise of corporations. Godkin refers to railroad corporations as "those large quasi-public enterprises." Godkin, "Reputation," 63.

27. *Griswold v. Connecticut,* 381 U.S. 479 at 485–86 (1965).

28. E. L. Godkin, "The Labor Crisis," *North American Review,* 105 (1867): 183.

29. *Maynard v. Hill,* 125 U.S. 190 at 211 (1887). The fact that a marriage contract is a special kind of contract that does not even come under contract law in the period complicates Tony Tanner's claim that "for bourgeois society, marriage is the all-subsuming, all-organizing, all-containing contract." *Adultery in the Novel: Contract and Transgression* (Baltimore: Johns Hopkins Univ. Press, 1979), p. 15.

30. *People v. Dawell,* 25 Mich. 247 at 257 (1872).

31. See n. 14 above.

32. Amy Dru Stanley, "Conjugal Bonds and Wage Labor: Rights of Contract in the Age of Emancipation," *The Journal of American History* 75 (1988): 477. For problems that the legal similarities between slavery and marriage cause Stowe in *Uncle Tom's Cabin,* see my *Cross-examinations of Law and Literature* (New York: Cambridge Univ. Press, 1987), pp. 113–37.

33. *Green v. State,* 58 Ala. 190 (1877), cited in Michael Grossberg, *Governing the Hearth: Law and the Family in Nineteenth-Century America* (Chapel Hill: Univ. of North Carolina Press, 1985), p. 138.

34. Quoted in Stanley, "Conjugal Bonds," 474. Woodhull's spiritualism granted her sense of the marriage contract the sanctity of a higher power as well. On feminism and spiritualism, see Ann Braude, *Radical Spirits* (Boston: Beacon Press, 1989).

35. It seems obvious to us today that Olive and Verena's relationship is based on homosexual rather than heterosexual attraction. I am not, however, convinced that James consciously constructed such an attraction between them. Whether he did or not does not affect my argument, which is merely that he removes from their relationship that force that determined the "natural" positions of status in marriage.

On feminist ideals of marriage, see William Leach, *True Love and Perfect Union: The Feminist Reform of Sex and Society* (New York: Basic Books, 1980). Leach's discussion of the feminist call for a doctrine of "no secrets" about the mysteries of marriage might seem to imply that the lack of secrets between Olive and Verena is an effort to live up to this ideal. But the "no secrets" doctrine was based on the belief that previously unspoken aspects of marriage (like sex) should be made public so as to demystify marriage and place it on a rational foundation. In contrast, the lack of secrets between Olive and Verena results from the similarity of their union to that of traditional marriage, in which, ideally, husband and wife had no secrets. Try to imagine Olive making public the details of her life with Verena.

36. Albion W. Tourgée has a character describe a law partnership as a marriage. "If lawyers are in a partnership they ought to be like husband and wife,—no secrets between them." *With Gauge & Swallow, Attorneys* (Philadelphia: J. B. Lippincott, 1890), p. 136.

37. Lynne Wardley, "Woman's Voice, Democracy's Body, and *The Bostonians,*" *English Literary History* 56 (Fall 1989): 639–65.

38. Fisher, "Appearing and Disappearing," p. 178.

39. On Verena's spiritualism, see Susan Wolstenholme, "Possession and Personality: Spiritualism in *The Bostonians,*" *American Literature* 49 (1978): 580–91, and Howard Kerr, *Mediums, and Spirit-Rappers and Roaring Radicals:*

Spiritualism in American Literature, 1850–1900 (Urbana: Univ. of Illinois Press, 1972), pp. 190–222.

40. Geoffrey Hartman writes that each Jamesian novel is a "story that exacts from its hero and often from the storyteller himself a contractual quid pro quo. Consciousness must be paid for, and the wages are usually sacrifice and death." *Beyond Formalism,* (New Haven: Yale Univ. Press, 1970), p. 55.

41. Henry James, *The Aspern Papers* in *The Atlantic Monthly* 61 (1888): 594.

42. For speculation on whether or not Miss Tina is Aspern's daughter, see Jacob Korg, "What Aspern Papers? A Hypothesis," *College English* 23 (1962): 378–81; James Gargano, " 'The Aspern Papers': The Untold Story," *Studies in Short Fiction* 10 (1973): 1–10; Bernard Richards, "How Many Children Had Juliana Bordereau?" *Henry James Review* 12 (1991): 120–28; and John Carlos Rowe, *The Theoretical Dimension of Henry James* (Madison: Univ. of Wisconsin Press, 1984), pp. 104–118.

43. For a different reading of this scene, see Rowe, *Theoretical Dimension* , p. 117.

44. Alfred Habegger, *Henry James and the "Women Business"* (New York: Cambridge Univ. Press, 1989), p. 58.

45. *The Notebooks of Henry James,* eds. F. O. Matthiessen and Kenneth B. Murdock, (Chicago: Univ. of Chicago Press, 1981), p. 82.

46. Habegger, *Henry James* , p. 248, n. 30.

47. Posnock argues that William's pragmatism cannot account for the "idle" curiosity so important for Henry. For Henry, a journalist's curiosity is not idle, nor always is the artist's or critic's. *The Trials of Curiosity* (New York: Oxford Univ. Press, 1991). Posnock's account of Jamesian subjectivity is similar to mine. For significant differences, see my last chapter, n. 17.

48. Godkin, "Reputation," 66.

49. Gary Scharnhorst, "James, 'The Aspern Papers,' and the Ethics of Literary Biography," *Modern Fiction Studies* 36 (1990): 211–17.

50. Harriet Beecher Stowe, *Lady Byron Vindicated* (Boston: Fields, Osgood, & Co., 1870).

51. George Knox, "Reverberations and *The Reverberator,*" *Essex Institute Historical Collections* 95 (1959): 348–54.

52. *The Notebooks of Henry James,* p. 83.

53. *Henry James Letters II,* pp. 216–17. Quoted in Scharnhorst, "Ethics of Literary Biography," 213.

54. The belief that literature presented to the public was public property, entered into discussions of privacy. Godkin, for instance, quotes an English writer on jurisprudence who stresses limits to a citizen's right to reputation. "A man doing an important public act, or addressing a literary treatise to his fellow-countrymen, has no right entitling him to shut the mouths even of harsh and severe critics, even though their general intention be unkindly, but not accompanied by that vehement desire, or distinct consciousness of doing evil, which alone the law denounces." Godkin, "Reputation," 63. Clearly, the writer is using "literary" here more broadly than our present use, which links it to aesthetic productions. My discussion in section VIII of the fact that James's

notion of aesthetic privacy depends on the idea that it is not possible to reduce a work of literature to ideas, suggests reasons why a certain notion of privacy and a particular notion of the literary arise in conjunction with one another.

55. While planning *The Bostonians* James recorded in his notebook, "There must be a type of newspaper man—the man whose ideal is the energetic reporter. I should like to *bafouer* the vulgarity and hideousness of this—the impudent invasion of privacy—the extinction of all conception of privacy, etc." *The Notebooks of Henry James,* p. 47.

56. For a fascinating reading see, Matei Calinescu, "Introducing Secrecy: Henry James's 'The Private Life,'" in *Rereading* (New Haven: Yale Univ. Press, 1993): 227–38.

57. Warren and Brandeis, "The Right to Privacy," 211.

58. See, for instance, Jean Fagan Yellin's remark: "Because James's young heroine Verena is essentially selfless, there is never any possibility that she will achieve autonomy." *Women & Sisters: The Antislavery Feminists in American Culture* (New Haven: Yale Univ. Press, 1989), p. 164.

59. Alfred Habegger, "The Disunity of *The Bostonians*," *Nineteenth-Century Fiction* 24 (1969): 193–209.

60. C. B. Macpherson, *The Political Theory of Possessive Individualism* (New York: Oxford Univ. Press, 1962). For a powerful feminist supplement to Macpherson's argument, see Carole Pateman, *The Sexual Contract* (Stanford: Stanford Univ. Press, 1988).

61. On the novel and Reconstruction, see Theodore C. Miller, "The Muddled Politics of *The Bostonians*," *Georgia Review* 26 (1972): 336–46; Barry Meinikoff, "A House Divided: A New Reading of *The Bostonians*," *CLA Journal* 20 (1977): 459–74; and Kenneth W. Warren, *Black and White Strangers* (Chicago: Univ. of Chicago Press, 1993), pp. 93–101.

Chapter 4. In the Hands of *The Silent Partner* and Spiritual Regulation in *The Bread-Winners*

1. Works that will be cited parenthetically within the text are: John Hay, *The Bread-Winners: A Social Study* (New York: Harper & Brothers, 1883), designated as BW; Henry James, *The Bostonians: A Novel* (New York: Macmillan and Co., 1886), designated as B; and Elizabeth Stuart Phelps, *The Silent Partner: A Novel,* afterward by Mari Jo Buhle and Florence Howe (Old Westbury, N.Y.: The Feminist Press, 1983), designated as SP.

2. Vernon Louis Parrington, *Main Currents in American Thought: The Beginnings of Critical Realism in America,* vol. 3 (New York: Harcourt and Brace, 1930), p. 173.

3. Susan K. Harris, *Nineteenth-Century American Women's Novels* (New York: Cambridge Univ. Press, 1990), p. 193. An unsigned 1871 review claimed that "if one-half of [Phelps's] picture is accepted as true," it provides a "terribly needed lesson" to New England mill-owners and Pennsylvania mine-owners. *Harper's New Monthly Magazine* 43 (1871): 301.

4. Louis Hartz, *The Liberal Tradition in America* (New York: Harcourt Brace, 1955); Gordon S. Wood, *The Creation of the American Republic* (Chapel

Hill: Univ. of North Carolina Press, 1969); and J. G. A. Pocock, *The Machiavellian Moment* (Princeton: Princeton Univ. Press, 1975). See also chapter 2, n. 58.

5. Quoted in Paul C. Nagel, *This Sacred Trust* (New York: Oxford Univ. Press, 1971), pp. 292–93, 250.

6. Herbert Hovenkamp, "The Political Economy of Substantive Due Process," *Stanford Law Review* 40 (1988): 403–4.

7. Ann Braude, *Radical Spirits* (Boston: Beacon Press, 1989), p. 6.

8. Howard Kerr, *Mediums and Spirit-Rappers, and Roaring Radicals* (Urbana: Univ. of Illinois Press, 1972), p. 220.

9. C. B. Macpherson, *The Political Theory of Possessive Individualism* (New York: Oxford Univ. Press, 1962), pp. 219–20.

10. Sacvan Bercovitch has argued most persuasively about the power of liberal thought in the United States to sustain itself by deferring rather than resolving contradictions. See *The American Jeremiad* (Madison: Univ. of Wisconsin Press, 1978), and *The Office of "The Scarlet Letter"* (Baltimore: Johns Hopkins Univ. Press, 1991). Bercovitch, however, does not engage the debate between republicanism and liberalism. He more or less assumes the triumph of liberalism over republicanism during the age of Jackson. In *The Office* he refers to "the dynamics of cohesion in the movement from republican to Jacksonian America" (xv).

11. See Christopher Lasch, *The True and Only Heaven* (New York: W. W. Norton & Co., 1991).

12. Pocock, *Machiavellian Moment,* p. 461.

13. James Fenimore Cooper, *The Chainbearer; or The Littlepage Manuscripts,* vol. 1 (New York: Burgess, Stringer, 1845), pp. 171–72.

14. "Clarence Hay's Introduction to the 1916 Edition," in *The Bread-Winners,* ed. Charles Vandersee (New Haven: College & University Press, 1973), p. 64. Vandersee superbly places the novel in its historical and critical context.

15. Field's citation of Smith is from the famous *Slaughter-House Cases,* 83 U.S. (16 Wall) 36, at 110 (1873).

16. Editorial, *Philadelphia Record,* 15 July 1884. On this belief, see Daniel T. Rogers, *The Work Ethic in Industrial America, 1850–1920* (Chicago: Chicago Univ. Press, 1978), pp. 35–36.

17. William Dean Howells, *"The Bread-Winners," Selected Literary Criticism,* ed. Ulrich Halfmann, vol. 1 (Bloomington: Indiana Univ. Press, 1993), p. 334.

18. Howells, *"The Bread-Winners,"* p. 334.

19. Quoted by Louis E. Wolcher, "The Privilege of Idleness: A Case Study of Capitalism and the Common Law in Nineteenth Century America," *The Journal of American Legal History* 36 (1992): 237.

20. William Graham Sumner, *What Social Classes Owe to Each Other* (New York: Harper & Brothers, 1883), p. 15.

21. Pocock, *Machiavellian Moment,* p. 523.

22. Quoted in Nagel, *Sacred Trust,* p. 292.

23. Jean-Jacques Rousseau, *Politics and the Arts: Letter to M. D'Alembert on the Theatre,* trans. Allan Bloom (Ithaca: Cornell Univ. Press, 1960), pp. 79, 80–81. On Rousseau's letter, see Lionel Trilling, *Sincerity and Authenticity* (Cambridge: Harvard Univ. Press, 1975), and Philip Fisher, "Acting, Reading, Fortune's Wheel: *Sister Carrie* and the Life History of Objects" in *American Realism,* ed. Eric Sundquist, (Baltimore: Johns Hopkins Univ. Press, 1982), pp. 259–77.

24. John William Ward, *Andrew Jackson, Symbol for an Age* (New York: Oxford Univ. Press, 1962); Arthur M. Schlesinger Jr., *The Age of Jackson* (Boston: Little, Brown, 1945); and Marvin Meyers, *The Jacksonian Persuasion* (Stanford: Stanford Univ. Press, 1957).

25. Rousseau, *Politics,* p. 109.

26. Jean-Jacques Rousseau, *Emile or on Education,* trans. Allan Bloom, (New York: Basic Books, 1979), p. 408.

27. Rousseau explains that when women "seek for men's looks, they are already letting themselves be corrupted by them." *Politics,* p. 83.

28. William Dean Howells, quoted in Charles Vandersee, "Introduction," p. 29.

29. For James's response to Hay's novel, see George Monteiro, *Henry James and John Hay* (Providence: Brown Univ. Press, 1965), pp. 39–40. It is not clear whether James was one of a few, including Howells, who knew that Hay wrote the book. Monteiro does, however, point out that Hay was in London for the summer of 1882, with portions of the novel. There is evidence that Howells may have read them. James may have done so also, but there is no evidence that he did. What is clear is that he was working on *The Bostonians* when *The Bread-Winners* appeared to much applause.

30. Harris, *Women's Novels,* p. 196.

31. Harris, *Women's Novels,* p. 195.

32. For a positive judgment of the novel's aesthetic value and a discussion of its relation to the period's religious beliefs, see Paul A. Carter, *The Spiritual Crisis of the Gilded Age* (Dekalb: Northern Illinois Univ. Press, 1971), pp. 73–77.

33. Judith Fetterly, "'Checkmate': Elizabeth Stuart Phelps's *The Silent Partner,*" *Legacy* 3 (1986): 17–29. On the back cover of the Feminist Press paperback edition, Fetterly notes that Phelps raises the question: "How does one communicate in a world where language has been debased, even rendered meaningless, by the reliance of power on dishonesty?" Phelps's answer, I have argued, is that our messages can be truly translated only when we become agents through whom God, our silent partner, can speak.

By imposing upon Phelps late twentieth-century liberal views, Phillip Brian Harper also misreads the strike scene. "Thus, Perley's impulse to reform is developed through her growing sense of the relation between the condition of the mill workers and her own rather more comfortable existence, which she actually comes to use as an index of the wrongs suffered by the workers. The consciousness that she thus develops (though it seems to slip in a way that betrays the entrenchedness of her class conditioning during her effort to mollify the workers when they consider striking over a cut in wages) influences her to eschew marriage altogether and devote her life to personal efforts at reform within the mills, which she undertakes as a means to realize her rather naive utopian vision of social equality among the classes." "Fiction and Reform II," *The Columbia History of the American Novel,* ed. Emory Elliott (New York: Columbia Univ. Press, 1991), p. 227.

In contrast, Amy Schrager Lang offers a sophisticated discussion of class in the novel. Recalling how evocations of wage slavery entered the debate between labor and capital, she points out how the factory worker Sip is figured as dark, thus evoking the moral force of arguments against chattel slavery on behalf of labor reform. But she also recognizes that for Phelps, class divisions become as naturalized as racial ones. Concluding that for Phelps, "Class divisions are . . . irremediable except by supernatural intervention" (284), she argues that the narrator's position and eventually Perley's become that of the emerging middle class. It is important to add, however, that not all in the emerging middle class shared Phelps's supernatural faith. Determining the novel's point of view, that faith helps to account for differences between her fiction and works of realism. See "The Syntax of Class in Elizabeth Stuart Phelps's *The Silent Partner,*" in *Rethinking Class,* eds. Wai-Chee Dimock and Michael T. Gilmore (New York: Columbia Univ. Press, 1994), pp. 267–85.

34. Elizabeth Stuart Phelps, "Why Shall They Do It?" *Harper's Monthly* 35 (1867): 219. See Susan Albertine, "Breaking the Silent Partnership: Businesswomen in Popular Fiction," *American Literature* 62 (1990): 238–61.

35. Elizabeth Stuart Phelps, *The Gates Ajar* (Boston: James Osgood and Co., 1869).

36. Elizabeth Stuart Phelps, "Women's Views of Divorce," *The North American Review* 150 (1890): 128, 130, 131, 129.

37. Douglas C. Baynton, " 'A Silent Exile on This Earth': The Metaphorical Construction of Deafness in the Nineteenth Century," *American Quarterly* 44 (1992): 216–43.

38. Erich Auerbach, *Mimesis* (Princeton: Princeton Univ. Press, 1953). See especially the chapter "Fortunata," pp. 24–49.

39. Nancy Schnog, " 'The Comfort of My Fancying': Loss and Recuperation in *The Gates Ajar,*" *Arizona Quarterly* 49 (1993): 40–41.

40. John Stuart Mill, *On Liberty* (Arlington Heights, Ill.: Crofts Classics, 1947), pp. 63, 10, 63.

41. Laurence Holland, *The Expense of Vision* (Princeton: Princeton Univ. Press, 1964).

42. Albion W. Tourgée has a minister stop a strike in *Murvale Eastman: Christian Socialist* (New York: Fords, Howard, & Hulbert, 1890). A strike is also put down and social order restored in Thomas Bailey Aldrich, *The Stillwater Tragedy* (Boston: Houghton, Mifflin, and Co., 1880), and Paul Leicester Ford, *The Honorable Peter Stirling and What People Thought of Him* (New York: Henry Holt & Co., 1894). In Aldrich's work, an Italian immigrant, whose rhetoric is more powerful than his reason, causes the strike. When order is restored, he takes his family back to Italy where, according to the narrator, it is better off. In Ford's, Peter, who is loosely based on Grover Cleveland, leads the

militia against strikers with whom he has great personal sympathy. His action is Ford's way of justifying Cleveland's response to the Pullman workers' strike.

43. For translation and agency in Howells, see the brief discussion of *A Hazard of New Fortunes* in the final chapter.

Chapter 5. *The Rise of Silas Lapham* and the Hazards of Realistic Development

1. William Dean Howells, *The Rise of Silas Lapham* (Bloomington: Indiana Univ. Press, 1971), p. 163. Future references to this edition will be cited parenthetically and designated as SL. Other texts by Howells cited parenthetically are *The Minister's Charge; or The Apprenticeship of Lemuel Barker* (Bloomington: Indiana Univ. Press, 1978), designated as MC; and *A Hazard of New Fortunes* (Bloomington: Indiana Univ. Press, 1976), designated as HNF.

2. Thomas G. Tanselle, "The Architecture of *The Rise of Silas Lapham*," *American Literature* 27 (1966): 434, and Wai-chee Dimock, "The Economy of Pain: The Case of Howells," *Raritan* 9 (1990): 113.

3. Dimock, "Economy," 112–13.

4. See Dennis E. Curtis and Judith Resnick, "Images of Justice," *Yale Law Journal* 96 (1987): 1727–72.

5. Thomas Galt Peyser, "Those Other Selves: Consciousness in the 1890 Publications of Howells and the James Brothers," *American Literary Realism* 25 (1992): 25.

6. Everett Carter, *Howells in the Age of Realism* (Philadelphia: Lippincott, 1954), p. 154. Carter mistakenly concludes of *Silas Lapham* that "the moral scheme envisioned by this work was ill-served by the simplicity of the book's structure" (164).

7. Donald Pizer, "The Ethical Unity of *The Rise of Silas Lapham*," *American Literature* 32 (1960): 322–27.

8. Donald E. Pease, introduction to *New Essays on "The Rise of Silas Lapham,*" ed. Donald E. Pease (New York: Cambridge Univ. Press, 1991), p. 20.

9. Pease, *New Essays*, p. 20.

10. On residual, dominant, and emergent, see Raymond Williams, *Marxism and Literature* (New York: Oxford Univ. Press, 1977). Examples of the use of uneven development are Mary Poovey, *Uneven Developments: The Ideological Work of Gender in Mid-Victorian England* (Chicago: Univ. of Chicago Press, 1988) and Wai-Chee Dimock, "Uneven Development: American Realism and Cultural History," *REAL* 11 (1995): 103–17.

11. Dominick LaCapra, *Emile Durkheim* (Ithaca: Cornell Univ. Press, 1972), p. 108.

12. Marxism is not the only form of economic determinism. Charles Beard had his own in *An Economic Interpretation of the Constitution of the United States* (New York: Macmillan, 1913), and much of the new historicist attention to the logic of the market provides another version.

13. For a use of the notion of relative autonomy prior to Althusser, see Jean-Paul Sartre, *Search for a Method,* trans. Hazel E. Barnes (New York: Vintage Press, 1968), pp. 48, 66, 111.

14. On Lukàcs's and temporality, see Paul de Man, "Georg Lukacs's *Theory of the Novel*," in *Blindness and Insight* (New York: Oxford Univ. Press, 1971), pp. 51–59. For "police academy" critics, see chapter 2, p. 14.

15. On Heidegger's *Verwindung* see Gianni Vattimo, *The End of Modernity*, trans. Jon R. Snyder (Cambridge: Polity Press, 1988). Vattimo uses *Verwindung* to characterize a postmodern era, one that is "post-historical." My use of *Verwindung* to describe an effect of Howells's novels suggests that *Verwindung* need not indicate an end to modernity. Indeed, we might need to rethink what we mean by modernity. Not all notions of modernity need be teleological. See, for instance, Hans Blumenberg, *The Legitimacy of the Modern Age,* trans. Robert Wallace (Cambridge: MIT Press, 1983). According to my reading, Howells's realism is intricately linked to a modern sense of temporality as described by both Blumenberg and Koselleck. (See n. 36.) This modern sense of temporality should not be confused with literary "modernism."

16. Tanselle, "Architecture," 482–83.

17. Dimock, "Economy," 110, 111, 111, 111, 119.

18. Dimock, "Economy," 109.

19. Amy Stanley, "Conjugal Bonds and Wage Labor: Rights of Contract in the Age of Emancipation," *The Journal of American History* 75 (1988): 471–500.

20. For an 1884 discussion, see "A Husband's Right to His Wife's Services," *The American Law Journal* 1 (1884): 422–23.

21. Elizabeth Cady Stanton, "The Need for Liberal Divorce Laws," *North American Review* 139 (1884): 220–42. For critical and historical studies, see James Harwood Barnett, *Divorce and the American Divorce Novel, 1858–1937* (Philadelphia: Univ. of Pennsylvania Press, 1939); Elaine Tyler May, *Great Expectations: Marriage and Divorce in Post-Victorian America* (Chicago: Chicago Univ. Press, 1980); and George R. Uba, "Status and Contract: The Divorce Dispute of the 'Eighties and Howells' *A Modern Instance*," *Colby Library Quarterly* 19 (1983): 78–89.

22. For a clarification of the legal status of marriage at the time of *Silas Lapham,* see Joel Bishop, *Commentaries on the Law of Marriage and Divorce and Evidence, Practice, Pleading, and Forms,* 6th ed., vol. 2 (Boston: Little, Brown, 1881) and M. S. Robinson, *Marriage and Divorce* (Chicago: M. S. Robinson, 1884). The laws of marriage and divorce vary from state to state.

23. Sir Henry Sumner Maine, *Ancient Law: Its Connection with the Early History of Society and Its Relation to Modern Ideas,* 10th ed. (1861; reprint, New York: Dorset, 1986), p. 104.

24. William Graham Sumner, *What Social Classes Owe to Each Other* (New York: Harper & Brother, 1883), pp. 17, 14, 18.

25. Silas's decision to cut off support for Zerrilla's husband might seem to be dictated by the logic of an economy of pain, since once again two benefit while one is left out. But pain has little to do with Silas's decision. Zerrilla's mother will continue to suffer because of her alcoholism as much as Zerrilla's husband continues to suffer because of his. Silas draws the limit in this case in terms of immediate blood relations to Jim.

26. For a recent account that suffers from arguing that realism is a naive attempt to imitate life, see Michael Davitt Bell, *The Problem of American Realism* (Chicago: Univ. of Chicago Press, 1993).

27. Leo Bersani, *A Future for Astyanax* (Boston: Little, Brown, 1976), and "The Subject of Power," *Diacritics* (1977): 2–21.

28. Walter Benn Michaels, *The Gold Standard and the Logic of Naturalism* (Berkeley: Univ. of California Press, 1987), p. 42.

29. Gyorgy Lukàcs, "Narrate or Describe?" in *Writer and Critic and Other Essays* (London: Merlin Press, 1970), pp. 110–48.

30. Michaels, *Gold Standard*, p. 46.

31. Corey's position is even more conservative. The house discussed is Mrs. Corey's. "*My* ancestral halls," he insists, "are in Salem, and I'm told you couldn't drive a nail into their timbers" (SL 192). Salem declined as Boston took away its commerce.

32. Michaels, *Gold Standard*, p. 36.

33. William Dean Howells, "Novel-Writing and Novel-Reading," *Selected Literary Criticism,* Ronald Gottesman, vol. 3 (Bloomington: Indiana Univ. Press, 1993), p. 222.

34. The debate over the value of sentimental fiction is too often seen as an issue of gender. But sentimentalism was not confined to women nor women to sentimentalism. One author of the titles I cite is male; one is female. E. P. Roe, *Barriers Burned Away* (New York: Dodd, Mead & Co., 1872) and Elizabeth Stuart Phelps, *Gates Ajar* (Boston: James Osgood, 1869).

35. Unlike Michaels, I would not classify *Sister Carrie* as sentimental. It is, however, a work of naturalism in which agency is more mechanical than in *Silas Lapham*.

36. For Howells's complication of people's noble efforts to take principled stands, see the brief discussion of *A Hazard of New Fortunes* in the final chapter.

37. Reinhart Koselleck, *Futures Past,* trans. Keith Tribe (Cambridge: MIT Press, 1985).

38. William Dean Howells, "Novel-Writing and Novel-Reading," p. 223.

39. Howells seems to conflate the novel and the sermon when he writes, "Let all the hidden things be brought into the sun, and let every day be the day of judgment. If the sermon cannot any longer serve this end, let the novel do it." But this statement does not urge the novelist to preach to his audience. In the same essay Howells warns that he should "not aim to instruct." His point is that judgment will follow if the novelist is not afraid to treat all sorts of subject matter, even the repressed ones of a society. If the novel takes over a function of the sermon, it accomplishes it in a different manner. William Dean Howells, "Novel-Writing and Novel-Reading," pp. 228, 221.

40. Nicholas St. John Green, "Proximate and Remote Cause," *American Law Review* 4 (1870): 211. See Morton J. Horwitz, "The Doctrine of Objective Causation," in *The Politics of Law,* ed. David Kairys (New York: Pantheon Books, 1982), pp. 201–13.

41. Thomas L. Haskell, "Capitalism and the Origins of Humanitarian Sensibility," Parts 1 and 2, in *The Antislavery Debate,* ed. Thomas Bender (Berke-

ley: Univ. of California Press, 1992), pp. 107–60. For literary critics' use of Haskell, see Dimock, "Economy," and Clare Virginia Eby, "*The Octopus:* Big Business as Art," *American Literary Realism* 26 (1994): 33–51. For a criticism of the doctrine of human sympathy in the law, see "Sympathy as a Legal Structure," *Harvard Law Review* 105 (1992): 1961–80.

42. Morton G. White, *Social Thought in America: The Revolt Against Formalism* (New York: Oxford, 1949).

43. Green, "Proximate and Remote Cause," 211. The rejection of metaphor by many legal realists suggests a way to distinguish them from adherents of the critical legal studies movement. Those in critical legal studies are generally more attuned to the importance of metaphor, and therefore rhetoric, in the law. For instance, their reliance on literary theory to study the law evokes the displeasure of some members of the law and society movement, whose dependence on the social sciences remains more indebted to legal realism. At the same time, some "in" critical legal studies, according to my distinction, would be more accurately labeled realists.

44. For Michaels to argue that he does, undercuts his claim that Howells's doctrine of realism as life offers no models. If Howells endorses agrarian values, he clearly offers them as a model for how to act. Indeed, Michaels associates Howells with the "genteel/progressive view" that "important works of art" are capable of "transcending or opposing the market" because he supposedly partakes of such moralism (Michaels, *Gold Standard* , p. 14, n. 16).

45. Andrew Delbanco, "Howells and the Suppression of Knowledge," *The Southern Review* 19 (1983): 771.

46. Charles W. Eliot, *The Conflict between Individualism and Collectivism in a Democracy* (Charlottesville: Barbour-Page Foundation, 1910), p. 15.

47. Pease, *New Essays,* p. 21.

48. Howells is not, in other words, one of those who, as Howard Horwitz argues, saw in the trust the possibility for a transcendental, corporate structure of agency. Instead, for him corporations were constituted by discrete individuals bound together by contractual relations. Howard Horwitz, "The Standard Oil Trust as Emersonian Hero," *Raritan* 6 (1987): 97–119.

49. G. W. F. Hegel, *Lectures on the Philosophy of History,* tr. J. S. Bree (New York: Colonial Press, 1900) pp. 85–88.

50. Numerous works at the end of the century conclude with characters thinking about or participating in opening foreign markets. Tourgée's protagonist in *A Fool's Errand* goes to South America. Henry Adams's Virginia lawyer in *Democracy* goes to Latin America. Robert, Edna's "lover" in Chopin's *The Awakening,* goes to Mexico. Farnham in Hay's *The Bread-Winners* contemplates going to Japan because "at the present rate of progress there is not more than a year's purchase of bric-a-brac left in the empire. I must hurry to get my share." John Hay, *The Bread-Winners* (New York: Harper & Brothers, 1883), p. 314.

51. David Crocker, "Functioning and Capability: The Foundations of Sen's and Nussbaum's Developmental Ethic," *Political Theory* 20 (1992): 584–612.

52. Joel Porte sees Howells's "wobbling point of view . . . caused presumably by Howells' own social anxieties" as "one of his great formal weaknesses

as a novelist." "Manners, Morals, and Mince Pie: Howells' America Revisited," *Prospects* 10 (1987): 447. I see his point of view as being calculated to create effects on his readers that cannot be accounted for totally by irony, as Arlene Young attempts to do in "The Triumph of Irony in *The Rise of Silas Lapham*," *Studies in American Fiction* 20 (1992): 45–55. Janet Holmgren McKay details Howells's point of view in relation to James and Twain in *Narration and Discourse in American Realistic Fiction* (Philadelphia: Univ. of Pennsylvania Press, 1982).

53. Howells warns that good intentions do not necessarily control outcomes. As Sewell puts it, "We must beware of the refined selfishness which shrinks from righteous self-assertion because it is painful" (MC 324).

54. Fritz Oehlschager, "An Ethic of Responsibility in *The Rise of Silas Lapham*," *American Literary Realism, 1870–1910* 23 (1991): 20–34, and Kermit Vanderbilt, introduction to *The Rise of Silas Lapham*, by William Dean Howells (New York: Penguin, 1986), pp. vii–xxviii. Vanderbilt is especially well-tuned to the complications that Howells presents to anyone seeking to make certain moral judgments about his characters.

Chapter 6. Charles W. Chesnutt: Race and the Re-negotiation of the Federal Contract

1. Texts by Charles W. Chesnutt cited parenthetically within the chapter are: *The House Behind the Cedars* (Boston: Houghton Mifflin & Co., 1900), designated as HBC; *The Marrow of Tradition* (Boston: Houghton Mifflin & Co., 1901), designated as MT; and *The Colonel's Dream* (New York: Doubleday, Page & Co., 1905), designated as CD. Those by William Dean Howells are: *The Shadow of a Dream* and *An Imperative Duty*, introduction by Martha Banta (Bloomington: Indiana Univ. Press, 1970), designated as ID; and *The Rise of Silas Lapham* (Bloomington: Indiana Univ. Press, 1971), designated as SL. Those by Albion W. Tourgée are: *An Appeal to Caesar* (New York: Fords, Howard, & Hulbert, 1884), designated as ATC; *The Invisible Empire*, introduction by Otto H. Olsen (Baton Rouge: Louisiana State Univ. Press, 1989), designated as IE; and *With Gauge & Swallow, Attorneys* (Philadelphia: J. B. Lippincott, 1890), designated as GS.

2. William Dean Howells, "A Psychological Counter-Current in Recent Fiction," *North American Review* 172 (1901): 873.

3. Contemporary African-American responses to Howells's treatment of race varied. W. E. B. Du Bois paid tribute to Howells in the Boston *Transcript*, 24 February 1912, pt. III, p. 2. Julia Cooper, a Washington, D.C., high school teacher, charged that "he had no business to attempt a subject of which he knew so little, or for which he cared so little." *A Voice from the South* (1892), quoted in David Shi, *Facing Facts* (New York: Oxford Univ. Press, 1994), p. 201.

4. William L. Andrews, *The Literary Career of Charles W. Chesnutt* (Baton Rouge: Louisiana State Univ. Press, 1980), pp. 163, 164, 166. Implying that a longer study is in the works, Richard H. Brodhead devotes a chapter to Chesnutt in *Cultures of Letters*, (Chicago: Univ. of Chicago Press, 1993), pp.

177–210. Eric J. Sundquist offers a superb analysis of Chesnutt in "Charles Chesnutt's Cakewalk," *To Wake the Nations* (Cambridge, Mass.: Belknap Press, 1993), pp. 271–454. Sundquist concentrates mostly on the short stories and *The Marrow of Tradition,* whereas I focus on *The House Behind the Cedars* and the neglected *The Colonel's Dream.* I hope that my synchronic examination of Chesnutt in relation to contemporaries treating issues other than race complements Sundquists's diachronic examination of him within a tradition of writers dealing with race.

5. Quoted in Harriet Beecher Stowe, *A Key to Uncle Tom's Cabin* (Boston: John P. Jewett, 1853), p. 78. For Stowe's use of the case, see my *Cross-examinations of Law and Literature* (New York: Cambridge Univ. Press, 1987), pp. 8, 117–19, 133–34. James Boyd White includes the decision in *The Legal Imagination* (Boston: Little, Brown, 1973), pp. 451–54.

6. Howells, "A Psychological Counter-Current," 882.

7. George W. Cable, "The Freedman's Case in Equity," *The Century Magazine* 29 (1885): 409–18.

8. Charles W. Chesnutt, "The Disfranchisement of the Negro," in *The Negro Problem* (New York: James Pott & Co., 1903), p. 124.

Sterling Brown concludes of Chesnutt, "Answering propaganda with propaganda, he might be expected to have certain faults. . . . He was melodramatic in plotting, but evidence of a skilled master's hand can still be found. He knew a great deal, and all things considered, he told it well." Of Howells's *An Imperative Duty,* he remarks, "The novel is sympathetic, but there were graver, less romantic problems of Negro life that a novelist of Howells' scope and ability might have presented." *The Negro in American Fiction* (Washington, D.C.: Associates in Negro Folk Education, 1937), pp. 76, 82.

9. William L. Andrews, foreword to *The House Behind the Cedars* (Athens: Univ. of Georgia Press, 1988), pp. vii–xxii.

10. Chesnutt possibly alludes to *Plessy v. Ferguson,* which declared that in deciding whether a law was a reasonable regulation, a legislature "is at liberty to act with reference to established usages, customs and traditions of the people." *Plessy v. Ferguson* 163 U.S. 537, 550 (1896). See also n. 48 of this chapter.

11. By emphasizing how John's and Rena's black descent is not immediately visible, Chesnutt counters the stereotypical view expressed by his racist Dr. Green that "God has marked [the negro] with the badge of servitude" (HBC 136). But Chesnutt's point of view on the stamp of descent is complicated. As a way of pointing out the high hereditary quality of some people of color, he insists that John's features were of "the high-bred, clean-cut order that marks the patrician type the world over" (HBC 167).

12. Chesnutt anticipates Jürgen Habermas's argument for the right to "cultural membership": the "right to develop and maintain" one's identity in the life and traditions into which one was born without a loss of status in civil society. Habermas also argues for the right to break from such membership, if one finds it constraining. "Multiculturalism and the Liberal State," *Stanford Law Review* 47 (1995): 850.

13. Howells's North-South marriage plot in *A Hazard* is striking, given

Basil March's questioning of the "demand for matrimony" that "comes from our novel-reading." *A Hazard of New Fortunes* (introduction by Everett Carter, Bloomington: Indiana Univ. Press, 1976), p. 479.

14. Quoted in Paul M. Gaston, *The New South Creed* (New York: Alfred A. Knopf, 1970), p. 85.

15. Thomas Bailey Aldrich, *The Poems of Thomas Bailey Aldrich* (Houghton, Mifflin and Co., 1885), pp. 210–11.

16. Henry W. Grady, "The New South," in *The Life of Henry W. Grady, Including His Writing and Speeches*, ed. Joel Chandler Harris, (1890; reprint, New York: Haskell House Publishers, 1972), p. 92. In *The Colonel's Dream* Grady had lectured at Clarendon's opera house, while Booker T. Washington had been refused (CD 197).

17. Grady, "The New South," p. 88. For an excellent examination of Grady's use of metaphors of currents in his description of racial blood and its implications for Twain's *Huckleberry Finn*, see Steve Mailloux, *Rhetorical Power* (Ithaca: Cornell Univ. Press, 1989), 65–69.

18. Kenneth W. Warren offers a reading of James's 1882 story "The Point of View" to document James's anxieties about issues of race. Critical of *The Bostonians* as well, he nonetheless admits that it "proved to be a devastatingly accurate reading of the period." *Black and White Strangers* (Chicago: Chicago Univ. Press, 1993), p. 93. For more on Warren, see the next chapter, especially n. 49.

19. On magazine stories about the Civil War and the figurative marriage between North and South, see Kathleen Diffley, *Where My Heart Is Turning Ever: Civil War Stories and Constitutional Reform, 1861–1876* (Athens: Univ. of Georgia Press, 1992). Novels that marry Southerners and Northerners include Henry Adams's *Democracy*, Owen Wister's *The Virginian*, and Thomas Dixon's *The Clansman*.

20. John David Smith, *An Old Creed for the New South: Proslavery Ideology and Historiography, 1865–1918* (Westport, Conn.: Greenwood Press, 1985). On how even Frederick Jackson Turner's "frontier thesis" participates in this reinterpretation, see my "Turner's 'Frontier Thesis' as a Narrative of Reconstruction," in *Centuries' Ends, Narrative Means*, ed. Robert Newman (Stanford: Stanford Univ. Press, 1996).

21. Quoted in Peter Novick, *That Noble Dream* (New York: Cambridge Univ. Press, 1988), p. 76.

22. Chesnutt's gender bias is also apparent in *The Colonel's Dream* when we compare Chesnutt's portrayal of a silent female partner in a corporation with that of Elizabeth Stuart Phelps's novel. Nonetheless, it is worth noting that in *A Japanese Nightingale*, written by a woman (Ondo Watana), the marriage of an American to a Euro-Asian woman cements the sense of brotherhood between the woman's husband and her brother. Howells favorably reviewed *A Japanese Nightingale* in the same article in which he reviewed Chesnutt. See "A Psychological Counter-Current in Recent Fiction." On Watana, which was the pen name of Winnifred Eaton, the daughter of a Chinese mother and an English father and the sister of Edith Maud Eaton (who wrote under the name Sui Sin

Far), see Amy Ling, *Between Worlds: Women Writers of Chinese Ancestry* (New York: Pergamon Press, 1990). On Chesnutt's support of female suffrage, see "Women's Rights," *Crisis* 10 (1915): 182–83.

23. *The Journals of Charles W. Chesnutt,* ed. Richard H. Brodhead, (Durham: Duke Univ. Press, 1993), pp. 139–40.

24. On such contracts, see Leon F. Litwack, *Been in the Storm So Long* (New York: Knopf, 1979), pp. 408–25.

25. Quoted in Benno C. Schmidt Jr., "Principle and Prejudice: The Supreme Court and Race in the Progressive Era. Part 2: *The Peonage Cases,*" *Columbia Law Review* 82 (1982): 649. I am deeply indebted to Schmidt's analysis, and I borrow heavily from it. Other works to consult on the peonage question are David A. Novak, *The Wheel of Servitude* (Lexington: Univ. of Kentucky Press, 1978); Theodore Wilson, *The Black Codes of the South* (University: Univ. of Alabama Press, 1965); William Cohen, "Negro Involuntary Servitude in the South, 1865–1940: A Preliminary Analysis," *Journal of Southern History* 42 (1976): 31–60, and Peter Daniel, *The Shadow of Slavery* (Urbana: Univ. of Illinois Press, 1972). See also Tourgée's discussion (IE 56–57).

26. Quoted in Schmidt, "Principle and Prejudice," 651.

27. See Walter Benn Michaels's discussion of contractual slavery in "The Phenomenology of Contract," *The Gold Standard and the Logic of Naturalism* (Berkeley: Univ. of California Press, 1987), pp. 113–36.

28. John Stuart Mill, *On Liberty* (Arlington Heights, Ill.: Crofts Classics, 1947), p. 104.

29. On the Supreme Court's laissez-faire paternalism, see Aviam Soifer, "The Paradox of Paternalism and Laissez-Faire Constitutionalism: United States Supreme Court, 1888–1921," *Law and History Review* 5 (1987): 249–79, and "Status, Contract, and Promises Unkept," *Yale Law Journal* 96 (1987): 1916–59. The paternalism of alternatives to convict leasing is shown by the rise of the chain gang. Considered a progressive advance over a system that both artificially lowered the wages of "free" laborers and abdicated the state's responsibility to care for prisoners, chain gangs put prison labor to work for the public welfare. See Alex Lichtenstein, "Good Roads and Chain Gangs in the Progressive South: 'The Negro Convict Is a Slave,'" *The Journal of Southern History* 59 (1993): 85–110. The racial politics of Progressivism in the South complicates Ernestine Williams Pickens's efforts to link Chesnutt with Progressivism. See *Charles W. Chesnutt and the Progressive Movement* (New York: Pace Univ. Press, 1994).

30. Quoted in Schmidt, "Principle and Prejudice," 709. Under slavery, courts had to decide whether a contract for the sale of a slave should be specifically enforced. Some ruled that it could. Others argued that the situation was no different from the sale of other chattels, *unless* "long family service, early association, or the like, had made the slave of particular value to one seeking specific performance." "Specific Performance of Contracts for the Sale of Goods and Chattels," *The American Law Journal* 2 (1885): 272.

31. *Hodges v. United States,* 203 U.S. 1 (1906).

32. *Bailey v. Alabama,* 219 U.S. 219, 231 (1911). Justice Holmes, along with Justice Lurton, dissented in *Bailey,* but not *Reynolds.* As Schmidt points

out, Holmes's dissent seems to contradict some of his views on contract in other writings. At the same time, there are many points of consistency. One relevant to my concerns is that, as in his comments on contract in "The Path of the Law," Holmes continues to assume legalistic "thin description" in contract law. He completely agrees with the majority that the race of those involved is irrelevant, although, as Schmidt points out, in *Reynolds* his language betrays a condescending attitude toward the black laborers involved. See chapter 2, n. 58.

33. There is clear evidence that those attacking Southern practices were concerned about its consequences for whites. Novak, *Wheel of Servitude,* suggests that the Roosevelt administration was sparked to action because of abuses to white immigrants (47).

34. Chesnutt reinforces the journalistic campaign against peonage and convict leasing. See Ray Stannard Baker, *Following the Color Line* (New York: Harper and Row, 1964), most of which appeared in the *American Magazine* April 1907–September 1908, and W. E. B. Du Bois, "The Spawn of Slavery: The Convict Lease System in the South," *The Missionary Review of the World* 14 (1901): 737–45. In addition, 1907 saw the reprint of an 1885 essay by Cable on the convict-lease system, together with "The Freedman's Case in Equity."

35. See Mark Tushnet, *The American Law of Slavery, 1810–1860* (Princeton: Princeton Univ. Press, 1981).

36. "The Strike Averted," in *The Short Fiction of Charles W. Chesnutt,* ed. Sylvia Lyons Render (Washington, D.C.: Howard Univ. Press, 1981), pp. 386, 383, 385.

37. Henry C. Carey, *Principles of Political Economy* (Philadelphia: Carey, Lea & Blanchard, 1837), 40.

38. Grady, "In Plain Black and White" in *The Century Magazine* 29 (1884–1885): 917.

39. Grady, "Black and White," 916.

40. Raymond Williams, *Marxism and Literature* (New York: Oxford Univ. Press, 1977), pp. 128–35.

41. Howells, "A Psychological Counter-Current," 882.

42. John Hay, "The Foster Brothers," *Harper's Monthly Magazine* 39 (1869): 535–66. Hay's close friend Clarence King was known to be attracted to nonwhite women. Whether this fact accounts for Clarence Brydges's first name is impossible to know.

43. Quoted by Paul C. Nagel, *This Sacred Trust* (New York: Oxford Univ. Press, 1971), p. 293.

44. "The Dumb Witness" in *The Conjure Woman and Other Conjure Tales,* ed. Richard H. Brodhead (Durham: Duke Univ. Press), pp. 158–71. Eric Sundquist claims that the version in *The Colonel's Dream* "diluted" the story's import (*To Wake,* p. 390). I offer a different reading.

45. "The Courts and the Negro," unpublished speech in the Fisk University archives. In "The Disfranchisement of the Negro" (1903), Chesnutt discusses Giles's appeal. Susan L. Blake argues that Chesnutt's novel dramatizes the thesis of that essay and thus points to the failure of Booker T. Washington's program for economic development. "A Better Mousetrap: Washington's Program and *The Colonel's Dream,*" *CLA Journal* 23 (1979): 49–50.

46. *Giles V. Harris,* 189 U.S. 475 (1903).

47. Rufus Choate, "The Importance of Illustrating New-England History by a Series of Romances Like the Waverley Novels," in *The Works of Rufus Choate with a Memoir of His Life,* ed. Samuel Gilman Brown, vol. 1 (Boston: Little, Brown, 1862), pp. 320, 343.

48. Chesnutt's response to *Plessy* is even more obvious in his portrayal of a Jim Crow car in *The Marrow of Tradition.* For an allusion to the case in *The House Behind the Cedars,* see n. 10 of this chapter. The role of the railroad in *A Colonel's Dream* is further complicated when the colonel's son and his servant, Peter, die as the result of a railroad accident. In a trial a jury decides that "there was no suggestion of blame attaching to any one; it had been an accident, pure and simple, which ordinary and reasonable prudence could not have foreseen" (CD 259).

49. Linguistic influence also flows in both directions. As the narrator notes, "the current Southern speech" was marked by "a touch" of black accent. "The corruption of the white people's speech was one element—only one—of the negro's unconscious revenge for his own debasement" (HBC 9).

50. Chesnutt's essay "What Is a White Man?" New York *Independent,* 30 May 1889, pp. 5–6, explicitly raises questions about the arbitrariness of defining racial purity. One of the most interesting metaphors at the time for the mixture of colors making up the human race comes in Helen Hunt Jackson's novel about a marriage between a Mexican and an Indian: *Ramona.* Late in the book the unsentimental Aunt Ri weaves a rag carpet for the Indian agent's wife. "It was of her favorite pattern, the 'hit or miss' pattern, as she called it: no set stripes or regular alternation of colors, but ball after ball of indiscriminately mixed tints, woven back and forth, on a warp of a single color. The constant variety in it, the unexpectedly harmonious blending of the colors, gave her delight, and afforded her a subject, too, of not unphilosophical reflection." *Ramona* (Boston: Roberts Brothers, 1884), pp. 472–73.

Chapter 7. Twain, Tourgée, and the Logic of "Separate but Equal"

1. Charles A. Lofgren, *The Plessy Case* (New York: Oxford Univ. Press, 1987), p. 41. My account of the Plessy case relies on Lofgren, Otto H. Olsen, *Carpetbagger's Crusade: The Life of Albion Winegar Tourgée* (Baltimore: Johns Hopkins Univ. Press, 1965); *The Thin Disguise,* ed. Otto H. Olsen, (New York: Humanities Press, 1967); and Keith Weldon Medley, "The Sad Story of How 'Separate but Equal' Was Born," *Smithsonian Magazine* 24 (1994): 105–17.

2. "A Grave Responsibility," *The Century Magazine* 29 (1884–1885): 462.

3. George Washington Cable, "The Freedman's Case in Equity," *The Century Magazine* 29 (1885): 418.

4. Henry W. Grady, "In Plain Black and White," *The Century Magazine* 29 (1885): 909–17.

5. Booker T. Washington, *Up from Slavery,* (New York: Doubleday Page & Co., 1901), pp. 219–20. The metaphor may have been inspired by former

President Rutherford B. Hayes in a May 20, 1880, speech at Hampton Institute, where Washington was teaching. Washington also uses the metaphor in an April 30, 1885, letter to the Montgomery *Advertiser* asking for equal railroad accommodations for equal pay.

6. *Plessy v. Ferguson,* 163 U.S. 537, 543 (1896). Future references to this decision will be included parenthetically in the text and designated as P. Other works referred to parenthetically include those by Samuel Langhorne Clemens: *A Connecticut Yankee in King Arthur's Court,* ed. Bernard L. Stein and Henry Nash Smith (Berkeley: Univ. of California Press, 1979), designated as CY; *The Love Letters of Mark Twain,* ed. Dixon Wector (New York: Harper, 1942), designated as LL; and *"Pudd'nhead Wilson" and "Those Extraordinary Twins,"* ed. Sidney E. Berger (New York: Norton, 1980), designated as PW. The one book by William Dean Howells is: *Their Wedding Journey,* ed. John K. Reeves (Bloomington: Indiana Univ. Press, 1968), designated as WJ. Works by Albion Winegar Tourgée include: *Murvale Eastman, Christian Socialist* (New York: Fords, Howard, and Hulbert, 1890), designated as ME; *Pactolus Prime* (New York: Cassell and Co., 1890), designated as PP; *A Royal Gentleman and Zouri's Christmas* (New York: Fords, Howard, and Hulbert, 1881), designated as RG; and *With Gauge and Swallow, Attorneys* (Philadelphia: J. B. Lippincott, 1889), designated as GS.

7. On the *Roberts* case, see *Jim Crow in Boston,* eds. Leonard W. Levy and Douglas L. Jones, (New York: DaCapo Press, 1974). On connections with Melville, see Brook Thomas, *Cross-examinations of Law and Literature,* (New York: Cambridge Univ. Press, 1987).

8. Brown's precedent was *Yick Wo v. Hopkins,* 118 U.S. 356 (1886), which concerned the discrimination against Chinese in San Francisco. The NAACP eventually used the logic of *Yick Wo* as part of its strategy to fight the *Plessy* decision.

9. There were some exceptions that revealed the intention of the law. For instance, nurses of children of the opposite race were exempted. There were not many white nurses of black children.

10. Introducing Olsen's *Carpetbagger's Crusade,* C. Vann Woodward makes a rare error when he attributes the dissent to Holmes (xiii).

11. W. E. B. Du Bois, "The Strivings of the Negro People," *The Atlantic Monthly* 80 (1897): 195.

12. For an excellent analysis of *Pudd'nhead Wilson* and the *Plessy* case, see Eric J. Sundquist, "Mark Twain and Homer Plessy," in *To Wake the Nations* (Cambridge, Mass.: Belknap Univ. Press, 1993), pp. 225–70.

13. Sterling Brown, *The Negro in American Fiction,* (Washington, D.C.: Associates in Negro Folk Education, 1937), p. 74.

14. Theodore L. Gross, *Albion Winegar Tourgée,* (New York: Twayne, 1963), p. 133.

15. Sterling Brown, *Negro in American Fiction,* p. 75. Brown feels that *Pudd'nhead* "falls a great way" from *Huckleberry Finn,* p. 68.

16. Helen M. Chesnutt, *Charles Waddell Chesnutt,* (Chapel Hill: Univ. of North Carolina Press, 1952). pp. 58–59.

17. Albion Winegar Tourgée, "The South as a Field for Fiction," *The Forum* 6 (1888): 406, 406, 411, 411.

18. Martha Banta, introduction to *The Shadow of a Dream and An Imperative Duty,* by William Dean Howells (Bloomington: Indiana Univ. Press, 1970), p. v.

19. Lee Clark Mitchell, "'De Nigger in You': Race or Training in *Pudd'nhead Wilson,*" *Nineteenth-Century Literature* 42 (1987): 310. For an example of recent essays concerned with this problem, see Susan Gillman and Forest G. Robinson, eds., *Mark Twain's "Pudd'nhead Wilson"* (Durham: Duke Univ. Press, 1990).

20. Evan Carton, "*Pudd'nhead Wilson* and the Fiction of Law and Custom," in *American Literary Realism,* ed. Eric Sundquist, (Baltimore: Johns Hopkins Univ. Press, 1982), p. 89.

21. Quoted in Olsen, *The Thin Disguise,* p. 83.

22. Earl F. Briden, "Idiots First, Then Juries: Legal Metaphors in Mark Twain's *Pudd'nhead Wilson,*" *Texas Studies in Literature and Language* 20 (1978): 169–80.

23. John S. Haller Jr., *Outcasts from Evolution* (Urbana: Univ. of Illinois Press, 1971).

24. Quoted in Lofgren, *Plessy,* pp. 105, 106.

25. Quoted in Lofgren, *Plessy,* p. 106.

26. Tourgée hoped that his book would affect the 1884 election, and he blamed mugwump support of Cleveland for undermining his educational program.

27. Mark D. Coburn, "'Training Is Everything': Communal Opinion and the Individual in *Pudd'nhead Wilson,*" *Modern Language Quarterly* 31 (1970): 210.

28. Sherwood Cummings, *Mark Twain and Science* (Baton Rouge: Louisiana State Univ. Press, 1988), p. 172. Cummings's discussion of Twain's neo-Lamarckianism is first-rate, although he and I interpret its effects differently.

29. The black student was Warner McGuinn. See Mark V. Tushnet, *Making Civil Rights Law* (New York: Oxford Univ. Press, 1994), p. 10.

30. Hershel Parker, *Flawed Texts and Verbal Icons* (Evanston: Northwestern Univ. Press, 1984), p. xiv.

31. Tourgée's brief for Plessy declares, "Justice is pictured blind and her daughter, the Law, ought at least to be color-blind" (Olsen, *The Thin Disguise,* p. 90). In *Pactolus* he writes, "As [Justice] is always represented as blind-folded we may infer she is not particular about her appearance and doesn't care who sees her;—though it seems inconsistent to speak of her as a woman if that is the case" (PP 91).

32. Albion W. Tourgée, *Bricks Without Straw* (New York: Fords, Howard, & Hulbert, 1880), p. 35. Although Andrew Kull is unaware of this quotation, it confirms his observation that Tourgée supported versions of affirmative action that existed in his time, which were not afraid of recognizing race as a legal category, a stand that Kull argues contrasts with Justice Harlan's position. Kull also cites Wendell Phillips and Theodore Tilton's use of the color-blindness

metaphor. *The Color-Blind Constitution* (Cambridge: Harvard Univ. Press, 1992), pp. 119–20. Whether Kull is right about Harlan is open to debate. For a different view of Harlan's dissent, see T. Alexander Aleinikoff, "Re-Reading Justice Harlan's Dissent in *Plessy v. Ferguson:* Freedom, Antiracism, and Citizenship," *University of Illinois Law Review* 1992: 961–77. In *Regents of the University of California v. Bakke* (1978) Justices Brennan, White, Marshall, and Blackmun argue that we cannot "let color blindness become myopia which masks the reality that many 'created equal' have been treated within our lifetimes as inferior both by the law and their fellow citizens" (438 U.S. 265 at 327).

33. The only suggestion that Tom might operate in the interests of the black race comes early in the book when Roxy imagines him, "her nigger son, lording it amongst the whites and securely avenging their crimes against her race" (PW 4). But Tom would lord it amongst whites only so long as he remained unaware that he had black blood. His superior attitude would certainly not be a self-conscious effort to help his black brothers and sisters. As we shall see, Pactolus will also argue that Benny can do more for his race by passing as white, but Benny would do so self-consciously.

34. Carton, "Fiction," p. 93.

35. Dorothy Ross, *The Origins of American Social Science* (New York: Cambridge Univ. Press, 1991), p. 130.

36. Stowe's "The True Story of Lady Byron's Life," and Twain's "The Defense of Harriet Shelley" have similar views on gender roles in marriage. In an editorial for the Buffalo *Express* 7 September 1869, Twain defended Stowe's essay. See *Mark Twain's Letters,* eds. Victor Fischer and Michael B. Frank, vol. 3 (Univ. of California Press, 1992), pp. 350–51, n. 6. On the controversy over Stowe's 1869 essay, see Frank Lentricchia Jr., "Harriet Beecher Stowe and the Byron Whirlwind," *Bulletin of the New York Public Library* 70 (1966): 218–28. Twain cites the "Byron Scandal" in "Unburlesquable Things" (1870), *Collected Tales, Sketches, Speeches, & Essays, 1852–1890* (New York: Library of America, 1992), pp. 421–24.

37. Elizabeth Perry Hedges argues that the scene in which Huck is shocked when Jim vows to buy his wife and children out of slavery can instruct law students in the relation between language and law. "Writing in a Different Voice," *Texas Law Review* 66 (1988): 630–33. See also Aviam Soifer, "Reviewing Legal Fictions," *Georgia Law Review* 20 (1986): 886–87. Soifer stresses that Twain's novel was written after the *Civil Rights Cases* (1883).

38. On Twain's economic liberalism, which comes closest to Manchester Liberalism, see Louis J. Budd, *Mark Twain: Social Philosopher* (Bloomington: Indiana Univ. Press, 1962).

39. Twain's portrayal of Judge Driscoll most likely drew on his father John Marshall Clemens. Named after the famous chief justice from Virginia even before the justice was appointed to the Supreme Court, Twain's father was a lawyer, local judge, and justice of the peace. Kim M. Roam, "Mark Twain: Doctoring the Laws," *Missouri Law Review* 48 (1983): 680–718. Justice Harlan was also named after Marshall.

40. See Myra Jehlen, "The Ties That Bind: Race and Sex in *Pudd'nhead Wilson*," in Gillman and Robinson, *"Pudd'nhead,"* pp. 105–20.

41. Tourgée, "The South as a Field for Fiction," 409. Chesnutt, who was influenced by Tourgée, more effectively makes connections between the conditions of slavery and emancipation in his fiction.

42. Steven Mailloux, *Rhetorical Power* (Ithaca: Cornell Univ. Press, 1989), p. 102. Mailloux lists one minor exception.

43. Tourgée frequently evokes equity when writing about race. For instance, in *With Gauge & Swallow* he dramatizes the dilemmas that result from differing state laws about interracial marriage, and notes, "Such conduct did not seem to be exactly in consonance with the principles of universal equity" (GS 164).

44. Pac stakes out his position, which is Tourgée's, by debating the proposed Blair bill with a senator getting a shine. In 1890 the Blair bill appropriated federal money to address the high rate of illiteracy in the South. Since a large percent of those illiterate were black, it would seem that Tourgée would support it. For Tourgée, however, it was flawed because the money would be distributed to the states. Since state governments were controlled by whites, Tourgée feared that they would spend most on white schools and then use the relatively poor progress of black children to prove their intellectual inferiority. Thus, he supported an alternative bill that gave money directly to counties or townships according to the number of illiterates in each, with the appropriate amount given to black and white schools. Tourgée was probably correct in his analysis. Nonetheless, his uncompromising stand placed him in an alliance with conservative Southerners who also opposed the bill. It failed. When the country fell into an economic depression, no new bill could possibly get support.

45. Olsen, *The Thin Disguise*, p. 79.

46. See, for instance, Jane Tompkins, *Sensational Designs* (New York: Oxford Univ. Press, 1985), and Philip Fisher, *Hard Facts*, (New York: Oxford Univ. Press, 1985).

47. Olsen, *The Thin Disguise*, p. 79.

48. Quoted in Louis D. Rubin, *George Washington Cable*, (New York: Pegasus, 1969), pp. 218–19. Chesnutt's refused essay gave a Negro's perspective on issues of race. See Herbert F. Smith, *Richard Watson Gilder*, (New York: Twayne, 1970), p. 71.

49. Kenneth W. Warren, *Black and White Strangers: Race and American Literary Realism* (Chicago: Univ. of Chicago Press, 1993), p. 38. Like me, Warren argues that the realists tried to imagine the "consequences that would ensue from an 'extension of the field of democratic struggles to the whole of civil society and the state' [Ernesto Laclau and Chantal Mouffe, *Hegemony and Socialist Strategy* (London: Verso, 1985), p. 176]" (p. 13). Nonetheless, he asserts, they retreated from those consequences when they involved race. Admiring greatly Warren's work, I have three points of difference. First, I try to distinguish the different effects that works by Howells, James, and Twain had on issues of race. Second, I try to clarify the importance of differences among social, civil, economic, and political rights. Third, I am more skeptical of the transcendental position of Tourgée. Instead, I measure the realists' retreat by the standard that Warren himself admits is enacted in their works, one that

imagines the consequences of basing the entire social order on what I have called the promise of contract. See also chapter 6, n. 18.

50. See, for instance, Amy Kaplan, *The Social Construction of American Realism* (Chicago: Univ. of Chicago Press, 1988) and Daniel Borus, *Writing Realism*, (Chapel Hill: Univ. of North Carolina Press, 1989), especially, "The Lure of Classlessness: The Antipolitics of Realism," pp. 139–82.

51. Albion W. Tourgée, *Our Continent*, 2 (Dec. 27, 1882): 797.

52. Albion W. Tourgée, "A Study in Civilization," *The North American Review* 143 (1886): 252, 253, 252.

53. Gyorgy Lukàcs, "Narrate or Describe?" in *Writer and Critic and Other Essays* (London: Merlin Press, 1970), pp. 110–48. Tourgée has a different distinction between realism and naturalism, which I mention in the final chapter.

54. Tourgée, "Study," 253.

55. Albion W. Tourgée, *Our Continent* 3 (April 18, 1882): 509.

56. Albion W. Tourgée, *Our Continent*, 3 (Jan. 31, 1883): 155.

57. Albion W. Tourgée, "Study," 250.

58. Albion W. Tourgée, "Study," 249–50. Tourgée's complaint that the realists do not present characters who woo in "true manly fashion" complicates Michael Davitt Bell's claim that Howells's call to present the real facts of life in fiction responded to a fear that novel writing itself was considered a feminine activity in the United States. For Tourgée, at least, the absence of proper sentiment and feeling in realistic works denied true manhood. For instance, in *Murvale Eastman* in a chapter entitled "Too Natural for Realism" he writes, "The 'realist' is always ready to believe anything mean; but anything decent and manly he declares at once to be unnatural" (ME 165). Bell seems to assume that sentimentalism in the period was seen as exclusively feminine. It was not. *The Problem of American Realism* (Chicago: Chicago Univ. Press, 1993).

59. Albion W. Tourgée, "Study," 246. Tourgée's praise of *Ramona* implies, of course, that it is better than *Uncle Tom's Cabin*. Tourgée lavishes high praise on *Uncle Tom's Cabin*. Nonetheless, he notes the inaccuracy of Stowe's portrayal of slaves who are "in intellectual and moral qualities simply 'blacked Yankees.'" Tourgée grants that the book's effect on its white audience might have depended on such a distortion. But having read the book aloud to former slaves and listening to their responses, he was convinced that Stowe had no real understanding of slave life. It is significant that he does not publish this criticism till after Stowe's death. "The Literary Quality of 'Uncle Tom's Cabin,'" *The Independent* 48 (August 20, 1896): 3–4, quotation on p. 3.

60. Albion W. Tourgée, *Our Continent*, 3 (May 23, 1883): 669.

61. The context of March's comment generates irony. Observing a lone Southerner at a hotel in Niagara Falls, March sentimentally imagines that he used to come every year before the war, spending lavishly. He also imagines that the black waiter serving the Southerner admires him "immensely," then admits, "The impoverished slaveholder *is* a pathetic figure, in spite of all justice and reason; the beaten rebel *does* move us to compassion, and it is of no use to think of Andersonville in his presence" (WJ 95).

62. Gross, *Tourgée*, p. 134.

63. Everett Carter links Tourgée with the realists because of his attack on sentimental lies about the South, but he also notes that Tourgée, like Bret Harte and Edward Eggleston, succumbs to other forms of sentimentalism. I have tried to show that the realists themselves were not completely free of sentimentalism, such as Twain's views on gender. Nonetheless, there is a relative, if not absolute, difference between them and others writing at the time, a difference that Tourgée himself noticed. *Howells and the Age of Realism* (Philadelphia: Lippincott, 1954), pp. 79–81, 154.

64. In 1883 Gilder wrote, "Negroes constitute a peasantry wholly untrained in, and ignorant of, those ideas of constitutional liberty and progress which are the birthright of every white voter; . . . they are gregarious and emotional rather than intelligent, and are easily led in any direction by white men of energy and determination." Quoted in Ray Ginger, *The Age of Excess* (New York: Macmillan, 1965), p. 74.

65. Albion W. Tourgée, *Our Continent* 3 (Feb. 7, 1883): 187. See also "Reform versus Reformation," *The North American Review* 132 (1881): 305–19. For a recent defense of the bureaucratic state in terms of citizen participation, see Mark Seidenfeld, "A Civic Republican Justification for the Bureaucratic State," *Harvard Law Review* 105 (1992): 1511–76.

Tourgée's mention of China recalls that he spoke out against anti-Chinese sentiment at its peak. *Our Continent* 3 (May 2, 1883): 572. See also Twain's "John Chinaman in New York" (1870), in *Collected Tales, Sketches, Speeches, & Essays, 1852–1890*, pp. 440–41. Tourgée's and Twain's support of Chinese is noteworthy. In contrast, in his *Plessy* dissent Justice Harlan refers to the Chinese as a "race so different from our own that we do not permit it to become citizens of the United States" (P 561). Two years after *Plessy* Harlan dissented in *United States v. Wong Kim Ark* (1898), which declared that someone of Chinese parents, born in the United States, is guaranteed citizenship by the 14th Amendment.

66. Thomas Haskell, *The Emergence of Professional Social Science* (Urban: Urbana Univ. Press, 1977), pp. 67–68.

67. On Holmes and the Metaphysical Club, see Max Fisch, "Justice Holmes, The Prediction Theory of Law, and Pragmatism," *Journal of Philosophy* 39 (1942): 85–97. On Holmes's pragmatism, see, among many others, Fisch, "Holmes, Pierce, and Legal Pragmatism," *Yale Law Journal* 84 (1975): 1123–31; Frederic Rogers Kellogg, "The Making of an American Legal Philosophy," in *The Formative Essays of Justice Holmes* (Westport, Conn.: Greenwood Press, 1984), pp. 3–74; Thomas C. Grey, "Holmes and Legal Pragmatism," *Stanford Law Review* 41 (1989): 787–870; and Richard Posner, *The Problems of Jurisprudence* (Cambridge: Harvard Univ. Press, 1990). Not everyone agrees that Holmes was a pragmatist. The most powerful dissenter is Yosal Rogat, who takes issue with Morton White's link between Holmes and Dewey. "The Judge as Spectator," *The University of Chicago Law Review* 31 (1964): 251–53, n. 194. H. L. Pohlman claims that Holmes was a utilitarian, in *Justice Oliver Wendell Holmes and Utilitarian Jurisprudence* (Cambridge: Harvard Univ.

Press, 1984), Patrick J. Kelley that he was a positivist in "Was Holmes a Pragmatist? Reflections on a New Twist to an Old Argument," *Southern Illinois University Law Journal* 14 (1990): 427–67.

The argument demonstrates how difficult it is to fit a complicated figure like Holmes under one label. It also shows how important it is for people claiming to be the true inheritors of the pragmatic tradition to decide whether or not Holmes is within that tradition. My own position is that, although his thought cannot be contained by what neopragmatists identify variously as the true legacy of pragmatism, Holmes was clearly influenced by pragmatic thinkers and helped to influence them. Holmes's pragmatic streak helps to clarify distinctions among classical republicanism, liberalism, mugwump reformism, and progressivism. Such distinctions are useful to help us chart historical transformations, even if no one thinker perfectly represents any one brand of thought. For instance, Holmes's formalization of contract reveals his positivism.

68. Robert Gordon, "Legal Thought and Legal Practice in the Age of American Enterprise, 1870–1920," in *Professions and Professional Ideologies in America,* ed. Gerald L. Geison (Chapel Hill: Univ. of North Carolina Press, 1983), pp. 70–110.

69. R. Jackson Wilson, *In Quest of Community* (New York: John Wiley, 1968), p. 43.

70. Charles Sanders Peirce, "The Fixation of Belief," in *Classic American Philosophers,* ed. Max H. Frisch (Englewood Cliffs: Prentice-Hall, 1951), pp. 62, 63.

71. Oliver Wendell Holmes Jr., *The Common Law,* ed. Mark De Wolfe Howe (Cambridge: Harvard Univ. Press, 1963), p. 5.

72. See Lofgren, *Plessy,* especially "The Intellectual Environment: Racist Thought in the Late Nineteenth Century," pp. 93–115. See also Robin West's use of *Pudd'nhead Wilson* to point out the fallacies in Owen Fiss's and Ronald Dworkin's appeals to interpretive communities. In this same essay she somewhat mistakenly refers to Stanley Fish's "subjective interpretivism," but uses John Barth's *The Floating Opera* to engage Fish. I am implying that *Plessy* and *Pudd'nhead* should make us reconsider the limitations of Fish's pragmatically derived notion of interpretive communities and his defense of professionalism. "Adjudication Is Not Interpretation: Some Reservations about the Law-As-Literature Movement," *Tennessee Law Review* 54 (1987): 203–78.

73. On Twain's use of science and its relation to legal realism, see John P. McWilliams Jr., "Innocent Criminal or Criminal Innocence: The Trial in American Fiction," in Carl S. Smith, John P. McWilliams Jr., and Maxwell Bloomfield, *Law and American Literature* (New York: Knopf, 1983), pp. 45–124. On Twain's use of fingerprinting and scientific racism, see Susan Gillman, *Dark Twins* (Chicago: Univ. of Chicago Press, 1989).

74. Of course, the representation of the past often has present political importance. As the works of Page indicate, the production of images of the slaveholding South played an important role in national debates over postbellum racial policies. *Pudd'nhead Wilson* is more than an imaginative work of memory; it is also a self-conscious parody of versions of the Southern past that

helped to reunite North and South after Reconstruction. For instance, Twain's portrait of Judge Driscoll and Pembroke Howard can be profitably juxtaposed to Page's idealized sketches of Virginia lawyers.

75. Eric J. Sundquist offers a similar interpretation of Pudd'nhead's role, but, as he acknowledges, it was influenced by reading an essay of mine that "modified his views." Compare, for instance, Sundquist's book and his early essay "Mark Twain and Homer Plessy," *Representations,* 24 (1988): 102–27. For the acknowledgment, see *Wake,* p. 650, n. 8.

76. John Carlos Rowe, *Through the Custom-House* (Baltimore: Johns Hopkins Univ. Press, 1982), p. 147.

77. Mark Twain, *Mark Twain in Eruption,* ed. Bernard De Voto (New York: Grosset & Dunlap, 1940), pp. 204, 206, 206–7.

78. See Mark Twain, "Mental Telegraphy" and "Mental Telegraphy Again," *In Defense of Harriet Shelley and Other Essays* (New York: Harper & Brothers, 1929), pp. 111–147. On Twain and mediumship, see Howard Kerr, *Mediums, and Spirit-Rappers, and Roaring Radicals* (Urbana: Univ. of Illinois Press, 1972), and Gillman, *Dark Twins.*

79. Wolfgang Iser, "Feigning in Fiction," in *Identity of the Literary Text,* eds. Mario J. Valdés and Owen Miller (Toronto: Univ. of Toronto Press, 1985), pp. 204–28.

80. *Brown v. Board of Education,* 347 U.S., 483, 494 (1954).

Chapter 8. Corporate Liberalism, the Politics of Character, and Professional Management in Phillips's *The Cost* and Lynde's *The Grafters*

1. Texts cited parenthetically in this chapter are: Samuel Clemens, *"Pudd'nhead Wilson" and "Those Extraordinary Twins,"* ed. Sidney E. Berger (New York: Norton & Co., 1980), designated as ET; David Graham Phillips, *The Cost* (Indianapolis: Bobbs-Merrill Co., 1904), designated as C; David Graham Phillips, "'Bev'" and "Secretary Root and His Plea for Centralization," in *Contemporaries,* ed. Louis Filler (Westport, Conn.: Greenwood Press, 1981), designated as B and R respectively; and Francis Lynde, *The Grafters* (Indianapolis: Bobbs-Merrill Co., 1904), designated as G.

2. On Twain's persistent financial difficulties, see Justin Kaplan, *Mr. Clemens and Mark Twain* (New York: Simon and Schuster, 1966).

3. Quoted in John D. Lewis, *The Genossenschaft-Theory of Otto von Gierke,* no. 25 (Madison: Univ. of Wisconsin Studies in the Social Sciences and History, 1935), p. 75. For more on Gierke in English, see Frederic William Maitland's introduction to his translation of Otto Gierke, *Political Theories of the Middle Ages* (Cambridge: Cambridge Univ. Press, 1900), pp. vii–lv. Gierke's argument for rights-bearing groups between the sovereign state and the individual could justify rights for various ethnic groups. Gierke, however, was himself extremely Eurocentric on issues of race. In a 1914 letter to Oliver Wendell Holmes on World War I, he declares that England will never "be able to free herself of the moral crime of having drawn Japan into the battle, and leading colored men of

all shades against the white race." Quoted in Sheldon M. Novick, *Honorable Justice* (Boston: Little, Brown, 1989), p. 312.

4. Quoted in Lewis, p. 169. In the United States at this time Horten Crooley was arguing that from birth, individuals were members of a society; that is, the family.

5. *Dartmouth College v. Woodward*, 4 Wheat. (U.S.), 518, 636 (1819).

6. See Morton Horwitz, "*Santa Clara* Revisited: The Development of Corporate Theory," *West Virginia Law Review* 88 (1985): 173–224.

7. Walter Benn Michaels, "Corporate Fiction," *The Gold Standard and the Logic of Naturalism* (Berkeley: Univ. of California Press, 1987), pp. 181–214.

8. See Brook Thomas, "Walter Benn Michaels and Cultural Poetics: Where's the Difference?" *The New Historicism and Other Old-Fashioned Topics* (Princeton: Princeton Univ. Press, 1991), p. 117–50.

9. Charles and Mary Beard subscribed to a conspiracy theory in which Republican framers of the 14th Amendment intentionally used "person" in order to expand corporate rights. *The Rise of American Civilization*, vol. 2 (New York: Macmillan Co., 1927), pp. 111–14. Horwitz makes a convincing argument that in *Santa Clara*, the Court was still intent on protecting the individual people making up the corporation, not the corporate personality itself. My reading of *In re Tiburcio Parrott* that follows confirms his argument.

10. Charles Wallace Collins, *The Fourteenth Amendment and the States* (Boston: Little, Brown, 1912), pp. 145–46. I have slightly adjusted Collins's statistics because he leaves out two cases concerned with blacks and one concerned with the citizenship of Chinese Americans.

11. On corporations and privacy, see Robert C. Post, "The Social Foundations of Privacy: Community and Self in the Common Law Tort," *California Law Review* 77 (1989): 986, n. 141.

12. Alan Trachtenberg, *The Incorporation of America* (New York: Hill and Wang, 1982).

13. Tiedeman, quoted in Horwitz, "*Santa Clara* Revisited," 206. See also Louise A. Halper, "Christopher G. Tiedeman, 'Laissez-Faire Constitutionalism' and the Dilemmas of Small-Scale Property in the Gilded Age," *Ohio State Law Journal* 51 (1990): 1347–84.

14. *In re Tiburcio Parrott*, 1 F. 481 (C.C.D. Cal. 1880), 494.

15. Quoted in Martin Sklar, *The Corporate Reconstruction of American Capitalism: 1890–1916* (New York: Cambridge Univ. Press, 1988), p. 88. Sklar coined the phrase "corporate liberalism" in his "Woodrow Wilson and the Political Economy of Modern United States Liberalism," *Studies on the Left* 1 (1960): 17–47. See also R. Jeffrey Lustig, *Corporate Liberalism* (Berkeley: Univ. of California Press, 1982). For recent work on legal aspects of the rise of corporate liberalism, see Morton Horwitz, *The Transformation of American Law, 1870–1960* (New York: Oxford Univ. Press, 1992); Tony Fryer, *Regulating Big Business* (Cambridge: Harvard Univ. Press, 1992); and Herbert Hovenkamp, *Enterprise and American Law* (Cambridge: Harvard Univ. Press, 1991). Earlier studies are Adolf A. Berle Jr. and Gardiner Means, *The Modern Corporation and Private Property* (Chicago: Commerce Clearing House, 1932); Oscar Handlin and Mary F. Handlin, "Origins of the American Business

Corporation," *Journal of Economic History* 5 (1945): 1–23; and James Willard Hurst *The Legitimacy of the Business Corporation in the Law of the United States, 1780–1970* (Charlottesville: Univ. of Virginia Press, 1970).

16. Oscar Lewis, *The Big Four* (New York: Knopf, 1938).

17. *Bartle v. Home Owners Cooperative*, 127 N.E. 2d 832 (N.Y. Ct. App., 1955).

18. See Sir Henry Sumner Maine, *Ancient Law: Its Connection with the Early History of Society and Its Relation to Modern Ideas,* 10th ed. (1861; reprint, New York: Dorset Press, 1986), pp. 17–36; and Kathy Eden, *Poetic and Legal Fiction in the Aristotelian Tradition* (Princeton: Princeton Univ. Press, 1986), pp. 45–46.

19. Twain's attitude toward corporations may have been influenced by Henry H. Rogers of Standard Oil, who helped him with financial advice. In 1893 Twain refused even to consider publishing an exposé of Standard Oil. When Ira Tarbell was working on hers, he tried to arrange a meeting between her and representatives of the corporation to soften her criticism. See Louis Budd, *Mark Twain: Social Philosopher* (Bloomington: Indiana Univ. Press, 1962), pp. 194–200.

20. In "Michaels" I point to intriguing corporate portrayals in works that stretch the novel's limits, such as Thomas Pynchon's *Gravity's Rainbow* and Herman Melville's *The Confidence-Man.*

21. *Literary Digest* 32 (1903): 503. This and other valuable references of use in examining Phillips's work are documented in Ala C. Ravitz, *David Graham Phillips* (New York: Twayne, 1966). Other useful works on Phillips are Isaac Marcosson, *David Graham Phillips and His Times* (New York: Dodd, Mead, 1932); Kenneth S. Lynn, *The Dream of Success* (Westport, Conn.: Greenwood Press, 1955), pp. 121–57; Louis Filler, *Voice of the Democracy: A Critical Biography of David Graham Phillips* (University Park: Penn State Univ. Press, 1978); and Christopher Wilson, *The Labor of Words: Literary Professionalism in the Progressive Era* (Athens: Univ. of Georgia Press, 1985), pp. 141–67. For an excellent summary of popular fiction responding to the rise of corporations, see Maxwell Bloomfield, "Fictional Lawyers and the Rise of the Corporate State," in Carl S. Smith, John P. McWilliams Jr., and Maxwell Bloomfield, *Law and American Literature* (New York: Knopf, 1983), pp. 148–72.

22. "Literature of Exposure," *Independent* 40 (1906): 690–91.

23. Theodore Roosevelt, "The Man with the Muck-Rake," *Outlook* 82 (1906): 884–87, a reprint of his 14 April 1906 speech on laying the cornerstone of the House Office Building, which elaborated on remarks made to the Gridiron Club on 17 March 1906.

24. Richard Hofstadter, *The Age of Reform* (New York: Alfred A. Knopf, 1955), p. 5.

25. David Graham Phillips, "New York's Misrepresentatives," *Cosmopolitan* 40 (1906): 488.

26. On progressivism's diversity, see Daniel T. Rogers, "In Search of Progressivism," *Reviews in American History* 10 (1982): 113–32.

27. C. Wright Mills, *White Collar* (New York: Oxford Univ. Press, 1953).

28. "The Fate of the Salaried Man," *Independent* 60 (1903): 2002.

29. David Graham Phillips, *The Treason of the Senate,* ed. George Mowry and Judson A. Grenier (Chicago: Quadrangle, 1964), p. 56. June Howard links naturalism to a middle-class fear of sliding toward working-class dependency. See *Form and History in American Literary Naturalism* (Chapel Hill: Univ. of North Carolina Press, 1985).

30. Albion W. Tourgée, "The Anti-Trust Campaign," *The North American Review* (July 1893): 41.

31. Warren Susman, " 'Personality' and the Making of Twentieth-Century Culture," in *Culture as History* (New York: Pantheon Books, 1984), pp. 271–85.

32. Examples are John Hicks, *The Populist Revolt* (Lincoln: Univ. of Nebraska Press, 1931); Matthew Josephson, *The Robber Barons* (New York: Harcourt, Brace and Co., 1934); Samuel Hays, *The Response to Industrialism* (Chicago: Univ. of Chicago Press, 1957). Challenges to the constraints of this narrative are Alfred D. Chandler Jr., *The Visible Hand* (Cambridge: Harvard Univ. Press, 1977); Olivier Zunz, *Making America Corporate: 1870–1920* (Chicago: Univ. of Chicago Press, 1990); and James Livingston, "The Social Analysis of Economic History and Theory: Conjectures on Late Nineteenth-Century American Development," *American Historical Review* 92 (1987): 69–85.

33. Phillips, *Treason,* pp. 82–83.

34. Albert J. Beveridge, "Trusts, A Development," *The Meaning of the Times* (Indianapolis: Bobbs-Merrill Co., 1908), p. 146. The speech was delivered on 28 September 1890.

35. The kiss that Scarborough delivers to a more than willing Gladys recalls the one Farnham delivers to Maud in *The Bread-Winners.* But although the scenes share similarities, they reveal how much Phillips's social vision is anchored in middle-class values. In Hay's novel a working-class woman tries to use her sexuality to rise socially. In Phillips's a woman of the powerful newly rich attempts to corrupt a man of solid middle-class values.

36. Albert J. Beveridge, "Trusts," p. 145.

37. W. J. Ghent, "The Next Step: A Benevolent Feudalism," *The Independent* 54 (1902): 781.

38. Walter Benn Michaels notes that in Bellamy's *Looking Backward,* people are "individualized by their place in the system." "An American Tragedy, or the Promise of American Life," *Representations* 25 (1989): 73.

39. On the corporate loyalty of middle-level management, see Chandler, *Visible Hand,* and Zunz, *Making America.* Zunz especially challenges Mills's thesis that the lives of the middle class were completely determined by the rise of corporate liberalism. He argues instead that "the diverse group of individuals that staffed the early corporation, not all of whom shared the same purpose, did not so much react to the corporation as they did design it. In doing so, they transformed their own lives" (8). The representation of corporate workers in *The Grafters* reinforces Zunz's argument and suggests the need to explore further the attitudes of those working for corporations. See Walter Licht's valuable *Working for the Railroad* (Princeton: Princeton Univ. Press, 1983).

40. William L. Riordon, *Plunkitt of Tammany Hall,* ed. Terrence J. McDonald (Boston: Bedford Books, 1994), pp. 49–51.

41. Like *The Cost* and *The Grafters,* Samuel Merwin-Webster's *The Short Line War* (New York: Macmillan Co., 1899) has an honorable judge (Judge Grey) and one in corporate pay (Judge Black).

42. Evoking the Gospel of Wealth's belief that "genius thrives on adversity," the narrator remarks of Kent's struggles: "Brutal as their blind gropings were, the Flagellants of the Dark Ages plied their whips to some dim purpose" (G 182). Kent's need to assert his primitive manhood confirms T. Jackson Lears's thesis that for middle-class moralists, worried about social decadence, the figure of the warrior promised both social and personal regeneration. See *No Place of Grace* (New York: Pantheon Books, 1981). Nonetheless, his thesis that the period's medieval nostalgia is a response to "modernity" is a bit too simple, since, as I have argued, it is not all that clear which forces stand for "modernity." If the middle class worried about loss of autonomy and romanticized medieval tests of manhood, it also feared and idealized "feudal" forms of organization that simultaneously threatened individual autonomy and promised to overcome the sense of alienation brought about by new economic conditions of life. Attitudes toward corporations dramatize this complexity. *The Grafters* shows how feudal tests of manhood can be imagined within a corporate model.

43. Charles Edward Russell, "Obstructions in the Way of Justice: Address before the Fourteenth Annual Convention of the National American Woman Suffrage Convention," Buffalo, New York, October 20, 1908. Quoted in Ravitz, *Phillips,* p. 101.

44. Hofstadter, *The Age of Reform.*

45. Robert Wiebe, *The Search for Order* (New York: Hill and Wang, 1967), p. 166.

46. Zunz, *Making America,* p. 35. Martha Banta also discusses the alliance in *Taylorized Lives* (Chicago: Univ. of Chicago Press, 1993). This chapter can do no more than provide a modest supplement to Banta's complex argument about narratives of managed efficiency.

47. Dewey Grantham, *Southern Progressivism: The Reconciliation of Progress and Tradition* (Lexington: Univ. of Kentucky Press, 1983).

48. David W. Noble, *The Paradox of Progressive Thought* (Minneapolis: Univ. of Minnesota Press, 1958).

49. Louis D. Brandeis, *The Curse of Bigness* (New York: Viking Press, 1934), p. 104.

50. Sklar, *Corporate Reconstruction,* p. 175. For a lucid and provocative summary of Sklar's argument, see Spencer Olin, "Free Markets and Corporate America," *Radical History Review* 50 (1991): 213–20.

51. On Civil Service reform, see Paul P. Van Riper, *History of the United States Civil Service* (Evanston, Ill.: Row, Peterson, 1958). We should remember that Albion W. Tourgée's traditional republican values made him fear that Civil Service reform would destroy participatory democracy by creating a class of professional bureaucrats. See "Reform versus Reformation," *The North American Review* 293 (1881): 305–19. Woodrow Wilson, in contrast, believing that the American people's character determined the character of its institutions rather than vice versa, was not worried that a "European-style" bureaucracy

would affect the political virtue of the country. See "The Study of Administration," *Political Science Quarterly* 2 (1887): 197–222.

52. Christopher Wilson, *The Labor of Words*.

Chapter 9. The Question of Agency and Delivering the Promise

1. P. S. Atiyah, *The Rise and Fall of Freedom of Contract* (Oxford: Clarendon Press, 1979), p. 6.

2. Hannah Arendt, *The Human Condition* (Chicago: Univ. of Chicago Press, 1958), p. 233. Future references to this text will be cited parenthetically in the text and designated as HC. Other works by Hannah Arendt that will be cited parenthetically are: *The Origins of Totalitarianism*, 2d ed. (New York: Meridian Books, 1958), designated as OT; *Between Past and Future* (New York: Viking Press, 1961), designated as PF; and *Eichmann in Jerusalem* (New York: Viking Press, 1963), designated as EJ. The one book by Kate Chopin is: *The Awakening*, ed. Margaret Culley (New York: Norton, 1976), designated as A. Works by William Dean Howells include: *The Rise of Silas Lapham* (Bloomington: Indiana Univ. Press, 1971), designated as SL; and *A Hazard of New Fortunes* (Bloomington: Indiana Univ. Press, 1976), designated as HNF. Also included is: Henry James, *The Golden Bowl*, in *The Novels and Tales of Henry James*, vols. 23 and 24 (New York: Scribners, 1908), designated as GB.

3. See Alan Keenan, "PROMISES, PROMISES: The Abyss of Freedom and the Loss of the Political in the Work of Hannah Arendt," *Political Theory* 22 (1994): 297–322.

4. J. G. A. Pocock, *The Machiavellian Moment* (Princeton: Princeton Univ. Press, 1975).

5. Richard Chase, *The American Novel and Its Tradition* (Garden City, NY: Anchor Books, 1957), p. 186 n.

6. Albion W. Tourgée, "The Claim of 'Realism,' " *North American Review* 148 (1889): 387, 386, 387.

7. Walter Benn Michaels, *The Gold Standard and the Logic of Capitalism* (Berkeley: Univ. of California Press, 1987), p. 201.

8. Mark Seltzer, *Bodies and Machines* (New York: Routledge, 1992), p. 26.

9. *Mark Twain-Howells Letters*, eds. Henry Nash Smith and William M. Gibson, vol. 2 (Cambridge: Harvard Univ. Press, 1960), p. 630.

10. Responding to charges that realism lacks a moral purpose, Howells writes, "Then shall the novel have no purpose? Shall it not try to do good? . . . No, and a thousand times, no! . . . The novel can teach, and for shame's sake, it must teach, but only by painting life truly." "Novel-Writing and Novel-Reading," *Selected Literary Criticism*, ed. Ronald Gottesman, vol. 3 (Bloomington: Indiana Univ. Press, 1993), p. 222.

11. *The Love Letters of Mark Twain*, ed. Dixon Wector (New York: Harper, 1942), p. 291.

12. Quoted in Leon Edel, *The Life of Henry James*, vol. 2 (Philadelphia: Lippincott, 1962), pp. 165–66.

13. David McWhirter argues that "James's fatalistic vision of human experience" invites further study of James's "affinity with the naturalist currents of his era." *Desire and Love in Henry James* (New York: Cambridge Univ. Press, 1989), p. 167. My brief reading of *The Golden Bowl* suggests a subtle, but crucial, distinction between James's sense of agency and that of the naturalists.

14. Deftly linking *The Golden Bowl* to turn-of-the century narratives of mechanical efficiency, Martha Banta offers a much more pessimistic reading of the novel, claiming that "James leaves Maggie and the prince with the terrible reality of *where* they are—the 'well hell' of the present moment." *Taylorized Lives* (Chicago: Univ. of Chicago Press, 1993), p. 79. But perhaps Banta expects too much. Criticizing narratives of efficient control, she still wants Maggie and the Prince to have sovereign control over their future together. James does not offer a final triumph, but in leaving his couple with the reality of the present moment, he gives it the chance not to turn back time and recover a lost innocence that never existed but to start anew. Maggie and the Prince now have the opportunity to create a better future through negotiating a new agreement about what their duties and responsibilities to one another will be. To be sure, that opportunity was achieved at great cost, but that cost should heighten their awareness of what is at stake in their negotiations—if they take place.

15. For instance, Jonathan Arac claims, "Huck Finn lives so as to feel right with no sanction beyond his own psyche, the imaginative construction of an autonomous self that is the cultural work of literary narrative." "Nationalism, Hypercanonization, and *Huckleberry Finn*," in *National Identities and Post-Americanist Narratives,* ed. Donald E. Pease (Durham: Duke Univ. Press, 1994), p. 33.

16. Helmuth Plessner, quoted by Wolfgang Iser, "Staging as an Anthropological Category," *New Literary History* 23 (1993): 879.

17. This structure of doubleness constituted by a space of emptiness is similar to what Ross Posnock "identifies" as nonidentity thinking in James. I play on Posnock's identification of nonidentity to emphasize a subtle difference in our work. Posnock derives his notion of Jamesian nonidentity mostly from Theodor Adorno, but also from George Herbert Mead. Mead speaks of the self as consisting of both a "me" and an "I." The "me" is linked to its normative social roles; the "I" never quite fits into particular social situations. Thus for Mead the self is constituted by a structure of doubleness, in which, according to Posnock, "We are never fully aware of what we are, since we exist in a kind of perpetual disequilibrium of internal division." For Posnock this disequilibrium is an example of nonidentity. But the fact that the elements making up the self are not identical does not necessarily create a condition of nonidentity, which is a negation of identity. Rather than negate identity, a structure of doubleness generates a performed or staged identity that, nonetheless, is not completely identical to the structure that allows it to be staged. Posnock implicitly acknowledges the staged aspect of Jamesian identity when he states that, "The Jamesian self is perpetually negotiating an *identity* out of its interaction with others" (my emphasis).

Posnock use of "nonidentity" grows out of his attempt to use James to link Mead's pragmatism with Adorno's negative dialectic. Adorno does work with a dialectic of identity and nonidentity. But, as Jürgen Habermas argues, Mead and Adorno have an important difference. Habermas celebrates Mead for first challenging the notion of selfhood as a substance and seeing it as constituted by intersubjective role-playing. Adorno's nonidentity also challenges the notion of the self as substance, but it does not allow for intersubjectivity and thus it resists socialization.

Despite Posnock's efforts to wed Mead and Adorno, this difference is crucial. For me the Jamesian self is closer to Mead's than Adorno's. Nonetheless, it does have an affinity with Adorno's that keeps it from being identical with Mead's pragmatic self and helps to explain James's similarity with the literary modernists championed by Adorno. Habermas champions Mead because his sense of the self's intersubjectivity confirms a rationality inherent in everyday communication, a rationality assumed by pragmatists like Peirce, Mead, and Dewey. Thus, like Habermas, their account of experience remains subordinate to critical reason. Adorno's nonidentity is threatening to Habermas because it resists that subordination. The vacancy at the heart of the Jamesian self does not generate a dialectic of identity and nonidentity. Even so, it keeps a staged Jamesian identity from being accounted for completely in terms of intersubjectivity. Therein lies the unpredictability of the Jamesian self and its "aesthetic" aspect that cannot be subordinated to critical reason. The quotations from Posnock are from *The Trial of Curiosity* (New York: Oxford Univ. Press, 1991), p. 136.

18. W. E. B. Du Bois, "The Strivings of the Negro People," *Atlantic Monthly* 80 (1897): 194.

19. W. E. B. Du Bois, *The Souls of Black Folk* (New York: Penguin, 1989), p. 5.

20. Hans Blumenberg, "An Anthropological Approach to the Contemporary Significance of Rhetoric," in *After Philosophy*, eds. Kenneth Baynes, James Bohman, and Thomas McCarthy (Cambridge: MIT Univ. Press, 1988), p. 456.

21. The novel's "plasticity, its elasticity," James wrote, "are infinite." *Literary Criticism: Essays on Literature, American Writers, English Writers* (New York: Library of America, 1984), p. 105.

22. Georges Poulet, "The Phenomenology of Reading," *New Literary History* 1 (1969): 54–72.

23. Yosal Rogat, "The Judge as Spectator," *University of Chicago Law Review* 31 (1964): 219, 220.

24. Mark DeWolfe Howe, *Justice Holmes: The Proving Years* (Cambridge: Harvard Univ. Press, 1963).

25. Lawrence Friedman, *Contract Law in America* (Madison: Univ. of Wisconsin Press, 1965), p. 20.

26. Holmes most likely believed in a subjective interior. As Rogat argues, he valued his own privacy to an extreme. It is even possible to argue, as Rogat does, that Holmes's legal rhetoric and judicial stance serve to hide the private man. What is at stake, however, is the sense of self that he constructs for the law.

27. Cynthia Griffin Wolff, "Thanatos and Eros: Kate Chopin's *The Awakening*," *American Quarterly* 25 (1973): 449–72.

28. Jules Chametsky, "Our Decentralized Literature: The Significance of Region, Ethnic, Racial, and Sexual Factors," in *Our Decentralized Literature*

(Amherst: Univ. of Massachusetts Press, 1986), pp. 43, 44. First delivered June 4, 1971, this essay influenced Wolff and Margot Culley, the editor of the Norton Critical Edition. Feminist readings include Sandra Gilbert, "The Second Coming of Aphrodite: Kate Chopin's Fantasy of Desire," *Kenyon Review* 5 (1983): 42–56, and Elaine Showalter, "Tradition and the Individual Talent: *The Awakening* as a Solitary Book," in *The Awakening,* ed. Nancy A. Walker, (Boston: Bedford Books, 1993), pp. 169–89.

29. Margit Stange, "Personal Property: Exchange Value and the Female Self in *The Awakening,*" in *The Awakening,* ed. Nancy A. Walker, pp. 201–17. Quotation on p. 209. For another account of the self-defeating logic of Edna's possessive individualism, see Wai-chee Dimock, "Rightful Subjectivity," *Yale Journal of Criticism* 4 (1990): 25–51. Michele A. Birnbaum faults many feminists for neglecting the role of race and argues that "Possessive individualism, with its myth of the inalienable self, is precisely what makes it so difficult to see the investment in race upon which the white female subject capitalizes." She concludes, "The racial politics of womanhood in Chopin's novel must complicate, if not compromise, our celebration of a nineteenth-century white woman's sexual liberation." " 'Alien Hands': Kate Chopin and the Colonization of Race," *American Literature* 66 (1994): 301–23, quotations at 316 and 317. Birnbaum still assumes that the novel is a celebration of Edna's sexual liberation.

30. Albion W. Tourgée, "The Reversal of Malthus," *The American Journal of Sociology* 2 (1896): 20, 22, 22.

31. Willa Cather disapprovingly noted the similarity between Edna and Madame Bovary in "Books and Magazines," *Leader* (8 July 1899): 6. This similarity is also stressed by the French translator, Cyrille Arnavon, "Les Débuts du Roman Réaliste Américain et l'Influence Française," in *Romanciers Américains Contemporains,* ed. Henri Kerst (*Cahiers des Langues Modernes* 1 (1946): 9–35, and Susan J. Rosowski, "The Novel of Awakening," *Genre* 12 (1979): 313–32.

32. Chametzky, "Decentralized Literature," p. 43.

33. On rights in the novel, see Dimock, "Rightful Subjectivity."

34. Carole Pateman, *The Sexual Contract* (Stanford: Stanford Univ. Press, 1988), pp. 49, 182, 183.

35. Contracts made with surrogate mothers might seem to present an exception, but in terms of sexual difference they do not. No children to date have been born to surrogate mothers who are male.

36. Peter H. Schuck and Rogers M. Smith, *Citizenship without Consent,* (New Haven: Yale Univ. Press, 1985), p. 39.

37. Michael T. Gilmore, "Revolt against Nature: The Problematic Modernism of *The Awakening,*" in *New Essays on "The Awakening",* ed. Wendy Martin (New York: Cambridge Univ. Press, 1988), pp. 59–87.

38. Hannah Arendt, "Reflections on Little Rock," *Dissent* 6 (1959): 45–56.

39. For discussions of Arendt's essay, see Elisabeth Young-Bruehl, *Hannah Arendt: For Love of the World* (New Haven: Yale Univ. Press, 1982), 308–18; Marie A. Failinger, "Equality versus the Right to Choose Associates: A Critique of Hannah Arendt's View of the Supreme Court's Dilemma," *University of Pittsburgh Law Review* 49 (1987): 143–88; and Werner Sollors, "Of Mules and

Mares in a Land of Difference; or Quadrupeds All?" *American Quarterly* 42 (1990): 167–90. Though refusing to take back most of her argument, Arendt did modify her sense of the children's role in the struggle for black rights, in response to an explanation offered by Ralph Ellison in 1964. See Ellison's contribution to *Who Speaks for the Negro?*, ed. Robert Penn Warren (New York: Random House, 1965), pp. 342–44.

40. See Dimock, "Rightful Subjectivity," and Birnbaum, " 'Alien Hands.' "

41. See Joseph Allen Boone's claim that James's texts bring readers "face-to-face with the issues implicit in their concluding uncertainty." *Tradition and Counter Tradition* (Chicago: Univ. of Chicago Press, 1987), p. 188. But open-endedness is not, as Boone claims, inherently subversive of existing social orders. Nor is it, as Thomas Galt Peyser argues about *The Golden Bowl,* inevitably a "strategy to appropriate the structures of power Boone suggests James wants to subvert." "James, Race, and the Imperial Museum," *American Literary History* 6 (1994): 68 n. 6. Instead, it allows readers to imagine alternatives, whose political consequences are themselves uncertain. What needs to be considered is the specific context in which open-endedness occurs. Peyser's nuanced reading pays attention to that context at the moment of production, but in creating a homology between it and James's form he does not do justice to the novel's relationship with its readers, which depends on a structure of doubleness created by the novel's lack of identity with the representations that it bears. By establishing a seamless connection between the text and its historical context, Peyser, like so many others, either traps readers within the text's network of controls or allows privileged ones, like himself, to adopt the imperial position of the present to stand outside it to judge it. In either case, such "historical" readings confine texts to a museum past rather than allow them to participate in a contract that grants both them and readers a future orientation. The realists' "contract" also challenges Posnock's embrace of a presentism that acknowledges the value of "letting the present interrogate the past," but does not stress the equal importance of having texts from the past judge our present condition. *The Trials of Curiosity,* p. ix.

Index

Compositor:	Braun-Brumfield, Inc.
Text:	10/13 Galliard
Display:	Galliard
Printer:	Braun-Brumfield, Inc.
Binder:	Braun-Brumfield, Inc.